D0662393

SAN ANTONIO, AUSTIN & THE HILL COUNTRY

1st Edition

Where to Stay and Eat
for All Budgets

Must-See Sights
and Local Secrets

Ratings You Can Trust

Portions of this book appear in *Fodor's Texas*
Fodor's Travel Publications   New York, Toronto, London, Sydney, Auckland
www.fodors.com

FODOR'S SAN ANTONIO, AUSTIN & THE HILL COUNTRY

Editors: Debbie Harmsen, Michael Nalepa

Editorial Contributors: Paul Eisenberg, Shannon Kelly, Suzanne Robitaille
Writers: Tony Carnes, Jessica Norman Dupuy, Jennifer Edwards, Wes Eichenwald, Daniel Huerta, Lisa Miller, Larry Neal, Roger Slavens, Fran Stephenson, Kevin Tankersley

Editorial Production: Linda K. Schmidt
Maps & Illustrations: maps.com, *cartographers;* Bob Blake, Rebecca Baer, *map editors;* William Wu, *information graphics*
Design: Fabrizio LaRocca, *creative director;* Guido Caroti, Siobhan O'Hare, *art directors;* Tina Malaney, Chie Ushio, Ann McBride, *designers;* Melanie Marin, *senior picture editor;* Moon Sun Kim, *cover designer*
Cover Photo: (bluebonnet pasture near San Antonio): America/Alamy
Production/Manufacturing: Angela L. McLean

First Edition

ISBN 978-1-4000-0718-9

ISSN 1941-0298

SPECIAL SALES

This book is available at special discounts for bulk purchases for sales promotions or premiums. Special editions, including personalized covers, excerpts of existing books, and corporate imprints, can be created in large quantities for special needs. For more information, write to Special Markets/Premium Sales, 1745 Broadway, MD 6-2, New York, New York 10019, or e-mail specialmarkets@randomhouse.com.

AN IMPORTANT TIP & AN INVITATION

Although all prices, opening times, and other details in this book are based on information supplied to us at press time, changes occur all the time in the travel world, and Fodor's cannot accept responsibility for facts that become outdated or for inadvertent errors or omissions. So **always confirm information when it matters,** especially if you're making a detour to visit a specific place. Your experiences—positive and negative—matter to us. If we have missed or misstated something, **please write to us.** We follow up on all suggestions. Contact the San Antonio, Austin & the Hill Country editor at editors@fodors.com or c/o Fodor's at 1745 Broadway, New York, NY 10019.

PRINTED IN THE UNITED STATES OF AMERICA

10 9 8 7 6 5 4 3 2 1

Be a Fodor's Correspondent

Your opinion matters. It matters to us. It matters to your fellow Fodor's travelers, too. And we'd like to hear it. In fact, we need to hear it.

When you share your experiences and opinions, you become an active member of the Fodor's community. That means we'll not only use your feedback to make our books better, but we'll publish your names and comments whenever possible. Throughout our guides, look for "Word of Mouth," excerpts of your unvarnished feedback.

Here's how you can help improve Fodor's for all of us.

Tell us when we're right. We rely on local writers to give you an insider's perspective. But our writers and staff editors—who are the best in the business—depend on you. Your positive feedback is a vote to renew our recommendations for the next edition.

Tell us when we're wrong. We're proud that we update most of our guides every year. But we're not perfect. Things change. Hotels cut services. Museums change hours. Charming cafés lose charm. If our writer didn't quite capture the essence of a place, tell us how you'd do it differently. If any of our descriptions are inaccurate or inadequate, we'll incorporate your changes in the next edition and will correct factual errors at fodors.com immediately.

Tell us what to include. You probably have had fantastic travel experiences that aren't yet in Fodor's. Why not share them with a community of like-minded travelers? Maybe you chanced upon a beach or bistro or B&B that you don't want to keep to yourself. Tell us why we should include it. And share your discoveries and experiences with everyone directly at fodors.com. Your input may lead us to add a new listing or highlight a place we cover with a "Highly Recommended" star or with our highest rating, "Fodor's Choice."

Give us your opinion instantly at our feedback center at www.fodors.com/feedback. You may also e-mail editors@fodors.com with the subject line "San Antonio, Austin & the Hill Country Editor." Or send your nominations, comments, and complaints by mail to San Antonio, Austin & the Hill Country Editor, Fodor's, 1745 Broadway, New York, NY 10019.

You and travelers like you are the heart of the Fodor's community. Make our community richer by sharing your experiences. Be a Fodor's correspondent.

Happy traveling in Central Texas!

Tim Jarrell, Publisher

CONTENTS

MAPS

ABOUT THIS BOOK

Our Ratings

Sometimes you find terrific travel experiences and sometimes they just find you. But usually the burden is on you to select the right combination of experiences. That's where our ratings come in.

As travelers we've all discovered a place so wonderful that its worthiness is obvious. And sometimes that place is so experiential that superlatives don't do it justice: you just have to be there to know. These sights, properties, and experiences get our highest rating, **Fodor's Choice**, indicated by orange stars throughout this book.

Black stars highlight sights and properties we deem **Highly Recommended**, places that our writers, editors, and readers praise again and again for consistency and excellence.

By default, there's another category: any place we include in this book is by definition worth your time, unless we say otherwise. And we will.

Disagree with any of our choices? Care to nominate a place or suggest that we rate one more highly? Visit our feedback center at www.fodors.com/feedback.

Budget Well

Hotel and restaurant price categories from ¢ to $$$$ are defined in the opening pages of each chapter. For attractions, we always give standard adult admission fees; reductions are usually available for children, students, and senior citizens. Want to pay with plastic? **AE, D, DC, MC, V** after restaurant and hotel listings indicate if American Express, Discover, Diners Club, MasterCard, and Visa are accepted.

Restaurants

Unless we state otherwise, restaurants are open for lunch and dinner daily. We mention dress only when there's a specific requirement and reservations only when they're essential or not accepted—it's always best to book ahead.

Hotels

Hotels have private bath, phone, TV, and air-conditioning and operate on the European Plan (aka EP, meaning without meals), unless we specify that they use the Continental Plan (CP, with a continental breakfast), Breakfast Plan (BP, with a full breakfast), or Modified American Plan (MAP, with breakfast and dinner), or are all-inclusive (including all meals and most activities). We always

list facilities but not whether you'll be charged an extra fee to use them, so when pricing accommodations, find out what's included.

Many Listings

★	Fodor's Choice
★	Highly recommended
⊠	Physical address
✛	Directions
⌖	Mailing address
☎	Telephone
🖷	Fax
⊕	On the Web
✎	E-mail
☜	Admission fee
☉	Open/closed times
Ⓜ	Metro stations
▭	Credit cards

Hotels & Restaurants

🏠	Hotel
⇥	Number of rooms
☖	Facilities
⑂	Meal plans
✕	Restaurant
☟	Reservations
⬉	Smoking
☗	BYOB
✕🏠	Hotel with restaurant that warrants a visit

Outdoors

🏌	Golf
⛺	Camping

Other

☺	Family-friendly
⇨	See also
⊠	Branch address
☞	Take note

WHAT'S WHERE

1 San Antonio. Remember the Alamo? The city's—and state's—famous landmark is here, though it sometimes gets lost amid the charm of the ever-popular River Walk, a shady pedestrian walkway along the San Antonio River that winds through town. Tourists gravitate to the scores of shops, hotels, and restaurants hugging the river's shore. If they're not at the River Walk, they're probably at Market Square, enjoying Tex-Mex or the real thing, as San Antonio is heavily Hispanic.

2 Austin. Keep it weird, y'all. Quirkiness is a big part of Austin's charm. But its motto really could be Keep it on the Move, as development continues to expand the city's borders and make it more and more urban. The state capital is home to the sprawling University of Texas campus and energetic 6th Street—where music thumps into the wee hours of the night—and treasures like the Bullock Story of Texas Museum, a repository for exhibits about the Lone Star State's fascinating history. Nestled in Texas's Hill Country, with myriad lakes and parks, Austin has its rural side. But Round Rock, where Dell Computers is headquartered, is nearby, giving the area a high-tech edge, too.

3 The Hill Country. Dude ranches, lakes, wineries, German-flavored Fredericksburg, and lots of hills comprise Central Texas's Hill Country, west of Austin and north and northwest San Antonio. Scenic drives and outdoor activities are popular here, and the best time of year to visit without a doubt is springtime, when the bluebonnets burst forth, coloring the landscape with their vibrant blue-violet hue.

QUINTESSENTIAL SAN ANTONIO, AUSTIN & THE HILL COUNTRY

Barbecue

Texas barbecue will make you forget all about Memphis, North Carolina, and Kansas City. Here barbecue can mean pretty much anything, smoked until it literally disintegrates in your mouth. Most of the time, though, we're talking about brisket. Not that dried-up hunk of meat Grandma used to make—Texas barbecue brisket is moist, tender, and thinly sliced, served over some bread and slathered with sauce. Grab some pickles and sides—baked beans, potato salad, fried okra, jambalaya, broccoli-rice-cheese casserole, corn on the cob, black-eyed peas, green beans, mac 'n' cheese . . . maybe even an SOS (side of sausage). Wash it all down with a sweet iced tea or a Shiner Bock, and you'll find culinary nirvana.

Tejano Traditions

Texas's Hispanic heritage goes back to the 16th century, when Spanish conquistadors first visited the region. These explorers were followed by settlers from Mexico, who extended their mission trails throughout the state and brought their religion, customs, and legal system along. They also unknowingly established the beginnings of Tejano (Spanish for "Texan") culture—eventually solidifying this new identity as they fought against Mexico alongside Anglo settlers in the Texas Revolution. Today you can see Tejano influences in San Antonio, Austin, and the Hill Country's architecture, music, food (don't leave the state without trying some Tex-Mex), and, yes, the language. The Census Bureau reports that 35.7% of the state's residents are of Hispanic or Latino origin—a figure that is expected to grow along with the Tejano impact on all Texans' identity.

Living in such a large and bold state, Texans sometimes seem to forget about the rest of the country. They've developed a culture all their own, which you can delve into by doing as the natives do.

Cowboy Culture

One of the first things you'll notice when you deplane in Texas is that people here are proud of their Western roots. Many of the real cowboys are long gone (though the state remains home to many working ranches), but Texans still dress the part. You're likely to see at least a handful of people wearing cowboy boots and hats in most public places, and hearing country music at some point during your stay is a given. The most Western of institutions, the rodeo, is alive and well here, and dude ranches—where you experience ranch life for yourself—populate the Hill Country. If you want to meet Texans who aren't "all hat and no cattle," leave the urban areas to visit places where farming and ranching are still a part of the daily rhythm of life.

Sports Fervor

Football in Central Texas is more religion than sport. In fall, normal life is put on hold on Friday nights, and it feels like everyone is at the high school game. (It's fitting that NBC's series *Friday Night Lights* is filmed in Austin, Pflugerville, and San Marcos.) On Saturday, burnt-orange-clad UT fans pack Darrell K Royal-Texas Memorial Stadium—capacity 90,000—to cheer on the Longhorns, a perennial college football powerhouse.

In recent years, though, the area has become a bit basketball crazy, too. Tim Duncan and Tony Parker's San Antonio Spurs are the closest thing to a dynasty in the NBA right now; the team won the title in 1999, 2003, 2005, and 2007.

IF YOU LIKE

Outdoor Adventure

There's no shortage of things to do in Texas for those who love spending time outdoors. And this is true not only in the Hill Country, but in the cities, too, where hike-and-bike trails and golf courses allow you to get away from the brick and mortar.

- **Enchanted Rock State Park, between Fredericksburg and Llano.** The "enchanted" pink granite dome, at 425 feet tall, makes this state park popular with rock climbers. Others come to hike or simply look at the sky—bird-watching by day, stargazing by night. (⇨ Chapter 3.)

- **La Cantera, San Antonio.** Play golf at the Arnold Palmer–designed course that San Antonioans have rated number-one. (⇨ Chapter 1.)

- **Natural Bridge Caverns, near New Braunfels and San Antonio.** Want to go below Earth's surface to cool off and get a different perspective? Here you travel down 180 feet and then walk through a maze of beautiful rock formations. (⇨ Chapter 1.)

- **Wild Basin Wilderness Preserve, Austin.** Ten different walking trails allow you to stretch your legs and provide stunning scenic views as well. At night it's a great place to look up at the stars. (⇨ Chapter 2.)

- **Zilker Park, Austin.** Canoe in Lady Bird Lake, view outdoor sculpture, walk through meditative gardens or under 100-year-old pecan trees, or go swimming at Austin's centrally located urban park, southwest of downtown. (⇨ Chapter 2.)

Art

Austin and San Antonio have traditional sprawling art museums, and little ones, too. Here are a few we like and think you will, too.

- **Blanton Museum of Art, Austin.** On the campus of the University of Texas, this is the largest university art museum. It holds works from across the ages, including Renaissance art and contemporary Latin-American art. (⇨ Chapter 2.)

- **Elisabet Ney Museum, Austin.** The preserved neoclassical studio of 19th-century Austin socialite Elisabet Ney includes dozens of Ney's sculptures, such as one of Texas founder Stephen F. Austin. (⇨ Chapter 2.)

- **McNay Art Museum, San Antonio.** This museum has a homey feel, which makes sense, given that it's housed in a private mansion once owned by artist and oil heiress Marion Koogler McNay. The 24 rooms showcase the talents of Cézanne, Gauguin, and Picasso, among others. (⇨ Chapter 1.)

- **San Antonio Museum of Art (SAMA), San Antonio.** The collection at this large downtown museum is diverse, from folk, American Indian, and Spanish-colonial art to European paintings, Western antiquities, and contemporary works. (⇨ Chapter 1.)

- **Umlauf Sculpture Garden and Museum, Austin.** Enjoy art outdoors at this tranquil spot in Austin's Zilker Park. More than 130 works of art are on display. (⇨ Chapter 2.)

Family Fun

Families have so much to choose from in the Lone Star State: from water parks, roller coasters, and outdoorsy options to museums with kids in mind.

- **Schlitterbahn, New Braunfels.** Though the park is also in Galveston and South Padre Island, the biggest of the three Texas Schlitterbahns is in New Braunfels, a convenient day trip from San Antonio or Austin. It's been voted the best water park for a decade now. The new ride Dragon's Revenge includes a two-story free fall, creepy caverns, special effects, and, as the name suggests, a dragon bent on revenge—everything a preteen boy wants. (⇨ Chapter 3.)

- **SeaWorld San Antonio.** The killer whale Shamu is enough of an enticement to get your kids here, but add to that all of the rides, large water park, and opportunities to see (and even feed) dolphins and stingrays, and you can't go wrong with a visit to the world's largest marine park. (⇨ Chapter 1.)

- **Six Flags Fiesta Texas, San Antonio.** The thrill-rides chain has two fun parks in Texas, but the San Antonio one maintains its unique personality among Six Flags' many properties due to its musical shows that have carried over from when it was owned by Opryland. (⇨ Chapter 1.)

- **Witte Museum, San Antonio.** Learning is fun at this small science museum with interactive exhibits. The tree house out back can keep curious young children entertained for hours. (⇨ Chapter 1.)

History

History lessons abound throughout Central Texas, often in plain sight for easy access.

- **The Alamo, San Antonio.** All Texans know about this site that inspired the battle cry for Texas independence, and John Wayne helped cement this historic mission firmly in the minds of everyone else. The building is small but significant for its role in the fight for Texas independence against Mexico. (⇨ Chapter 1.)

- **Bob Bullock Texas State History Museum, Austin.** If you want to envelop yourself in Lone Star State history, don't miss this 176,000-square-foot museum named after Texas's 38th lieutenant governor. (⇨ Chapter 2.)

- **King William Historic District, San Antonio.** This 25-block area is where prosperous merchants of the late 19th century lived. You can visit historic homes such as the 1876 Steves Homestead and 1860 Guenther House, both influenced by the Victorian era. (⇨ Chapter 1.)

- **Menger Hotel, San Antonio.** This hotel near the Alamo has been the overnight stop for famous folks from all walks of life—Oscar Wilde, Robert E. Lee, and Teddy Roosevelt among them. (⇨ Chapter 1.)

- **Treaty Oak, Austin.** Legend has it that under this tree the "Father of Texas," Stephen F. Austin, negotiated the first boundary agreement between American Indian tribes and European settlers. (⇨ Chapter 2.)

GREAT ITINERARIES

HILL COUNTRY DRIVING TOUR

The Hill Country is one of Texas's most scenic regions. It spans 23 counties and is filled with small towns, popular lakes, several caves, and historic attractions. The drive can be done in a few days or in a week, depending on how often you stop along the way. For the purpose of this itinerary, we've set it up as a four-day trip, with a full day in Fredericksburg and an afternoon in Austin. We've set it up from San Antonio, but you can jump in anywhere along the route.

Day 1: Cowboys & Art

Leaving from San Antonio, travel about 52 mi northwest to **Bandera**. It's known as the "Cowboy Capital of the World," both a reminder of its Wild West history and a symbol of its present-day Western theme-inspired tourism. The town is surrounded by numerous dude ranches that offer you a chance to take to the saddle for a few days of cowboy fun. Rodeos, country music, and horse racing are also found in the area. If you want to get out and walk a bit, Hill Country State Natural Area is a good place to do it. It has 5,300 acres of hills, creeks, and live oaks.

For lunch, stop in at the Full Moon Café, if you're after healthy fare, or at the O.S.T. Restaurant if you want that artery-busting, but oh-so-good chicken-fried steak.

In the afternoon, head north on Highway 173 for approximately 25 mi to **Kerrville**. Attractions in the area include the Y.O. Ranch, one of the most famous in the nation (you can call ahead for a tour; 830/257–4440), and the Museum of Western Art. If you want to stay overnight here, you can try the Y.O. or Guadalupe RV Resort (which has cabins with kitchens as well as campsites). Otherwise, take a brief detour west for 7 mi to **Ingram** to peruse the small cluster of art galleries and shops. (Note that most of the shops are closed Monday.) When you're ready to call it a day, drive 32 mi (via Highway 16 from Kerrville) to Fredericksburg, the most popular city in the Hill Country (⇨ Chapter 3 for the many lodging options here).

Day 2: German Infusion

Welcome to Texas's enclave of German heritage. **Fredericksburg** is a longtime favorite with shoppers and bed-and-breakfast lovers. Downtown, the National Museum of the Pacific War honors Fredericksburg native Admiral Chester Nimitz, World War II commander-in-chief of the Pacific, and Wildseed Farms is the largest working wildflower farm in the United States.

If hiking rather than shopping is your thing, venture to nearby Enchanted Rock State Natural Area. This park contains the largest stone formation in the West; both easy and challenging climbs are available. In summer, climbers should start the hike early to avoid midday heat. For dinner, try some German cuisine at one of the restaurants on Main Street.

Day 3: LBJ Day

On Day 3, head east on U.S. 290 for about 10 mi to **Stonewall**, the birth and burial place of Lyndon B. Johnson. At the Lyndon B. Johnson State Historical Park, you can catch a guided tour of the LBJ Ranch.

Approximately 10 mi east of Stonewall on U.S. 290 is **Johnson City**. Named for LBJ's grandfather's nephew, the then future president moved here from Stonewall when he was five years old. The Lyndon B. Johnson National Historic Park (dif-

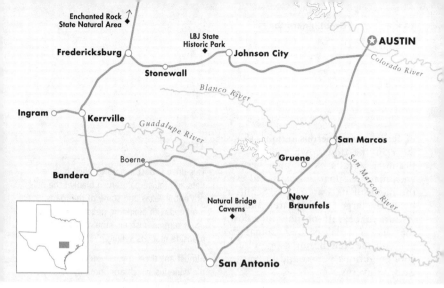

ferent from the state park noted above) is here; it is the simply titled Boyhood Home of LBJ. Have lunch at the Silver K Café in Johnson City.

From Johnson City, head east on U.S. 290 for about 40 mi, then north on I–35 into **Austin**. The centerpiece of the city as well as the state government is the state capitol. Guided tours of the statehouse that stands taller than the national capitol are offered daily. If you have time, visit the Governor's Mansion, just south of the capitol. It is filled with historic reminders of the many governors of the Lone Star State. You're taken past the main staircase, through the formal parlor, and finally into the dining room.

But if your time is limited, head north of the capitol to learn more about LBJ at the University of Texas at Austin, the largest university in the nation. The Lyndon Baines Johnson Library and Museum traces the history of his presidency. Tour a model of the Oval Office as it looked during LBJ's administration. Spend the evening in Austin (⇨ Chapter 2 for dining, lodging, and nightlife options); if you love live music, be sure to visit 6th Street.

Day 4: The I–35 Strip

Approximately 40 mi south of Austin at Exit 206 off I–35 is **San Marcos**, a favorite with shoppers from around the state who come to browse its two massive outlet malls. Summer visitors find recreation along the banks of the San Marcos River. It's popular with snorkelers for its clear waters, and is home to many fish (including some white albino catfish) and various types of plant life.

When you've finished shopping, continue south to **Gruene** (pronounced Green), a former town and now technically a neighborhood in New Braunfels. From its founding in the 1870s, Gruene was a happening place with a swinging dance hall and busy cotton gin. But when the boll weevil arrived in Texas with the Great Depression on its heels, Gruene became a ghost town. Today that former ghost town is alive with small shops and restaurants as well as Texas's oldest dance hall, Gruene Hall—as lively today as it was in the late 1800s.

From Gruene, reach **New Braunfels** by returning to I–35 and continuing south, or by traveling south on Gruene Road. The self-proclaimed "Antiques Capital of Texas" has numerous antiques shops, most in the downtown region. New Braunfels recalls its German heritage with many German festivals and even the name of its water park, Schlitterbahn (the largest in the state). Summer visitors canoe, raft, or inner tube down the city's Guadalupe and Comal rivers. Outside New Braunfels, you'll find cool conditions year-round in Natural Bridge Caverns.

From New Braunfels, take Highway 46 West for about 50 mi back to Bandera, or continue on I–35 back to San Antonio.

TIPS

This drive is best in spring, when bluebonnets and Indian paintbrush blanket the hills of Central Texas and some of the roads are lined with blooming peach trees. If you go in summer instead, stop at one of the roadside markets selling peaches.

Almost any time of year you can stop at the wineries, which are primarily bunched around Fredericksburg.

Be wary of this tour during heavy rains; many roads have low water crossings that can be prone to flash flooding.

San Antonio

WORD OF MOUTH

"Many visitors miss King William Historic District, not far from the River Walk. Most of the homes were built in the mid to late 1800s, were beautiful at one time, fell into disrepair, became a slum, then were rescued, and are once again simply gorgeous. . . . One of the better breakfast/lunch places in town, Guenther House, is located there, so you could do a drive-by or walk by of the area, and have a terrific lunch at Guenther House the same day. Eat outside on their patio. So pleasant!"

—OO

By Debbie
Harmsen,
Suzanne
Robitaille,
Rogers
Slavens,
and Kevin
Tankersley

WAKE UP IN THE ALAMO City with the scent of huevos rancheros in the air, the sound of mariachis, and the sight of barges winding down the San Antonio River, and you know you're some place special.

San Antonio is quite possibly Texas's most beautiful and atmospheric city, so it's no wonder it's the state's number-one tourist destination. Remember the Alamo? It's here, sitting in a plaza right downtown, so you can easily walk to it from your hotel. But while most visitors check out this famous symbol of Texas liberty when they come to town, the historic mission is by no means the only reason to visit San Antonio.

In fact, the heart of the visitor area is the *Paseo del Rio*—the River Walk—a festive, almost magical place that winds through downtown at 20 feet below street level. Nestled by tall buildings and cypress trees, and tucked away from the noise of traffic above, the River Walk draws crowds to its high-rise and boutique hotels, specialty shops, and plethora of restaurants with alfresco dining.

Families are drawn to the big theme parks on the northwestern edge of town. San Antonio's SeaWorld is the largest marine-adventure park in the SeaWorld chain, and has what every kid wants in a park: animals, roller coasters, waterslides, and swimming pools. Meanwhile, Six Flags Fiesta Texas also boasts a water park and roller coasters, plus many other rides and Branson-like musical shows.

Snuggled firmly in south-central Texas, San Antonio acts as the gateway to the Hill Country—a landscape punctuated with majestic live oaks, myriad lakes, and flush-with-wildflowers hills—as well as the beginning of South Texas, the huge triangular tip of the state that is home to the Rio Grande Valley and South Padre Island, favorite destinations for bird-watchers and beachgoers. San Antonio also isn't far from the Mexico–Texas border—between two and three hours to Del Rio to the west and Laredo to the south.

Given the city's close proximity to Mexico and its onetime position as the chief Mexican stronghold in Texas (prior to Texas's independence), it's not surprising that the rich tapestry of San Antonio's heritage has a good deal of Hispanic culture woven into it. Visitors can peruse shops selling Mexican crafts and jewelry, dine on Tex-Mex food, and enjoy Spanish music and mariachi bands at Market Square.

If experiencing San Antonio's multifaceted ethnicity—including not only its Latino side but also its German, French, African, and even Japanese influences—is of prime importance to you, then the best time for you to visit may well be during Fiesta each April. An event that began in the late 1800s to pay tribute to the soldiers who died in the Battle of the Alamo and San Jacinto, the 10-day citywide celebration captures the city's many cultures, with music, food, festivals, fairs, parades, a carnival, and more.

PLANNING YOUR TRIP

WHEN TO GO

October and April are the prime months for a comfortable visit to San Antonio, though spring (when it's not raining) is ideal for seeing the scenery if you're planning to visit the missions or take an excursion into the Hill Country. Also in spring, a celebratory mood overtakes the town during the annual Fiesta event.

From June through September, intense heat bakes the city, with high humidity to boot. If you come then, you can escape the heat with well-air-conditioned inside attractions and at the popular water parks of SeaWorld and Six Flags Fiesta Texas.

Though not out of the question, winter snows are very rare, as are light ice storms. More expected are the heavy spring rains, which can result in flash flooding in the Hill Country.

GETTING THERE & AROUND

Three interstate highways converge in central San Antonio; I–35, which links San Antonio with Dallas and Austin to the north and Laredo and the Mexican border to the south; I–10, which connects San Antonio to Houston to the east and then veers northwest before heading to El Paso and the west coast; and I–37, which connects San Antonio to Corpus Christi on the Gulf of Mexico. A number of U.S. highways and Texas state roads also lead into the city, including U.S. 281 to the north and south and U.S. 90 to the east and west. Two other highways loop around the city; I–410 encircles the heart of San Antonio, and Texas Highway 1604 makes a wider circle that encompasses areas beyond the city limits.

In most cases, having a car in San Antonio is extremely helpful. Like most Texas cities, things are quite spread out. That being said, if you're focusing on the River Walk and the area immediately surrounding it, you'll probably want to park your car at your hotel and tackle sightseeing on foot (or via the downtown streetcars, www.viainfo.net/busservice/streetcar.aspx).

EXPLORING SAN ANTONIO

Much of downtown San Antonio can be explored on foot or by way of the trolley system that runs frequently between points of interest (⇨ *San Antonio Essentials for trolley information*).

Depending on whom you ask, the number of neighborhoods in San Antonio varies. The San Antonio Convention & Visitors Bureau breaks the city into quadrants—Northside, Eastside, Southside, and Westside, with museums in the north, heritage sites on the east and west, and missions in the south.

For the purposes of this guidebook, we've broken San Antonio into five primary neighborhoods that fit where visitors tend to go. In the dining and lodging sections we've given the River Walk its own category due to the multitude of restaurants and hotels around the river's banks.

SAN ANTONIO TOP 5

■ **Peace Like a River Walk:** Meandering through the heart of downtown, the San Antonio River won't elude you. Walk along its cypress-draped serenity for a relaxing stroll, or take a dinner cruise aboard a barge.

■ **On a Mission Trail:** Five missions from the 1700s, including the Alamo, are all within city limits. Follow the signs to find these exquisite buildings with Spanish-colonial architecture.

■ **An Art Attack:** At museums, galleries, and a school devoted to arts education, the arts—and artists—are

flourishing in San Antonio. Take in an exhibition while in town, or watch an artist at work.

■ **Hispanic Culture:** From the new Alameda museum focusing on Latino arts to the shops, restaurants, and entertainment at Market Square, a Mexican sensibility saturates San Antonio.

■ **Family Fun:** Thrill rides, Shamu sightings, serious splashing at the water parks, and a science-theme tree house at the Witte Museum are the reasons kids (and their parents) want to keep coming back to San Antonio.

DOWNTOWN & THE RIVER WALK

Coming from the northeast and heading southwest, I–35 slices through San Antonio, curving around its main downtown area, which is primarily composed of the region south and east of I–35, west of I–37, and north of I–10. The San Antonio River falls along the western part of downtown but makes a little loop into the downtown area around Market and Commerce streets, producing the ideal conditions for a winding River Walk set a level below the main hubbub of traffic. That's not to say the River Walk is quiet. Although the cars and horns are out of sight and earshot, the festive, largely developed River Walk is often bustling with people—both visitors and locals. All of San Antonio comes here to dine, shop, and eat with friends along the river's banks.

Four prime areas downtown are Alamo Plaza, Market Square, La Villita, and HemisFair Park. Alamo Plaza is, of course, where the Alamo is located, but it also serves as a bit of a town square, with many hotels (like the famous Menger Hotel) and tourist traps (such as the wax museum) either off the plaza or nearby.

The three-block area comprising Market Square (⌧ *West Commerce and Dolorosa Sts.* ⊕ *www.marketsquaresa.com*) includes the Farmer's Market, a former produce market now filled with crafts, open-air boutiques, and El Mercado, the largest Mexican market in the United States. The history of Market Square dates back to the early 1800s. This was the birthplace of *chili con carne,* the spicy meat-and-bean mixture that today is generally considered the state dish of Texas. Enjoy the music of roaming mariachis and the delicious foods offered at stalls along the way, and pick up some *pan dulce* (sweet bread) at the famed Mi Tierra Café and Bakery, open 24 hours a day. The new Alameda museum and its accompanying *botanica* (a curio shop) and outdoor

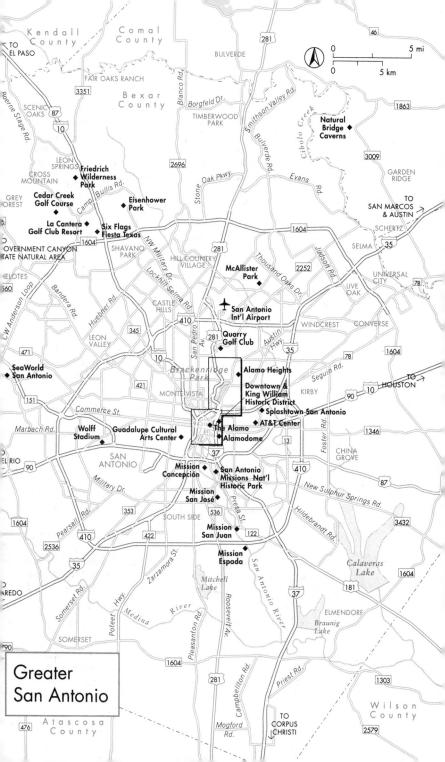

Greater San Antonio

performing space is also part of the outdoor-mall-like complex.

A relative newcomer to San Antonio, the Torch of Friendship (La Antorcha de Amistad), installed in 1994, stands tall and slightly twisted at the intersection of Losoya, Commerce, Market, and Alamo streets near the River Walk. The bright orange sculpture, 65 feet high and weighing 50 tons, symbolizes the city's friendly ties with Mexico.

> ### CRUISIN' ON A RIVER
>
> **Rio San Antonio Cruises**
> (☎ 210/244–5700 or 800/417–4139 ⊕ www.riosanantonio.com 🚢 $7.75) provides narrated boat tours and charter dinner cruises. Try to take your trip near twilight, when the sounds and light begin to soften.

Meaning Little Village, La Villita (⊠ *S. Alamo St., at the River Walk, Downtown* ⊕ *www.lavillita.com*), a prime place for shopping *(⇨ Shopping)* and entertainment *(⇨ Arts & Entertainment)*, was the original settlement in Old San Antonio, with adobe, brick, and stone structures in varying architectural styles. Workshops and boutiques of many of the city's artisans and jewelers are here, as well as a few good restaurants. The historic structures have been well preserved.

The biggest of these areas is HemisFair Park (⊠ *S. Alamo St. between Market and Durango Sts., Downtown*), a 15-acre green space near the convention center that was the site of the 1968 World's Fair. The park is landscaped with waterfalls and a playground, and features a trio of attractions: the Tower of the Americas, the Institute of Texas Cultures, and the Mexican Cultural Institute.

The River Walk, with its twisting way, is near all of these areas and connects many of the main sites visitors go to downtown. If downtown is San Antonio's heart, the river's many arms are its arteries, bringing everyone to where the action is.

MAIN ATTRACTIONS

❶ The Alameda. The Museo Alameda, in partnership with the Smithsonian Institution (its first formal affiliate outside Washington, D.C.), uses continually changing exhibitions to explore the Latino experience in America. Recent installations include "Nosotras: Portraits of Latinas," and "¡Azúcar! The Life and Music of Celia Cruz." The museum, based in San Antonio's historic Market Square (look for the watermelon-colored building), opened in spring 2007 with much fanfare. ⊠ *101 S. Santa Rosa, Market Square, Downtown* ☎ *210/299–4300* ⊕ *www.thealameda.org* 🚢 *$4* ⊗ *Tues.–Sat. 10–6 (until 8 on Wed.), Sun. noon–6.*

Numbers in the margin correspond to numbers on the Downtown San Antonio & King William Historic District map.

❿ Alamo. At the heart of San Antonio, this onetime Franciscan mission stands as a repository of Texas history, a monument to the 189 Texan volunteers who fought and died here during a 13-day siege in 1836 by Mexican dictator General Antonio López de Santa Anna. The Texans lost, but the defeat inspired a later victory in Texas's bid

Fodor'sChoice
★

San Antonio's Missions

Once referred to as the Queen of the Missions due to its vastness, the Mission San José y San Miguel de Aguayo reflects the 18th-century Spanish Colonial period.

During the Spanish-colonial period, San Antonio was home to five missions that were used by the Spanish in their attempts to Christianize the American Indians. Among them was the Alamo, originally called San Antonio de Valero. It was established by Franciscan priests in 1718 in temporary buildings. The first permanent chapel collapsed in 1744. Work on another—a building later known as the Alamo—began in the 1750s, but it was never completed, and the mission's small Indian population left the area.

The Alamo's military significance eclipsed its religious role when, in February 1836, 189 Texas revolutionaries fought Mexico leader Santa Anna's troops. Santa Anna demanded the mission's surrender. The Texans answered with a cannon shot. Santa Anna ran up the red flag—no quarter, no surrender, no mercy—from atop San Fernando Cathedral and laid siege in what would come to be called the Battle of the Alamo. On the list of defenders were Davy Crockett, James Bowie, and William Barret Travis. The revolutionaries fought from the walls and then hand to hand, until—as legend has it—they all died. (There is some indication that a half dozen men surrendered and were immediately executed.) The April afterward, Texas leader Sam Houston and his men attacked and defeated Santa Anna near the San Jacinto River on Vince's Bayou, near Houston. "Remember the Alamo" was their great battle cry.

San Antonio's other four missions—Concepción, San Francisco de la Espada, San José, and San Juan Capistrano—are located along the San Antonio River in southern San Antonio. These four are operated by the National Park Service, though they also are still active parishes.

—Excerpted from *Fodor's Compass American Guides: Texas, 3rd Edition*

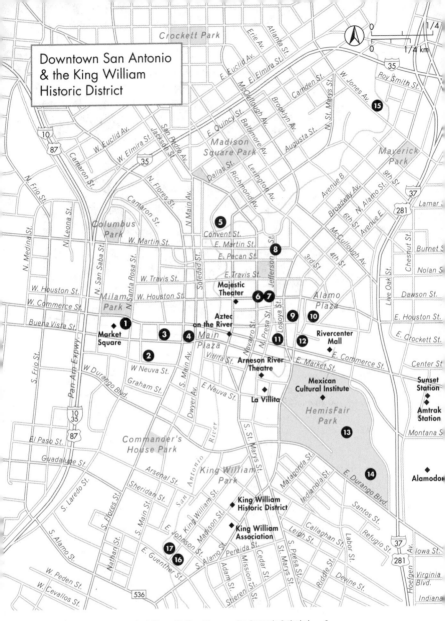

Downtown San Antonio & the King William Historic District

for independence with the rallying cry "Remember the Alamo" spurring the soldiers on toward success. Today the historic shrine and barracks contain the guns and other paraphernalia used by such military heroes as William Travis, James Bowie, and Davy Crockett, who all died defending the Alamo. You can step inside the small mission and tour on your own, and then listen to a 20-minute history talks (talks occur every 30 minutes during operating hours except at noon, 12:30, and 1). Outside in the peaceful courtyard, a history wall elucidates the story of the Alamo, including its days as a religious mission. The site is operated today by the Daughters of the Republic of Texas, who saved it from ruin a century ago. ⊠*300 Alamo Plaza, Houston and Crockett, Downtown* ☎*210/225–1391* ⊕*www.the alamo.org* ⊠*Free* ☉*Mon.–Sat. 9–5:30, Sun. 10–5:30 (it generally stays open until 7 Fri. and Sat. July and Aug.).*

> ### TAKE A TOUR
>
> **Gray Line bus tours.** Guided, narrated tours of San Antonio's top visitor attractions. ⊠*216 Alamo Plaza* ☎*210/226–1706* ⊠*Prices vary.*
>
> **VIA San Antonio Streetcar.** These motorized, open-air trolleys make stops at all the major hotels and attractions such as Market Square, the Alamo, and the Spanish Governor's Palace. Trolleys follow four different routes that encompass most of downtown. ☎*210/362–2020* ⊠*$1.*

14 **Institute of Texan Cultures.** Beyond the Tower of the Americas, this interactive museum affiliated with the University of Texas focuses on the 25 ethnic groups who have made Texas what it is today. Walk through a re-created sharecropper's house, or listen to an animated, recorded conversation that might have taken place between a Spanish governor and a Comanche chief in the 1790s. Most days costumed docents mill about the museum, ready to educate visitors on the role of a chuckwagon cook on a cattle drive or the rigors of frontier life for women. ⊠*801 S. Bowie St., Downtown* ☎*210/458–2300* ⊕*www.texan cultures.com* ⊠*$7* ☉*Tues.–Sat. 10–5, Sun. noon–5.*

11 **River Walk.** The *Paseo del Rio* is the city's (and the state's) leading tourist attraction. Built a full story below street level, it comprises about 3 mi of scenic stone pathways lining both banks of the San Antonio River as it flows through downtown, connecting many of the city's tourist attractions. (Soon, however, it will expand to 13 mi, connecting downtown with Brackenridge Park to the north and the missions to south.) In some places the walk is peaceful and quiet; in others it is a mad conglomeration of restaurants, bars, hotels, shops, and strolling mariachi bands, all of which can also be seen from river taxis and charter boats. Throughout downtown, there are 35 access points to the River Walk. ⊠*Access from many points downtown; it starts near the Rivercenter Mall at 849 E. Commerce St.* ☎*210/227–4262* ⊕*www. thesanantonioriverwalk.com* ⊠*Free.*

15 **San Antonio Museum of Art (SAMA).** The museum houses choice collections of pre-Columbian, American Indian, and Spanish colonial art,

The River Walk: Past, Present, and Future

The San Antonio River snakes through the city for 15 mi, while advancing a mere 6 mi north to south in terms of city blocks. Because of its many curves, the Indians called the river "drunken old man going home at night."

In 1921, the river flooded, killing 50 people and caused millions of dollars in damage. The city proposed building an underground channel for the river, essentially hiding it away under concrete as it flowed through downtown. Enraged residents, led by the San Antonio Conservation Society, persuaded the city to turn their sow's ear into a silk purse. The combined beautification and flood-control plan, executed under the aegis of the Depression-era Works Progress Administration, also called for the building of retaining walls, walkways, footbridges, and pretty stone stairways leading from the river up to street level.

Local old-timers remember the River Walk as an almost neglected area, where for most of the year one could stroll in complete peace, hearing only one sound: the clicking of linotypes on the other side of print-shop windows. In spring months, one sometimes heard a more-alarming sound—shotgun fire, as police and parks personnel, in annual pest control campaigns, blew blackbirds out of trees on the banks and filled the river with little corpses.

Today, for better or for worse, all of that has changed. The River Walk is now lined with restaurants, cafés, nightclubs, boutiques, hotels, and a shopping mall, and barges take visitors on river cruises. Cypress, oaks, and willows shade the waterway. At

Christmastime, lights adorn the river and walkway.

The River Walk currently extends for about 3 mi from the city's Municipal Auditorium on the north end to the King William district at the southern end. However, construction is underway to expand the River Walk to 13 mi, making it the country's largest linear park. The developed walk will connect downtown San Antonio with Brackenridge Park and its attractions (San Antonio Botanical Gardens, San Antonio Zoo and Aquarium, Japanese Tea Gardens, the McNay Art Museum, and the Witte Museum, among them) to the north, as well as to the Spanish missions (Concepción, San Francisco de la Espada, San José, and San Juan Capistrano) to the south. The $216-million project, estimated to be completed by 2014, provides for 20,000 planted trees, additional pedestrian bridges and walkways, and more.

—Part of this was excerpted from *Fodor's Compass American Guides: Texas, 2nd and 3rd editions.*

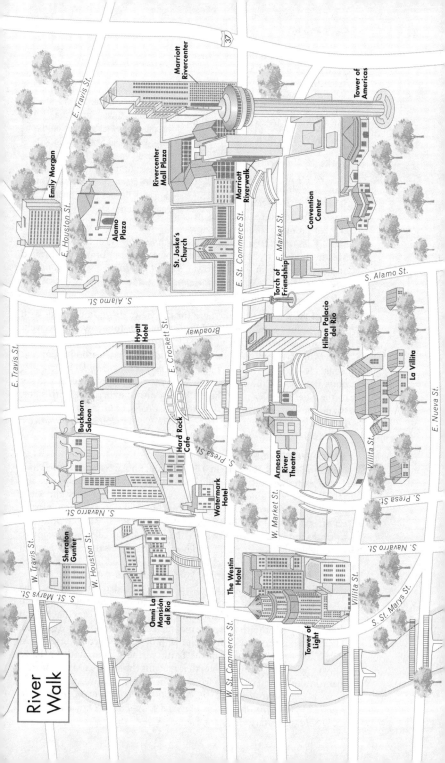

River Walk

as well as the Nelson A. Rockefeller Center for Latin American Art—the nation's largest such facility, with more than 2,500 folk-art objects, and an extensive collection of Asian art, with more than 70 pieces featured in its own wing. Past exhibitions have included works by Impressionists, lacquer over wood and other art by Japanese artist Shibata Zeshin, and lithographs by 20th-century Mexican master David Siquerios. One permanent painting to consider view-

ing is *Passion Flowers with Three Hummingbirds,* an 1875 piece by Martin Johnson Heade depicting a tropical forest in Brazil; it is located on the third floor in the east tower. ⊠*200 W. Jones Ave., Downtown* ☎*210/978–8100* ⊕*www.samuseum.org* ⊠*$8* ☉*Tues. 10–8, Wed.– Sat. 10–5, Sun. noon–6.*

⓭ Tower of the Americas. Come here for the views, including dining with a view. Built for the 1968 World's Fair, the 750-foot tower underwent a $15 million renovation in 2006. It features the popular Flags Over Texas Observation Deck and the rotating steak-and-seafood restaurant Chart House (⇨ *Where to Eat), which makes one complete turn every hour.* Included in the Tower of the Americas admission price is a ticket to the **Skies Over Texas 4D Theater Ride,** a movie experience with sight, sound, movement, and smell. ⊠*600 HemisFair Plaza Way, in Hemis-Fair Park, Downtown* ☎*210/223–3101* ⊕*www.toweroftheamericas. com* ⊠*$10.95* ☉*Sun.–Thurs. 11–10, Fri. and Sat. 11–11.*

ALSO WORTH SEEING

❻ Buckhorn Saloon & Museum. In 1881 the Buckhorn Saloon opened as a Texan watering hole, and Teddy Roosevelt and his Rough Riders are said to have been among its patrons, as were writer O. Henry and Mexican Revolution leader Francisco "Pancho" Villa. Its primary customers after it opened were hunters and trappers, eager for a cold brew and to trade furs and horns. Owner Albert Friedrich collected the horns, some which his father made into horn chairs. The saloon serves a full menu of mostly American fare (burgers, BBQ, catfish, chicken, and steak). In the museum portion, you can see an assortment of marine trophies, fishing lures, and mounted birds on guided tours through the property's many halls: the Buckhorn Hall of Fins, the Buckhorn Hall of Feathers, and the Buckhorn Hall of Horns. Famous artifacts (and they number in the thousands) include one of Gene Autry's saddles. There's also a wax museum on-site with objects related to Texas's history, such as a re-creation of the Battle of the Alamo; and the Texas Ranger Museum, with exhibits that recount the stories of law enforcement in the Lone Star State from Stephen Austin forward. ⊠*318 E. Houston, Downtown* ☎*210/247–4000* ⊕*www.buckhornmuseum. com* ⊠*$11.99 (museum)* ☉*Memorial Day–Labor Day, daily 10–6; early Sept.–late May, daily 10–5.*

2 **Casa Navarro State Historic Site.** A signer of the Texas Declaration of Independence, lawyer and legislator José Antonio Navarro, built these three limestone, brick, and adobe buildings in the 1850s for his residence and law office. He had sold his ranch near Seguin and moved to San Antonio to be active on the city council. Open to visitors, the 0.5-acre site in old San Antonio's Laredito area features period furniture and copies of Navarro's writings—he wrote about the history of Texas from a Tejano's perspective and in the Spanish language. It is San Antonio's only historic site focused on the Mexican history and heritage of Texas from the viewpoint of a native Texan with Mexican ancestry. A fund-raising effort is underway to expand the attraction with more interpretive exhibits. ⊠*228 S. Laredo St., Downtown* ☎*210/226–4801* ⊲*$2* ⊙*Tues.–Sun. 9–4.*

DID YOU KNOW? In the 1900s, a section of San Antonio was called Laredito. It was where working-class Tejanos lived, including merchant–turned–influential statesman José Antonio Navarro, a man of Mexican descent who was born in San Antonio.

9 **Louis Tussaud's Plaza Wax Museum/Ripley's Believe It or Not!** The Plaza Wax Museum depicts the famous, from Jesus to John Wayne. Many figures are displayed in elaborate sets featuring movie scenes. Alamo visitors will appreciate the "Heroes of the Lone Star" exhibits on the fateful battle. Ripley's displays an assortment of more than 500 oddities ranging from miniatures to freaks of nature. ⊠*301 Alamo Plaza, Downtown* ☎*210/224–9299* ⊕*www.plazawaxmuseum.com* ⊲*$16.99 for 1 visitor, $21.99 for 2* ⊙*Daily Mon.–Thurs. 10–8, Fri.–Sat. 9–10, Sun. 9–8.*

12 **Menger Hotel.** After you visit the Alamo, stop by this adjacent 1859 property. It's San Antonio's most historic lodging, and offers a history book full of "who's who"s who've slept here. Some of its most famous guests include Civil War generals Robert E. Lee and William Sherman, Mount Rushmore sculptor Gutzon Borglum (who had a studio at the hotel), playwright Oscar Wilde, and author William Sydney Porter (O. Henry), who mentioned the hotel in several of his short stories. As legend has it, William Menger built the Victorian hotel to accommodate the many carousers who frequented his brewery, which stood on the same site. Step inside the hotel to see its moody, mahogany bar, a precise replica of the pub in London's House of Lords. Here cattlemen closed deals with a handshake over three fingers of rye, and Teddy Roosevelt supposedly recruited his Rough Riders—hard-living cowboys fresh from the Chisholm Trail. Note that Buckhorn Saloon & Museum also makes the same claim; either someone's been playing too much poker and can't stop bluffing, or Teddy had to go recruiting more than once. (⇨ *Where to Stay for a review of its accommodations.*) ⊠*204 Alamo Plaza, Downtown* ☎*210/223–4361* ⊕*www.mengerhotel.com.*

7 **San Antonio Children's Museum.** Are your kids getting bored with the Alamo? Then head to the San Antonio Children's Museum, where they can provide energy to run the museum's kid-powered elevator, drive a

San Antonio for Kids

San Antonio is a terrific Texas spot to take the kids for a weekend getaway or a family vacation. Here are some of the best places for kids in the city:

■ **San Antonio Children's Museum, Downtown.** Learning is fun at this downtown museum, where kids can do anything from blowing bubbles to creating a thunderstorm.

■ **SeaWorld San Antonio, North/ Northwest.** Shamu is the character all the kids love, but the many other animals—including sharks, sea lions, and stingrays—along with roller coasters, and the big water park are all hits with youngsters, too.

■ **Six Flags Fiesta Texas, North/ Northwest.** The new Goliath ride is all the rage right now, but this 105-foot-tall, inverted roller coaster is just one of many attractions at this long-time Central Texas theme park. Moms and Dads especially love the inside entertainment, because they can get out of the heat and let the little ones rest their feet for a bit, all while watching fun shows.

■ **Skies Over Texas 4D Theater Ride, Downtown.** At the base of the

The new Goliath, the ultimate inverted coaster, thrills riders at Six Flags Fiesta Texas.

Tower of the Americas in HemisFair Park, boys and girls (and their parents, too) can experience a fun simulator ride that even has a 4D element (hint: you might get a little wet).

■ **The Witte Museum, Breckenridge Row.** The tree house out back lets kids explore and burn off energy after they've learned all about animals related to Texas's history inside the museum. But, shhh. Don't tell them, but there are learning activities for them in the tree house, too.

kid-size front-end loader, and learn about a variety of topics, including bank accounts, skeletons, and flying a plane. ⊠ *305 E. Houston St., Downtown* ☎ *210/212–4453* ⊕ *www.sakids.org* ⊠ *$4* ⊙ *Mar.–Aug., weekdays. 9–5, Sat. 9–6, Sun. noon–4; Sept.–Feb., Tues.–Fri. 9–4, Sat. 9–6, Sun. noon–4.*

❹ **San Fernando Cathedral.** Still an active parish, San Fernando's was built in 1738 by the city's Canary Island colonists. Later, Mexican general Santa Anna raised a flag of "no quarter" here before he stormed the Alamo in 1836, signifying to the Texans that he would take no prisoners. In 1873, following a fire after the Civil War, the chapel was replaced with the present-day construction. Although a tomb holds the remains of some unknown soldiers, modern historians do not believe these were the bodies of the Alamo defenders because evidence of military uniforms, never worn by the Texans, has turned up among the remains. ⊠ *115 Main Plaza, Downtown* ☎ *210/227–1297*

⊕*www.sfcathedral.org* ✉*Free* ⊙*Daily masses starting at 6 AM. Tours available when church isn't in use.*

❺ Southwest School of Art & Craft. Situated along the river with access to the River Walk, the school is housed in the former Ursuline Convent and Academy. Built in 1851, the Ursuline became the first girls' school in the city. The long halls of the once busy dormitory are now filled with photography, jewelry, fibers, paper making, painting, and the like. The school offers adult and youth classes and workshops, and the annual Fiesta Arts Fair is held in April. The Gallery Shop sells handcrafted items, including silver Southwestern jewelry, hand-painted plates, and wooden Christmas ornaments. Grab a sandwich or salad at the School's Copper Kitchen Café, or some sweets at the Garden Room. ✉*300 Augusta, Downtown* ☎*210/224–1848* ⊕*www.swschool.org* ✉*Free* ⊙*Mon.–Sat. 10–5, Sun. 11–4.*

❸ Spanish Governor's Palace. The beautiful 18th-century seat of Spanish power in Texas has period furnishings throughout its 10 rooms. Relax on the cobblestone patio and make a wish in the wishing well. ✉*105 Plaza de Armas, Downtown* ☎*210/224–0601* ✉*$2* ⊙*Mon.–Sat. 9–5, Sun. 10–5.*

❽ Vietnam War Memorial. Created by combat artist Austin Deuel, this sculpture in front of Municipal Auditorium represents a Marine holding a wounded soldier looking skyward as he awaits evacuation. ✉*E. Martin and Jefferson Sts., Downtown.*

ING WILLIAM & MONTE VISTA HISTORIC DISTRICTS

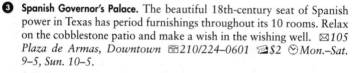

In the late 19th century, leading German merchants settled the 25-block King William Historic District south of downtown. Today the area's Victorian mansions, set in a quiet, leafy neighborhood, are a pleasure to behold. Madison, Guenther, and King William streets are particularly pretty for a stroll or drive. Each December, on the first Saturday, you can tour several of the homes during the King William Home Tour, and during the citywide Fiesta each April the area puts on a fair. For a map of the area and information on district events, contact the **King William Association** (✉*1032 S. Alamo St., King William Historic District, San Antonio* ☎*210/227–8786* ⊕*www.kingwilliamassociation.org*).

Northwest of downtown and southwest of Alamo Heights, the Monte Vista Historic District encompasses 100 blocks and features homes from the turn of the 19th century, when San Antonio's "Gilded Age" brought affluent residents to the area. Dozens of architectural styles define the homes; among them are Beaux-Arts, Craftsman, Dutch Colonial, Georgian, Greek Revival, Italianate Renaissance, Mediterranean, Mission, Modern, Neoclassical, Prairie School, Pueblo Revival, Queen Anne, Ranch, Tudor, and Victorian. The entire district is on the National Register of Historic Places. For a map of the area, contact the **Monte Vista Historical Association** (✉*Box 12386, San Antonio 78212* ☎*210/737–8212* ⊕*www.montevista-sa.org*).

Numbers in the margin correspond to numbers on the Downtown San Antonio & King William Historic District map.

MAIN ATTRACTIONS

16 **Guenther House.** This 1860 home of the family that founded the adjacent Pioneer Flour Mills welcomes self-guided tours. At the latter you'll find a small museum of mill memorabilia, a gift shop, and a cheerful restaurant serving fine German pastries and full breakfasts and lunches. ✉*205 E. Guenther St., King William Historic District* ☎*210/227–1061* ⊕*www.guentherhouse.com* ✆*Free* ⏲*Mon.–Sat. 8–4, Sun. 8–3.*

17 **Steves Homestead.** This 1876 Victorian home is one of the few in the
★ King William Historic District open for touring. It's always been a trendsetter. Not only was its eclectic architecture—a blend of French Second Empire and Italian Villa styles—copied by other well-to-do San Antonians, but the estate was the city's first to have a telephone (1881) and among the first to install electric lights (1894). Completed in 1876, the house, occupied by lumber magnate Edward Steves, also has a slate mansard roof and delicate floral stenciling on the ceilings. Admission includes a guided tour. ✉*509 King William St., King William Historic District* ☎*210/225–5924* ✆*$.* ⏲*Daily 10–4:15; last tour begins at 3:30.*

ALAMO HEIGHTS & BRACKENRIDGE PARK

The area north of downtown (but south of the airport) is known as Alamo Heights. This affluent residential neighborhood contains an abundance of cultural establishments, a top university, and the lush, locally loved (and much used) Brackenridge Park.

Numbers in the margin correspond to numbers on the Alamo Heights & Brackenridge Park map.

MAIN ATTRACTIONS

4 **Brackenridge Park.** The 343-acre green space between U.S. 281 and
Fodor'sChoice Broadway Street (also known as State Spur 368) makes an excellent
★ setting for a picnic or a stroll, and also offers jogging trails, public art, athletic fields, a golf course, concessions, and rides on a carousel and miniature train (⇨*Sports & the Outdoors for recreational options at the park*). However, the park is much more than just an outdoorsy retreat. It's home to—or in the vicinity of—many noteworthy attractions: the San Antonio Zoo, the San Antonio Botanical Gardens, the Japanese Tea Gardens, McNay Art Museum, and the Witte Museum (*for more information on these, see their individual listings in this section and also under Also Worth Seeing*). Families should budget at least half a day here. ✉*3700 N. Saint Mary's St., Alamo Heights* ☎*210/207–7275* ✆*Free* ⏲*Daily 5 AM–11 PM.*

8 **San Antonio Botanical Gardens.** Step into 33 acres of formal gardens, wildflower-spangled meadows, native Texas vegetation, and a "touch and smell" garden specially designed for blind people. Among the gardens are older flower varieties, an extensive rose garden, and a Japanese

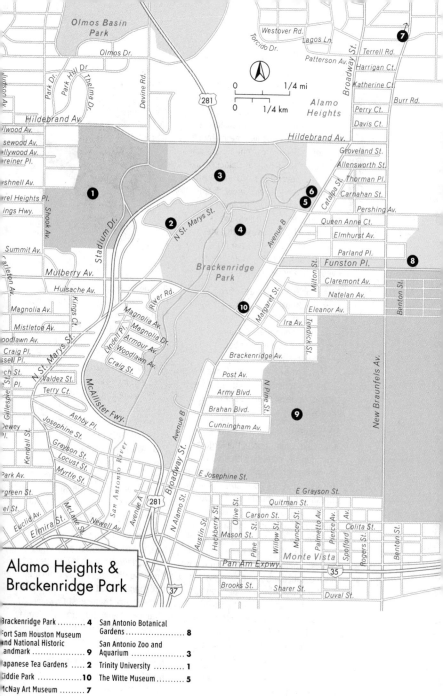

Alamo Heights & Brackenridge Park

Mega-Spirited Texas

If you see motorcycles flying overhead while you're in Texas, forget the state fair or rodeo, you just might be in church. As surely as Texas history is seen in its missions like the Alamo, a slice of the state's current culture can be seen in its Battlestar Galactica–like churches. Beyond their sociological significance, the sheer "wow" factor alone (generated by their immense size and offerings) makes Texas's megachurches tourist-worthy sites. In fact, many of them even cater to tourists, with building tours, special events, and book signings.

Inspirational author Max Lucado pastors one of San Antonio's mega-churches.

Texas has more than 182 mega-churches (those with a weekly attendance greater than 2,000)—many more per capita than California, which has about the same number of big churches but twice as many residents. Statisticians say that Texas ranks first in the nation in the number of evangelical Protestants and third in the number of Catholics.

Houston features the truly stupendous Lakewood Church, the largest church in the country with a Sunday attendance of 45,000, spread out over three services. Its Texas-size slogan is "Dreaming Big," and its leaders, Joel and Victoria Osteen, have plunked the church into the sports arena formerly occupied by the Houston Rockets. With a Texas-twanged smile Joel welcomes people to "our big living room." His most recent book, *Become a Better You*, released in October 2007, is expected to sell more than 5 million copies. Visitors can take self-guided tours of the church, or stop in for music concerts, seminars, conferences, and classes held throughout the week.

Houston has lots of other "biggest of the big" religious sites to visit. Rev. Kirbyjon Caldwell, who presided over George W. Bush's presidential inaugurations, also presides over the largest Methodist Church in the country: Kingdom Builders Center. Mega-synagogue Beth Yeshurun is the largest Conservative Jewish congregation in the country (with more than 4,000 attendees), and in 2008 Catholics—not to be outdone—built a mega-European style Co-Cathedral of the Sacred Heart with 32 million pounds of concrete and one-half million pounds of steel. Even Rick Warren has an outpost in Houston; at Fellowship of the Woodlands, Pastor Shook's services are known for dramatic sermon illustrations like motorcycles leaping over his head when he discussed having faith.

If you're single and looking, then be sure to visit Second Baptist Church, which claims it hosts the largest adult singles gatherings at any church in the country—7,313 to be exact. And every March, the largest Cowboy Church in the world forms on Sunday at the world's largest rodeo, the Houston Livestock Show and Rodeo.

Not to be religiously out-bigged by Houston, Dallas proclaims itself as the newest buckle of the Bible belt. The city is a sort of Disneyland of

Basketball fans may recognize Lakewood Church. Until 2003 it was the Summit/Compaq Center, where the Houston Rockets played.

big churches. You can attend various churches' weekday power lunches, use their mega–sports centers to play ball, or attend conferences that attract more than half a million attendees. On 140 acres (and growing rapidly), Dallas-area's Prestonwood Baptist gathers 28,000 every Sunday to listen to Dr. Jack Graham and the 650-member choir, the largest in Texas. If you like the Texas Rangers, Dallas Cowboys, or other Texas sports teams, then Prestonwood's PowerLunch on Tuesday is the place to hear the athletes talk.

T.D. Jakes's Potter's House sponsors the biggest conferences, including, in 2008, a men's conference featuring excursions, concerts, and seminars in one of Texas's grand cowboy-styled resorts. Author of the megahit book *Woman, Thou Art Loosed,* Jakes held a four-day Megafest in 2004 that had more than half a million attendees. On Sunday 30,000 congregants pack his church, along with a Grammy-winning choir. Bishop Jakes has twice been featured on the cover of *Time* magazine as "America's Best Preacher" and one of this nation's "25 most influential evangelicals."

But if you want to visit the mega-author of Texas churches who has written more books than any pastor in the United States, then one must go to San Antonio to Max Lucado's Oak Hills Church. After 14 refusals, Lucado finally found a publisher and then batted out more than 100 books and counting (with more than 55 million in print). He preaches—simply and directly—three times a month at his very tourist-friendly megachurch of 5,300 weekly attendees.

—Tony Carnes

garden. The centerpiece is the Halsell Conservatory, a 90,000-square-foot structure composed of seven tall glass spires. A self-guided tour of the climate-controlled conservatory takes visitors through the plants and flowers found in different environments around the world, from desert to tropics. The conservatory sits partially underground for a cooling effect in the hot Texas summers—a definite draw! ⊠ *555 Funston Pl., Alamo Heights* ☎ *210/207–3250* ⊕ *www.sabot.org* ⊠ *$7* ⊙ *Daily 9–5.*

❸ **San Antonio Zoo and Aquarium.** Set on 35 acres with more than 3,500
☾ animals of 600 species, the San Antonio Zoo is consistently ranked as
Fodor'sChoice one of the best zoos in the country, and with the nation's third-largest
★ animal collection, most in outdoor habitats. The zoo is best known for its excellent collection of African antelopes, as well as other hoofed species. Exhibits include the butterfly house, where about 20 species fly freely about, often coming to rest on visitors; animals from the African plains and the Amazon; critters from the prairies—both dogs and chickens; and cranes from around the world. The Children's Zoo, a $3 million addition, features rides, a nursery, a playground, an education center, and, the highlight, the "Round-the-World Voyage of Discovery" exhibit. ⊠ *3903 N. Saint Mary's St., Alamo Heights* ☎ *210/734–7184* ⊕ *www.sazoo-aq.org* ⊠ *$9* ⊙ *Memorial Day–Labor Day, daily 9–6 (though visitors can remain until 8); otherwise daily 9–5 (visitors can remain until 6).*

❺ **The Witte Museum.** Teach your kids about science in an adventurous way,
☾ with hands-on exhibits and log cabins to explore. The history, science,
★ and culture museum covers all things Texan, from the area's dinosaur inhabitants to the white-tailed deer that roam the region today. Children especially love the tree house out back—some kids (though perhaps not their aunts and grandmas!) also love the exhibits of slithering animals (think snakes and the like). The museum is near the zoo in Brackenridge Park, which lies between Broadway and Highway 281, south of East Hildebrand Avenue and north of I–35. ⊠ *3801 Broadway, Alamo Heights* ☎ *210/357–1900* ⊕ *www.wittemuseum.org* ⊠ *$7* ⊙ *Mon. and Wed.–Sat. 10–5, Tues. 10–8, Sun. noon–5.*

ALSO WORTH SEEING

❾ **Fort Sam Houston Museum and National Historic Landmark.** This National Historic Landmark, an army base dating back to 1870, has almost 900 historic structures (about nine times as many as Colonial Williamsburg). These include the residence where General John J. Pershing lived in 1917; the Chinese Camp, which was once occupied by Chinese who fled Mexico to escape Pancho Villa; and the home where Lieutenant and Mrs. Dwight Eisenhower lived in 1916. Visitors can stroll past the structures (most are not open to the public). The Fort Sam Houston Museum is filled with exhibits on the site's early days, with items on display ranging from old uniforms and personal papers to firearms and vehicles. ⊠ *1210 Stanley Rd., Fort Sam Houston, Alamo Heights* ☎ *210/221–1886* ⊠ *Free* ⊙ *Wed.–Sun. 10–4.*

② **Japanese Tea Gardens.** A rock quarry–turned–lily pond and more, this serene oasis blossoms with lush flowers, climbing vines, tall palms, and a 60-foot-high waterfall. The ponds, with beautiful rock bridges and walkways, are home to hundreds of koi (a type of carp). The vibrant garden celebrated its grand reopening in 2008, after a more than $1.5 million restoration. ⊠ *3853 N. Saint Mary's St., in Brackenridge Park, Alamo Heights* ☎ *No phone* ☎ *Free* ⊙ *Daily 8–dusk.*

⑩ **Kiddie Park.** Established in 1925, this is America's original and old-
Ⓒ est children's amusement park. The Herschell-Spillman Carousel's 36 jumping horses have been revolving since it opened in 1925. A Ferris wheel, a small roller coaster, and many other rides will keep your kids busy for hours. You can get popcorn, pizza, and more at the snack bar. ⊠ *3015 Broadway, in Brackenridge Park, Alamo Heights* ☎ *210/824–4351* ⊕ *www.kiddiepark.com* ☎ *$1.50 per ride or $9.25 for a day of unlimited rides* ⊙ *Mon.–Sat. 10–dusk, Sun. 11–dusk.*

⑦ **McNay Art Museum.** In a private mansion with a Moorish-style courtyard, this museum reopened in summer 2008 with a new 45,000-square-foot exhibition center that gives a modernist twist to the landmark home once owned by artist and oil heiress Marion Koogler McNay. Housing a collection of Postimpressionist and modern paintings and sculpture, along with an arts library, the walls of the 24-room house are adorned with works by Gauguin, Cézanne, Matisse, Picasso, and Van Gogh. Twenty-three acres of landscaped gardens surround the museum. ⊠ *6000 N. New Braunfels Ave., Alamo Heights* ☎ *210/824–5368* ⊕ *www.mcnayart.org* ☎ *$5 suggested donation* ⊙ *Tues., Wed., and Fri. 10–4; Thurs. 10–9; Sat. 10–5; Sun. noon–5.*

⑥ **Memorial Hall Museum.** This repository houses history and original lore of Texas pioneers and 19th-century trail drivers, with exhibits covering everything from badges to saddlebags. Western art is displayed here as well. ⊠ *3805 Broadway, Alamo Heights* ☎ *210/822–9011* ☎ *$5* ⊙ *Mon.–Sat. 11–4, Sun. noon–4.*

① **Trinity University.** Situated to the west of Brackenridge Park, this well-regarded institution of higher education spreads out over 117 acres, with sweeping views of downtown. Walk around the campus and you may see some of the nearly 2,700 enrolled students sitting under the live oak trees or walking to and from class in one of the school's trademark redbrick buildings. If the timing is right, attend a show at the Stieren Theater or Laurie Auditorium. Campus tours are also offered to prospective students and their families. ⊠ *1 Trinity Pl. (at McAllister Freeway /U.S. 281 and Mulberry), Alamo Heights* ☎ *210/999–7011* ⊕ *www.trinity.edu.*

SOUTHSIDE

The main attractions south of downtown are the historic missions. See the Greater San Antonio map for the locations of these sites.

★ Except for the Alamo, San Antonio's missions constitute **San Antonio Missions National Historical Park**. Established along the San Antonio River in the 18th century by Franciscan friars, the missions stand as reminders of Spain's most-successful attempt to extend its New World dominion northward from Mexico: the missions had the responsibility of converting the natives (primarily American Indians) to Catholicism. The missions were also centers of work, education, and trade. They represented the greatest concentration of Catholic missions in North America, and were the basis of the founding of San Antonio. Today, the four missions are active parish churches, and each illustrates a different concept of mission life. All are beautiful, in their own ways. ⊠ *2202 Roosevelt Ave., Southside* ☎ *210/932–1001 visitor center, 210/534–8833 headquarters* ⊕ *www.nps.gov/saan* ☎ *Free* ☉ *Daily 9–5.*

Start your tour at the stunning **Mission San José,** the "Queen of Missions." It's adjacent to the visitor center, where a National Park Service Ranger or docent illuminates the history of the missions. San José's outer wall, American Indian dwellings, a granary, a water mill, and workshops have been restored. Here you can pick up a driving map of the Mission Trail that connects San José with the other missions. ⊠ *6701 San Jose Dr., Southside* ☎ *210/922–0543* ☎ *Free* ☉ *Daily 9–5.*

Mission Concepción, the oldest unrestored stone church in the nation, is known for its colorful frescoes, or wall paintings. The most striking fresco is the Eye of the God, a face from which rays of light emanate. ⊠ *807 Mission Rd., at Felisa St., Southside* ☎ *210/534–1540* ☎ *Free* ☉ *Daily 9–5.*

Mission San Juan Capistrano, with its Romanesque arches, has a serene chapel. This mission once supplied all its own needs, from cloth to crops, and a trail behind the mission winds along the low river-bottom land and provides a look at the many indigenous plants formerly used by the mission. ⊠ *9101 Graf Rd., Southside* ☎ *210/534–0749* ☎ *Free* ☉ *Daily 9–5.*

Mission San Francisco de la Espada, the southernmost mission, was named for St. Francis of Assisi, founder of the monastic order of Franciscans. The mission's full name is Mission San Francisco de la Espada. It includes an Arab-inspired aqueduct that was part of the missions' famous *acequia* water management system. ⊠ *10040 Espada Rd., Southside* ☎ *210/627–2021* ☎ *Free* ☉ *Daily 9–5.*

NORTH & NORTHWEST

See the Greater San Antonio map for the locations of these sites.

MAIN ATTRACTIONS

SeaWorld San Antonio. Sprawled across 250 acres northwest of the city, this Texas-size marine-theme amusement park (the world's largest such park) delights animal lovers with its whales, dolphins, sharks, seals, sea lions, otters, penguins, and even two Clydesdale horses, as well as thrilling rides—including the Great White, Texas's first inverted steel coaster; and the Steel Eel, a "hypercoaster" reaching speeds of 65 mph. SeaWorld's newest coaster, Journey to Atlantis, has a water compo-

Fodor's Choice
★

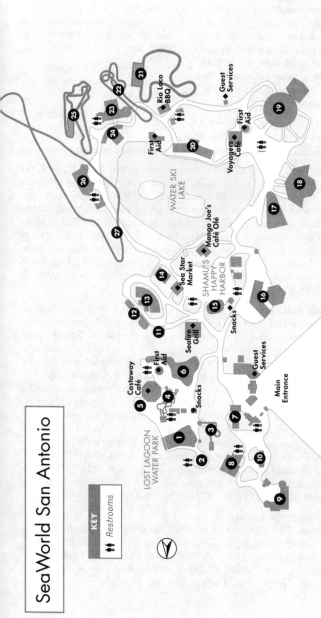

SeaWorld San Antonio

KEY
♦♦ *Restrooms*

Wave Wash Pool **1**
Splash Attack **2**
Sky Tubin' **3**
Buckaroo Mountain **4**
Lil' Gators Lagoon **5**
Castaway Cruisin' **6**
Clydesdale Hamlet **7**
Anheuser Busch
Hospitality House **8**
Sharks/ The Coral Reef **9**
Dolphin Cove **10**
Lorikeet Feeding **11**
Sea Lion Feeding **12**
Sea Lion Stadium **13**
Sea Star Theater **14**
Shamu Express **15**
Beluga Stadium **16**
Journey to Atlantis **17**
Nautilus Amphitheater **18**
Shamu Theater **19**
Ski Stadium **20**
Rio Loco **21**
Great White **22**
Boardwalk Games **23**
Penguin Plaza **24**
Texas Splashdown **25**
Penguin Encounter **26**
Steel Eel **27**

LOST LAGOON
WATER PARK

WATER SKI
LAKE

Castaway
Café

First
Aid

Snacks

Main
Entrance

Guest
Services

Seafire
Grill

Sea Star
Market

SHAMU'S
HAPPY
HARBOR

Snacks

Mango Joe's
Café Olé

Rio Loco
BBQ

First
Aid

First
Aid

Voyagers
Café

Guest
Services

My Trip to SeaWorld San Antonio

Last year I went to SeaWorld with my family and I got to go on a behind-the-scenes tour (it was called the Ultimate Seafari Tour). On the tour I got to pet a baby shark, and I tried to feed and touch a bottlenose dolphin, but I couldn't reach him. But I was able to throw fish down at the sea lions. They were very loud and very hungry.

Then I went to watch Shamu. He splashed me really, really hard. I got soaking wet. He splashed me twice. After that my mom bought me and my brothers some ice cream, and that's where we got the Shamu bowl. We still have it. We call it the fishy bowl.

After lunch we went to the water park. There, we swam and went on the slides. It was really fun.

—Daniel Huerta, age 9

nent and spins you backward. Amid acres of manicured gardens, the huge park also offers marine shows, trick waterskiing performances, and a water park with swimming pools and waterslides—a guaranteed hit with water-lovin' kids on a hot spring or summer day. Shamu, of course, is the most beloved animal in the park. His performance tank/arena has lots of water—5 million gallons of it, in fact (except when it's being splashed all over audience members who dare to sit to close). Special tours take you behind the scenes. ⊠ *10500 SeaWorld Dr., Northwest* ☎ *800/700–7786* ⊕ *www.seaworld.com/sanantonio* ⊡ *$50.99* ☉ *Mar.–Dec., hrs vary.*

Fodor'sChoice
★

☉ **Six Flags Fiesta Texas.** Set within 100-foot quarry walls, this amusement park features sectors highlighting Texas's rich diversity, from the state's Mexican and German culture to its rip-roarin' Western past. Eight take-it-to-the-max roller coasters are here, including Superman: Krypton Coaster (the Southwest's largest steel coaster) and the new Goliath, a suspended looping coaster that opened in spring 2008. The more than 40 other rides include a white-water rapids flume and a tower drop. Rounding out the offerings are many excellent family-friendly musical shows (a lasting feature from when the property was owned by Opryland)—Fiesta Texas has won the Golden Ticket award for best theme-park shows in the country for nine straight years. Some of the shows invite audience participation. Concerts with big-name artists are also held periodically throughout the season. ⊠ *17000 I–10W, at junction of Loop 410, Northwest* ☎ *210/697–5050* ⊕ *www.sixflags.com/fiestaTexas* ⊡ *$46.99* ☉ *Mar.–Dec., hrs vary.*

ALSO WORTH SEEING

☉ **Splashtown.** This 20-acre park north of downtown has dozens of slides, a kids' activity pool, a giant wave pool, and six sand volleyball courts. ⊠ *3600 N. IH-35 (I–35 at Exit 160), North* ☎ *210/227–1100* ⊕ *www.splashtownsa.com* ⊡ *$24.99* ☉ *June–Aug., Mon.–Thurs. 11–8, Fri.–Sun. 11–9; Apr., May, and Sept., weekends 11–7.*

My First Shamu

Whales delight at SeaWorld San Antonio.

I will never forget the first time I saw a killer whale. It was a warm spring afternoon in 1985. The surface of the water was calm, smooth as glass, when suddenly the quiet was shattered by a massive turbulence of churning water, splashing, and then, breaking the surface was this massive black-and-white animal, as big as a school bus.

Unknowingly, I was holding my breath, watching this sleek torpedo arc over and, as quickly as I felt myself exhale, he slipped back into the depths. The displaced water crashed back and forth, slipping and splashing over the edges of the pool, until only a ripple was left.

Moments later, Shamu hoisted himself up and slid onto the stage, his mouth open as if to smile. A brief whistle from his trainer indicated "good job," and then Shamu raised his tail in a salute.

Over time, my reaction has been duplicated by thousands of people when they first encounter Shamu at SeaWorld San Antonio. It is the sheer delight of a moment of discovery that is nearly indescribable, but has kept me coming back every day.

I have seen it written on my son's face the first time he saw a Shamu show. His eyes got so big I thought his eyebrows would pop off. But what was equally surprising was seeing that same expression on my husband's face at the same encounter. So every time I hear someone say "Oh, SeaWorld is just for kids." I reply, "It certainly is . . . no matter how old you are."

—Fran Stephenson, director of communications, SeaWorld San Antonio

Six Flags Fiesta Texas

SHOPPING

1

With its rich ethnic heritage, this city is a wonderful place to buy Mexican imports, most of them inexpensive and many of high quality. A good number of San Antonio's shopping options are centered on the popular River Walk area that winds through downtown. There you'll find plenty of restaurants and bars that make perfect pit stops as you stroll from one shop to the next.

DOWNTOWN & THE RIVER WALK

MALLS & SHOPPING CENTERS

Fodor'sChoice
★

El Mercado is the Mexican market building that is part of **Market Square** (⊠ *514 W. Commerce St., Downtown* ☎ *210/207–8600* ⊕ *www.market squaresa.com*). The building contains about 35 shops, including stores selling blankets, Mexican dresses, men's guayabera shirts, and strings of brightly painted papier-mâché vegetables; it's open from 10 to 8 in summer and 10 to 6 in winter. The lively **Farmer's Market Plaza,** with more shops and a food court, and the **Produce Row Shops** are other shopping areas in Market Square worth visiting. Also in Market Square is **Botanica,** run by artist-author Franco Mondini-Ruiz. Located in the new Alameda Museum, the shop carries a little bit of everything from dozens of local artisans. "I want this to be a fun store," says Mondini-Ruiz, "profitable and a celebration of culture."

LA VILLITA

It's noteworthy for its Latin American importers and demonstrations by its resident glassblower.

The shops and galleries at San Antonio's first residential area, on the southern edge of downtown, **La Villita** (⊠ *418 Villita St., just off E. Nueva St., Downtown* ☎ *210/207–8610* ⊕ *www.lavillita.com*), delight shoppers bent on discovering homemade treasures. Some of the shops in this block-long historic arts village along the San Antonio River are in adobe buildings dating from the 1820s. Stores are open daily from 10 to 6, with some staying open later. A few of the stores are noted below.

Peruse paintings (oil, acrylic, and watercolor), pottery, prints, sculpture, and more at **Artistic Endeavors Gallery** (⊠ *418 Villita St., just off E. Nueva St., No. 2500, Downtown* ☎ *210/222–2497* ⊕ *www.artend.com* ⊙ *Mon.–Sat. 10–6*), which specializes in original works by regional artists, many of which turn their artistic eye toward San Antonio's charms. **Rivercenter** (⊠ *849 E. Commerce St.* ☎ *210/225–0000* ⊕ *www. shoprivercenter.com* ⊙ *Mon.–Sat. 10–9, Sun. noon–6*) is a fairly standard shopping mall right on the river, whose stores include Macy's, Dillard's, and major retail chains. At **Village Weavers** (⊠ *418 Villita St., just off E. Nueva St., No. 800, Downtown* ☎ *210/222–0776* ⊕ *www. artend.com* ⊙ *Daily 8–8*), the four designers weave rugs, baskets, blankets, clothes, jewelry, and even toys from a variety of fabrics.

SOUTHSIDE

ART GALLERY

Garcia Art. No two pieces of glass work are the same when Gini Garcia custom designs chandeliers and other requests, all of which go into her 2,150° furnace. Tuesday through Saturday she or one of her 12 assistants are blowing glass, so you might be treated to a demonstration if you stop by the shop, which is next to the Azúca Bar. ✉ *715 S. Alamo St.,* ☎ *210/354–4681* ⊕ *www.garciaartglass.com.*

OUTSIDE SAN ANTONIO

Outlet mall shoppers will delight in the more than 200 stores at **Prime Outlets San Marcos** (✉ *3939 IH-35S, exit Centerpoint Rd., San Marcos* ☎ *512/396–2200 or 800/628–9465* ⊕ *www.primeoutlets.com* ☉ *Mon.–Sat. 10–9, Sun. 10–7*), located between San Antonio and Austin (about a 45-minute drive from San Antonio). It's the largest outlet mall in the state of Texas—which is definitely saying something.

SPORTS & THE OUTDOORS

There's plenty for the sports lover in San Antonio. If you like to get outdoors, the city has several fantastic parks and natural areas within its borders, and many others are just beyond the city limits. There are also a number of great golf courses in and around San Antonio. If you'd rather watch a game, the San Diego Padre's AA affiliate, the San Antonio Missions, play America's pastime in "the Wolf" (Nelson Wolff Municipal Stadium), the jewel of the Texas League. The city is also home to an AHL hockey team, the San Antonio Rampage.

The hottest ticket in town, though, is definitely the NBA's World Champion San Antonio Spurs. Tim Duncan, Manu Ginobili, Tony Parker, and Co. put the Spurs into contention for a title every year; the team has won the Larry O'Brien Championship trophy in 1999, 2003, 2005, and 2007.

PARKS & NATURAL AREAS

For relaxation and recreation, San Antonio boasts several city parks—Crownridge Canyon, Eisenhower, McAllister, Stone Oak, and Walker Ranch among them. The city's star park, however, is picturesque **Brackenridge Park**, at Broadway and Funston, northeast of downtown in the Alamo Heights neighborhood. In 2006 the comfortably aged park emerged from a five-year, $7.5-million makeover that, among other improvements, transformed roads once used by cars into paved trails for bicyclists and joggers. Additional recreational opportunities at the park include golf *(⇨Golf, below)*, picnicking (grills are provided), pedal boating, fishing, and, for the little ones, burning off energy on the playground equipment. Another option is simply unwinding with a stroll and feeding the ducks. The San Antonio River runs through the park, as does one main thoroughfare, Red Oak Drive. *(⇨Explor-*

ing San Antonio under the Alamo Heights & Brackenridge Park section for information on the cultural attractions in and near the park.)

For more information on Brackenridge Park and other parks in San Antonio, visit the San Antonio Parks and Recreation Department's Web site, www.sanantonio.gov/sapar.

WILDFEST

San Antonio's annual birding and nature festival is held in early May. For more information, visit wildfestsanantonio.com.

NORTH/NORTHWEST

Friedrich Wilderness Park. On the outskirts of town (about 20 mi from downtown off I–10), this 600-acre hilly haven for rare birds and orchids offers more than 5 mi of hiking trails, including one handicapped-accessible trail (Rollerblades and bicycles are not allowed). Bird-watchers from around the world are often spotted here. Some species are seasonal, such as blue jays (fall and winter), eastern meadowlarks (spring), red-winged blackbirds (spring and summer), scissor-tailed flycatchers (spring, summer, and fall), and double-crested cormorants (winter). See turkey vultures, finches, Carolina wrens, doves, northern woodpeckers, northern cardinals, mockingbirds, and more year-round. ✉ *21395 Milsa St., North/Northwest* ☎ *210/564–6400* ⊕ *www.fofriedrichpark. org* ✒ *Free* ⊙ *Daily 7:30–sunset.*

Government Canyon State Natural Area. Home of numerous varieties of trees and several species of rare birds, such as the golden-cheeked warbler, this 8,600-acre park just outside San Antonio opened in 2005. It offers views of surrounding Bexar County and glimpses of San Antonio. Protected Habitat Area trails are open September through February; other trails are available year-round. The park is for day-use only, and, like any good outdoor area, offers Wi-Fi. ✉ *12861 Galm Rd., North/Northwest* ☎ *210/688–9055* ⊕ *www.tpwd.state.tx.us* ✒ *$6* ⊙ *Fri.–Mon. 8–6.*

PARTICIPANT SPORTS

BIRD-WATCHING

Mitchell Lake. Bird-watchers worldwide come here to see the more than 300 species that visit each year. This 624-acre complex is located on a natural migratory route and serves as a stopping point for thousands of birds annually. ✉ *10750 Pleaston Rd, South San Antonio* ☎ *210/628–1639* ⊕ *www.saws.org/environmental/mitchelllake* ✒ *$2* ⊙ *Weekends 8–4.*

GOLF

Its enviable position as the southern gateway to the Hill Country makes San Antonio a great destination for golfers. If you have wannabe golf pro youngsters in tow, the **San Antonio Golf Operations Department** (🗋 *Box 839966, San Antonio 78283* ☎ *210/225–3528*) has set up Saturday clinics year-round for junior golfers (ages 6 to 18).

Brackenridge Golf Course. This historic course was the first inductee of the Texas Golf Hall of Fame. Located in San Antonio's Brackenridge Park, it first opened for play in 1916 and is the oldest municipal course in the city. Brackenridge closed in January 2008 for renovations that will include reworked tee boxes, greens, and fairways, and a return to the original layout of 15 holes; it is scheduled to reopen in late fall 2008 as a 6,185-yard par-71. ⊠ *2315 Ave. B, Alamo Heights* ☎ *210/225–3528* ⊕ *www.playsanantoniogolf.com.*

> **RODEO TIME!**
>
> The annual San Antonio Stock Show and Rodeo draws about 1.3 million people to the AT&T Center over a 2½-week period. If you're in town during this time, be sure to attend—you'll find out all about steer wrestling, team roping, and barrel racing.

Cedar Creek Course. Enjoy scenic views—and isn't that a big part of what golfing is all about?—while perfecting your swing at this 18-hole, par-72, course in the hills. Hazards include waterways and waterfalls. Greens fees are $35 weekdays and $41 weekends; price includes cart. ⊠ *8250 Vista Colina* ☎ *210/695–5050* ⊕ *www.playsanantoniogolf. com.*

La Cantera. This 18-hole, par-72 course was voted the best in San Antonio by readers of both the *San Antonio Express-News* and the *San Antonio Current.* The resort course offers views of Six Flags Fiesta Texas as well as the Texas Hill Country, while the signature number 4 on the 18-hole, par 71 Arnold Palmer course—designed by the legendary golfer—requires a long carry over a waterfall-fed lake at the lip of the green. Greens fees range from $125 to $150. ⊠ *16641 La Cantera Pkwy.* ☎ *210/558-46453* ⊕ *www.lacanteragolfclub.com.*

Quarry Golf Club. The front 9 here play like a links-style course, with no trees and an ever-present breeze to deal with. The back 9, however, are set in a limestone quarry with 100-foot perimeters. Greens fees range from $89 to $109. Overall the course is par 71. ⊠ *444 E. Basse Rd.* ☎ *210/824–4500* ⊕ *www.quarrygolf.com.*

SPELUNKING

Natural Bridge Caverns. Trek down 180 feet below the earth's surface for a half-mile walk through this beautiful, historic cavern system. Visitors can take the popular North Cavern tour for a look at stalagmites, stalactites, flowstones, chandeliers, and soda straw formations. The Jaremy Room encompasses two huge underground chambers that use both light and dark to showcase rare formations. ⊠ *26495 Natural Bridge Cavern Rd. (FM 3009), 30 mi north of San Antonio* ☎ *210/651–6101* ⊕ *www.naturalbridgecaverns.com* ⊠ *$16.95–$25.95* ☉ *Daily 9–4, 5, 6, or 7, depending on season.*

SPECTATOR SPORTS

BASEBALL

Enjoy a night at the ballpark watching the **San Antonio Missions** (☏210/675–7275 ⊕*www.samissions.com*), the Double-A affiliate of the San Diego Padres. The Missions play more than 50 home games a year, from April through early September, at **Nelson W. Wolff Stadium** (✉*5757 Hwy. 90W, West San Antonio*). Admission is $6.50 to $9.50, and, as with any minor-league baseball team, expect lots of promotions, giveaways, and fun on-field activities during the game.

BASKETBALL

The pride and joy of the Alamo City, the NBA's **San Antonio Spurs** (☏210/444–5000 ⊕*www.spurs.com*), play home games at the **AT&T Center** (✉*1 AT&T Center Pkwy., Downtown* ☏*210/444–5000* ⊕*www.attcenter.com*) from October through April. Seats are available in every price range; a seat in the rafters can be had for as little as $10—or you can sit courtside for about $900.

Catch great women's hoops action when the Women's National Basketball Association's **San Antonio Silver Stars** (✉*1 AT&T Center Pkwy., Downtown* ☏*210/444–5050* ⊕*www.sasilverstars.com*) play at the AT&T Center from May to September. Tickets for the Silver Stars range from $10 to $200.

FOOTBALL

Alamodome. This 65,000-seat, $186 million sports arena is a busy place. Home of the Valero Alamo Bowl each December, featuring teams from the Big 12 and Big 10 conferences, the site hosts other sporting events as well as concerts, trade shows, and conventions. The Alamodome is the only place in North America with two permanent Olympic-size ice rinks under the same roof. If you're not here during a game, you can still visit during a behind-the-scenes tour, which must be scheduled in advance. ✉*100 Montana St., just east of HemisFair Park, across I–37, Downtown* ☏*210/207–3652 or 800/884–3663* ⊕*www.alamodome. com* 🖾*Prices vary with events* ⊗ *Weekdays 8–5.*

HOCKEY

If hard-hitting ice hockey is your style, the **San Antonio Rampage** (☏*210/444–5554* ⊕*www.sarampage.com*) of the American Hockey League play from October through May at the **AT&T Center** (✉*1 AT&T Center Pkwy., Downtown* ☏*210/444–5000* ⊕*www.attcenter.com*). Tickets are priced from $8.50 to $39.

ARTS & ENTERTAINMENT

THE ARTS

Guadalupe Cultural Arts Center. Founded in 1980 to preserve and develop Latino arts and culture, the GCAC stages regular dance, music, and theatrical performances. It also displays the art of emerging artists and schedules various classes. Of the center's major annual events, the

Tejano Conjunto Music Festival, with more than 42 hours of live performances, is in May, and the Cinefestival, five days of Latino film, is in January. ⊠ *1300 Guadalupe St., Southside* 210/271–3151 ⊕ *www.guadalupeculturalarts.org* Free ⊙ *Weekdays 9–5.*

MUSIC & CONCERTS

Mexican Cultural Institute. Mexican culture is depicted in film, dance, art, and more. ⊠ *600 HemisFair Plaza Way, Downtown* 210/227–0123 ⊕ *www.saculturamexico.org* Free ⊙ *Weekdays 10–5, weekends 11–5.*

THEATER

Arneson River Theatre. Erected in 1939, this unique outdoor music

and performing-arts venue in the heart of La Villita was designed by River Walk architect Robert Hugman and built by the WPA. Have a seat on the grass-covered steps on the river's edge and watch performers on the small stage. In this open-air format, the river, not a curtain, separates performers from the audience. Some of San Antonio's top events take place here, including Fiesta Noche del Rio, a summer show presented for more than five decades. ⊠ *418 Villita St., Rriver Walk.* 210/207–8610 ⊕ *www.lavillita.com/arneson* Prices vary, with shows starting at $5.

Aztec on the River. Closed for construction in 2008, the Aztec's theater doors are scheduled to reopen by 2009. Showing movies and more, the historic theater's crowning glory is its highly ornamented Wurlitzer organ, which was used for its early-day silent films and is still played today. The organ has 1,700 pipes, ranging from the size of a pencil up to 17 feet long. In the grand lobby, a special-effects show occurs every 75 minutes. ⊠ *201 E. Commerce St., Suite 300, Downtown* 210/227–3930 Ext. 301, 877/432–9832 box office ⊕ *www.aztecontheriver.com.*

Majestic Theater. A masterpiece of baroque splendor with Spanish Mission and Mediterranean-style influences, this 1929 movie-and-vaudeville theater one time showcased such talents as Jack Benny, Bob Hope, and George Burns. Today the fully restored, 2,311-seat theater spotlights current and up-and coming stars while serving as a venue for touring Broadway shows like *Miss Saigon, The Color Purple,* and *Phantom of the Opera.* It is also the resident performance space for the San Antonio Symphony Orchestra. ⊠ *224 E. Houston St, Downtown.* 210/226–5700, 210/226–3333 box office ⊕ *www.majesticempire.com* ⊙ *Weekdays 9–5.*

FESTIVALS & EVENTS

JAN. River Walk Mud Festival and Mud Parade. Parts of the river are drained to clear the bottom of debris, and locals revel in the subsequent parties, parades, and the crowning of a Mud King and Queen. ☎210/227–4262 ⊕www.the sanantonioriverwalk.com.

FEB. Livestock Exposition and Rodeo Held at the AT&T Center, this event features country, Tejano, and rock music, along with a rodeo and livestock show. ☎210/225–5851 ⊕www.sarodeo.com.

Mardi Gras Parade. The colorfully festooned floats create a spectacle. If you miss an event, don't worry—there are at least two a month, each with food, music, and lots of entertainment. ☎210/227–4262 ⊕www.thesanantonioriverwalk.com.

MAR. Irish Festival. The San Antonio River is dyed green, and live music, food, arts and crafts, and dances fill the city in honor of St. Patty. ⊕www.harpandshamrock.org.

Remembering the Alamo Weekend. Educational exhibits about those involved with both sides of the Battle of the Alamo are on display at 300 Alamo Plaza during this commemorative weekend. ☎210/225–1391 ⊕www.thealamo.org.

APR. Fiesta. The city's top annual event comes to town each spring for 10 days of celebrations throughout the city. Approximately 100 events are held during the festival, which honors the heroes of the Alamo and the Battle of San Jacinto. ☎210/212–4917 ticket information ⊕www.fiesta-sa.org.

JUNE Texas Folklife Festival. During this summertime event more than 40 cultures exhibit their contributions to the development of Texas through music, food, dance, and folktales at the Institute of Texan Cultures in HemisFair Park. ☎210/458–2300 ⊕www.texan cultures.com.

DEC. Fiestas Navidenas. Held in Market Square during the first three weekends of December, this event features children's choirs, folkloric dance groups, mariachi bands, and a visit by Pancho Claus. ☎210/207–8600 ⊕www.sanantonio.gov.

NIGHTLIFE

BARS

Around the 3000 block of San Antonio's **North Saint Mary's Street** lie a colorful assortment of bars and restaurants in converted commercial buildings, many with live entertainment.

DOWNTOWN & THE RIVER WALK

Sip your drink while taking in a bird's-eye view of the city at the Tower of the Americas' **Bar 601** (⊠600 HemisFair Park, Downtown ☎210/223–3101).

With a great location right on the river, **Dick's Last Resort** (⊠406 Navarro St., Downtown ☎210/224–0026) is a nice place to grab a drink in the afternoon—provided you have a thick enough skin to withstand the intentionally surly staff.

Juan Seguin: Texican

Juan Seguin was a man of contradictions.

Born into the landed Mexican gentry of San Antonio in 1806, he unaccountably fell in with Stephen F. Austin and the gathering Anglo forces of revolution. Seguin was commissioned a captain in the Texas army and survived the Alamo—he was not among the 189 soldiers, all of whom died, because he had left the battle early as a courier. He reached General Sam Houston in time to help rout Santa Anna at San Jacinto.

After three sessions in the new Republic of Texas's senate, Seguin's rising fortunes abruptly collapsed. The hero of the revolution encountered financial reverses, ethnic tension, and a spreading rumor of Mexican collaborations. As if to confirm the complaint, he fled the Texas he'd helped create and settled in Mexico.

Following the Mexican War, the ex-turncoat was back, reestablishing himself in Texas business and politics. He died in 1890, and is interred at the city east of San Antonio that bears his name.

—Larry Neal

Drink (⊠*200 Navarro St., Downtown* ☎*210/224–1031*) serves tapas and has 85 signature cocktails, 150 wines by the bottle, and 75 wines by the glass.

Durty Nellie's Pub (⊠*Hilton Palacio del Rio, 200 S. Alamo St., Downtown* ☎*210/222–1400*), where sing-alongs are popular, is a favorite on the River Walk.

Howl at the Moon (⊠*111 Crockett St., Downtown* ☎*210/212–4770*) is a dueling-piano bar—don't hesitate to sing along!

Near the Aztec Theater,**Iron Cactus Mexican Grill and Margarita Bar** (⊠*200 Commerce St., near the corner of St. Marys and Crockett, Downtown* ☎*210/224–9835*) has an extensive selection of tequilas and margaritas; it also serves tequila flights for the indecisive.

Mad Dogs British Pub (⊠*123 Losoya St., Downtown* ☎*210/222–0220*) has a wide selection of imported beers; entertainment includes DJs, karaoke, and live acts.

★ Don't miss the **Menger Bar** (⊠*204 Alamo Plaza, Downtown* ☎*210/ 223–4361 or 800/345–9285* ⊕*www.mengerhotel.com*) at the Menger Hotel, a fun place to go with friends for a drink, and a great place to go to meet the locals. The historic hotel is one of San Antonio's great cultural treasures (⇨ *Where to Stay*).

The San Antonio outpost of New Orleans institution **Pat O'Brien's** (⊠*121 Alamo Plaza,, Downtown* ☎*210/220–1076*) serves the bar's wickedly strong hurricane.

At night, **Republic of Texas** (⊠*526 River Walk, Downtown* ☎*210/226– 6256*) transforms into a nightclub. Enjoy one of the nightly drink specials, or order the massive 46-ounce margarita.

Open until 2 AM, **Vbar** (⊠ *150 E. Houston St., Downtown* ☎ *210/227–9700*), inside Hotel Valencia on the River Walk, is one of the hottest, hippest places in town—at least this week. San Antonio's Downtown Alliance has rated it the best place to see and be seen. A slew of stars have stayed at the boutique hotel, and, well, they get thirsty, too.

Waxy O'Connor's Irish Pub (⊠ *234 River Walk, Downtown* ☎ *210/229–9299*) was actually built in County Monaghan, Ireland, and shipped to San Antonio, where it was reassembled.

KING WILLIAM HISTORIC DISTRICT

★ **Azúca Nuevo Latino** (⊠ *713 S. Alamo St., King William Historic District* ☎ *210/225–5550*) puts a salsa or merengue in your step (on Friday and Saturday nights). When you aren't dancing, you'll be sipping on a Latin or specialty cocktail—more than 15 types of mojitos are available. A full dinner menu is available.

MUSIC & DANCING

World-class Jim Cullum's Jazz Band plays superb Dixieland at the **Landing** (⊠ *Hyatt Regency, 123 Losoya St., Downtown* ☎ *210/223–7266*).

Sunset Station. Four live-music stages, five dance floors, and three restaurants entertain in a turn-of-the-20th-century Southern Pacific train depot at the heart of downtown San Antonio. There's something for everyone here: the nightly music choices range from country and western to merengue, and the food runs the gamut from Aldaco's Mexican Cuisine to Ruth's Chris Steak House. The depot is open during the day, but the bands take the stage after dark. Call ahead to see whether any nationally known acts are scheduled. ⊠ *1174 E. Commerce, Downtown* ☎ *210/222–9481* ⊕ *www.sunset-station.com* ⊠ *Varies by performance.*

WHERE TO EAT

THE SCENE

San Antonio is a terrific dining town. It's big enough and has enough demanding conventioneers to support fine dining you'd usually find in much larger cities. But it still has a relaxed small-town feel that makes it easy to eat out almost anywhere without much fuss. You can count on one hand the number of restaurants requiring jackets; the dress codes at most other nice restaurants pretty much stops at "no shorts, please." Reservations and long waits are rare except at a few high-end restaurants and at peak times on the River Walk.

Essentially, San Antonio cuisine is about two things: Mexican-inspired flavors and meat. Mexican, Tex-Mex, Latin, and a variety of other fusion variations crowd this bicultural town. You'll find wonderful Mexican breads and pastries, rich sauces with complex flavors heavy with chilies, fresh peppers, even chocolate. Margaritas and local beers, courtesy of the local German immigrant brewing tradition, remedy the occasional chili overdose (though not all Latin food here is spicy—far from it). If your idea of a perfect meal is a steak, ribs,

WHERE SHOULD I DINE IN SAN ANTONIO?

	Neighborhood Vibe	Pros	Cons
Alamo Heights	San Antonio's toniest neighborhood is also where you'll find many of its best restaurants, among residential streets and the occasional upscale strip mall. You'll definitely feel like you're eating where the locals eat (at least the well-heeled ones), but don't expect exotic vistas around every corner—the environs can be quaint but also often nondescript.	Ten minutes from downtown by car; adjacent to the San Antonio Zoo, Brackenridge Park, and other attractions; excellent and varied restaurants; caters to locals, so lacks tourist prices and congestion.	Getting here from downtown requires a car or $15 cab fare each way; the area is not particularly scenic or memorable.
Downtown	Outside the River Walk tourist district, San Antonio's downtown is a mixed bag. Some areas showcase its many historic buildings with cute local restaurants and shops. Others are just plain run-down. Drive or grab a cab if you're going more than four or five blocks from the tourist district.	Many local dining institutions lie just off the beaten path of the River Walk (usually within walking distance) and yet don't draw the usual tourist crowds; possibility to experience something truly Texan.	Some ratty areas not so easy on the eyes and feel unsafe; long distances between some attractions plus busy streets make walking something of a challenge.
North/Northwest	San Antonio's northern neighborhoods have a suburban feel, and popular chain restaurants and stores are in plentiful supply. Though there are many local gems to be found, often tucked away in nondescript shopping centers, strips of familiar restaurants line the major highway frontage roads north of the city.	Many reliable, inexpensive choices; near Fiesta Texas, SeaWorld, and some great shopping; most restaurants are kid-friendly; ample parking.	Suburban feel; highway driving necessary; packed with locals for lunch and dinner.
River Walk	Finding a variety of local dining options is as easy as taking a stroll along the river, where dozens of restaurants are stacked atop one another. Many have patio dining, for watching the barges go by. National chains join the local spots. Be prepared for large crowds at all of them.	Several top-quality local restaurants; many have patios with views of the boats and passersby strolling along the river.	Tourist and convention crowds can be overwhelming; waits are long at peak times; prices are high.
King William/ Monte Vista Historic District	Several of the city's best upscale restaurants are just south of downtown in this National Historic District. Drive or take the trolley to this beautifully preserved neighborhood that seems a world apart from the bustle of downtown.	Peaceful area with tree-canopied streets and restored antebellum homes; top-notch local chefs.	Few lower-priced options; neighborhood feels a little sketchy for late-night dining.

or just a killer hamburger, this is your kind of town. But San Antonio isn't stuck remembering the Alamo at every meal: chef-driven restaurants with a wide range of offerings, including sushi, offer a break from beef and tortillas.

Most restaurants, especially downtown and at the River Walk, are open seven days a week. Outside the downtown tourist area, restaurants generally close at around 10 on weekdays, 11 on weekends. River Walk restaurants and bars stay open later, generally until 2 AM. San Antonio bans smoking in all restaurants except in designated outdoor areas (bars do allow it). Tipping conventions are standard, generally 15% for lunch, 20% for dinner.

WHAT IT COSTS				
	¢	$	$$	$$$	$$$$
Restaurants	under $8	$8–$12	$13–$20	$21–$30	over $30

Restaurant prices are per person for a main course at dinner.

ALAMO HEIGHTS

FRENCH
$–$$$

✕**Bistro Vatel.** The bistro is named Vatel, the chef is named Watel, but no matter how you spell it, this up-and-coming spot takes fine French dining to new levels in its elegant dining room. You can go with the reasonable prix-fixe option (lunch is a steal) or mix-and-match entrées such as succulent duck breast, or tempura lobster tail with a range of salads and sides. Daily blackboard specials take advantage of the freshest foods and never fail to surprise. ⊠*218 E. Olmos Dr., Olmos Park (near Alamo Heights)* ☎*210/828–3141* ⊟*AE, D, DC, MC, V* ⊘*Closed Mon. No lunch weekends.*

AMERICAN
$–$$$$
★

✕**Cappy's Restaurant.** The antidote to big and brash national chains, Cappy's caters to a local crowd craving innovative food, classy but cheerful environs, and solid service. You can score great cheap eats like a Kobe burger or splurge for the chef's three-course prix-fixe menu which lets you pick a salad, entrée, and dessert. A simple but exceptional brunch, where eggs are whipped up in unusual ways, is served on Sunday. The main dining room takes advantage of funky brick architecture, tall windows, and an ever-changing gallery of art. The covered outdoor seating is hard to get on a busy night. ⊠*5011 Broadway St., Alamo Heights* ☎*210/828–9669* ⊟*AE, D, DC, MC, V.*

BURGER
¢–$$

✕**Casbeers.** Since 1932, Casbeers has been serving up live music with their famous enchiladas and mammoth hamburgers. Its down-home approach has made it a local institution, with Kinky Friedman among its many fans. In fact, there's a burger named after him. Come here for the rustic environs, some good music, and a slice of old San Antonio, but don't expect a culinary revelation. Beer and wine flow freely. ⊠*1719 Blanco Rd., Alamo Heights* ☎*210/732–3511* ⊟*AE, MC, V* ⊘*Closed Sun. and Mon.*

BURGER
¢–$

✕**Cheesy Jane's.** Big burgers, milk shakes and malts, and nostalgic decor dominate this throwback to old-time malt shops. But Jane's is any-

BEST BETS FOR SAN ANTONIO DINING

San Antonio offers just about everything you're looking for in a dining experience, with a wide choice of cuisines ranging from local flavors to French haute cuisine, and a host of atmospheres from casual fun to a luxurious, romantic night out on the town.

Fodor'sChoice ★

Biga on the Banks, $$–$$$$, River Walk

Francesca's at Sunset, 4, Northwest

Le Rêve, $$$$, Downtown

Mi Tierra Café and Bakery, $–$$$, Downtown

Silo Elevated Cuisine, $$–$$$$, North

By Price

¢

Casbeers, Alamo Heights

Cheesy Jane's, Alamo Heights

Magnolia Pancake Haus, North

Rudy's Country Store & Bar-B-Q, Outskirts

$

Chris Madrids, North

Earl Abel's, Alamo Heights

El Jarro de Arturo, North

Guenther House, King William Historic District

Josephine Street Café, North Central

La Fonda on Main, Alamo Heights

Liberty Bar, Alamo Heights

Schilo's Deli, Downtown

$$

Acenar, River Walk

Azúca Nuevo Latino, King William Historic District

Boudro's, River Walk

Cappy's Restaurant, Alamo Heights

Mi Tierra Café and Bakery, Downtown

Paesanos, River Walk

Paloma Blanca, Alamo Heights

$$$

Antlers Lodge, Northwest

Citrus, River Walk

Fig Tree Restaurant, River Walk

Frederick's, Alamo Heights

Las Canarias, River Walk

Little Rhein Steak House, River Walk

$$$$

Biga on the Banks, River Walk

Bohanan's Prime Steaks and Seafood, Downtown

Francesca's at Sunset, Northwest

Le Rêve, Downtown

L'Etoile, Alamo Heights

Silo Elevated Cuisine, North

By Cuisine

AMERICAN

Biga on the Banks, $$–$$$$, River Walk

Cappy's Restaurant, $–$$$$, Alamo Heights

Citrus, $$$–$$$$, River Walk

Earl Abel's, $–$$$, Alamo Heights

Liberty Bar, ¢–$$$, Alamo Heights

Silo Elevated Cuisine, $$–$$$$, North

BARBECUE

Barbecue Station Restaurant, ¢–$, Northeast

County Line Barbecue, $–$$, River Walk

Rudy's Country Store & Bar-B-Q, ¢–$$, Outskirts

BREAKFAST OR BRUNCH

Bawdsey Manor British Tea Room, $–$$$, Outskirts

Crumpets Restaurant & Bakery, $$–$$$$, North Central

Guenther House, ¢–$, King William Historic District

Magnolia Pancake Haus, ¢–$, North

CONTINENTAL

Azúca Nuevo Latino, $$–$$$, King William Historic District

Fig Tree Restaurant, $$$–$$$$, River Walk

Las Canarias, $$$–$$$$, River Walk

FRENCH

Bistro Vatel, $–$$$, Olmos Park

Frederick's, $$$–$$$$, Alamo Heights

Le Rêve, $$$$,
Downtown

L'Etoile, $$$–$$$$,
Alamo Heights

HAMBURGERS

Casbeers, ¢–$$,
Alamo Heights

Cheesy Jane's, ¢–$,
Alamo Heights

Chris Madrids, $,
North

Timbo's, ¢–$$, Alamo
Heights

ITALIAN

Aldo's Ristorante
Italiano, $$–$$$$,
Northwest

La Focaccia Italian
Grill, $–$$$, King William Historic District

Paesanos, $–$$$$,
River Walk

MEXICAN

El Jarro de Arturo,
$–$$$, North

La Fogata, $–$$$,
North

La Fonda on Main,
$–$$, Alamo Heights

Los Barrios, $–$$,
North Central

Paloma Blanca, $$–
$$$$, Alamo Heights

Rosario's Café y Cantina, $–$$$, King William Historic District

SEAFOOD

Chart House at Tower
of the Americas,
$$$–$$$$, Downtown

Landry's Seafood
House Inn, $$–$$$$,
River Walk

Pesca on the River,
$–$$$$, River Walk

SOUTHWESTERN

Antlers Lodge, $$$–
$$$$, Northwest

Boudro's, $$–$$$$,
River Walk

Francesca's at Sunset,
$$$$, Northwest

STEAK HOUSE

Bohanan's Prime
Steaks and Seafood,
$$$$, Downtown

Josephine Street
Café, ¢–$$, North
Central

Little Rhein Steak
House, $$$–$$$$,
River Walk

Morton's The Steakhouse, $$$–$$$$,
River Walk

Ruth's Chris Steak
House, $$$$,
Downtown

By Experience

CLASSIC SAN ANTONIO

Casbeers, ¢–$$,
Alamo Heights

Earl Abel's, $–$$$,
Alamo Heights

La Fonda on Main,
$–$$, Alamo Heights

Los Barrios, $–$$,
North Central

Mi Tierra Café and
Bakery, $–$$$,
Downtown

Schilo's Deli, $,
Downtown

DINING ALFRESCO

Cappy's Restaurant,
$–$$$$, Alamo Heights

Fig Tree Restaurant,
$$$–$$$$, River Walk

La Fonda on Main,
$–$$, Alamo Heights

Las Canarias, $$$–
$$$$, River Walk

Mi Tierra Café and
Bakery, $–$$$,
Downtown

Paesanos, $–$$$$,
River Walk

FAMILY FRIENDLY

Cheesy Jane's, ¢–$,
Alamo Heights

Chris Madrids, $,
North

La Hacienda de
los Barrios, $–$$$,
Outskirts

Mi Tierra Café and
Bakery, $–$$$,
Downtown

Rainforest Café,
$–$$$, River Walk

Schilo's Deli, $,
Downtown

ON THE RIVER WALK

Acenar, $$–$$$, River
Walk

Biga on the Banks,
$$–$$$$, River Walk

Boudro's, $$–$$$$,
River Walk

Little Rhein Steak
House, $$$–$$$$,
River Walk

Paesanos, $–$$$$,
River Walk

Pesca on the River,
$–$$$$, River Walk

ROMANTIC

Azúca Nuevo Latino,
$$–$$$, King William
Historic District

Biga on the Banks,
$$–$$$$, River Walk

Citrus, $$$–$$$$,
River Walk

Fig Tree Restaurant,
$$$–$$$$, River Walk

Francesca's at Sunset,
$$$$, Northwest

Le Rêve, $$$$,
Downtown

SINGLES SCENE

20nine Restaurant
and Wine Bar, $$–$$$,
Alamo Heights

Liberty Bar, ¢–$$$,
Alamo Heights

Rosario's Café y Cantina, $–$$$, King William Historic District

Silo Elevated Cuisine,
$$–$$$$, North

thing but vanilla—literally. Shake and malt flavors include amaretto-espresso, peanut butter and jelly, and peppermint double fudge. The ground chuck burgers come in sizes ranging from ¼ to 1 pound. On the nonmeat side there's a good bean burger or triple grilled-cheese sandwich. Adventurous diners should definitely partake of the jalapeño "slivers"—battered and fried slices of onion and peppers. ⊠*4200 Broadway St., Alamo Heights* ☎*210/826–0800* ▭*AE, MC, V.*

AMERICAN
$–$$$

✕**Earl Abel's.** This hip San Antonio restaurant changed owners in 2007 and moved to a new neighborhood, but the food is still top-notch. The crispy fried catfish is a winner, as is the fried chicken. You can get your fried-chicken fix (and other artery-clogging favorites) from the to-go stand in the parking lot, but if you take the time to sit, you can also savor a slice of homemade coconut or lemon meringue pie. ⊠*1201 Austin Hwy., Alamo Heights* ☎*210/822–3358* ⚔*Reservations not accepted* ▭*AE, D, DC, MC, V.*

FRENCH
$$$–$$$$

✕**Frederick's.** Chef Perrin marries French and Asian cuisine to create some fantastic fusion dishes in relaxing yet romantic surroundings. Seafood is a particular standout, especially the truffle-baked sea bass and curry-crusted red snapper—both fine examples of complex flavor and stylish presentation. French staples such as veal tenderloin and rack of lamb have been jazzed up with Asian flourishes. A deep wine cellar offers many choices to complement your meal. ⊠*7701 Broadway St., at West Nottingham, Alamo Heights* ☎*210/828–9050* ▭*AE, D, DC, MC, V* ☉*Closed Sun.*

MEXICAN
$–$$
★

✕**La Fonda on Main.** Open for business in San Antonio since 1932, this family-friendly restaurant in a hacienda-like building is fun and casual, but still upscale. The beautiful dining room opens onto an inviting outdoor patio. The traditional Mexican fare includes such dishes as steak Tampiquena ("Tampico-style": grilled tenderloin strips with a green enchilada and *charro* beans [pinto beans in a slightly spicy sauce]) and a variety of enchiladas. Several Tex-Mex specialties also populate a robust menu. Flan and *tres leches* cake ("three milks" cake—a butter cake soaked in sweetened condensed milk, evaporated milk, and cream) are made daily, and the vibrant bar delivers tasty margaritas. ⊠*2415 N. Main Ave., Alamo Heights* ☎*210/733–0621* ▭*AE, D, DC, MC, V.*

FRENCH
$$$–$$$$

✕**L'Etoile.** Progressive but classic French cuisine, beautifully executed, makes L'Etoile a local favorite. You might find perfectly grilled lamb chops, lobster theatrically flamed in cognac and presented on a bed of julienned vegetables, or veal *piccata* (sautéed and drizzled with lemon-caper sauce). The menu changes daily. The chocolate Grand Marnier soufflé is incredible; order it when you order your meal, as it takes 45 minutes to prepare. Great deals include an early-bird special (a 20% discount before 6:30 PM) and a $15 three-course lunch on Tuesday and Thursday. ⊠*6106 Broadway St., Alamo Heights* ☎*210/826–4551* ▭*AE, D, DC, MC, V* ☉*Closed Sun.*

AMERICAN
¢–$$$

✕**Liberty Bar.** Built in 1890 and leaning conspicuously on its foundation (attributed to a 1921 flood), Liberty Bar is a hip, funky restaurant that's a place to see and be seen. The menu features basic, old-time favorites such as pot roast, peppered steak, and pasta. Dessert may be what they

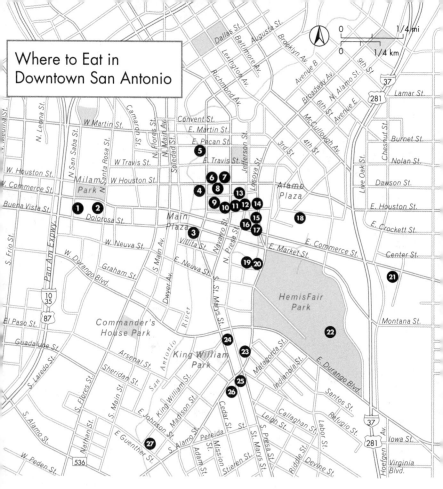

Where to Eat in
Downtown San Antonio

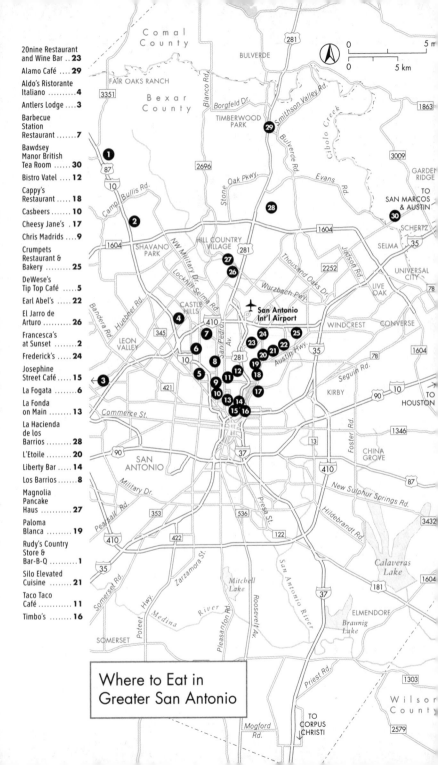

Where to Eat in
Greater San Antonio

do best: try the chocolate cake or a slice of homemade pie. Guinness is on tap. ⊠ *328 E. Josephine St., Alamo Heights* ☎ *210/227–1187* ▤ *AE, D, DC, MC, V.*

MEXICAN
$$–$$$$
✕ **Paloma Blanca.** A warm, almost clubby atmosphere—especially in the bar, with its fireplace and leather sofas—lets you know to expect more than the typical Mexican fare at this Alamo Heights mainstay. Tempting offerings as varied as grilled snapper, enchiladas *verdes* (covered with green tomatillo salsa), pozole, handmade flautas, and tacos *al pastor* (marinated pork with pineapple) are sure to please. And don't skip out on dessert—the rich flan and decadent tres leches cake are alone worth the trip to this hacienda-inspired spot. A scrumptious brunch with mimosas is served weekends. ⊠ *Cambridge Shopping Center, 5800 Broadway St., Alamo Heights* ☎ *210/822–6151* ▤ *AE, D, DC, MC, V.*

MEXICAN
¢–$
✕ **Taco Taco Café.** If you've never had a breakfast taco, this is the place to be initiated. Don't be afraid of the long lines out the door, as the morning crowd moves quickly. However, newbies may pause at the enormous number of possibilities, including *barbacoa* (shredded meat barbecue, Mexican style) and *migas* (eggs scrambled with fried tortilla strips, cheese, and peppers) tacos. Daily specials, a children's menu, and substantial lunch plates round out the taco extravaganza. ⊠ *145 E. Hildebrand Ave., Alamo Heights* ☎ *210/822–9533* ▤ *AE, D, DC, MC, V* ⊗ *No dinner.*

BURGER
¢–$$
✕ **Timbo's.** The owner of legendary San Antonio restaurant Little Hipps later opened this destination for fabulous burgers, tater tots, and fresh salads. Don't miss the shypoke eggs: toasted bread with two kinds of cheese on top (no eggs in sight). Many tables have their own personal jukeboxes, adding to the modern diner look. ⊠ *1639 Broadway, at Pearl Pkwy., Alamo Heights* ☎ *210/223–1028* ▤ *AE, D, DC, MC, V* ⊗ *Closed weekends.*

AMERICAN
$$–$$$
✕ **20nine Restaurant and Wine Bar.** Part of the Alamo Quarry Market shopping complex, this upscale spot may make you wonder whether you're going to dinner or a wine tasting. Well, why not have both? The selection of vintages is overwhelming, but the sommelier will help you make the right choices to pair with a small menu of entrées ranging from Stilton-stuffed chicken breast to a NY strip. This is also a great place to wind down from a day at the boutiques with dessert and a glass of port. ⊠ *Alamo Quarry Market, 255 E. Basse Rd., Suite 940, Alamo Heights* ☎ *210/798–9463* ▤ *AE, MC, V* ⊗ *No lunch weekends.*

DOWNTOWN

STEAK HOUSE
$$$$
✕ **Bohanan's Prime Steaks and Seafood.** Executive chef and owner Mark Bohanan dishes up only prime-grade, center-cut Aberdeen Angus beef with exclusive selections of ultramarbled Japanese Akaushi beef. The restaurant also has more than 35 varieties of seafood flown directly to the restaurant from the Gulf of Mexico. Add a selection of single-malt Scotches, a cigar bar, a cognac cart, and an expansive wine list, and it's no wonder that the place attracts a power crowd. ⊠ *219 E. Houston St., Suite 205, Downtown* ☎ *210/472–2600* ▤ *AE, D, MC, V* ⊗ *No lunch weekends.*

STEAK HOUSE
$$$–$$$$

✕ **Chart House at Tower of the Americas.** This steak house, opened in 2007, reigns over the San Antonio skyline, perched at the top of the Tower of the Americas. Its predecessor was primarily popular as a destination for drinks, but Chart House serves up some great steaks and seafood to keep you occupied for an entire night out while enjoying one-of-a-kind views of the city. It's a short stroll and elevator ride from the River Walk and other downtown attractions. ⊠*Tower of the Americas, 600 HemisFair Pkwy., Downtown* ☎*210/223–3101* ▤*AE, D, DC, MC, V.*

TEX-MEX
$$–$$$
★

✕ **La Margarita Mexican Restaurant & Oyster Bar.** In the heart of Market Square, you can eat Mexican fare or oysters or both while surrounded by Spanish tile and light music. Try the fajitas, enchiladas, or puffy tacos, seated inside or on the patio under colorful umbrellas with a great view of the city. Want it all? Go for the Fiesta San Antonio appetizer plate for yourself or to share with friends over a fantastic array of margaritas—it's what the restaurant is named for, and the moniker is justified. There's plenty of live entertainment, and mariachis will serenade your table upon request (and please do tip a couple of dollars). ⊠*120 Produce Row, Downtown* ☎*210/227–7140* ▤*AE, D, MC, V.*

FRENCH
$$$$
Fodor'sChoice
★

✕ **Le Rêve.** Largely hailed as one of the finest restaurants in the United States, the elegant and formal La Rêve serves up romance and fine French food in equal measure. Chef Andrew Reissman marries the contemporary with the classic in (frequently updated) dishes that feature ingredients ranging from foie gras to diver sea scallops. The eight-course tasting menu with matched wines is the best way to enjoy a leisurely dining experience—be prepared to devote two-plus hours—perfect for special celebrations. ⊠*Historic Exchange Bldg., 152 E. Pecan St., Downtown* ☎*210/212–2221* ⚎*Reservations essential* ▤*AE, D, DC, MC, V* ☉*Closed Sun. and Mon.*

TEX-MEX
$–$$$
Fodor'sChoice
★

✕ **Mi Tierra Café and Bakery.** In the heart of Market Square lies one of San Antonio's most venerable culinary landmarks. Opened in 1941 as a place for early-rising farmers to get breakfast, the colorful, helium-balloon-filled Mi Tierra is now a traditional Mexican restaurant, bakery, and bar that brings in locals and visitors (even John Wayne once stopped by). Its hallmark breakfasts are served all day, and the *chilaquiles famosas*—eggs scrambled with corn tortilla strips and topped with *ranchero* (mild tomato-based) sauce and cheese—are alone worth coming back for again and again. Truly memorable tacos, enchiladas, chalupas, and house specialties, all made from fresh ingredients, are served at lunch and dinner. The giant, carved oak bar serves up aged tequilas, authentic margaritas, draught beer, and mixed drinks. The bakery has an enormous selection of *pan dulces* (Mexican pastries) and excellent coffee. The atmosphere is partylike, and the restaurant is open 24 hours. ⊠*218 Produce Row, Market Square, Downtown* ☎*210/225–1262* ⚎*Reservations not accepted* ▤*AE, D, DC, MC, V.*

STEAK HOUSE
$$$–$$$$

✕ **The Palm Restaurant.** The San Antonio location of this classic New York–style steak house maintains the chain's efforts to bring back the supper clubs of decades gone by. Premium seafood, including jumbo Nova Scotia lobster, and Italian specialties add plenty of diversity to a menu populated by prime aged porterhouses and veal rib chops. The dining room is elegant and stately, putting you in the right frame of mind to down some serious turf or surf or both. ⊠ *233 E. Houston St., Downtown* ☎ *210/226–7256* ▭ *AE, D, DC, MC, V* ⊘ *No lunch weekends.*

STEAK HOUSE ✗**Ruth's Chris Steak House.** It's a mainstay in almost every convention
$$$$ town, but you can't go wrong with this upscale purveyor of fillets and T-bones. The menu's à la carte approach allows you to mix and match to your heart's content, but be wary of tab creep. Try a cowboy rib eye for a truly flavorful cut or venture outside the norm for the seared ahi tuna. ⊠ *1170 E. Commerce St., Downtown* ☎ *210/227–8847* ▭ *AE, D, DC, MC, V.*

DELI ✗**Schilo's Deli.** This venerable downtown institution has been serving up
$ hearty German soul food at breakfast (served daily), lunch, and dinner since 1917. Fuel up for a walking tour of downtown with thick split-pea or lentil soup, corned beef, sausage, deli sandwiches, or weekday lunch specials such as chicken and dumplings or meat loaf. Wash it down with fantastic homemade root beer and top off your meal with cheesecake—if you have room. ⊠ *424 E. Commerce St., Downtown* ☎ *210/223–6692* ▭ *AE, D, DC, MC, V* ⊘ *Closed Sun.*

KING WILLIAM & MONTE VISTA HISTORIC DISTRICT

CARIBBEAN ✗**Azúca Nuevo Latino.** If you want something different from San Anto-
$$–$$$ nio's usual Mexican or Tex-Mex offerings, venture south to find festive fare hailing from the Caribbean, Spain, and South and Central America. Executive Chef Rene Fernandez mixes up flavors and styles *con pasion.* Start out with an Amazonian tamale or Bolivian empanada and move onto plantain-crusted salmon and meats basted with *chimichurri,* a tangy basil sauce. A good array of steaks plus a children's menu ensure that everyone leaves happy. There's live salsa music and dancing Friday and Saturday. ⊠ *713 S. Alamo St., King William Historic District* ☎ *210/225–5550* ▭ *AE, D, DC, MC, V.*

MEXICAN ✗**El Mirador.** Nuevo Mexican and traditional Tex-Mex flavors collide
$–$$$ at this family-owned restaurant, a much-loved King William–district mainstay since 1967. Owner Dona Marie's mole enchiladas shine here, with the extra-sweet but smoky sauce designed to be sopped up by homemade corn tortillas. Shrimp and fish play a major role, bringing new life to tacos, nachos, and chiles rellenos. And if you've never had a breakfast taco, this is the place to try one in any of almost a dozen ways. A full bar during dinner and an outdoor dining patio seal the deal on a quintessential San Antonio eating experience. ⊠ *722 S. Saint Mary's St., King William Historic District* ☎ *210/225–9444* ▭ *AE, D, MC, V* ⊘ *No dinner Sun. and Mon.*

BREAKFAST ✗**Guenther House.** This popular restaurant in downtown San Antonio
¢–$ is housed in a stately 1860 home built by the founder of Pioneer Flour
★ Mills. Breakfast goodies—fluffy Pioneer Brand biscuits, breakfast tacos (with eggs, beans, and potatoes), waffles, and pastries—are half of the reason to eat here. The other half is the 1920s art-nouveau decor of stained glass, beveled glass, etched glass, and plant motifs that creates the illusion of a fine home's conservatory. ⊠ *205 E. Guenther St.,*

King William Historic District ☎210/227–1061 ▭AE, MC, V ⊘No dinner.

ITALIAN ✕**La Focaccia Italian Grill.** A family-owned, classic Italian restaurant, La
$–$$$ Focaccia has been luring folks to the King William district for pasta, steaks, and seafood since 1996. House specialties include veal saltimbocca, fresh linguine *pescatora* (with fresh shellfish), and wood-fired pizzas. Match such food with a warm, lush dining room and top-notch service, and you almost forget you're deep in the heart of Texas. ⊠*800 S. Alamo St., King William Historic District* ☎210/223–5353 ▭AE, D, DC, MC, V.

MEXICAN ✕**Rosario's Café y Cantina.** A fitting gateway to the city's Blue Star Arts
$–$$$ District, this vibrant, colorful spot has a contemporary decor enhanced by striking paintings by local artists. The authentic Mexican food includes crowd-pleasing favorites such as supernachos (packed with nearly every topping you could want) and enchiladas to delicacies like tender tips of beef tongue. Many consider their margaritas the best in the city. Live entertainment on weekends kicks the festivities into high gear. ⊠*910 S. Alamo St., King William Historic District* ☎210/223–1806 ▭AE, D, DC, MC, V.

NORTH/NORTHWEST

MEXICAN ✕**Alamo Café.** A perennial favorite with locals, the Alamo Café is far
$–$$ from the actual Alamo, but you'll still remember it for its fresh tortillas (made while you watch) and no-frills approach to Mexican dishes. This is a good place to try some puffy tacos with grilled chicken or steak, or dive into a mega combination platter of enchiladas, tamales, and chiles rellenos. It's extremely family-friendly, with a kids' menu that serves up near-adult-size portions. ⊠*14250 U.S. 281N, Northwest* ☎210/495–2233 ▭AE, D, MC, V.

ITALIAN ✕**Aldo's Ristorante Italiano.** This outpost of northern Italian fare near the
$$–$$$$ Southwest Texas Medical Center and USAA is in a warm and homey century-old house. Fresh, simple fish, chicken, beef, game, and pasta dishes are paired with attentive service. A small patio allows you to dine alfresco, but you may prefer sitting in the bar, which has live piano music in the evenings. ⊠*8539 Fredericksburg Rd., Northwest* ☎210/696–2536 ▭AE, D, DC, MC, V ⊘No lunch weekends.

SOUTH- ✕**Antlers Lodge.** Known for upscale takes on Texan fare—rattlesnake
WESTERN fritters, quail with chorizo and grits, bison tenderloin—this restaurant
$$$–$$$$ in the Hyatt Hill Country Resort also has lighter options like chili-dusted ahi tuna steak. The centerpiece of the elegant dining room is a huge chandelier with more than 500 naturally shed pairs of antlers. The dress code requires collared shirts for men and equally polished "dress resort wear" for women. ⊠*Hyatt Regency Hill Country Resort & Spa, 9800 Hyatt Resort Dr., Northwest* ☎210/520–4001 ▭AE, D, DC, MC, V.

BARBECUE ✕**Barbecue Station Restaurant.** When you walk into a true Texas smoke-
¢–$ house, expect to see smoke and taste fire. Though the location is inconspicuous—apart from the long line of hungry patrons—the restaurant meets and exceeds any barbecue hankerings. Mouthwatering, dry-rubbed beef brisket, smoked turkey, pork ribs, and sausages are served

TEX-MEX: A SPICY AFFAIR

Of the many things Texans take pride in, one of the things they boast about the most is Tex-Mex, a cuisine influenced by their south-of-the-border neighbor. Similar to Mexican cuisine, Tex-Mex is slightly different (more shredded cheese, no mole sauce, for example). And it's important to note that despite being lumped into the realm of Tex-Mex, steak burritos hail from San Francisco, chimichangas are from Tucson, and fish tacos are strictly a Southern Californian thing.

Every Tex-Mex restaurant typically offers at least one, if not multiple, versions of the following:

Chalupas. The word "chalupas" means "canoes." The modern form of Tex-Mex chalupas are served as a flat fried corn tortilla topped with taco fixings including ground taco meat, diced tomato, lettuce, and cheese. (Ground beef is often substituted with, or added on top of, refried beans.)

Chile con queso. A popular accompaniment to the standard chips and salsa served at most Tex-Mex restaurants (you can also dunk pieces of fresh flour tortillas—ask your server for some, they're usually free). Chile con queso simply means cheese with chilies; it's a rich, liquid concoction of melted cheese (usually including the processed Velveeta-type cheese), chilies or hot sauce, and occasionally tomatoes and onions.

Enchiladas. One of the more-"messy" dishes, enchiladas are piping-hot rolled corn tortillas filled with either cheese or meat and covered in melted cheese and sauce (chili, ranchero, and tomatillo are common options).

Fajitas. Somewhat of a misnomer, fajitas are literally a cut of grilled skirt-steak, chopped and served with condiments to be rolled in flour tortillas. Today, though, fajitas can be pretty much any type of grilled meat (steak, chicken, or even shrimp), sautéed onions and peppers, and a side of sour cream, pico de gallo, guacamole, and shredded cheese. Roll your own, and enjoy!

Nachos. Rumored to be a last-minute snack idea by Ignacio "Nacho" Anaya in the border town of Piedras Negras, Mexico, this simple appetizer consists of fried tortilla chips covered in melted cheese (usually cheddar) and slices of jalapeño peppers. More-over-the-top versions include extra toppings (meat, sour cream, etc.).

Quesadillas. A commonly recognized appetizer equivalent to the American grilled cheese—but substituting pan-grilled tortillas for bread (and sometimes including meats and vegetables along with the cheese).

Salsa picante. Commonly seen in small dishes next to a heaping basket of tortilla chips when seated at a Tex-Mex restaurant, salsa is the chunky tomato, vegetable, and chili sauce. Chips and salsa are usually complimentary with your meal—if they're not, consider dining elsewhere.

Tacos. Traditionally served as crunchy U-shape fried tortillas stuffed with ground meat, diced tomatoes, lettuce, and cheese. Soft tacos are made with pliable flour tortillas.

–Jessica Norman Dupuy

up with tangy sauce (on the side), pickles, and slices of white bread. Beer, wine, and creamy sides help soothe the palate. There's a sizable outdoor patio. ✉*1610 N.E. Loop 410, Northeast* ☎*210/824–9191* *Reservations not accepted* *D, MC, V* *Closed Sun.*

BURGER $ ✕**Chris Madrids.** Founded in 1977, this burger and nacho joint goes by the motto "Cook Each Item as if You Were Cooking It for a Friend," and it shows. The six varieties of hamburgers—which locals and tourists alike consider among the best in the world—come in two sizes: regular and macho. The only other items on the menu are fresh-cut fries, nachos, *chalupas* (open-faced tacos), and a grilled chicken sandwich. Tex-Mex decor adorns the old gas station and cantina, which is a full-service bar with iced-down longnecks and frozen margaritas. It all makes for a fun, family-friendly meal out. ✉*1900 Blanco Rd., North* ☎*210/735–3552* *Reservations not accepted Fri. and Sat.* *AE, D, DC, MC, V* *Closed Sun.*

AMERICAN $$–$$$$ ✕**Crumpets Restaurant & Bakery.** The name sounds stuffy, but the dining room is everything but at this European-inspired location far removed from downtown's urban closeness. Views of the forest through large windows and comfortable seating prepare you for a greatest-hits approach to continental cuisine, with some unexpected twists such as ostrich fillet. Savory sauces drape chicken, prime rib, and rack of lamb. The on-site bakery serves up fresh breads and pastries. Outdoor dining is plentiful, but beware mosquitoes after dark. ✉*3920 Harry Wurzbach Rd., North Central* ☎*210/821–5454* *AE, D, DC, MC, V.*

DINER $–$$ ✕**DeWese's Tip Top Café.** Put the diet on hold if you're coming to this San Antonio institution. And leave white-tablecloth expectations behind, too. Bathrooms are outside, stuffed heads hang on the paneled walls, and the food is definitely home-style. Not much has changed since DeWese's opened in 1938, and that's its great charm. The onion rings and chicken-fried steaks draw a loyal local following. Homemade desserts made fresh every morning, such as banana icebox pie, disappear quickly. ✉*2814 Fredericksburg Rd., Northwest* ☎*210/732–0191* *D, MC, V* *Closed Sun. and Mon.*

MEXICAN $–$$$ ✕**El Jarro de Arturo.** For more than 30 years this has been a favorite San Antonio spot for upscale and innovative Mexican cuisine. It's tough to choose between the beautiful, festive dining room and the garden-lush outdoor dining patio. And it's also tough to choose from among the diverse entrées, *antojitos* (appetizers), and desserts. Start out with the *botano* (sampler) platter to get a sample of the flavors, and then consider the house-specialty fajitas or chicken *fundido* (swathed in melted, white Mexican cheese) for the main course. The best value, however, is the extensive lunch buffet served weekdays 11–2. There's a full bar, live music on the weekends, and a kids' menu. ✉*13421 San Pedro Ave., North* ☎*210/494–5084* *AE, D, DC, MC, V.*

SOUTHWESTERN $$$$ Fodor's Choice ★ ✕**Francesca's at Sunset.** As the name would suggest, stunning views of the evening sky are part of the draw at the Westin La Cantera's showcase restaurant. But chef Ernie Estrada, a San Antonio native, also adds considerable local flare to a Southwestern menu originally crafted by world-renowned restaurateur Mike Miller. Those wanting a truly memorable dining experience can choose from powerful eclectic dishes ranging from fillet of antelope to spicy grilled duck legs to chili-rubbed buffalo rib eye. If you can nab a reservation, it's well worth the trip across town. ⊠ *Westin La Cantera Resort, 16641 La Cantera Pkwy., Northwest* ☎*210/558–6500 Ext. 4803* ⌾ *Reservations essential* ⊟*AE, D, DC, MC, V* ⊘*No lunch.*

STEAK HOUSE
¢–$$

✕**Josephine Street Café.** This "café" is actually a Texas roadhouse famous for dishing up "steaks & whisky" since 1979. In an early 1900s building on the outskirts of downtown, Josephine's is decidedly casual and friendly. Steaks come in all shapes and sizes, from a tasty chicken-fried variety to a 16-ounce Texas T-bone. Those looking for something different on the menu can opt for choices like Pacific snapper and Cajun chicken breast. The beer on tap and full bar are to be expected—what isn't is the baked-fresh-daily peach cobbler, for a belly-busting finish. ⊠*400 E. Josephine St., North Central* ☎*210/224–6169* ⊟*AE, D, DC, MC, V* ⊘*Closed Sun.*

MEXICAN
$–$$$

✕**La Fogata.** The open and airy spaces of La Fogata's rambling, hacienda-style indoor dining areas plus lush, tropical outdoor patio put you in the mood for some authentic Mexican food. A top-shelf, hand-shaken margarita helps you relax and enjoy an enormous selection of dishes ranging from chicken mole to *calabacita con carne de puerco* (a pork stew with fresh squash). The expected Mexican cornucopia of tacos, enchiladas, quesadillas, and everything in between is kicked up a notch with made-on-the-premises tortillas. Live music is common, and mariachis are known to roam, so have a request in mind—besides "La Cucaracha." ⊠*2427 Vance Jackson Rd., Northwest* ☎*210/340–1337* ⊟*AE, D, MC, V.*

MEXICAN
$–$$

✕**Los Barrios.** Diana Barrios Trevino—a frequent Food Network guest—oversees the kitchen at this family-run restaurant, known for its authentic gourmet Mexican dishes. Eat in a relaxed, casual atmosphere with lots of light. Try the fajitas, tacos, or classic enchiladas. There's a kids' menu and entertainment on the weekend. ⊠*4223 Blanco Rd., North Central* ☎*210/732–6017* ⊟*AE, D, DC, MC, V.*

AMERICAN
¢–$

✕**Magnolia Pancake Haus.** Opened in 2000 and already a much-loved breakfast institution, Magnolia prides itself on dishes made from fresh and wholesome ingredients. Fluffy buttermilk pancakes are a mainstay, but for something different, try the jambalaya omelet, smoked-turkey hash, or puffed apple pancakes made with Granny Smith apples, cinnamon, and powdered sugar. Breakfast is served all day, but at lunchtime a diverse selection of salads, soups, burgers, and deli sandwiches rounds out the menu. However, the real reason to come here is for your morning pancake pilgrimage. It's open 7 AM–2 PM daily. ⊠*13444 West Ave., Suite 300, North* ☎*210/496–0828* ⌾*Reservations not accepted* ⊟*AE, D, DC, MC, V* ⊘*No dinner.*

AMERICAN
$$–$$$$

Fodor's Choice
★

✕**Silo Elevated Cuisine.** Just a few miles northeast of downtown, Silo has beautiful views of the city from its sleek first-floor bar and second-floor restaurant. The dining room is modern and modestly glamorous, but not at all pretentious, bringing some of the fun up from the popular bar downstairs. Start out with the chicken-fried oysters or blue-crab spring rolls and move onto the grilled and braised Kurobuta pork shank or seared sea scallops. If you catch a table before 6:30 PM Sunday through

---

SAN ANTONIO SPECIALTIES

The dish that San Antonio invented is also its best-kept secret: the puffy taco. It starts by cooking a salad-plate-size disc of corn masa (corn-meal dough) until it becomes chewy and crispy. While it's still warm, it's folded and stuffed with seasoned chicken or beef, shredded lettuce, tomatoes, guacamole, and other fillings. When you're in San Antonio you owe it to yourself to become a tortilla snob. At most Mexican or Tex-Mex restaurants, the meal begins with freshly made tortillas (flour or corn). Locals butter them and eat them as you would a dinner roll. Fresh tortillas bear little resemblance to their grocery-store cousins: they're soft, fluffy and have a buttery taste that you may lie awake nights craving.

Texas-style barbecue generally serves up beef brisket that's been cooked low and slow with dry spices rubbed into the meat. Sauce is served on the side after cooking. It's generally thick and tomato-based with strong flavors (but not particularly hot or spicy). Side dishes include a local style of baked beans that's more smoky than sweet, along with white bread and maybe cole-slaw. Prices for barbecue are generally quite reasonable, so even if your budget is limited, you can go big with your barbecue.

Thursday, opt for the prix-fixe three-course dinner: it puts a whole new spin on the typical "early bird" special by allowing you to put together many of the restaurant's specialties for under $30. ⊠ *1133 Austin Hwy., Northeast* ☎ *210/824–8686* ⊟ *AE, D, DC, MC, V.* ·

OUTSKIRTS

CAFÉ   ✕ **Bawdsey Manor British Tea Room.** You may feel like you've stumbled
$–$$$ into stately cottage on the other side of the pond at this restaurant, where British sensibilities abound in decor and menu. For those seeking something a little more genteel than a typical Texas fiesta, Bawdsey complies with high tea—finger sandwiches, scones, the works—and Brit faves like fish-and-chips and meat pies. It's just north of Highway 1604 in Bracken Village. ⊠ *18771 FM 2252 (Nacogdoches Rd.), Outskirts* ☎ *210/651–7500* ⊟ *D, MC, V* ☉ *Closed Sun. No dinner Mon.*

TEX-MEX   ✕ **La Hacienda de los Barrios.** It may feel like you're walking into a cen-
$–$$$ turies-old hacienda at this enormous outpost just outside the Highway 1604 loop, but the tacos (regular or puffy), nachos, tamales, grilled chicken, and steaks have a slightly modern twist. If you can't decide what to pick from the enormous menu, hedge your bets by going for the enchilada platter—five delectable takes on a Mexican staple. With lots of space and an impressive playground, there's no doubt the place was built with families in mind. It's ideal for large groups and is a sister restaurant to Los Barrios (⇨ *above*). ⊠ *18747 Redland Rd., Outskirts* ☎ *210/497–8000* ⊟ *AE, D, DC, MC, V.*

BARBECUE   ✕ **Rudy's Country Store & Bar-B-Q.** What looks like an old gas station
¢–$$ on the outside pumps out some of San Antonio's favorite barbecue.
★   The wait to place your order is worth it once you bite into some tender brisket (the "sause" is on the side) or smoked turkey dry-rubbed

with flavor and cooked in wood-fired pits. Everything here—including the ribs, sausages, slaw, and potato salad—is dished up on plastic plates and necessitates lots of napkins. Outdoor picnic-table seating completes the picture. ⊠ *24152 W. I–10, Outskirts* ☎ *210/698–2141* 🖃 *AE, D, DC, MC, V.*

RIVER WALK

To find the locations of these River Walk restaurants, see the Where to Eat in Downtown San Antonio map earlier in this section.

TEX-MEX
$$–$$$
★

✕ **Acenar.** This nouvelle Tex-Mex hot spot sits astride a less-traveled section of the River Walk. Start out with excellent margaritas—many made from exotic ingredients, such as pear cactus—and guacamole made table-side or fresh ceviche. For the main course, move onto fish tacos (grilled or fried) or a host of seasonal fare, all with a fresh, contemporary flare. The outdoor dining area is small, but worth the wait for views of the river. ⊠ *146 E. Houston St. (N. Saint Mary's St.), River Walk* ☎ *210/222–2362* 🖃 *AE, D, MC, V.*

AMERICAN
$$–$$$$
Fodor'sChoice
★

✕ **Biga on the Banks.** Like Texas, enthusiastic chef Bruce Auden's menu is big and eclectic, and the dining atmosphere manages to be both bigger than life and romantic. Dishes change daily to take advantage of the freshest food available, ranging from seared red grouper grits to 11-spice axis venison chops. Don't skip out on dessert, which may be the best in town: the sticky toffee pudding is a must. This is one of the best spots for a leisurely dinner on the River Walk, if you can get a reservation. ⊠ *203 S. Saint Mary's St. (W. Market St.), River Walk* ☎ *210/225–0722* 🍴 *Reservations essential* 🖃 *AE, D, MC, V* ⊘ *No lunch.*

SOUTH-
WESTERN
$$–$$$$
★

✕ **Boudro's.** A little bit Gulf Coast, a little bit Mexican, and a whole lotta Texan, this landmark River Walk establishment caters to almost every taste with exceptional good taste. Fresh fish is the star of the menu, including an unusual seafood platter that matches together a glazed lobster tail, blackened fillet du jour, crawfish, chicken-fried oysters, and a shrimp taco. Spicy-charred prime rib gives an extra kick for landlubbers. The main dining room is almost cavelike, and provides several nooks for conversation and romance, but the patio on the river is where you want to be when the weather's fine. ⊠ *421 E. Commerce St., River Walk* ☎ *210/224–8484* 🖃 *AE, D, DC, MC, V.*

AMERICAN
$$$–$$$$

✕ **Citrus.** This über-cool restaurant at the Hotel Valencia (⇨ *Where to Stay*) overlooks the River Walk and serves New American and Spanish-influenced cuisine. Its creative paella and pasta bar (you choose the ingredients) is popular at lunch, while dinner fare ranges from hickory-plank-roasted redfish to honey-orange-glazed duck. Executive chef Jeff Balfour puts on a pretty good show with fresh produce and a diverse repertoire. An extensive wine list and creative cocktails make it a one-stop shop for an evening's enjoyment. ⊠ *150 E. Houston St., River Walk* ☎ *210/230–8412* 🖃 *AE, D, DC, MC, V.*

BARBECUE
$–$$

✕ **County Line Barbecue.** Texas is famous for its barbecued ribs, smoked brisket, and related fare, and this contender definitely holds its own among the competition. The barbecue here is dry rubbed with the sauce on the side, and the various combo platters and family-style options let you sample from smoked turkey and sausage, brisket, beef and pork ribs, and more. The atmosphere is rustic–casual, so don't be afraid to put your elbows on the table. ⊠ *111 W. Crockett, Suite 104, River Walk* 🕿 *210/229–1941* ▤ *AE, D, DC, MC, V.*

<aside>
DINING WITH KIDS

It's easy to eat out with kids in San Antonio. Most restaurants have children's menus or an à la carte selections that work well for young diners. An affordable, kid-friendly alternative to fast food is Taco Cabana, a local chain with fast, fresh, and straightforward Mexican food. Some upscale restaurants on the River Walk can be less accommodating during peak times and often lack diaper-changing stations. For older kids, Rainforest Café on the River Walk is a popular (but pricey) option.
</aside>

ECLECTIC
$$$–$$$$

✕**Fig Tree Restaurant.** Exquisite food and impeccable service are mainstays of this French-inspired restaurant with a cozy interior and an outdoor villa-style terrace overlooking the San Antonio River. Crisp linens drape tables set with fine china and sparkling crystal in elegant yet homey surroundings. Delicate, highly composed dishes such as *tournedos Rossini* (seared beef fillets wrapped around foie gras and truffles), mint-crusted rack of lamb, and prosciutto-wrapped yellowfin tuna are menu standouts. Table-side flamed desserts include bananas Foster and traditional baked Alaska. ⊠ *515 Villita St., River Walk* 🕿 *210/224–1976* ▤ *AE, D, DC, MC, V.*

SEAFOOD
$$–$$$$

✕**Landry's Seafood House.** In the thick of things right on the San Antonio River, this upscale national seafood chain is a pleasurable oasis from the hustle and bustle. Dozens of varieties of fresh fish (reportedly flown in by helicopter each day) prepared in a number of ways include blackened swordfish and Parmesan-crusted sea bass; top steak cuts appease those who prefer turf to surf. The atmosphere is classy yet relaxed; there's a large wine list, a capable bar, and a prompt and knowledgeable waitstaff. ⊠ *517 N. Presa St., River Walk* 🕿 *210/229–1010* ⌕ *Reservations not accepted* ▤ *AE, D, DC, MC, V.*

MEDITERRANEAN
$$$–$$$$
Fodor's Choice
★

✕**Las Canarias.** In the Omni La Mansion del Rio, this three-level restaurant is known for its sophistication and romance, and has one of the most relaxing and beautiful outdoor dining areas on the San Antonio River. The menu mixes traditional and contemporary Mediterranean fare with Southwest influences. Creative, flavorful dishes of note include blue crab–stuffed swordfish tempura, buffalo carpaccio, and an unusual, delectable array of Spanish tapas. Gentle, live piano or guitar accompanies dinner. There is a stunning dessert tray, a full bar, and on Sunday an à la carte brunch menu. ⊠ *Omni La Mansion del Rio, 112 College St., River Walk* 🕿 *210/518–1063* ▤ *AE, D, DC, MC, V.*

STEAK HOUSE
$$$–$$$$

✕**Little Rhein Steak House.** Housed in a structure built in 1847, this rustic restaurant was originally used as a residence and store by German immigrant Otto Bombach. It's a historically protected site, with antique brass lights, wooden booths, and a smattering of Old West antiques. Specialties include center-cut filet mignon, bone-in prime strip loin, and fresh Norwegian salmon. Terrace dining gives diners views of the San

God Bless Texas (and Taco Cabana)

You can't visit the Lone Star State without indulging in some good Tex-Mex. South-of-the-border fare can be found everywhere—from trendy, upscale spots to mobile taco trucks—but only Taco Cabana has managed to deliver fresh Tex-Mex (and adult beverages) at fast-food prices.

The first Taco Cabana opened in 1978; it was essentially a taco stand in the parking lot of a Dairy Queen, serving cheap grub to college students leaving a nearby bar.

Founder Felix Stehling's patio furniture was stolen after the first day of business, and he decided that the best way to deter future theft was to stay open 24 hours. (Many Taco Cabana locations still offer 'round-the-clock service.)

Taco Cabana's food isn't gourmet. That being said, you'll be hard-pressed to find better Tex-Mex value (and this is certainly one of the best fast-food chains in the country). There are a variety of entrées, including Chicken Flameante (marinated rotisserie chicken), fajitas served on hot iron skillets (at roughly half the price

you'd pay in a sit-down joint), and Tex-Mex breakfast (including great breakfast tacos, served from midnight to mid-morning each day). But TC really makes three things extremely well: flour tortillas (fresh-pressed to order on an awesome machine), salsa (seven freshly made varieties, with varying levels of heat), and queso (delicious hot cheese sauce). For the quintessential Taco Cabana experience, order a stack of tortillas, a bowl of queso, and hit the salsa bar—it's like heaven for $3. Best of all, you can wash down your Taco Cabana with a cold margarita or cerveza, including Texas's own Shiner Bock and, of course, Corona.

Taco Cabana now has more than 140 locations in Texas, Oklahoma, and New Mexico, which means diners can take advantage of warm weather and sit on the patio or in the (weather permitting) open-air dining room.

The original restaurant, at 3310 San Pedro, is still in operation, and there are 35 other Taco Cabana restaurants around San Antonio.

–by Kevin Tankersley

Antonio River, and a full bar reminds you that the spot once served as a saloon. Expect the same dedication to excellence as sister restaurant the Fig Tree (they have the same owner). ⊠*231 S. Alamo St., River Walk* ☎*210/225–2111* ▭*AE, D, DC, MC, V.*

STEAK HOUSE
$$$–$$$$
✕**Morton's The Steakhouse.** A block from the Alamo and near the River Walk, this branch of the Morton's chain is appropriately elegant and contemporary. Fabulous steaks, the selection and size of which are truly impressive, range from double-cut fillets to prime rib to Cajun rib eye, and are matched with exquisite wines and service. This is not a spot for vegetarians, who are relegated to side dishes (albeit relatively healthful ones), but non-red-meat options include sesame-encrusted yellow tuna and whole baked Maine lobster. ⊠*Rivercenter Mall, 300 E. Crockett St., River Walk* ☎*210/228–0700* ▭*AE, D, MC, VC.*

ITALIAN
$–$$$$
★
✕**Paesanos.** This deservedly popular spot at a bend on the San Antonio River melds fine Italian dining with a Mediterranean approach.

The range of foodie-friendly dishes includes the signature shrimp *paesano*, a delicate and flavorful lightly breaded and baked concoction accented with lemon, butter, and garlic, which you can have as an appetizer or as an entrée. Other standouts include wood-fired pizzas, baked ziti with Italian sausage, cioppino (a seafood stew), and lemon-pepper salmon. Arrive

early to nab a primo table on the outdoor patio, right next to the river. ⊠*111 W. Crockett St., River Walk* ☎*210/227–2782* ⌖*Reservations not accepted* ▭*AE, D, DC, MC, V.*

SEAFOOD
$–$$$$

✕**Pesca on the River.** A relatively young addition to the River Walk dining scene, Pesca is a rising star in San Antonio, thanks to executive chef Scott Cohen's dedication to excellence. This high-energy, but romantic dining room "fishes" for seafood from around the world and matches it with locally grown herbs and produce. Pesca also has an oyster bar, a great wine list, and terrace dining with spectacular views of the river. ⊠*212 W. Crockett St., River Walk* ☎*210/396–5817* ▭*AE, D, DC, MC, V.*

AMERICAN
$–$$$

✕**Rainforest Café.** Ideal for kids, this fun chain near the Rivercenter Mall offers up a tropical theme and some decent food. The menu is varied, and dishes range from jambalaya to burgers—pretty basic but solid fare. It's a bit pricey, but well worth ducking out of the hustle-and-bustle to placate your kids even if you have to put up with animatronic jungle antics and overt merchandising. Inventive, colorful cocktails help you cope. ⊠*110 E. Crockett St., River Walk* ☎*210/277–6300* ▭*AE, D, DC, MC, V.*

SOUTH-
WESTERN
$$–$$$$

✕**Zuni Grill.** Although its eclectic Southwestern food is nothing special, loftlike Zuni Grill certainly ranks heads above the many tourist traps on the River Walk. The real draws are the views of the river, the spot-on cocktails—including a margarita made with real cactus juice—and a host of great appetizers. If you stay for a meal, you can't go wrong with the scorpion-shrimp-stuffed red chilies or the blue-corn chicken enchiladas. The outdoor patio right on the river is where to roost no matter your dining objective. ⊠*223 Losoya St., River Walk* ☎*210/227–0864* ▭*AE, D, DC, MC, V.*

WHERE TO STAY

THE SCENE

San Antonio's hotel scene is sizzling with new energy and excitement. In the next few years alone, the city's landscape will alter as more than 40 hotels open throughout the urban area. The biggest new hotel is the Grand Hyatt, which opened in spring 2008. Adjoining the Convention Center, the Grand Hyatt offers 79,000 square feet of business space and nearly 1,000 guest rooms.

San Antonio is a major convention destination, so it's feast or famine for hotel rooms; peak seasons are generally spring and late fall. At the right time you can get some great deals for top-quality accommodations, but during special events (Fiesta week, the NCAA Final Four tournament, major conventions) expect to pay top dollar and make reservations months in advance. Because of the city's appeal for business travelers, you can actually find lower rates on weekends at many hotels.

Many visitors choose to stay downtown to be close to the Alamo, River Walk, museums, and other attractions. Once you're downtown, almost everything is accessible on foot or via river taxi or trolley; a car isn't needed and parking can be expensive. The city has one shuttle service from the airport that serves all downtown hotels ($14 one way, $24 round-trip). It runs from 7 AM to 11 PM right from the airport. Several national chain hotels are concentrated along the River Walk and adjacent to the convention center. The Menger and Crockett hotels lead the list of historic hotels next to the Alamo. In recent years several boutique hotels have opened up, promoting spa weekends and indulgent getaways. Downtown has also seen the opening of some larger, value-oriented and extended-stay chains.

Several full-service resorts within the city limits, most near SeaWorld and Fiesta Texas amusement park, offer golf, tennis, on-site water parks, children's activities, restaurants, and the services you'd expect from a resort—a good option for families. Most major resorts are a 15- to 20-minute drive from downtown.

Bed-and-breakfasts are concentrated in a few of the national historic districts but still offer selections that are mid-range as well as pricier room options. Virtually all are no-smoking, and only a few accept children younger than 12.

WHAT IT COSTS					
	¢	$	$$	$$$	$$$$
Hotels	under $75	$75–$125	$126–$175	$176–$225	over $225

Hotel prices are per night for two people in a standard double room in high season, excluding taxes (16.75% for San Antonio) and service charges.

DOWNTOWN

$$ **Clarion Collection O'Brien Historic Hotel.** This reasonably priced downtown hotel is a great value with a hint of historic charm. Don't expect it to ooze history (the name oversells that a bit). Amenities are more likely to make you remember the 2003 renovation than the Alamo. With only 39 rooms, it's much smaller than the large convention hotels. Room sizes are modest and common areas aren't memorable but you're within a block of the River Walk. Parking is inexpensive ($10 a night) but is limited. **Pros:** Friendly staff, good location. **Cons:** Small rooms, limited parking. ⊠*116 Navarro St., Downtown,* ☎*210/527–1111*

WHERE SHOULD I STAY IN SAN ANTONIO?

	Neighborhood Vibe	Pros	Cons
Downtown	Staying here, you can walk past one historic building after another within blocks of several attractions. You can also often find some better deals than along the eminently popular River Walk. There's a mix of luxury, boutique, and value hotels to choose from.	Historic hotels, close to all the action but without the noise or bustle (and prices) of the River Walk.	High prices, especially at peak times, packed with tourists, limited and pricey parking.
North/Northwest	Family-friendly resorts and reliable national hotel chains cluster along highways with ready access to shopping, restaurants, and attractions north of Loop 410 in a massive sprawl that's technically urban but feels more suburban. Depending on traffic, getting there from downtown could take 15 to 30 minutes.	Easy access to the entire city via highway, many family-friendly amenities, many less-expensive lodging options than at the city's center.	Highway driving unavoidable; restaurants are primarily chains; generic, suburban feel.
River Walk	From charming boutiques to national chains, overlook the slow currents, towering trees, winding pathways, and arched bridges. Although the River Walk may evoke the romance of Venice, the seemingly endless array of restaurants, shops, and nightclubs also makes it the city's number-one location for fun.	The city's main attractions and restaurants are here, some rooms have balconies overlooking the river.	High premium for convenience and ambience, parking expensive and often inconvenient, many hotels not kid-friendly, late-night noise can be a problem.
King William/Monte Vista Historic District	Inns are tucked amid beautifully restored homes along tree-lined streets in this peaceful National Historic District just a short trolley ride from downtown.	Quiet, quaint, close to downtown (via trolley), easy parking.	B&Bs are the only option, and some lack amenities of conventional hotels.

⊕*www.obrienhotel.com* ➯*39 rooms* ⌂*In-room: Ethernet. In-hotel: gym, laundry facilities, laundry service, public Wi-Fi, parking (fee), no-smoking rooms* ⊟*AE, D, DC, MC, V* ⦿*CP.*

$$-$$ ⬚ **The Columns on Alamo.** Once the Anton Heinen house, this 1892 Greek Revival mansion was converted to a bed-and-breakfast in 1994. Victorian details fill every corner of the large home and garden. Many rooms have fireplaces and two-person whirlpool tubs. The adjacent Rock House is a two-bedroom cottage and the only part of the B&B that allows children. **Pros:** Warm and cozy environs, fairly inexpensive and accessible. **Con:** Nothing terribly special for a B&B.   ⊠*1037 S. Alamo St., Downtown,* ☎*210/271–3245 or 800/233–3364* ⊕*www. columnssanantonio.com* ➯*11 rooms, 1 suite, 1 cottage* ⌂*In-room: kitchen (some), refrigerator, Wi-Fi. In-hotel: laundry facilities, public Wi-Fi, parking (no fee), no-smoking rooms* ⊟*AE, D, DC, MC, V* ⦿*BP.*

$$–$$$ **Crockett Hotel.** Built in 1909 and listed on the National Register of
★ Historic Places, this hotel (named for frontiersman Davy Crockett) is a
relic of turn-of-the-20th-century San Antonio. Location is the big selling point here: you're 10 steps from the Alamo, River Walk, and many
sights. The seven-story, light-filled, sandstone-brick atrium lobby with
leather club chairs is impressive; some rooms look out onto it. Rooms
were thoroughly updated in 2007; they are contemporary and spotless
though a bit bland in the decor department. **Pros:** Great location, new
furnishings. **Cons:** Immediate area packed with tourists, bland room
decor, views nothing to write home about. ⊠ *320 Bonham St., Downtown,* ☎ *210/225–6500 or 800/292–1050* ⊕ *www.crocketthotel.com*
⇥ *126 rooms, 12 suites* ♿ *In-room: Ethernet. In-hotel: room service,
bar, pool, gym, laundry service, public Wi-Fi, parking (fee), no-smoking rooms* ☰ *AE, D, MC, V* ⏍ *BP.*

$$$$ **Emily Morgan Hotel.** Built in the 1920s and named for the woman
who inspired the song "The Yellow Rose of Texas," this boutique hotel
sits across from the Alamo on a triangular piece of land. Originally
built as a medical school, its neo-Gothic design stands out from other
downtown landmarks. Sleek furnishings and whirlpool tubs in marble
bathrooms make it a posh destination steeped in period romance. As
in many historic hotels, room size varies greatly, and quarters can be
tight. **Pros:** So close to the Alamo, you can see it from some rooms; nice
marriage of modern amenities and classic features. **Cons:** Relatively
expensive, a bit of a hike to the River Walk. ⊠ *705 E. Houston St.,
Downtown,* ☎ *210/225–5100* ⊕ *www.emilymorganhotel.com* ⇥ *154
rooms, 23 suites* ♿ *In-room: Wi-Fi. In-hotel: restaurant, room service,
bar, pool, gym, laundry facilities, laundry service, public Internet, public Wi-Fi, parking (fee), some pets allowed, no-smoking rooms* ☰ *AE,
D, DC, MC, V.*

$–$$ **Fairfield Inn & Suites San Antonio Downtown.** This Fairfield Inn looks
like every other, but it's clean and comfortable, with ready access to
all of San Antonio's sights. Two blocks from Market Square and a ride
on the trolley (which stops in front of the hotel) to the River Walk and
Alamo. The free parking is a major plus and a rarity downtown. **Pros:**
Refreshingly straightforward, relatively inexpensive, did we mention
the free parking? **Cons:** Cookie-cutter chain hotel with ho-hum decor.
⊠ *620 S. Santa Rosa, Downtown,* ☎ *210/229–1000* ⊕ *www.marriott.
com/satfi* ⇥ *73 rooms, 37 suites* ♿ *In-room: refrigerator (some), Ethernet, Wi-Fi. In-hotel: pool, gym, laundry facilities, laundry service,
public Internet, public Wi-Fi, parking (no fee), no-smoking rooms*
☰ *AE, D, DC, MC, V* ⏍ *CP.*

$$$$ **The Fairmount.** This historic luxury hotel made the *Guinness Book*
Fodor's Choice *of World Records* when its 3.2-million-pound brick bulk was moved
★ six blocks in 1985 to its present location. At the pinnacle of boutique,
luxury hotels in San Antonio, it offers premium amenities such as flat-
screen TVs, canopy beds, verandas, marble baths, and a courtyard
with a fountain. The hotel is full of quirks, with the hotel dog, Luke
Tips, manning the concierge desk, and different decor in each room.
Across from HemisFair Park, it's fairly close to the River Walk, convention center, and La Villita. **Pro:** Dripping with character and charm.

BEST BETS FOR SAN ANTONIO LODGING

With more than 330 hotels within the city limits, San Antonio offers the whole gamut of lodging options, from bed-and-breakfasts and ultrahip boutiques to full-service resorts and family-friendly venues. The following are our favorite accommodations across a variety of price points, types, and experiences. San Antonio aims to please, and we think you'll find something here for whatever your taste.

Fodor'sChoice ★

Brackenridge House, $$$–$$$$, King William Historic District

The Fairmount, $$$$, Downtown

Hotel Contessa Suites on the River Walk, $$$$, River Walk

Hyatt Regency Hill Country Resort, $$$$, North/Northwest

Ogé House, $$$$, King William Historic District

Watermark Hotel & Spa, $$$$, River Walk

By Price

¢

La Quinta Inn San Antonio I-35 N at Toepperwein, North/Northwest

$

A Yellow Rose, King William Historic District

Bonner Garden, King William Historic District

$$

El Tropicano Holiday Inn Riverwalk, River Walk

Hyatt Place San Antonio/River Walk, River Walk

Riverwalk Vista, River Walk

$$$

Brackenridge House, King William Historic District

Drury Plaza Hotel Riverwalk, River Walk

$$$$

The Fairmount, Downtown

Grand Hyatt, Downtown

Hotel Contessa Suites on the River Walk, River Walk

Hyatt Regency Hill Country Resort, North/Northwest

Ogé House, King William Historic District

Watermark Hotel & Spa, River Walk

Westin River Walk, River Walk

By Type

B&B

Brackenridge House, $$$–$$$$, King William Historic District

Jackson House, $$$–$$$$, King William Historic District

Ogé House, $$$$, King William Historic District

BOUTIQUE HOTEL

Emily Morgan Hotel, $$$$, Downtown

Hotel Contessa Suites on the River Walk, $$$–$$$$, River Walk

Hotel Valencia Riverwalk, $$$$, River Walk

Watermark Hotel & Spa, $$$$, River Walk

LARGE HOTEL

Grand Hyatt, $$$$, Downtown

Hilton Palacio del Rio, $$$$, River Walk

Marriott Rivercenter, $$$–$$$$, River Walk

Marriott River Walk, $$$–$$$$, River Walk

Omni La Mansión del Rio, $$$$, River Walk

Westin River Walk, $$$$, River Walk

RESORT

Hyatt Regency Hill Country Resort, $$$$, North/Northwest

Marriott Plaza San Antonio, $$$–$$$$, Downtown

Radisson Hill Country Resort & Spa, $$$–$$$$, North/Northwest

Westin La Cantera, $$$$, North/Northwest

By Location

ON THE RIVER WALK

Drury Plaza Hotel Riverwalk, $$$, River Walk

El Tropicano Holiday Inn Riverwalk, $$–$$$, River Walk

Hilton Palacio del Rio, $$$$, River Walk

Hotel Contessa Suites on the River Walk, $$$–$$$$, River Walk

Hotel Valencia Riverwalk, $$$$, River Walk

Hyatt Place San Antonio/Riverwalk, $$–$$$, River Walk

Omni La Mansión del Rio, $$$$, River Walk

Riverwalk Vista, $$–$$$, River Walk

Watermark Hotel & Spa, $$$$, River Walk

NEAR SIX FLAGS & SEAWORLD

Drury Inn & Suites Northwest, $$–$$$, North/Northwest

Hyatt Regency Hill Country Resort, $$$$, North/Northwest

Radisson Hill Country Resort & Spa, $$$–$$$$, North/Northwest

Westin La Cantera, $$$$, North/Northwest

By Experience

BEST VALUES

Bonner Garden, $–$$, King William Historic District

Drury Inn & Suites Northwest, $$–$$$, North/Northwest

Fairfield Inn & Suites San Antonio Downtown, $$–$$$, Downtown

Radisson Hill Country Resort & Spa, $$$–$$$$, North/Northwest

FAMILY FRIENDLY

El Tropicano Holiday Inn Riverwalk, $$–$$$, River Walk

Hilton Palacio del Rio, $$$$, River Walk

Holiday Inn San Antonio Riverwalk, $$–$$$, River Walk

Hyatt Regency Hill Country Resort, $$$$, North/Northwest

Marriott Plaza San Antonio, $$$–$$$$, Downtown

Radisson Hill Country Resort & Spa, $$$–$$$$, North/Northwest

GREAT VIEWS

Hilton Palacio del Rio, $$$$, River Walk

Menger Hotel, $$$–$$$$, Downtown

Omni La Mansión del Rio, $$$$, River Walk

Riverwalk Vista, $$–$$$, River Walk

Westin La Cantera, $$$$, North/Northwest

HISTORIC

Brackenridge House, $$$–$$$$, King William Historic District

Crockett Hotel, $$–$$$, Downtown

Emily Morgan Hotel, $$$$, Downtown

The Fairmount, $$$$, Downtown

Menger Hotel, $$$–$$$$, Downtown

Sheraton Gunter Hotel, $$$–$$$$, Downtown

ROMANTIC

Aaron Pancoast Carriage House, $$$–$$$$, King William Historic District

Emily Morgan Hotel, $$$$, Downtown

Hotel Contessa Suites on the River Walk, $$$–$$$$, River Walk

Hotel Valencia Riverwalk, $$$$, River Walk

Watermark Hotel & Spa, $$$$, River Walk

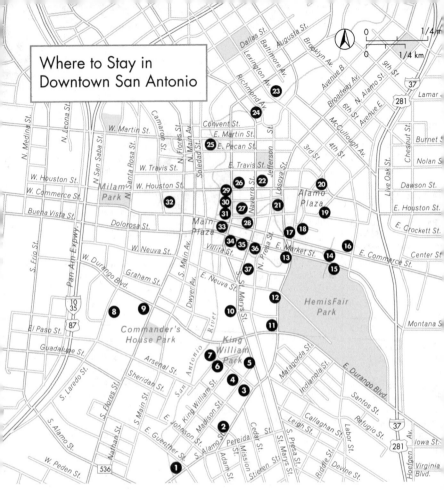

Where to Stay in Downtown San Antonio

Cons: Expensive, not exactly right in the thick of the River Walk/down-town action. ⊠*401 S. Alamo St., Downtown,* ☎*210/224–8800 or 800/996–3426* ⊕*www.fairmountsa.com* ☞*37 suites* 🔥*In-room: Ethernet, Wi-Fi. In-hotel: restaurant, room service, bar, gym, laundry service, concierge, executive floor, public Internet, public Wi-Fi, parking (fee), some pets allowed, no-smoking rooms* ▤*AE, D, DC, MC, V.*

$$$$ 🏨**Grand Hyatt.** After much anticipation, the newest of the mega convention hotels opened in spring 2008 and changed the city's skyline. The Grand Hyatt brings San Antonio the biggest array of amenities for business travelers, convention goers, and family vacationers. Adjacent to the convention center and the River Walk, it's sure to be the hotel of choice for business travelers. But even leisure travelers can enjoy flat-panel TVs and premium beds in every room. And a date with the "fitness concierge" in its premium gym might be just the thing to work off San Antonio's famous puffy tacos. **Pros:** State-of-the-art amenities, brand-new look and feel. **Con:** It has just opened—so you're the guinea pig. (If you stay here, go to www.fodors.com and write a review!) ⊠*600 E. Market St., Downtown,* ☎*210/224–1234* ⊕*www.grandsanantonio. hyatt.com* ☞*940 rooms, 63 suites* 🔥*In-room: safe, kitchen (some), refrigerator (some), Ethernet, Wi-Fi. In-hotel: restaurant, room service, bar, pool, gym, spa, laundry service, concierge, executive floor, public Internet, parking (fee), no-smoking rooms* ▤*AE, D, MC, V.*

$$$–$$$$ 🏨**Havana Riverwalk Inn.** San Antonio's most bohemian boutique hotel
★ occupies a Mediterranean Revival structure built in 1914 and feels as though you've wandered into an exotic British-colonial gentleman's club. You'll find teak and wicker chairs from India, beds fashioned from the grillwork of old buildings, and vintage chairs from French hotels and bistros. Don't miss Club Cohiba, the martini bar in the basement. It's a good 10-minute walk to most River Walk restaurants and bars, which is not all bad if you want to avoid the noise of late-night revelers. A trolley stop serving all downtown attractions is a block away. **Pros:** One of the city's truly unique lodging experiences, decadent and sophisticated, first-rate staff. **Cons:** Must book many months in advance, extremely pricey in peak season, not family friendly. ⊠*1015 Navarro St., Downtown,* ☎*210/222–2008 or 888/224–2004* ⊕*www. havanariverwalkinn.com* ☞*24 rooms, 3 suites* 🔥*In-room: Wi-Fi. In-hotel: restaurant, room service, bar, laundry service, public Internet, public Wi-Fi, parking (fee), no kids under 15, no-smoking rooms* ▤*AE, D, DC, MC, V.*

$$–$$$ 🏨**Hyatt Regency San Antonio.** You couldn't pick a more-central location than that of this hotel between the Alamo and the River Walk. The facility is what you'd expect from a large convention-oriented hotel—not the most memorable design or style but clean, updated, and convenient, with lots of services. The decor is an attractive modern-Texas style. **Pro:** Location, location, location. **Cons:** Pricey parking, fee for Internet, tiny pool. ⊠*123 Losoya St., Downtown,* ☎*210/222–1234* ⊕*www.sanantonioregency.hyatt.com* ☞*604 rooms, 28 suites* 🔥*In-room: refrigerator (some), Wi-Fi. In-hotel: restaurant, room service, bar, pool, gym, spa, laundry service, concierge, public Wi-Fi, parking (fee), no-smoking rooms* ▤*AE, D, DC, MC, V.*

$-$$ La Quinta Inn & Suites Downtown. A few blocks east of the River Walk mall you'll find this good alternative to the big full-service convention hotels. Free parking and continental breakfast top the list of perks that make your dollar go further than at many nearby hotels. Decor is of the uninspired mid-priced chain-hotel variety. Rates are significantly cheaper on weekends. **Pros:** Close to all the action, free parking. **Cons:** No air-conditioning in corridors, continental breakfast is small. ✉ *100 W. Durango Blvd., Downtown,* ☎ *210/212–5400* ⊕ *www. lq.com* 🛏 *151 suites* ⚬ *In-room: refrigerator, Wi-Fi. In-hotel: pool, gym, laundry facilities, laundry service, public Internet, public Wi-Fi, parking (no fee), some pets allowed, no-smoking rooms* ⊟ *AE, D, DC, MC, V* ⊚ *CP.*

$$$-$$$$ Marriott Plaza San Antonio. This 6-acre resort in the middle of downtown San Antonio has a full health club, jogging and bicycle routes, a heated pool and whirlpool, and lighted tennis courts in a setting of fountains and lush gardens. Most memorable are the Chinese pheasants and peacocks that roam the grounds. It's three blocks from the Alamo and a few steps from the River Walk's myriad attractions. The hotel does a brisk convention and meeting business. Chauffeured transportation to the downtown business district is complimentary on weekdays. The owners allow guests free use of bicycles and there are twice-daily maid service and plush bath robes. **Pros:** Close to River Walk, attentive staff. **Cons:** Fees for extras like parking and Internet. ✉ *555 S. Alamo St., Downtown,* ☎ *210/229–1000 or 800/421–1172* ⊕ *www.plazasa. com* 🛏 *246 rooms, 5 suites* ⚬ *In-room: Ethernet. In-hotel: restaurant, room service, bar, tennis court, pool, gym, spa, bicycles, laundry service, concierge, executive floor, public Internet, public Wi-Fi, parking (fee), some pets allowed, no-smoking rooms* ⊟ *AE, D, DC, MC, V.*

$$$-$$$$ Menger Hotel. Since its 1859 opening, the Menger has lodged, among
★   others, Robert E. Lee, Ulysses S. Grant, Theodore Roosevelt, Oscar Wilde, Sarah Bernhardt, Roy Rogers, and Dale Evans. You'll be the envy of many an overheated tourist strolling immediately across the street from the entrance to the Alamo into the cool lobby and up to your room. Balcony rooms overlook the Alamo. Inside, the hotel has a three-story Victorian lobby, sunny dining room, flowered courtyard, and four-poster beds (in the older section). Menger's famous bar, built in 1887, is styled after the House of Lords Pub in London. **Pros:** Close to Alamo, good food. **Con:** Rooms are more worn than at newer properties. ✉ *204 Alamo Plaza, Downtown,* ☎ *210/223–4361 or 800/345– 9285* ⊕ *www.mengerhotel.com* 🛏 *290 rooms, 26 suites* ⚬ *In-room: kitchen (some), Ethernet. In-hotel: restaurant, room service, bar, pool, gym, spa, laundry service, concierge, public Internet, public Wi-Fi, parking (fee), no-smoking rooms* ⊟ *AE, D, DC, MC, V.*

$$$-$$$$ Sheraton Gunter Hotel. Since 1909 this attractive downtown hotel has been a favorite of cattlemen and business travelers. The marble lobby has a beautiful coffered ceiling supported by massive columns. Rooms have antique reproduction furniture, large desks, and a masculine-contemporary design. The hotel is in a less-developed part of downtown, but is less than a block from the River Walk. It's generally a better value than hotels directly on the river, especially for a historic hotel. **Pros:**

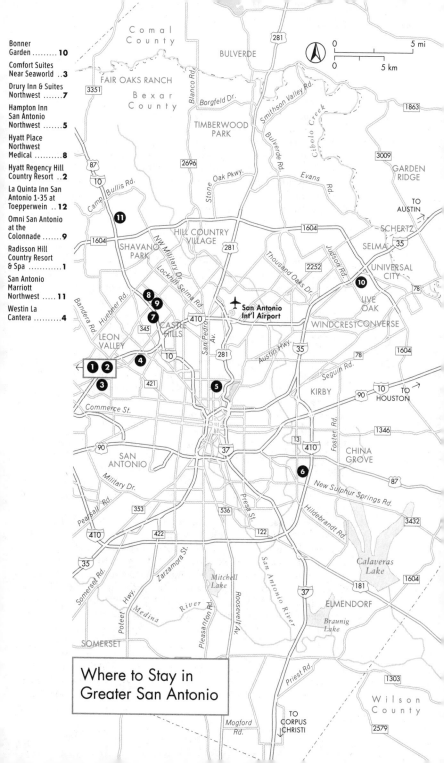

Where to Stay in Greater San Antonio

Excellent location, doesn't feel like a chain hotel. **Con:** Many extras and amenities require an additional charge. ⊠*205 E. Houston St., Downtown,* ☎*210/227–3241 or 800/325–3535* ⊕*www.gunterhotel. com* ⮑*322 rooms, 2 suites* ⌂*In-room: DVD, Ethernet, Wi-Fi. In-hotel: restaurant, room service, bar, pool, gym, laundry service, concierge, public Internet, public Wi-Fi, parking (fee), no-smoking rooms* ▤*AE, D, MC, V.*

$$$–$$$$ **Wyndham St. Anthony Hotel.** This somewhat formal 1909 historic hotel is decorated with oil paintings, chandeliers, and a handsome central staircase. It is in the center of downtown and near all the major attractions, including the Alamo and River Walk, and is within a short drive of Six Flags, SeaWorld, the San Antonio Zoo, and area golf courses. Rooms are posh, if overly rococo-esque—with four-poster beds, jacquard linens, and ornate antiques—and the service is what you'd expect in a first-rate establishment. **Pros:** Oozes historic elegance, good-size rooms. **Con:** Rooms could use an update. ⊠*300 E. Travis St., Downtown,* ☎*210/227–4392 or 800/355–5153* ⊕*www.wynd ham.com* ⮑*308 rooms, 42 suites* ⌂*In-room: Wi-Fi. In-hotel: restaurant, room service, bar, pool, gym, laundry service, concierge, public Internet, public Wi-Fi, parking (fee), no-smoking rooms* ▤*AE, D, DC, MC, V.*

KING WILLIAM & MONTE VISTA HISTORIC DISTRICTS

$$$–$$$$ **Aaron Pancoast Carriage House.** The local flavor of a B&B is wonderful; close quarters with other guests isn't. That's not a problem here, where each suite has its own kitchen (where breakfast is delivered), dining area, and private entrance. Also unusual for a B&B, children are welcome. Suites look out onto pool and patio with statuary and pecan trees, and have a marble bath, fireplace, and early-1900s antiques. In the King William Historic District, it has easy trolley access to the River Walk and the Alamo. **Pros:** Charming, romantic, convenient to attractions. **Cons:** Relatively expensive, a little stuffy. ⊠*202 Washington St., King William Historic District,* ☎*800/242–2770* ⊕*www.nobleinns. com* ⮑*3 suites* ⌂*In-room: kitchen, Wi-Fi. In-hotel: pool, parking (no fee), no-smoking rooms* ▤*AE, D, DC, MC, V* ⦿*BP.*

$–$$ **A Yellow Rose.** Built in 1878, this B&B is found in the leafy King William Historic District, five blocks from downtown. Traditional English decor with private porches and entrances in all rooms makes it perfect for a quiet weekend for two. Breakfast is delivered to your room, with several menus available. **Pros:** Charming and quaint, reasonably priced. **Con:** A long-ish walk to the main downtown sights. ⊠*229 Madison St., King William Historic District,* ☎*210/229–9903 or 800/950–9903* ⊕*www.ayellowrose.com* ⮑*6 rooms* ⌂*In-room: refrigerator, Wi-Fi. In-hotel: public Wi-Fi, parking (no fee), no kids under 12, no-smoking rooms* ▤*AE, D, MC, V* ⦿*BP.*

$–$$ **Beckmann Inn and Carriage House.** This 1886 Victorian with a Greek influence is filled with antiques, Oriental carpets, and floral prints. The two-course breakfast, served on china and crystal, is superb. The inn is convenient to all the River Walk attractions. Only one room has a bathtub; others have a shower only. **Pros:** Romantic and posh; feels like you're stepping back in time, despite being in a big, bustling city. **Cons:** Not many rooms available, difficult to book, lacking full-service amenities. ⊠*222 E. Guenther St., King William Historic District,* ☎*210/229–1449 or 800/945–1449* ⊕*www.beckmanninn.com* ⟡*5 rooms* ♿*In-room: refrigerator, Wi-Fi. In-hotel: parking (no fee), no kids under 12, no-smoking rooms* ▭*AE, D, DC, MC, V* ❙◎❙*BP.*

$–$$ ▦ **Bonner Garden.** Part of the Monte Vista Historic District (larger but less known than nearby King William), this inn sits amid some of the city's most beautiful homes and best restaurants. Built in 1910 for a Louisiana aristocrat and home to artist Mary Bonner, the 5,000-square-foot Italianate villa is decorated with Bonner's art and retains many of the details of the original building, such as hand-painted porcelain fireplaces (in three rooms) and tile floors. Suites have luxurious whirl-pool baths. The rooftop patio has a panoramic view of downtown San Antonio. **Pros:** Quiet, charming and relaxing, reasonably good value for an in-town B&B. **Cons:** Relatively small rooms, neighborhood a little sketchy at night. ⊠*145 E. Agarita St., Monte Vista Historic District, North/Northwest,* ☎*210/733–4222 or 800/396–4222* ⊕*www.bonnergarden.com* ⟡*4 rooms, 2 suites* ♿*In-room: DVD, VCR, Wi-Fi. In-hotel: pool, parking (no fee), no-smoking rooms* ▭*AE, D, MC, V* ❙◎❙*BP.*

$$$–$$$$ ▦ **Brackenridge House.** The first B&B in the King William Historic
Fodor's Choice District, Brackenridge House has a two-story veranda overlooking a
★ tree-lined street. The three-course breakfast is a highlight, with signature dishes of Texas eggs Benedict (thick Texas toast replaces the English muffin) and pancakes with homemade blueberry sauce. Enjoy the view from front-porch rockers and porch swings as you watch the horse-drawn trolleys go by. Rooms are lushly decorated with turn-of-the-20th-century accoutrements, and the service is top-notch. **Pros:** Reasonably priced for one of San Antonio's most sought-after B&B spots, one of the best breakfasts in town. **Cons:** Rooms are smallish and often difficult to book, especially at peak tourist times. ⊠*230 Madison St., King William Historic District,* ☎*210/271–3442 or 800/221–1412* ⊕*www.brackenridgehouse.com* ⟡*2 rooms, 4 suites* ♿*In-room: refrigerator, DVD, VCR. In-hotel: pool, parking (no fee), no kids under 12, no-smoking rooms* ▭*AE, D, DC, MC, V* ❙◎❙*BP.*

$$$–$$$$ ▦ **Jackson House.** Built in 1894 and listed in the National Register of Historic Places, this B&B in the historic King William area has elegant Victorian decor. The front porch, parlor, and gardens reflect the period with their antique furnishings and style. All rooms have their own fire-places, and first-floor rooms have two-person whirlpool tubs; one room has only a shower (no bathtub). The real highlight of the house is the conservatory with stained-glass windows looking out into the garden. The conservatory also houses the heated "swim spa," where guests can unwind. The River Walk and downtown are accessible via trolley. **Pros:** Quiet area, free parking, good three-course breakfast. **Cons:** Immediate area is residential, a brisk 10- to 15-minute walk from the River Walk area. ⊠*107 Madison St., King William Historic District,* ☎*210/225–4045 or 800/221–4045* ⊕*www.nobleinns.com* ⟡*6 rooms* ♿*In-room: Wi-Fi. In-hotel: pool, no elevator, public Wi-Fi, parking (no fee), no kids under 13, no-smoking rooms* ▭*AE, D, MC, V* ❙◎❙*BP.*

$$$$ ⛁ **Ogé House.** This gorgeous B&B sits on 1.5 acres that back up to a
Fodor'sChoice quiet section of the river running through the King William Historic
★ District. From the first steps up the wide staircase to the first-floor
veranda, the house captures your imagination about what antebellum
life must have been like in South Texas. Each room is individually decorated; yours might have a four-poster carved-wood bed, toile uphol-
stery, and Oriental rugs. Modern conveniences include flat-panel TVs,
Wi-Fi, and electric fireplaces (some rooms). One room has a shower
only—no tub. The Alhambra Room has less natural light than other
rooms. Breakfast, with a menu that changes daily, is served in the dining room or on the veranda. The quiet garden and grounds offer many
places to relax—perhaps on a seat in the gazebo or in one of the hammocks. **Pros:** Exquisitely decorated, staff goes beyond the call of duty.
Cons: Pricey, River Walk area not within easy walking distance. ⊠209
Washington St., King William Historic District, ☎210/223–2353 or
800/242–2770 ⊕www.nobleinns.com ⤶10 rooms ♿In-room: refrigerator, dial-up, Wi-Fi. In-hotel: laundry service, public Internet, public
Wi-Fi, parking (no fee), no kids under 16, no-smoking rooms ⊟AE,
D, DC, MC, V ⎮⊙⎮BP.

NORTH/NORTHWEST

$ ⛁ **Comfort Suites Near Seaworld.** A 5-mi drive from SeaWorld and the
Lackland Air Force base, this hotel also has easy access to the 1604
beltway, which takes you to major shopping at La Cantera mall, Six
Flags Fiesta Texas, and many restaurants. Easy highway access means
it's also a quick 20 minutes from downtown. All rooms are suites, so if
you're willing to stay outside downtown, you're rewarded with extra
elbow room. **Pros:** Close to SeaWorld, clean and updated, separate liv-
ing-room area. **Cons:** Far from downtown, surrounded by highways.
⊠8021 Alamo Downs Pkwy., North/Northwest, ☎210/681–6000
⊕www.sacomfortsuites.com ⤶74 suites ♿In-room: refrigerator, Ethernet, Wi-Fi. In-hotel: pool, gym, laundry facilities, public Internet,
public Wi-Fi, parking (no fee), no-smoking rooms ⊟AE, D, MC, V
⎮⊙⎮CP.

$$–$$$ ⛁ **Drury Inn & Suites Northwest.** The multistory atrium is filled with glow-
ing glass chandelier, a classy touch that sets it apart from other more-
mundane suburban hotels. The selling points are lots of perks, nicer
finishes, and good service at a moderate price. The hotel is immediately
off I-10 about 15 minutes north of downtown in a major restaurant
and shopping area. It's close to Six Flags Fiesta Texas and several large
malls. Your view is likely to be of the highway, so don't expect vistas but you'll definitely get more for your money here. **Pros:** Good
value, attentive staff, cocktail hour and other freebies. **Con:** Rooms are
nothing special. ⊠9806 I-10W, North/Northwest, ☎210/561–2510
⊕www.druryhotels.com ⤶115 rooms, 85 suites ♿In-room: kitchen
(some), refrigerator, Ethernet, Wi-Fi. In-hotel: pool, gym, laundry facilities, laundry service, public Internet, public Wi-Fi, parking (no fee),
some pets allowed, no smoking rooms ⊟AE, D, DC, MC, V ⎮⊙⎮BP.

$ Hampton Inn San Antonio Northwest. A straightforward hotel at a good price, the Hampton Inn is near the intersection of two major highways northwest of downtown. It's a quick drive to all parts of town and about 10 mi from SeaWorld and Lackland Air Force base. Rooms are modestly sized compared to similar hotels and it's definitely for travelers with a DIY mentality. **Pros:** Helpful staff, clean and well-maintained rooms. **Cons:** Far from downtown, rooms are small. ✉ *4803 Manitou Dr., North/Northwest,* ☎ *210/684–9966* ⊕ *www.hamptoninn.com* ➪ *124 rooms* ⚒ *In-room: refrigerator, Ethernet. In-hotel: pool, public Internet, public Wi-Fi, parking (no fee), no-smoking rooms* ⊟ *AE, D, MC, V* ❑ *CP.*

$$–$$$ Hyatt Place Northwest Medical. This Hyatt hotel with a sleek, technophile spin has the conveniences and price of a suburban hotel without a frumpy feel. It's set back from the highway in what feels like a suburban office park, offering a bit of quiet from one of the major shopping and restaurant corridors. You'll be north of downtown, near Six Flags Fiesta Texas, movie theaters, and a wide range of upscale shops. **Pros:** Free Wi-Fi, free shuttle for short trips, friendly staff. **Cons:** Removed from downtown, breakfast plan is a bit convoluted. ✉ *4308 Hyatt Place Dr., North/Northwest,* ☎ *210/561–0099* ⊕ *www.hyatt. com* ➪ *126 rooms* ⚒ *In-room: refrigerator, Wi-Fi. In-hotel: pool, gym, laundry service, public Internet, public Wi-Fi, parking (no fee), no-smoking rooms* ⊟ *AE, D, DC, MC, V* ❑ *CP.*

$$$$ Hyatt Regency Hill Country Resort. Step into relaxation at this sophisticated yet homey country resort with lots of shade—a key feature when the mercury soars during a San Antonio summer. On the western edge of the city, it occupies 200 acres of former ranch land, so you feel far removed, even though you're just a few minutes from SeaWorld, about 15 minutes from Six Flags, and 20 minutes from downtown. Family-friendly touches abound, from the man-made "lazy river," where you can float along with the current in an inner tube to Camp Hyatt's day camp and nightly s'mores at the fire pit; older kids can hang out at the Underground, with Internet and games. If you're not interested in the 4-acre water park, there are 27 holes of golf, a 0.75-mi nature trail, and a spa with a full range of treatments and salon services (and a shop for "retail therapy," quips staff member Jeanne). **Pros:** Great value for an expansive resort, tons of activities to keep the kids busy, great general store on-site. **Cons:** far from the city's main downtown and riverside attractions, fee for Internet use. ✉ *9800 Hyatt Dr., North/Northwest,* ☎ *210/647–1234* ⊕ *www.hillcountry.hyatt.com* ➪ *428 rooms, 72 suites* ⚒ *In-room: safe, refrigerator, Ethernet, Wi-Fi. In-hotel: 3 restaurants, room service, bar, golf course, tennis court, pools, gym, bicycles, children's programs (ages 3–12), laundry facilities, concierge, public Internet, public Wi-Fi, parking (no fee), no-smoking rooms* ⊟ *AE, D, DC, MC, V.*

Fodor'sChoice
★

¢–$ La Quinta Inn San Antonio I-35 N at Toepperwein. You can be a quick drive from major sights in San Antonio for a reasonable price. Rooms, service, and style are no-frills, but the rooms are clean and you'll be near major highways as well as the AT&T center and Alamo Heights. It's a straight shot up to Austin from here. **Pros:** Good price, good service.

Con: Far from downtown sights. ⊠*12822 I–35N, North/Northwest,* ☏*210/657–5500* ⊕*www.lq.com* ⇱*123 rooms, 13 suites* ⌂*In-room: Ethernet, Wi-Fi. In-hotel: pool, gym, laundry facilities, laundry service, public Wi-Fi, parking (no fee), some pets allowed, no-smoking rooms* ▤*AE, D, DC, MC, V.* ⓥ*CP.*

$$$–$$$$ ⚇ **Omni San Antonio at the Colonnade.** If the River Walk is only one stop on your tour of San Antonio, consider driving 15 minutes north on I–10 to the Colonnade. It's minutes from Six Flags, convenient to SeaWorld, shopping, movies, restaurants, upscale shopping, and the Hill Country to the north of San Antonio—and you'll avoid the parking fees and hassles of downtown. The hotel runs shuttle service to major shopping centers in the area. Services include spa treatments and a highlight is the rooftop ballroom with magnificent view of the San Antonio skyline. **Pros:** Above-average and sizable rooms. **Cons:** Service gets poor marks from some, River Walk is a 15-minute drive. ⊠*9821 Colonnade Blvd., North/Northwest,* ☏*210/691–8888* ⊕*www.omnihotels.com* ⇱*326 rooms, 3 suites* ⌂*In-room: Wi-Fi. In-hotel: restaurant, room service, bar, pool, gym, spa, laundry service, concierge, public Internet, public Wi-Fi, airport shuttle, parking (no fee), some pets allowed, no-smoking rooms* ▤*AE, D, DC, MC, V.*

$$$–$$$$ ⚇ **Radisson Hill Country Resort & Spa.** A 15-minute drive northwest of downtown you'll find a full-service resort at the base of Texas Hill Country. The hotel is one of the more-upscale Radisson properties, with a full golf course, tennis courts, a spa, and even children's programs. The huge, multilevel pool is a favorite with kids. This is the official hotel of SeaWorld and has package deals available. Free shuttles to and from the park save you from parking fees. **Pros:** Helpful staff, good-size rooms. **Con:** Driving everywhere (except to SeaWorld) is a necessity. ⊠*9800 Westover Hills Blvd., North/Northwest,* ☏*210/509–9800* ⊕*www.radisson.com* ⇱*174 rooms, 53 suites* ⌂*In-room: refrigerator (some), Ethernet, Wi-Fi. In-hotel: restaurants, room service, bar, golf course, tennis courts, pool, gym, spa, children's programs (ages 1–18), laundry facilities, laundry service, concierge, public Internet, public Wi-Fi, parking (no fee), no-smoking rooms* ▤*AE, D, DC, MC, V.*

$$$–$$$$ ⚇ **San Antonio Marriott Northwest.** This hotel just outside Loop 410 is built for business travelers but its great location and amenities appeal to all. Since it's business-oriented, other travelers may have the place to themselves on weekends. You need a car to get around and this isn't the ideal place to stay if you're here to hit the River Walk and Alamo, which are about a 20-minute drive away. But if you're a sucker for a bargain, or you like to be close to the airport (5 mi away), this could suffice. **Pros:** Staff gets accolades, clean rooms, comfortable beds. **Cons:** Rooms outdated, far from downtown. ⊠*3233 N.W. Loop 410, North/Northwest,* ☏*210/377–3900* ⊕*www.marriott.com* ⇱*295 rooms, 1 suite* ⌂*In-room: Ethernet, Wi-Fi. In-hotel: restaurant, room service, bar, pool, gym, laundry facilities, laundry service, concierge, executive floor, public Internet, public Wi-Fi, airport shuttle, parking (no fee), no-smoking rooms* ▤*AE, D, DC, MC, V.*

$$$$ ⚇ **Westin La Cantera.** Make a list of the things you'd look for in a luxury, ★ full-service resort, and La Cantera has it. The limestone quarry (*can-*

tera, in Spanish) on which it's built was a natural foundation for its golf course. It also offers the full compliment of resort services—including a spa, kids' programs, and tennis—and is immediately adjacent to upscale shopping, dining, and movies. On the northern edge of San Antonio, the resort is a short drive to Six Flags and SeaWorld, 30 minutes to the Alamo and River Walk. Its restaurant, Francesca's at Sunset *(⇨ Where to Eat),* is among the best in the city and has spectacular views of the start of Texas Hill Country. **Pros:** San Antonio's top resort hotel, lush common areas and rooms, virtually every amenity you could ask for. **Cons:** Removed from downtown and the River Walk, expensive. ⊠*16641 La Cantera Pkwy., North/Northwest,* ☎*210/558–6500* ⊕*www.westinlacantera.com* ⟳*450 rooms, 58 suites* ⌂*In-room: safe, kitchen (some), Ethernet. In-hotel: restaurant, room service, bar, golf course, tennis courts, pool, gym, spa, children's programs (ages 2–13), laundry facilities, laundry service, concierge, executive floor, public Internet, public Wi-Fi, parking (no fee), no-smoking rooms* ⊟*AE, D, DC, MC, V.*

RIVER WALK

To find the locations of these River Walk hotels and inns, see the Where to Eat in Downtown San Antonio map earlier in this section.

$$–$$$ ▦**Comfort Inn Alamo Riverwalk.** You can tell your friends you spent a night in jail on your stay in San Antonio. The former Bexar County Jail, built in 1878, is now a moderately priced hotel between the Alamo and Market Square. It's much closer to the latter, which is easily walkable. The River Walk and the Alamo are a long-ish walk, but a trolley stop is just down the street. The building has been completely renovated, meaning consistent room quality but not much historic feel. **Pros:** Good price for central downtown location, spotless, more character than the average chain. **Con:** Jail theme—with bars on some windows—is a turn-off for some. ⊠*120 Cameron St., River Walk,* ☎*210/281–1400* ⊕*www.choicehotel.com* ⟳*78 rooms, 4 suites* ⌂*In-room: refrigerator, Ethernet. In-hotel: pool, gym, laundry facilities, laundry service, public Internet, public Wi-Fi, parking (fee), no-smoking rooms* ⊟*AE, D, DC, MC, V* ⦿*CP.*

$$$$ ▦**Crowne Plaza San Antonio Riverwalk Hotel.** This hotel is popular for its easy access to the River Walk scene. Soak in a view of the river from the sundeck, taste the inventive Mediterranean offerings of the hotel's Restaurant Marbella, or cheer on the Spurs in the Players Sports Bar. It has a typical corporate-chain decor, with attractive common areas, large rooms, and tons of amenities. The staff is helpful and friendly. **Pros:** At the center of the action on the River Walk, equally good for business and leisure travelers. **Con:** You pay a premium for location when other full-service hotels a little farther from the action are better values. ⊠*111 Pecan St. E, River Walk,* ☎*210/354–2800 or 800/444–2326* ⊕*www.adamsmark.com* ⟳*450 rooms* ⌂*In-room: dial-up. In-hotel: restaurant, room service, bar, pool, gym, laundry facilities, parking (fee), no-smoking rooms* ⊟*AE, D, DC, MC, V.*

$$ 🖳 **Drury Inn & Suites San Antonio Riverwalk.** One of the best values among River Walk hotels, the Drury Inn & Suites is in the landmark Petroleum Commerce Building on the riverfront. Ask for a room with a terrace overlooking the river. This isn't a posh or luxurious getaway, but if you're on a budget or want a kid-friendly hotel, you can't beat it. **Pros:** Great value for families and business travelers, premium location for sightseeing, free nightly cocktail reception. **Cons:** Rooms and decor nothing to write home about. ✉ *201 N. Saint Mary's St., River Walk,* ☎ *210/212–5200* ⊕ *www.druryhotels.com* ⤶ *90 rooms, 60 suites* ⌂ *In-room: refrigerator, Ethernet, Wi-Fi. In-hotel: pool, gym, laundry facilities, laundry service, public Internet, public Wi-Fi, parking (fee), some pets allowed, no-smoking rooms* ▭ *AE, D, DC, MC, V* �“❘*BP.*

$$$ 🖳 **Drury Plaza Hotel Riverwalk.** In the restored Alamo National Bank
★ building right on the river, the Drury Plaza is giving many of the pricier full-service hotels some competition. It sticks to the formula that makes Drury hotels popular with many budget and leisure travelers: good prices and lots of perks (full breakfast, complimentary cocktail hour). There's a rooftop pool, and riverfront rooms have excellent views. At this writing, a major expansion planned for fall 2008 will bring an indoor pool and two restaurants, one with riverside dining. **Pros:** Ideal for families, just a few steps from the city's top attractions. **Cons:** Needs the planned updates to spruce up decor and amenities; the lobby makes you feel like you're in a bank from the '70s. ✉ *105 S. Saint Mary's St., River Walk,* ☎ *210/270–7799* ⊕ *www.druryhotels.com* ⤶ *231 rooms, 64 suites* ⌂ *In-room: kitchen (some), refrigerator, Ethernet, Wi-Fi. In-hotel: pool, laundry facilities, laundry service, public Internet, public Wi-Fi, parking (fee), some pets allowed, no-smoking rooms* ▭ *AE, D, DC, MC, V* ❘◎❘*BP.*

$$–$$$ 🖳 **El Tropicano Holiday Inn Riverwalk.** If you like "tropical, Latin, and glitzy," then this is the hotel for you. The lobby, restaurant, and common areas capture the feel of an Acapulco resort. A major renovation in 2006 updated common areas and rooms, although the building sometimes shows its age. Kids love the aviary filled with tropical birds, and exotic drinks available at the bar make parents feel like they're one step closer to paradise. Make sure to ask for a riverfront room. The hotel hosts many conferences, so staff are ready to serve a business traveler's needs. In-house Mangos restaurant has alfresco dining along a quiet stretch of the River Walk. **Pros:** Fun and festive, kid-friendly, good value. **Cons:** Somewhat noisy, some consider the theme too touristy. ✉ *110 Lexington Ave., River Walk,* ☎ *210/223–9461* ⊕ *www. eltropicanohotel.com* ⤶ *300 rooms, 8 suites* ⌂ *In-room: Wi-Fi. In-hotel: restaurant, room service, bar, pool, gym, laundry facilities, concierge, public Internet, public Wi-Fi, parking (fee), no-smoking rooms* ▭ *AE, D, DC, MC, V.*

$$$$ 🖳 **Hilton Palacio del Rio.** A towering complex with a central location on the busy part of the River Walk, this Hilton is steps away from many top restaurants and attractions. Ask for a balcony overlooking the river, and watch the barges and tourists go by. Noise at night can be a problem on some lower floors. It is across the street from the Rivercenter Mall, the Alamo, and the convention center. As a large convention hotel, it doesn't have a lot of local flavor, but the service and amenities are top-notch. **Pros:** Great location, facilities to accommodate longer stays. **Cons:** Expensive, even for a nice Hilton; lacks character. ⊠ *200 S. Alamo St., River Walk,* ☎ *210/222–1400* ⊕ *www. palaciodelrio.hilton.com* ⇆ *473 rooms, 10 suites* ♿ *In-room: Wi-Fi. In-hotel: restaurant, room service, bar, pool, gym, parking (fee), laundry facilities, laundry service, concierge, public Internet, public Wi-Fi, no-smoking rooms* ☰ *AE, D, DC, MC, V.*

$$–$$$ 🏨**Holiday Inn San Antonio Riverwalk.** Reliably predictable, this Holiday Inn has a nice location, with views of the River Walk from some rooms—albeit partial ones in some cases (be specific when you book if this is important). It's an older hotel and not necessarily indulgent but has a full range of services and a friendly staff. The food gets high marks and there are a few nice perks, like free meals for kids under 10. **Pro:** Excellent location for the price. **Con:** Many rooms without views or with only partial, neck-craning views of the River Walk. ⊠ *217 N. Saint Mary's St., River Walk,* ☎ *210/224–2500* ⊕ *www.holidayinn. com* ⇆ *301 rooms, 12 suites* ♿ *In-room: kitchen (some), Wi-Fi. In-hotel: restaurant, room service, bar, pool, gym, laundry service, concierge, public Interest, public Wi-Fi, parking (fee), no smoking rooms* ☰ *AE, D, DC, MC, V.*

$$$–$$$$ 🏨**Homewood Suites Riverwalk by Hilton.** This is one of the few heart-of-
★ the-tourist-district hotels whose suites have full kitchens. Although it doesn't look like a hotel from the outside, it's a pleasant surprise to visit the lobby and see the inlaid marble floors and stylish appointments. The suites are big, roomy, and packed with comfort, making for a perfect home base for exploring San Antonio and environs for more-extended stays. **Pros:** Reasonably priced suites downtown are certainly sweet for families and business travelers alike, service staff is good. **Con:** Still a cookie-cutter hotel, despite the location. ⊠ *432 W. Market St., River Walk,* ☎ *210/222–1515* ⊕ *www.homewoodsuitesriverwalk.com* ⇆ *146 suites* ♿ *In-room: kitchen, refrigerator, Ethernet. In-hotel: pool, gym, laundry facilities, laundry service, public Internet, public Wi-Fi, parking (fee), no-smoking rooms* ☰ *AE, D, DC, MC, V* ¶◎¶ *CP.*

$$$–$$$$ 🏨**Hotel Contessa Suites on the Riverwalk.** This exceptional boutique hotel,
Fodor's Choice built in 2005, takes visitors away from the hustle and bustle of the
★ River Walk, and gives them pause to relax in luxury. The decor is contemporary, but warm, with rooms and common areas featuring exposed brick, stone walls, and flora. The service is solid, and not too fussy. Suites are rare among hotels right on the river, and these have some indulgent amenities, such as fireplaces and marble bathrooms. The hotel also has an Aveda spa, as well as a heated outdoor pool (rare in San Antonio) and a hot tub. Definitely a destination for romantic weekends, though it's popular with those traveling for business as well; the hotel also hosts many weddings. **Pros:** A truly sophisticated, unique upscale hotel; top-notch concierge; full-service spa. **Con:** Reservations hard to obtain. ⊠ *306 W. Market St., River Walk,* ☎ *210/229–9222 or 866/435–0900* ⊕ *www.thehotelcontessa.com* ⇆ *265 suites* ♿ *In-room: safe, Ethernet, Wi-Fi. In-hotel: restaurant, room service, bar,*

pool, gym, spa, laundry service, concierge, public Internet, parking (fee), no-smoking rooms $\equiv$*AE, D, MC, V.*

$$$$ **Hotel Valencia Riverwalk.** One of a crop of new boutique hotels on
★ the river, Hotel Valencia has puffed pillows for Hollywood big names like *American Idol's* Ryan Seacrest, Paula Abdul, and Simon Cowell. From floor to ceiling, the decor is a modern take on traditional, mixing design elements such as Spanish archways and columns with leather headboards, polished concrete posts, and sleek dark-wood furniture. Rooms have custom-designed beds, imported designer linens, and faux mink throws; all rooms have a big leaning mirror and a flat-screen plasma television. Balcony rooms overlook the lushly landscaped banks of the River Walk. The restaurant, Citrus *(⇨ Where to Eat)*, is highly acclaimed. **Pros:** Hip, posh place to stay; great location on a quiet part of the river; its very popular bar has been rated one of the best places to see and be seen. **Cons:** High demand means difficult to book, especially at peak times; requires a hike to major River Walk attractions. ⊠*150 E. Houston St., River Walk,* ☏*210/227–9700, 866/842–0100 reservations* ⊕*www.hotelvalencia.com* ⇋*212 rooms, 1 suite* ⋏*In-room: Wi-Fi. In-hotel: restaurant, room service, bar, gym, laundry facilities, laundry service, concierge, public Internet, public Wi-Fi, no-smoking rooms* $\equiv$*AE, D, DC, MC, V.*

$$–$$$ **Hyatt Place San Antonio/Riverwalk.** Many established all-suites and extended-stay hotels provide plenty of space but fall short on style. Hyatt Place, opened in late 2007, challenges the status quo with their customary, luxurious "Grand Bed," and sleek furnishings in every room. Technology lovers enjoy the Wi-Fi throughout, flat-panel TVs, touch-screen room service, automated check-in kiosks, and the "e-room," with free computing and printing. On one of the quiet sections of the river, the hotel is a short walk from the entertainment district. **Pros:** Brand-new furnishings in 2007, hip and modern feel, tech-friendly. **Con:** Caters primarily to business travelers, so not great for families. ⊠*601 S. Saint Mary's St., River Walk,* ☏*201/227–6854* ⊕*www.hyattplace.com* ⇋*131 rooms* ⋏*In-room: refrigerator, Ethernet, Wi-Fi. In-hotel: restaurant, bar, pool, gym, laundry service, concierge, public Internet, public Wi-Fi, parking (no fee), no-smoking rooms* $\equiv$*AE, D, DC, MC, V.*

$$$–$$$$ **Marriott Rivercenter.** With more than 1,000 rooms, more than 80,000 square feet of meeting space, and a 40,000-square-foot ballroom, this 38-story hotel (attached to sister hotel Marriott River Walk) has all the pluses—and minuses—of a very large hotel. You will likely have all the services you could want and you're in the heart of the action, but if you're looking for a secluded getaway, this isn't it. An update of common areas completed in February 2008 modernized the restaurant and two-story lobby. **Pros:** Great location, friendly staff. **Cons:** Pricey parking, outrageous fees for extras like bottled water. ⊠*101 Bowie St., River Walk,* ☏*210/223–1000* ⊕*www.marriott.com/satrc* ⇋*916 rooms, 85 suites* ⋏*In-room: refrigerator (some), Ethernet. In-hotel: restaurant, room service, bar, pool, gym, spa, children's programs (ages 2–12), laundry facilities, laundry service, concierge, executive floor,* *public Internet, public Wi-Fi, parking (fee), some pets allowed, no-smoking rooms* ⊟*AE, D, DC, MC, V.*

$$$$ 🖼 **Marriott River Walk.** As one of the major convention hotels in the city, the 30-story Marriott River Walk has more than 10,000 square feet of ballroom space. But you don't have to be attending a conference to enjoy the location, between the convention center and the River Walk (it's also attached to sister hotel Marriott Rivercenter). Half the rooms face the river and have balconies from which you can watch the barges go by. The place is definitely full-service, with all the things you'd expect from a top hotel. The carpet, furniture, textiles, and lobby were updated in February 2008 and HDTV was added to rooms. **Pros:** Ideal location, some rooms with great River Walk views. **Cons:** Expensive, pricey parking. ⊠*889 E. Market St., River Walk,* ☎*210/224–4555* ⊕*www.marriott.com/satdt* ⇝*512 rooms, 5 suites* ⌂*In-room: Ethernet. In-hotel: restaurant, room service, bar, pool, gym, spa, laundry facilities, laundry service, concierge, executive floor, public Internet, public Wi-Fi, parking (fee), some pets allowed, no-smoking rooms* ⊟*AE, D, DC, MC, V.*

$$$$
Fodor's Choice
★
🖼 **Omni La Mansión del Rio.** The hotel was originally built as a school in 1852 and then converted to a hotel for the HemisFair, the 1968 World's Fair. Inside and out it's replete with Spanish tiles, archways, exposed beams, and soft, earthy tones. Many rooms share balconies or verandas looking out on the river—be sure to request a river-view room. Location is a big selling point for this hotel, in a quiet section of the river but still steps away from the entertainment district. **Pros:** Right on River Walk, frequent online discounts on third-party sites. **Cons:** Some complaints about service, undiscounted rooms pricey for quality, lower-level street-facing rooms noisy. ⊠*112 College St., River Walk,* ☎*210/518–1000* ⊕*www.lamansion.com* ⇝*307 rooms, 31 suites* ⌂*In-room: Ethernet, dial-up. In-hotel: restaurant, room service, bar, pool, gym, spa, laundry service, concierge, public Internet, public Wi-Fi, some pets allowed, no-smoking rooms* ⊟*AE, D, DC, MC, V.*

$$–$$$ 🖼 **Riverwalk Vista.** What began as a wholesale grocer's warehouse in the mid-1800s is now one of San Antonio's most noteworthy boutique hotels. The feeling in the hotel is of a converted loft—hardwood floors, exposed-brick walls—with heavy South Texas influences. Many rooms have floor-to-ceiling windows looking out on Alamo Plaza or the River Walk. All rooms have slate-tile walk-in showers. The location can be noisy, particularly on Saturday nights. The hotel doesn't have its own parking so guests have to unload and park at a garage down the street (which doesn't offer in-and-out rates). **Pros:** Central location, unique design. **Cons:** No on-site parking, hard-to-spot entry, can be noisy. ⊠*262 Losoya St., River Walk,* ☎*210/223–3200* ⊕*www. riverwalkvista.com* ⇝*17 rooms* ⌂*In-room: safe, Ethernet, Wi-Fi. In-hotel: gym, laundry facilities, laundry service, concierge, public Internet, public Wi-Fi, no-smoking rooms* ⊟*AE, D, DC, MC, V.*

$$$$
Fodor's Choice
★
🖼 **Watermark Hotel & Spa.** World-class luxury accommodations and services are offered at this hotel enclosed in the shell of the historic 19th-century L. Frank Saddlery Building with an entrance facing the River Walk. The Watermark has sleek modern rooms and suites, ranging in

size from 425 to 600 square feet, and 12-foot ceilings. Sink into luxury in the and marble baths with whirlpool tubs and plush linens. Some rooms have balconies, for river views. A full-service, European-style spa occupies almost the entire second floor, offering the ultimate in pampering: a hair and nail salon, massages, scrubs, soaks, and other therapies. Combining a massage with dinner and an overnight stay is popular. The restaurant, Pesca, does many tequila tastings. **Pro:** Everything a five-star hotel professes to be. **Cons:** Pricey, some extra charges for sundries, expensive parking. ⊠*212 W. Crockett St., River Walk,* ☎*210/396–5800 or 866/605–1212* ⊕*www.watermarkhotel.com* ⬐*97 rooms, 2 suites* ⌂*In-room: safe, Ethernet. In-hotel: restaurant, room service, bar, pool, gym, spa, laundry service, concierge, public Wi-Fi, parking (fee), some pets allowed, no-smoking rooms* ⊟*AE, D, DC, MC, V.*

$$$$ 🖫**Westin River Walk.** This premium hotel has premium prices but you get what you pay for in location and over-the-top service. Rooms have marble bathrooms, the chain's signature Heavenly Bed and now the Heavenly Bath—both promising luxurious comfort—and specially imported Venezuelan chocolates are left on your pillow. Some rooms have French doors leading onto verandas, with views of the River Walk. If you're a basketball fan, this might be the overnight spot for you. The hotel is the official NBA hotel, so all the players stay here. **Pros:** Fantastic location, smart staff. **Cons:** Some of the river-view rooms have only partial views, expensive breakfast. ⊠*420 W. Market St., River Walk,* ☎*210/224–6500* ⊕*www.westin.com/riverwalk* ⬐*413 rooms, 60 suites* ⌂*In-room: safe, Ethernet, Wi-Fi. In-hotel: restaurant, room service, bar, pool, gym, spa, laundry service, concierge, public Internet, public Wi-Fi, parking (fee), some pets allowed, no-smoking rooms* ⊟*AE, D, DC, MC, V.*

SAN ANTONIO ESSENTIALS

TRANSPORTATION

BY AIR

San Antonio International Airport (SAT) is in northeast San Antonio between Highway 281 and I–410, about 8 mi from downtown. By car it's only about 15 minutes to any major River Walk hotel. The Pan Am Expressway leads directly from the airport to San Antonio's central business district.

San Antonio's public transportation system, VIA Metropolitan Transit (⇨ *By Bus, below*), provides daily bus service between the airport and downtown. SATRANS offers shared-van shuttle service from the airport; the typical fare to a downtown hotel is $9 one-way or $16 round-trip. There are also several taxi companies providing 24-hour service at a standard metered rate of $1.60 at pickup plus $0.30 per 0.2 mi. From the airport there is a minimum departure charge of $8.50. A typical airport-to-downtown fare is $15 to $17, plus tip.

Airport Information San Antonio International Airport (✉ 9800 Airport Blvd., San Antonio ☎ 210/207–3450 ⊕ www.sanantonio.gov/aviation).

Shuttle Service Information SATRANS (☎ 210/281–9900).

Taxi Information Yellow Cab Co. (☎ 210/222–2222 ⊕ www.yellowcab sanantonio.com). **San Antonio Taxi** (☎ 210/444–2222 ⊕ www.sataxi.com). **Yellow Checker Cab** (☎ 210/226–4242 ⊕ www.yellowcabsa.com).

BY BUS & TROLLEY

Greyhound connects San Antonio with cities in Texas and beyond. The city's local bus line, Via Metropolitan Transit, takes travelers throughout the city and to the airport. Local fare is $1 (or $2 for the express). A one-day pass is $3.75 and includes service on the historic streetcars, which weave through downtown. The streetcars (also called trolleys) come about every 10 minutes.

> ### SA STREETCARS
>
> Traveling around downtown San Antonio without a car? Then you'll want to hop on one of VIA Metropolitan Transit's four downtown streetcar lines. The streetcars hit all of the major downtown attractions, including the Alamo, El Mercado/Market Square, Hemis-Fair Park, the Institute of Texan Cultures, the King William Historical District, Rivercenter Mall, and La Villita. Best of all, a one-day pass only costs $3.75. For more information, visit www.viainfo.net/busservice/streetcar.aspx.

Information Greyhound (✉ 500 N. Saint Mary's St., San Antonio ☎ 210/270–5824 or 800/231–2222 ⊕ www.greyhound.com).**Via Metropolitan Transit** (✉ 1021 San Pedro (main office) or 260 E. Houston St. (downtown station), San Antonio ☎ 210/362–2020 ⊕ www.viainfo.net).

BY CAR

Driving in San Antonio can be daunting. Though the city is said to be laid out in a grid, which is evident in the King William District, the best way to describe San Antonio's layout is as a spider web of major highways coming together in a radial loop around the city. If you can follow signs quickly, you'll be in good shape, but be prepared to exit from the left lane on occasion, a scenario that trips up many drivers new and old to the city.

The main arteries that feed into San Antonio are I–10, I–37, I–35, and U.S. 281. All connect to Loop 410, which makes an almost perfect circle around the city. I–10 lies on the west of town and takes you north to Hill Country towns such as Boerne and Comfort. I–37 leads south to coastal cities such as Corpus Christi and Port Aransas. U.S. 281 takes you north toward Hill Country and towns such as Johnson City and Marble Falls and puts you on the path to Fredericksburg. I–35 is the most direct route south from Austin and continues through San Antonio to the border town of Laredo.

BY TRAIN

Amtrak provides daily passenger service to and from San Antonio. Its Texas Eagle line arrives and departs daily, connecting San Antonio to Austin, Ft. Worth, Dallas, and other cities en route north to Chicago.

The Sunset Limited line serves San Antonio three times a week, running east–west across the country between Orlando and Los Angeles.

Train Information **Amtrak** (⊠ *Sunset Station, 350 Hoefgen St., San Antonio* ☎ *210/223–3226 or 800/872–7245* ⊕ *www.amtrak.com*).

CONTACTS & RESOURCES

EMERGENCIES

In an emergency dial 911. Each of the following medical facilities has an emergency room open 24 hours a day.

Hospitals **University Health Center Downtown** (⊠ *527 N. Leona, San Antonio* ☎ *210/358–3400*). **University Hospital** (⊠ *4502 Medical Dr., San Antonio* ☎ *210/358–4000*).

VISITOR INFORMATION

Contact **San Antonio Visitor Convention & Visitors Bureau** (⊠ *203 S. Saint Mary's St., Suite 200, San Antonio* ☎ *210/207–6700 or 800/447–3372* ⊕ *www.visitsanantonio.com*).

Austin

WORD OF MOUTH

"Austin is very family friendly. We have tons of parks, greenbelts, lakes, rivers, and a small zoo. We also have a great children's museum."

—nma

By Wes
Eichenwald;
Arts &
Nightlife
by Jessica
Norman
Dupuy

THERE'S A MYSTIQUE ABOUT AUSTIN. Even if you've lived for years in this small town–turned–big city, the reasons why this city functions as it does, and why it seems so different from other U.S. cities, may not be readily apparent.

Austin is an extraordinarily open and welcoming place—a city where you're not only allowed but *expected* to be yourself, in all your quirky glory. The people you encounter are likely to be laissez-faire and may even be newcomers themselves (Austin's population grew 47% during the 1990s, and continues to expand at a healthy pace: 65,800 new residents were added to the Austin–Round Rock metropolitan area from July 2006 to July 2007, according to the U.S. Census Bureau).

It's not pushing it too much to liken Austin to San Francisco: in the middle of a big state and the golden destination where people who are just a bit different and quite self-directed come to realize their fullest selves. Many who would never consider living anywhere else in Texas have relocated here after dreaming the Austin dream. The city ranks high on many national best-places-to-live lists. If it's sometimes hard for Austin to live up to its hype (some of it is self-generated), it's still a place where creativity and maverick thinking are valued.

Such things weren't on the mind of Mirabeau B. Lamar, president-elect of the Texas Republic, when he set out to hunt buffalo in 1838 but returned home with a much greater catch: a home for the new state capitol. He fell in love with a tiny settlement called Waterloo, surrounded by rolling hills and fed by cool springs. Within a year the government had arrived, and the town, renamed Austin (after Stephen F. Austin, the "Father of Texas"), was on its way to becoming a city. About a half a century later, in 1883, the University of Texas at Austin was founded.

Fed by the 1970s salad days of the "outlaw country" movement popularized by Willie Nelson, Waylon Jennings, and others, through the growing viewership of *Austin City Limits,* a showcase for bands that began taping for a local PBS station in 1976, Austin's reputation as a music center has grown to the point that the city now bills itself as the Live Music Capital of the World. This is especially true every March, when the city hosts the South by Southwest Conferences and Festivals (widely known as SXSW), which draw people from throughout the world: bands, record-company executives, filmmakers, Internet celebrities, and, of course, legions of fans.

Today, Austin is in the midst of reinventing itself yet again. High-tech industries have migrated to the area, making it Texas's answer to Silicon Valley. The city has also become an important filmmaking center. For the moment, Austin retains a few vestiges of a small-town atmosphere—but a quick scan of its rapidly growing downtown skyline will tell you that its days as a sleepy college town are long gone.

Despite all the changes that have occurred (and are occurring) in this capital city, Austin is still a town whose roots are planted firmly in the past—a past the city is proud to preserve and show off to visitors.

AUSTIN TOP 5

- **Great Live Music.** Whether it's country, rock, country-rock, folk, punk, jazz, classical, Celtic, or blue-grass music you're after, Austin's got the musicians and bands to suit your fancy—and the venue could be in an old-time dance hall, grimy hole-in-the-wall, or large, modern performance space. Music festivals happen year-round, with marquee names performing during SXSW in March and the Austin City Limits Music Festival in September, but also local affairs like the Armadillo Christmas Bazaar (December) and the Old Pecan Street Arts Festivals occurring in spring and fall.

- **World-class BBQ & Ethnic Food.** Austinites are passionate seekers of, and arguers about, great restaurants and food, not only of the old standbys (barbecue joints and authentic Mexican and Tex-Mex eateries), but a wide spectrum of world cuisines, for all tastes and budgets.

- **City of the Future.** Austin isn't only one of the best cities in the United States for free wireless Internet access (practically every hotel lobby has it), it's forward-looking in such areas as sustainability (green buildings, parkland), revitalizing its downtown through encouraging mixed-use residential and retail space, and promoting free and low-cost public transit. As a result, Austin's downtown is a hip, happening place.

- **Cowboy Culture.** The Star of Texas Fair & Rodeo in March is a prime opportunity to immerse yourself and your family in a classic rodeo-and-cattle atmosphere, complete with cook-offs, comedy, concerts, and other wholesome entertainment. Your kids will never forget it, and the odds are you won't, either. And if you'd like to bring home some genuine cowboy boots, those are easy to find around here.

- **The Great Outdoors.** Austinites take full advantage of their city's mostly mild, sunny climate and abundant green space. When they're not working, they're likely running or riding on the hike-and-bike trails along Lady Bird Lake, swimming at Barton Springs or Deep Eddy Pool, golfing at a public course like Lions Municipal, or boating on Lake Travis.

EXPLORING AUSTIN

Austin lies in Central Texas, about 163 mi southeast of the state's true center, Eden. On Austin's western border is the Hill Country, its eastern border the much flatter Blackland Prairie. Dallas is about 190 mi to the north, Houston 160 mi to the east.

The logical place to begin an exploration of the city is downtown, where the pink-granite Texas state capitol, built in 1888, is the most visible man-made attraction. The Colorado River, which slices through Austin, was once an unpredictable waterway, but it's been tamed into a series of lakes, including two within the city limits. Twenty-two-mile-long Lake Austin, in the western part of the city, flows into Lady Bird Lake (formerly Town Lake), a narrow stretch of water that meanders for 5 mi through the center of downtown.

PLANNING YOUR TRIP

WHEN TO GO

Austin has a humid, subtropical climate, with about 300 days of sunshine. The best times to visit are spring and late fall.

It's no accident that many visitors fall in love with the city when they visit during the SXSW festivals in March—that's when the weather is most pleasant and temperate, and wildflowers cut multicolor swaths on the rolling hills and roadsides.

In summer, when the high is 96° and weeks of daily triple-digit highs are not uncommon, every Austinite able to escape to cooler climes does so. It's usually not before October (average high 81°, average low 60°) that people again start to forego air-conditioned restaurant interiors for outdoor patios. Austin has mild winters, with the average high and low in the coldest month, January, at 60° and 40°, respectively. Snow, while not unheard of, is rare. The wettest month is May, with average precipitation of just over 5 inches.

If you visit in late September, be prepared for music-crazed fanatics flooding the city for the Austin City Limits Music Festival. Austinites and out-of-towners alike migrate in zombielike droves toward the bass-pumping, heart-thumping, rhythm-jumping beacon of Zilker Park, where the three-day affair takes place.

GETTING THERE

The major entryway into Austin is I-35. Loop 1 (also known as MoPac) joins with I-35 on Austin's northern and southern outskirts, dispersing traffic to the west side of the city. U.S. 183 runs at a slight north–south diagonal through Austin. Although it doesn't serve any major cities, U.S. 183 does serve as a major thoroughfare through town, eventually meandering northward to western Oklahoma and southward toward the gulf. East–west Highway 71 and U.S. 290 connect Austin and Houston.

GETTING AROUND

Although the highways are clearly marked, many of them have been granted other names as they pass through Austin (some joke that every road has at least two names). Keep in mind that U.S. 183 runs parallel to Research Boulevard for one stretch, Anderson Lane at another, and Ed Bluestein Boulevard at yet another, and Highway 71 is also known as Ben White Boulevard. Congress Avenue serves as the major north–south thoroughfare in the downtown area; it is interrupted by the state capitol, Austin's heart and soul.

The rest of downtown is laid out in a conventional grid of numerical streets. The majority of these are one-way streets: even-numbered streets generally run one way to the west, and odd-numbered streets generally run one way to the east.

With 19 million annual visitors, more than 50,000 university students, and a large commuter population, Austin meets the demand with having more roads per capita than the other major cities in Texas—and it needs all of them. In fact, even with new highways and toll roads added in recent years, Austin's population growth has brought congestion, and it seems that every year rush hour gets longer, running weekdays from 7 to 9:30 AM and 4 to 7 PM, with Friday-afternoon's rush starting a bit earlier. Driving can be irksome during rush hours, but Austin is generally navigable and car-friendly.

The sprawling University of Texas, one of the largest universities in the United States, flanks the capitol's north end. Among other things, it is home to both the Blanton Museum of Art and the Lyndon Baines Johnson Presidential Library and Museum. UT's northwestern border is flanked by Guadalupe Street, which for these blocks is known as the Drag, a fun and funky student-centered commercial strip.

The downtown's Warehouse District and 2nd Street District, which run from west of Congress to roughly Nueces Street, and north from the lake to 6th Street, are where you'll find some of Austin's liveliest (and newest) restaurants, bistros, and pubs, along with hip boutiques and other shops.

RULES OF THE ROAD

Speed limits in Austin are strictly enforced, and fines are stiff. Tickets run $139–$297 (more in school zones, and higher still in construction zones). Depending on the area, speed limits range from 20 to 25 mph in residential and downtown areas, 30–45 mph on larger streets and boulevards, and 55–70 mph on local highways.

Seat belts are mandatory. Right turns (and left turns on one-way streets) are permitted on red lights after a full stop. Using a cell phone while driving is currently legal in Texas, but it's best to reserve it for emergencies or use a hands-free device.

In the late afternoon hours, locals grab their sneakers and head to Zilker Park, just west and a bit south of downtown, for a jog or a leisurely walk. When the sun sets on summer days, everyone's attention turns to the lake's Congress Avenue Bridge, under which the country's largest urban colony of Mexican free-tailed bats hangs out (literally). The bats make their exodus after sunset to feed on insects in the surrounding Hill Country, putting on quite a show in the process.

Finally, no visit to Austin is complete without venturing south of the river to savor the unique creative vibe of South Congress, with its colorful antiques shops and oh-so-cool clubs and eateries, and the laid-back charms down South 1st and many side streets. (Note that Congress Avenue is known as South Congress—or SoCo for short—below the river. North of the river, in downtown Austin, it's generally called simply Congress Avenue.)

Wherever you go in town, be on the lookout for art: Austin boasts one of the highest per-capita concentrations of artists in the nation. Tangible proof of this are the many pieces of public art on display around town, from bronze statues of Southern statesmen to oversize, colorfully painted electric guitars.

■**TIP**➜**If it's your first time in Austin, your first stop should be the Austin Visitor Center (209 East 6th Street, between Brazos and San Jacinto, Downtown) for brochures galore and friendly dispensing of advice.**

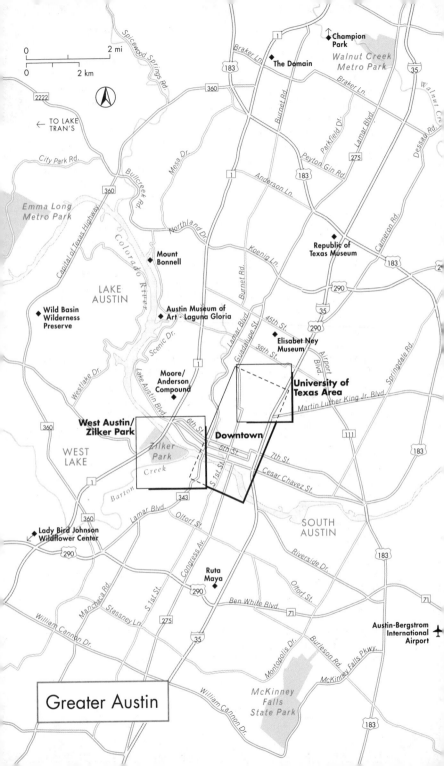

Greater Austin

DOWNTOWN & CAPITOL AREA

Downtown Austin is the natural starting point for seeing the city's sights, and is home to many of them, including the state capitol. Its boundaries are generally regarded as being I–35 to the east, Lamar Boulevard to the west, UT to the

MUSEUM DISCOUNTS
Many museums have free or reduced admission one day per week (the day varies per museum; research ahead).

north, and the river to the south. It's relatively compact and well served by buses and the free 'Dillo trolleys, so if you're primarily interested in touring downtown, you won't need a car. The capitol complex is the most visible landmark, of course, but most of the important museums (save for the Blanton) and many historic buildings are between the capitol and the river.

Areas within downtown are the Market District, the Warehouse District, 2nd Street District, Congress District, 6th Street, and the Red River District (⇨ *the Downtown Austin & Capitol Area map, above for a visual reference to these areas; numbers in the margin correspond to numbers on the map*). Some of these districts are so distinct that we've given them their own neighborhood section within this chapter for categories like shopping, dining, and lodging.

For the sake of soaking up the atmosphere and getting a sense of the city, we highly recommend walking the 10 blocks up Congress Avenue between 11th Street and the bridge, in either direction. And at some point, walk down 6th Street between Congress Avenue and I–35.

MAIN ATTRACTIONS

❶ **Austin Children's Museum.** Kids (and adults) of all ages will get a kick out of this well-designed museum. An open floor plan leads from one diversion to another, including a kid-size "global diner" and rotating exhibits to stimulate growing imaginations. ⊠ *201 Colorado St., Downtown & Capitol Area* ☎ *512/472–2499* ⊕ *www.austinkids.org* ⊠ *$5.50* ⊗ *Tues., Thurs.–Sat. 10–5, Wed. 10–8, Sun. noon–5.*

❾ **Austin Museum of Art–Downtown.** AMOA, as it's known, doesn't have a huge amount of space at either its downtown location or at the gorgeous 1916 Italianate villa of its West Austin Laguna Gloria site, but the exhibitions tend to be well curated, and interesting—Laguna Gloria is worth visiting for the ambience alone. ⊠ *823 Congress Ave., Downtown & Capitol Area* ☎ *512/495–9224* ⊠ *3809 W. 35th St., West Austin* ☎ *512/458–8191* ⊕ *www.amoa.org.*

❻ **Bob Bullock Texas State History Museum.** Bob Bullock, Texas's 38th lieutenant governor and a potent political force in his day, lobbied hard
Fodor's Choice to establish a museum of state history in his years of public service.
★ Bullock didn't live to see it happen—he died in 1999—but his dream came true in 2001 with the opening of this 176,000-square-foot museum. Four blocks north of the capitol, the museum hosts exhibitions of archaeological objects, documents, and other materials from regional museums throughout the state and also presents historical and

educational programs. Exhibits include everything from the letters of Sam Houston to Indian artifacts. The museum has a 400-seat IMAX. ⊠*1800 Congress Ave., Downtown & Capitol Area* ☎*512/936–8746* ⊕*www.thestoryoftexas.com* ⊡*Museum $5.50, IMAX $7* ☽*Mon.– Sat. 9–6, Sun. noon–6.*

❸ Bremond Block Historic District. A number of high-style Victorian homes built between 1854 and 1910 fill this area. They were once owned by wealthy Austinites, including several members of the Bremond family of merchants and bankers. Inquire at the Austin Visitor Center about self-guided walking tours. ⊠*Bounded by 7th and 8th Sts., and Guadalupe and San Antonio Sts., Downtown & Capitol Area.*

❼ Texas State Capitol. Built in 1888 of Texas pink granite, this impressive structure is even taller than the U.S. Capitol (yes, everything *is* bigger in Texas). The building dominates downtown Austin. The surrounding grounds are nearly as striking. Stand in the center of the star on the ground floor under the rotunda and look up, up, up into the dome—it's a Texas rite of passage. Catch one of the free historical tours, offered daily 8:30–4:30. ⊠*1100 Congress Ave., Downtown & Capitol Area* ☎*512/463–0063.*

Fodor'sChoice
★

ALSO WORTH SEEING

❿ ArtHouse at the Jones Center. Set in a squarish building on the northwest corner of 7th Street and Congress Avenue is this center with rotating installations by contemporary Texas artists. It also offers a number of art-related programs. ⊠*701 Congress Ave., Downtown & Capitol Area* ☎*512/453–5312* ⊕*www.arthousetexas.org.*

❷ Austin City Hall. The home of municipal government since November 2004 and the anchor of the 2nd Street District, City Hall is a striking modern showcase of the New Austin, loaded with energy-saving features like solar panels and decorated with modern art. The angular, four-story limestone-and-concrete building is clad in 66,000 square feet of copper. A 40-foot waterfall flows inside, and bands play on the outdoor plaza during free Friday concerts in spring and fall. Tours are available by appointment. ⊠*301 W. 2nd , Downtown & Capitol Area* ☎*512/974–7131* ⊕*www.ci.austin.tx.us/cityhall.*

❹ Austin History Center. Part of the Austin Public Library system (and next door to the central branch building), this is the central repository of all historical documents relating to Austin and Travis County (of which Austin is a part). Its more than 1 million items, including more than 700,000 photographic images, form a priceless collection of all things relating to Austin. ⊠*810 Guadalupe St., Downtown & Capitol Area* ☎*512/974–7480* ⊕*www.ci.austin.tx.us/library/ahc.*

NEED A BREAK?

Old Bakery and Emporium—In 1876, Swedish baker Charles Lundberg built this charming, affectionately renovated building near the capitol and operated it as a bakery for the next 60 years. Rescued from demolition by the Austin Heritage Society, the bakery is now a registered historic landmark owned by the city and run by the Parks and Recreation Department. The Old

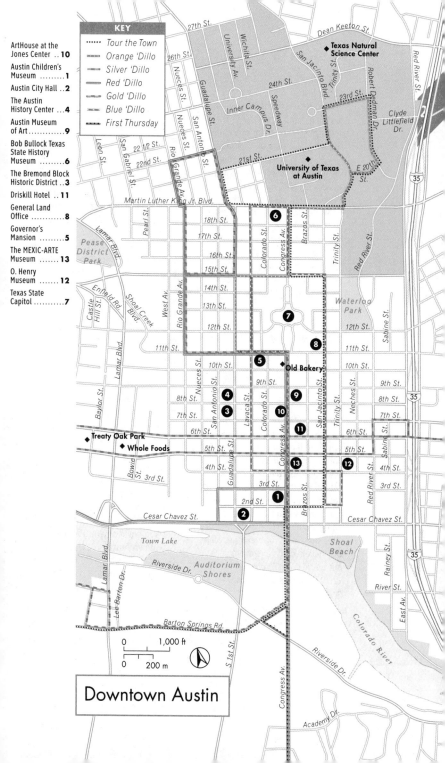

KEY

••••••• *Tour the Town*

Orange 'Dillo

Silver 'Dillo

Red 'Dillo

Gold 'Dillo

Blue 'Dillo

First Thursday

Downtown Austin

FESTIVALS & EVENTS

MAR. Zilker Park Kite Festival. Austin is also known for enjoying the outdoors. On the first Sunday of March, head down to the soccer fields at Zilker Park for this annual kite event. Be sure to bring a picnic basket, the kids, and even your furry friends for beautiful kite creations and amazing tricks. You can bring a kite or you can just watch the festivities—and if the mood strikes, purchase a kite on-site or attend one of the kite-building workshops. The festival is an ideal way to take in the Austin skyline. ✉ *2100 Barton Springs Rd., West Austin* ☎ *512/448–5483* ⊕ *www.zilkerkitefestival.com* ✑ *Free.*

APR. Texas Hill Country Wine and Food Festival. With the flagship Whole Foods Market on West 6th Street and two locations for the foodie-heaven Central Market, it's clear that Austin is a food-loving town. Each April at this fun-filled festival, celebrity chefs, winemakers, and food lovers alike join together to celebrate fabulous culinary creations and trends, as well as the up-and-coming Texas wine scene. Tickets can be expensive (with some events costing near $150), but the cooking demonstrations, speaker series, and general celebration of food and wine do make for an exciting affair. Buy tickets early; this event sells out quickly. ✉ *Throughout Austin* ☎ *512/249–6300* ⊕ *www.texas-* *wineandfood.org* ✑ *Prices vary per event, starting at $35.*

MAY & OCT. Old Pecan Street Art Festival. Austin is no stranger to the arts and hosts a number of art-driven festivals including this biannual event. Few may know that 6th Street was once Pecan Street, but twice a year (in spring and fall), old Austin roots surface, the street closes during the day and artists set up booths with paintings, jewelry, crafts, and much more for the public to peruse—and hopefully buy. Add to this live musical performances, cold beer, and smoked sausage wraps, and you've got an afternoon of good times. ✉ *6th St. Downtown* ☎ *512/443–6179* ⊕ *www.oldpecanstreetfestival.com* ✑ *Free.*

DEC. First Night Austin. For a family-friendly way to bring in the new year, stroll the plazas and parks of downtown Austin. Each New Year's Eve the city serves as the stage for a variety of artists, street performers, musicians, puppeteers, and dancers. This interactive festival features children-friendly workshops for creating puppets, festive hats, and origami cranes for the final event parade. Admission is free, and parents can feel safe with children in the alcohol-free environment. Throughout Downtown Austin ✉ *Throughout Downtown Austin* ☎ *512/374–0000* ⊕ *www.firstnightaustin.org* ✑ *Free.*

Bakery sells sandwiches and coffee these days, but its real appeal is as an outlet for handmade crafts made by older citizens (50 and over). It makes for a nice stop before or after touring the capitol. ✉ *1006 Congress Ave., Downtown & Capitol Area* ☎ *512/477–5961* ☽ *Weekdays 9–4 (also Sat. 10–2 Dec. only).*

 Driskill Hotel. If you make time to stroll through one Austin hotel even though you're not staying there, make it the Driskill. A monument

PARKING IN AUSTIN

Both street and garage parking are plentiful in downtown Austin. Metered parking costs $1 an hour (be warned that many downtown meters have two-hour limits); it is free after 5:30 PM and on week-ends. Parking lots and garages charge from $5 to $15 a day (prices increase during special events). For visits to the state capitol, a free, two-hour parking lot is adjacent to the building. Austin's City Hall has a large garage with free parking on Thursday (the day City Council meets) and on Friday from 11 AM to 1:15 PM whenever bands perform on City Hall Plaza; the maximum fee otherwise is $10 a day, $5 on weekends. Visitors to City Hall can generally get their parking validated, and many 2nd Street District retail-ers can validate tickets for two hours on weekdays, 8 AM to 5 PM. Parking regulations are strictly enforced in Austin, and a ticket will run $15–$35 (fines double if not paid in 21 days), and $250 for parking in a handi-capped spot ($300 after 21 days).

to Richardsonian Romanesque style, this delightful—and some say haunted—grande dame is embellished with stone busts of its original owner, cattle baron Jesse Driskill, and his sons. Two-story porches with Romanesque Revival columns surround the arched entrances. Over the years, countless legislators, lobbyists, and social leaders have held court behind its limestone walls, and it seems a few of them never left: according to guests, lights turn on by themselves, pipes bang eerily, elevators without passengers go up and down during the night, and luggage is mysteriously moved. But hotel management is quick to point out that the ghosts seem benign. *(Also see Where to Stay.)* ⊠ *604 Brazos St., Downtown & Capitol Area* ☎ *512/474–5911* ⊕ *www.driskill hotel.com.*

❽ **General Land Office.** The only surviving government building from Austin's first 30 years owes its Gothic style to its German-born and -trained architect, Conrad Stremme. This 2½-story structure of stuccoed stone and brick was opened for business in spring of 1858 as the first home of the Land Office. Writer O. Henry worked as a draftsman here and used the building as the setting for two of his short stories. In 1989 the legislature approved a $4.5 million renovation project to restore the building to its 1890s appearance. The structure now houses the Capitol Visitors Center and a gift shop, and has space on the second floor for traveling exhibits. ⊠ *112 E. 11th St., at Brazos St., Downtown & Capitol Area* ☎ *512/305–8400 visitor center* ⊠ *Free* ☉ *Mon.–Sat. 9–5, Sun. noon–5.*

❺ **Governor's Mansion.** Abner Cook, a leading architect of his day, designed the mansion, one of Austin's most elegant dwellings. The 1865 home has been the home of every Texas governor since the state's fifth, Elisha Marshall Pease. Constructed of bricks made in Austin and wood from nearby forests, the two-story mansion bears the marks of those who have lived here, including Governor James Hogg, who, to keep his children from speedballing down the banister on their rears, hammered tacks into the railing. The tack holes are still visible. The mansion has many fine furnishings, paintings, and antiques, including Sam Houston's bed and Stephen F. Austin's desk. Unfortunately, in order to visit, you'll have to wait until 2009, when it is expected to reopen after extensive renovations. A fire in June 2008 caused some structural damage; at press time, arson was suspected. ⊠*1010 Colorado St., Downtown & Capitol Area* ☎*512/463–5518* ⊕*www.governor. state.tx.us/mansion.*

⑬ MEXIC-ARTE Museum. Founded in 1984, this museum is a beguiling, moderate-size museum devoted to traditional and contemporary Mexican and Latino art. The permanent collection includes lithographs, prints, silk screens, etchings, and traditional ritual masks. If you're in town in time for the museum's popular annual Day of the Dead celebration, you're in for a treat. ⊠*419 Congress Ave., Downtown & Capitol Area* ☎*512/480–9373* ⊠*$5* ⊙*Mon.–Thurs. 10–6, Fri. and Sat. 10–5, Sun. noon–5.*

⑫ O. Henry Museum. Writer William Sydney Porter, better known as O. Henry, rented this modest cottage from 1893 to 1895. Moved a few blocks from its original location, the home today contains O. Henry memorabilia and period furniture. It has hosted the popular O. Henry Pun-Off World Championships in its backyard every May since 1977; it also sponsors student writing workshops. ⊠*409 E. 5th St., Downtown & Capitol Area* ☎*512/472–1903* ⊕*www.ci.austin.tx.us/parks/ ohenry.htm* ⊠*Donation suggested* ⊙*Wed.–Sun. noon–5.*

UNIVERSITY OF TEXAS

Envisioning Austin without the University of Texas is wellnigh impossible. The sprawling campus itself is home to both intimate charm (winding pathways past stone university buildings) and spectacle (the landmark UT Tower, the ultranew Blanton Museum of Art, the LBJ Library and Museum, and of course Memorial Stadium, home of those Longhorns). Parking can be a problem anywhere on or around campus (most parking spaces are reserved for students, faculty, and staff, and the Drag is always crowded when school is in session—and don't even think of driving down there on Longhorn football home game days).

You'll know you're in a college town when you stroll down Guadalupe Street, also known as "the Drag." Guadalupe borders the west side of the UT campus and is lined with trendy boutiques, vintage-clothing shops, and restaurants. See the University of Texas Area map, below. Numbers in the margin correspond to numbers on the map.

MAIN ATTRACTIONS

❶ Blanton Museum of Art. Austin's new showcase museum, formerly the Huntington Art Gallery, is the largest university art museum in the United States and holds one of the country's largest private collections of old-master paintings and drawings. Although it's home to a teaching school—this is a center for research and training in conservation studies and visual arts—the Blanton avoids the stifling tendencies of academe, frequently mounting daring special exhibitions. In addition

WALKING TOUR OF AUSTIN

Allow 3½ hours for this walk focused on Texas history and culture.

Begin at the **Paramount Theatre** at Congress Avenue and 8th Street. This restored neoclassical city landmark built in 1915 has hosted performances by Katharine Hepburn, Sarah Bernhardt, and the Marx Brothers.

Continue north on Congress to 10th Street. Turn left and walk up the hill one block. At 10th and Colorado is the Greek Revival–style **Governor's Mansion,** home to every Texas governor since 1856. (The mansion is currently closed for extensive renovations until 2009.)

Walk north one block on Colorado to 11th Street. **Texas's State Capitol,** the largest in the country, will be in front of you. Go inside to see the giant dome that reaches nearly 300 feet, as well as the terrazzo floor commemorating the centennial of Texas's independence from Mexico. To get to the **Capitol Visitors Center,** continue down 11th Street to the end of the block. The center is on your left, inside the capitol gates, in the **General Land Office Building.** (This is the oldest remaining Texas state office building.) After your visit, walk from the north side of the building 100 yards to the **Lorenzo de Zavala State Archives and Library Building.** Inside, the giant mural "Texas Moves Toward Statehood" depicts 400 years of tumultuous Texas history.

From the north side of the building, turn right on 12th Street and walk two blocks to Trinity. Turn left on Trinity and continue six blocks to Martin Luther King Boulevard. You are now at the southern boundary of the **University of Texas,** the country's largest public university. Cross MLK and continue through campus on what becomes San Jacinto Boulevard. Notice the **Lee and Joe Jamail Texas Swimming Center and Darrell K. Royal–Texas Memorial Stadium,** both on your right. Just past the stadium, take a right on 23rd Street and walk up the hill toward the large grassy area. This lawn is flanked on the left by the **Lyndon Baines Johnson Library and Museum.** Have a look inside this vast memorial to learn about one of the country's most colorful leaders, then walk back down 23rd Street. On your right is **Bass Concert Hall,** the largest and most impressive venue of the **UT Performing Arts Center** (closed for renovations until late 2008).

At Trinity, take a right. The **Texas Memorial Museum,** where you can view extensive geological and archaeological collections, is inside the **Texas Natural Science Center,** the second building on your left at 2400 Trinity. Head south on Trinity, take a right on 23rd and walk south down San Jacinto to MLK, and take a right. You are now near the entrance to the **Blanton Museum of Art.** This museum, one of Austin's best, displays permanent and rotating exhibits by national and international artists.

Return to San Jacinto, going south, and turn right onto 11th Street. Walk two blocks and the state capitol building will be on your right. At Congress, take a left and walk three blocks back to the Paramount Theatre.

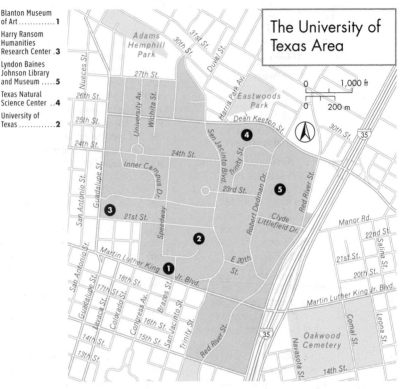

to European holdings rich in Renaissance and baroque works (many by Tiepolo, Poussin, Veronese, Rubens, and Correggio), the museum has a superior sampling of 20th- and early-21st-century American art, with an emphasis on abstract painting. Prints and drawings span the ages, from Albrecht Dürer to Jasper Johns, and the collection of modernist and contemporary Latin-American art is one of the country's largest, encompassing 1,600 works in various mediums. The Blanton's stunning new home, the Mari and James A. Michener Gallery Building, opened its doors in 2006; the adjacent Edgar A. Smith Building will open in fall 2008, adding an auditorium, event spaces, classrooms, a larger museum shop, and a café to the complex. ⊠ *Martin Luther King Jr. Blvd. and Congress St., University of Texas* ☎ *512/471–7324* ⊕ *www.blantonmuseum.org* ☞ *$5.* ☾ *Tues.–Fri. 10–5, Sat. 11–5, Sun. 1–5.*

❸ Harry Ransom Humanities Research Center. Part of the University of Texas, this is one of the world's greatest collectors and exhibitors of important literary papers and other artifacts related to the arts and humanities. Among its fantastic riches are the papers of Norman Mailer, Isaac Bashevis Singer, and Arthur Miller; Woodward and Bernstein's Watergate research materials; more than 10,000 film, television, and radio scripts; more than 10,000 film posters; 1 million rare books, including

2

CLOSE UP
Lady Bird: A Natural Beauty

Nobody didn't love Lady Bird. Born Claudia Alta Taylor in the East Texas town of Karnack, the first lady was 94 when she died at home in Austin in 2007. The nickname that everyone knew came as a toddler when a maid called her "pretty as a lady bird."

Within months of graduating from UT in 1934, she had met and married the boisterous Lyndon Johnson. It was a whirlwind courtship, but there was nothing tornadic about the quintessentially graceful Lady Bird Johnson. She seemed determined to offset LBJ's legendary crudity and relentless ambition with subtlety and good humor.

Some count her the nation's premier environmentalist, and she was the first presidential wife honored by a

The former first lady sits among the wild-flowers she loved so much.

Congressional Gold Medal for her work. Lady Bird also was active for six decades in operating the family's broadcasting outlets in Austin.

—Larry Neal

a Gutenberg Bible; and 5 million photographs. ⊠ *21st and Guadalupe Sts., University of Texas* ☎ *512/471–8944* ⊕ *www.hrc.utexas.edu.*

⑤ Lyndon Baines Johnson Library and Museum. The artifacts and voluminous documents on exhibit here provide some insight into the 36th president's mind and motivations, and though his foibles are downplayed, a clear sense of the man—earthy, conniving, sensitive, and wry—emerges. That he was able to function at all may surprise visitors born during the high-tech era. In an age when the average car is loaded with digital gadgets and 12-year-olds with cell phones are commonplace, Johnson's black Lincoln limousine and clunky, command-central telephone seem quaintly archaic, though they were state-of-the-art during his presidency. If you schedule your visit to the reading room in advance of your arrival, you can listen to recordings of conversations Johnson had using that telephone. The 30-plus hours of tape recordings include ruminations on Vietnam, economic inflation, and a New York City transit strike. Gordon Bunshaft designed the monolithic travertine building that houses the library; like the limo and the phone, it's a bit of a period piece. There are rotating temporary exhibits on the ground floor. Be sure to check out the second floor, where a life-size audio-animatronic figure of LBJ spins humorous anecdotes; it's a hoot. ⊠ *2313 Red River St., University of Texas* ☎ *512/721–0200* ⊕ *www.lbjlib.utexas.edu* ⊠ *Free* ⊙ *Daily 9–5.*

❷ University of Texas. The 350-acre campus breeds Texas Longhorns, as passionate about football (and other sports) as they are about academics (it has one of the country's top research libraries). The university is the largest employer in Austin (even more than the state government), employing more than 80,000 people. The number of students here is staggering, too: 39,000 undergraduates and 11,000 at the graduate level. Come to the grounds any time to stroll on your own, visit one of the museums or libraries (the Ransom Center, for example, is the repository for the Watergate papers), or attend a fun annual event like Explore UT, Gone to Texas, and commencement, which includes fireworks. ☎512/475–7348 ⊕ *www.utexas.edu.*

ALSO WORTH SEEING

Texas Natural Science Center. French architect Paul Cret's 1936 plans for the Texas Memorial Museum (now the exhibit hall of the Texas Natural Science Center) called for north and south wings to extend from a central building, a tailored limestone box with subtle art deco flourishes. The wings were scuttled because of funding difficulties, leaving only Cret's alabaster midsection. But the chic interior, with brass doors, glass embellishments, and blood-red marble walls, floors, and ceilings, mitigates any sense of abridgement. Among the popular draws at the museum are the dinosaur models (including a 30-foot-long mosasaur and a 40-foot-long pterosaur) and the life-size dioramas, which depict buffalo, roadrunners, cougars, mountain lions, and flying squirrels. ⊠2400 *Trinity St., University of Texas* ☎512/471–1604 ⊕*www. utexas.edu/tmm* ☑*Free* ☉ *Weekdays 9–5, Sat. 10–5, Sun. 1–5.*

WEST AUSTIN/ZILKER PARK

Zilker Park is Austin's regular daily backyard and playground, where Austinites go to swim, jog, and hang back with a barbecue platter and a beer. West Austin generally refers to the area just west of Lamar Boulevard (not to be confused with West Lake, which is the tony area west of Lake Austin). It's a laid-back, pleasant area with some good shopping strips and restaurants.

MAIN ATTRACTION

Treaty Oak. Many local legends attach themselves to Austin's most famous tree. At least 500 years old, the live oak, on Baylor Street in the West End between 5th and 6th streets, is the last survivor of a group of trees known as the Council Oaks, used in ceremonies and meetings by local American Indian tribes. The tree's name derives from a legend (which may or may not be true) that underneath its branches Stephen F. Austin negotiated the first boundary agreement between the tribes and settlers. In 1989 a disturbed individual attempted to poison the tree with a powerful herbicide; he was later apprehended. Intensive efforts to save the tree were successful, although nearly two-thirds of the Treaty Oak died and it is now a shadow of its former self. Still, it's well worth a visit to pay your respects to this venerable survivor. ⊠*Treaty Oak Park, on Baylor between 5th and 6th Sts., Downtown & Capitol Area.*

Zilker Park. Many people and companies have moved to Austin for a quality of life enhanced by pristine waterways and extensive greenbelts

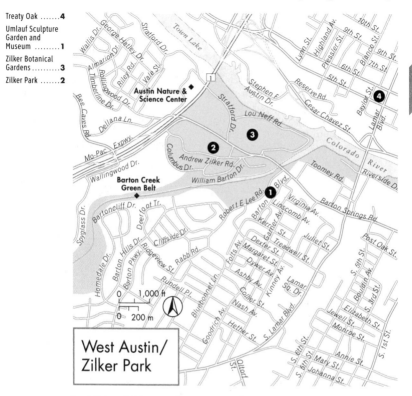

2

West Austin/ Zilker Park

for hiking, biking, and running. Zilker Park is the city's largest and connects to **Lady Bird Lake's hike and bike trail.** There's a parking fee on weekends. (⇨ *Sports & the Outdoors for more on Zilker Park and outdoor offerings in Austin.*) ✉ *2100 Barton Springs Rd., West Austin* ☎ *512/974–6700* ☉ *Daily 5 AM–10 PM.*

ALSO WORTH SEEING

❶ **Umlauf Sculpture Garden and Museum.** This pleasant space at the south end of Zilker Park houses more than 130 works of sculptor Charles Umlauf in the house where he lived and worked. Umlauf, who taught at the University of Texas Art Department from 1941 to 1981, created an incredibly diverse body of work that ranged in style from realistic to abstract, using such materials as granite, marble, bronze, wood, and terra-cotta. His subjects were equally wide-ranging, from religious figures to nudes, from whimsical animals to family groupings. ✉ *605 Robert E. Lee Rd., West Austin* ☎ *512/445–5582* ⊕ *www.umlauf sculpture.org* ▣ *$3.50* ☉ *Wed.–Fri. 10–4:30, weekends 1–4:30.*

❸ **Zilker Botanical Gardens.** Across from Zilker Park, this 26-acre botanical garden features such horticultural delights as butterfly trails and xeriscape gardens with plants native to the arid Southwest. ✉ *2220 Barton Springs Rd., West Austin* ☎ *512/477–8672* ⊕ *www.zilkergarden.org* ▣ *Free* ☉ *Daily 7 AM–6 PM.*

NORTH AUSTIN/HYDE PARK

One of Austin's oldest residential neighborhoods, Hyde Park is a calm area near the University of Texas, filled with charming older houses. North Austin will be familiar to most visitors via the I–35 corridor, chockablock with hotels and motels of all sorts, but there's a lot more to the neighborhood than that one relatively small part. North Austin may seem like one big commercial working-class strip (apart from myriad medical offices, clinics, and hospitals), but it's also home to the gourmet supermarket Central Market (Whole Foods' main competitor in town), many interesting independent upscale shops, and some outstanding ethnic restaurants.

MAIN ATTRACTIONS

★ **Elisabet Ney Museum.** The 19th century lives on at this delightfully eccentric museum, where German Romanticism meets the Texas frontier. The 70-plus sculptures and busts on display show an artist straining against convention. The career of Ms. Ney began auspiciously in her native Germany, where she sculpted eminent figures like the philosopher Arthur Schopenhauer and Germany's "Iron Chancellor" Otto von Bismarck. A nonconformist from birth, Ney eventually tired of social mores on the continent and in 1871 moved to Georgia; two years later, she headed to East Texas. In the early 1890s, Ney, then in her late fifties, designed a house and studio in quiet Hyde Park, calling it Formosa, Portuguese for "beautiful." Over the next several years, Ney would produce some of her most renowned sculptures here, including those of Stephen F. Austin and Sam Houston. Her studio here is set up as she knew it, with sculpting tools, hat, teacup, and other items all in their proper places. The sculptures on view include many Texas heroes. ⊠ *304 E. 44th St., North Austin/Hyde Park* ☎ *512/458–2255* ⊕ *www. ci.austin.tx.us/elisabetney* ⊠ *Free* ⊙ *Wed.–Sat. 10–5, Sun. noon–5.*

☾ **Republic of Texas Museum.** The Daughters of the Republic of Texas (which also oversees the Alamo in San Antonio), also headquartered in this building, maintains this collection of artifacts from the Republic of Texas era (1836–46), including hands-on exhibits like a scavenger hunt. ⊠ *510 E. Anderson La., North Austin/Hyde Park* ☎ *512/339–1997* ⊕ *www.drt-inc.org/museum.htm* ⊠ *$2* ⊙ *Weekdays 10–4.*

ELSEWHERE IN AUSTIN

For locations, see the Greater Austin map.

★ **Austin Museum of Art–Laguna Gloria.** Set on a lush Lake Austin peninsula, this 1915 Mediterranean-style villa was once home to Clara Driscoll Sevier, who led the fight to save the Alamo from demolition in the early 20th century. In this lovely if relatively diminutive setting, the museum showcases its expanding collection of 20th-century American paintings, sculpture, and photographs, and hosts outside exhibits and family-focused art programs. An art school shares the idyllic setting of this building, which is listed on the National Register of Historic Places. Staffers are extremely helpful and informative. ⊠ *3809 W. 35th St.*

☎ *512/458–8191* ⊕ *www.amoa.org* ✉ *$3 suggested donation* ☉ *Daily 11–4 (villa); Mon.–Sat. 9–5, Sun. 11–5 (grounds).*

NEED A BREAK? Those ubiquitous KEEP AUSTIN WEIRD bumper stickers are talking about places like **Ruta Maya** (✉ *3601 S. Congress Ave., South Austin* ☎ *512/707-9637* ⊕ *www.rutamaya.net*), a coffeehouse with a strong community vibe where people go to have fun and actually *talk* to each other, not stare into laptops (though Wi-Fi is available and free). In a converted military hangar, Ruta Maya hosts many special programs, including a free Sunday-morning kids' show, and a Tuesday open-mike poetry night. It's a great place to hear live music—oh, and the coffee's pretty good, too.

Moore/Andersson Compound. A rather plebian, nondescript exterior belies the madcap, joyous interior of the former home and office compound of influential postmodern architect and teacher Charles W. Moore (1925–93). Called "a tiny village that wants to be a cathedral" and compared to such architectural treasures as Monticello and Frank Lloyd Wright's Taliesin, the compound of small houses was preserved in the nick of time following Moore's death, thanks to the Charles W. Moore Foundation. The current owners cooperate with the foundation in arranging tours (available by appointment only) and fund-raisers here. ✉ *2102 Quarry Rd.* ☎ *512/220-7923* ✉ *$25.*

☾ **Mt. Bonnell.** Several miles northwest of Barton Creek Greenbelt stands Mt. Bonnell. At 750 feet, the crag offers a sweeping panorama of Austin, the rolling hills to its west, and the Colorado River. You can't get much higher than this in the Austin area, and if the view itself doesn't convince you of that, the 100 steps to the top surely will. (Seriously, though, the short hike shouldn't present a problem to anyone in reasonably good shape.) ✉ *3800 Mount Bonnell Rd., off Scenic Dr., North Austin* ☎ *512/974-6700* ✉ *Free* ☉ *Daily 5 AM–10 PM.*

BEYOND AUSTIN

☾ **Champion Park.** Kids can dig for stone casts of dinosaur bones (specifically *Mosasuraus Maximus*) buried under sand at a covered children's playscape at this innovative park that opened in October 2007 in Austin's northwest suburbs. Features include a "whale's tail sprayscape" for cooling off overheated kids (and perhaps parents) on warm days, fabricated boulders for climbing, a fishing area, and a picnic pavilion. ✉ *3900 Brushy Creek Rd., Cedar Park* ☎ *512/260-42839* ✉ *Free.*

SHOPPING

The best way to plumb the depths of any city's character is to go shopping. And once you start browsing in Austin, you'll quickly discover that this city is quite the character.

Sure, Austin has the same chain stores that you'll find anywhere—but the city's true charm dwells in its independently owned establishments.

To see the real Austin, browse the funky shops along revitalized South Congress, gaze at the hip downtown storefronts of the up-and-coming 2nd Street District, and stroll among the high-end galleries, antiques, and home furnishings emporia of the West End. You can trek to legions of book, computer, and music stores, then peruse the handicrafts of local artisans. Along the way, fuel up on organic foods and fresh-roasted coffee.

Out in Northwest Austin and Round Rock, upscale shopping malls are popping up all over the place. The Domain in North Austin, which opened in 2007, is an ambitious project of mixed-use retail, office, and residential space that's extending the affluent downtown vibe practically into the suburbs.

All stores are open daily unless stated otherwise.

UNIVERSITY OF TEXAS

The Drag (⊠ *Guadalupe St. from Martin Luther King Jr. Blvd. to 26th St. and 3 blocks west to Rio Grande between 23rd and 26th Sts. on the western edge of UT's campus*) elicits moans from people upset about its recent semi-invasion by outsiders like Starbucks and Urban Outfitters. But look closely; you'll find plenty of old-timers still around, selling books, imports, vintage clothing, gifts, and pizza by the slice. In truth, it hardly looks gentrified at all.

The crowd here is mostly students, so most shoppers and others you'll encounter are dressed casually or trendy on the hippie side, with a lot of backpacks slug across shoulders. Note that the Drag is not a good place to shop for clothes unless you're into the thrift-store and vintage-clothing look—or of course UT apparel. Books, however, you'll find aplenty.

■**TIP**→Note that parking on the streets surrounding campus is a chronic pain day and night anytime school is in session. Within the UT campus, only a very small number of spots are not reserved for students or staff. A good bet for visitors is the San Antonio Parking Garage at 2420 San Antonio Street, one block from Guadalupe; it's a large, multilevel covered facility open weekdays only from 6 AM to 11 PM, with reasonable rates. Another option, this one open 24/7, is the Brazos Garage (at a central location at the south end of campus, at 210 East Martin Luther King Boulevard).

BOOKS

If you want textbooks, you can find them on UT's campus at the University Co-Op (⇨ *UT Wear & Souvenirs, below)*, but for general trade books, head to Follett's.

Follett's Intellectual Property. This two-story bookstore, formerly a Tower Records, sells trade books even though it's owned by a large retailer of college and other school textbooks. It's a great bookstore, with CDs, DVDs, a large magazine selection, and even computers. ⊠ *2401 Guadalupe St., University of Texas* ☎ *512/478–0007* ⊕ *www.intellectual propertyaustin.com.*

Being a Texan 101

Texans have their own history, their own culture, and even their own language. Here's a little primer to help you fit in with the folks of the Great State.

TALK LIKE A LOCAL

Whether it's the slower, drawn-out speech, the never-ending y'alls, or how they drop off the hard "h" sound when they say things like humble (therefore pronouncing it "umble"), Texans talk differently than the rest of the country. They also fix their verbs quite a bit, as in "I'm fixin' to go the store," "I'm fixin' to drive my pickup truck over there right now." Also, if you're from the Midwest, word to the wise: don't even commit the social blunder of calling a carbonated beverage a pop. Everything here is Coke (even if it's a 7Up). Occasionally you'll hear someone say "sodie water."

EAT MEAT

It's hard to be a vegetarian in Texas. Not impossible, but challenging, at least if you're a visitor who will be dining out most of the time. (The exception to this is Texas's bigger cities, where dining options cover almost every cuisine type imaginable.) From barbecued brisket to "real" Texas chili (meat but no beans), solid meat options are what tend to fill menus.

DRINK DR PEPPER OR BIG RED

Created in Waco, Texas, within 50 some years of each other, these drinks are the state's alcohol-free beverages of choice. Not too far in the distant past, the live bear mascots of Baylor University used to even guzzle a bottle of Dr Pepper at the home football games. We must warn you that Big Red is an acquired taste.

WEAR YOUR BOOTS RIGHT

Please do *not* tuck your jeans into your boots. Unless you're wearing the big rubbery kind to wade through mud, or are doing some serious ranch work, you should wear your jeans overtop (this is why they have the "boot cut" jeans, after all).

LISTEN TO COUNTRY MUSIC

You don't have to have half of your set stations tuned to country music in your car or know the lyrics to all (or any) of the songs, but do keep it to yourself if the genre makes you want to run away screaming. Country music in Texas is mainstream, and it's the one type of music you're guaranteed to hear on your radio throughout the state. Prep in advance if you haven't at least heard of Toby Keith, Garth Brooks, and the Dixie Chicks.

BE FRIENDLY

By and large, Texans tend to be friendly, wishing you a good day and telling you to come back soon. In the smaller towns, they may even wave or say hello as they pass you. So smile and be nice, even to the guy who just cut you off on the freeway—in fact, especially to that guy, because in Texas on the road, rude gestures can land you a ticket.

OPEN-AIR MARKET

★ **Renaissance Market.** This year-round open-air market with roots stretching back to the early '70s is the soul of the Drag. The unreconstructed hippie ambience is at least as much of a draw as the actual merchandise crafted and sold by various local artisans. The wares include jewelry, leatherwork, candles, photographs, paintings, sculpture, textiles, and the inevitable tie-dyed T-shirts. (Note that the market is firmly regulated by the city, and all vendors must be licensed by a commission.) ⊠ *Guadalupe St. at W. 23rd St., University of Texas* ☎ *No phone* ⊕ *www.austinartistsmarket.com.*

TOYS & OTHER DIVERSIONS

↻ **Toy Joy.** This fantastic place is so much the ultimate toy store of your
Fodor'sChoice childhood fantasies that it's too good to save for actual children—don't
★ be embarrassed to come in even if you don't have little ones of your own. It's *the* place to get Marie Antoinette, Shakespeare, and Einstein action figures, red rubber duckies with devil horns, puppets of boxing nuns, repros of fave toys you played with as a kid, and floor-to-ceiling diversions for all ages, including science toys, metal robots, stuffed animals, hard-to-find candy, baubles and bangles, and more. On Friday and Saturday it's open until midnight. ⊠ *2900 Guadalupe St., University of Texas* ☎ *512/320–0090* ⊕ *www.toyjoy.com.*

UT WEAR & SOUVENIRS

★ **The University Co-Op.** The beating burnt-orange heart of Longhorn Nation is on display at the ultimate showcase of UT sports paraphernalia. You can find burnt-orange-and-Longhorn-logo'd everything at this three-level emporium, from Crocs and dress shirts to bath mats, a full set of luggage, even a $350 pair of Lucchese cowboy boots and a $600 acoustic guitar. An entire room is devoted to children's wear, from the nursery on up. Founded in 1896 and modeled after a similar co-op at Harvard, UT's Co-Op (which offers discounts to faculty, students, and staff) claims to be the largest seller of used textbooks in the country. Even if you have no direct (or indirect) connection to UT, if you're in the neighborhood, do stop in; it's gawk-inducing and unforgettable. ⊠ *2246 Guadalupe St., University of Texas* ☎ *512/476–7211* ⊕ *www.universitycoop.com.*

DOWNTOWN

Austin's vibrant downtown is home to too many businesses to list them all in this section, but as always, we've culled out the best places for your hard-earned dollars and shopping pleasure. Throngs of Austinites and visitors shop in downtown Austin every day, especially on the main thoroughfares like Lamar Boulevard, a long and diverse commercial strip, and on and near Congress Avenue, a stylish area featuring shops and galleries with high-quality goods. (Note that Congress Avenue south of the river is known as SoCo, or simply "The Avenue" by locals. *See the South Austin section, below, for shops in that neighborhood.*)

BOOKSTORES

Book People. Texas's largest independent bookstore is a homegrown alternative to the monster chain stores. It began in 1970 as Grok Books, and now stocks best-sellers along with books on topics such as women's studies, personal growth, and alternative home building; there's also a good children's section. Browse magazines; shop for quirky, hard-to-find gifts; and catch readings by local authors as well as literati like Richard Ford, Amy Tan, Jonathan Franzen, and David Sedaris. Former presidents Jimmy Carter and Bill Clinton and celebrities such as Lauren Bacall, David Byrne, and Jane Fonda have also made stops here while on book tours. ⊠*603 N. Lamar Blvd., Downtown* ☎*512/472–5050* ⊕*www.bookpeople.com.*

GALLERIES

Authenticity Gallery. Colorful glass, ceramic, and metal *objets* and paintings from American and Canadian artists and artisans find a home in Mary Ober's sunny two-story gallery. Wooden items and art cards are also on view. ⊠*910 Congress Ave., Suite 100, Downtown* ☎*512/478–2787* ⊕*www.authenticitygallery.com.*

Wild About Music. Looking for the perfect present for the music nut in your life? Part gallery, part gift shop, this popular shop across from the Driskill Hotel carries everything from hand-painted guitars to scarves, socks, ties, and jewelry. Past featured artists have included such well-known musicians as Joe Ely and the Rolling Stones' Ron Wood. ⊠*115 E. 6th St., Downtown* ☎*512/708–1700* ⊕*www.wild aboutmusic.com.*

HOME FURNISHINGS & IMPORTS

Eclectic. Eclectic it is: an explosion of bright colors, mainly painted wooden furniture, but also folk art galore, including Mexican *milagros* (small metallic votive offerings in various forms), elephants crafted in Africa from metal shavings, French and Israeli jewelry, and Peruvian and Bulgarian knickknacks. The store also has in stock handcrafted, folk-art-inspired pine cabinets, and other furniture from the workshop of well-known Houston craftsman David Marsh. ⊠*700 N. Lamar Blvd., Downtown* ☎*512/477–1816.*

Wildflower. "Organic luxury" is the motto of this bedroom-and-bath-focused shop, which stocks everything from luxe natural-fiber linens, pillows, and bathrobes to high-end furniture, nursery items, and baby clothes, even home saunas. Not a cheap place to shop, though some items are marked down in the "bargain room" (of course, even this room would never be confused with a thrift store). A second location flourishes in the Davenport Village (3801 Capitol of Texas Highway, D-180) in Austin's West Lake neighborhood. ⊠*908 N. Lamar Blvd., Downtown* ☎*512/320–0449* ⊕*www.wildflowerorganics.com.*

MARKETS

Fodor'sChoice ★ **Whole Foods Market.** This 80,000-square-foot flagship store for the natural/organic supermarket chain's world headquarters in downtown Austin is both a showcase for the company's philosophy and one of the most entertaining supermarkets you'll ever visit. It's been a major tourist attraction (we kid you not) since it opened in 2005. There are several places inside the massive store to enjoy a casual sit-down lunch, and the options are abundant, whether you're craving sushi, pizza, or seafood (we recommend the Fifth Street Seafood Corner). The store also has one of Austin's largest wine selections and a walk-in beer cooler (to keep those six-packs cold). There's ample free garage parking available. ☒*525 N. Lamar Blvd., Downtown* ☎*512/476–1206* ⊕*www.wholefoods.com.*

MUSIC

★ **Cheapo Discs.** Hunting for the really elusive CDs and LPs on your want list? If you can't find it at Waterloo, try Cheapo (and vice versa). A slightly more downscale version of Waterloo, Cheapo is a large, no-frills used-CD-and-LP emporium, where Austin goes to unload its unwanted music and look for replacements. The clerks will probably buy your used products, too—but don't expect to make a mint from 'em. The store hosts frequent free daytime live concerts, and it's open until midnight. ☒*914 N. Lamar Blvd., Downtown* ☎*512/477–4499* ⊕*www.cheapotexas.com.*

Fodor'sChoice **Waterloo Records & Video.** This large independent shop is an Austin insti-
★ tution that's been an integral part of the local music scene since 1982. Its outstanding selection, customer service, and free in-store concerts (including some pretty impressive names during SXSW week) mean it may be the only Austin record store you'll ever need. ☒*600A N. Lamar Blvd., Downtown* ☎*512/474–2500* ⊕*www.waterloorecords.com.*

OUTDOOR OUTFITTERS

♻ **Whole Earth Provision Co.** South Congress gets more attention from travel writers, but stores like this huge, sun- and fun-filled outdoor/travel outfitters (the local branch of a Texas chain) are why Austinites prize North Lamar as a real-life shopping destination. It carries a lot of the same things you'd find at any REI—backpacks, tents, sleeping bags, running shoes, rugged clothing—but it's much more diverting in several ways: jazz is on the speakers, the front space is filled with kids' toys (and a few adults-only selections), and there's a good variety of books for all ages. The staff is laid-back, but friendly and ever-willing to help. The store also has branches on the UT campus (2410 San Antonio Street) and at the Westgate Mall (4477 South Lamar) in South Austin. ☒*1014 N. Lamar Blvd., Downtown* ☎*512/476–1414* ⊕*www. wholeearthprovision.com.*

NORTH AUSTIN

It's easy for newcomers to get a bit lost in North Austin, but if you know what you're looking for, you can find some great deals in antiques markets, bookstores, boutiques, and thrift stores.

Kerbey Lane/Jefferson Square (☒*38th St. from N. Lamar Blvd. to MoPac*) is a seemingly infinite shopping district; it's hard to say where this area along 38th Street begins or ends. At the hub are the specialty shops along Kerbey Lane and in Jefferson Square that sell everything from pasta to dollhouses to fresh-roasted coffee to high-style fashions. Radiating from this center as far east as Central Market and as far west as MoPac are shops dedicated to gardening, architectural artifacts, ergonomic furniture, kids' clothing, plus much, much more. Most shops close Sunday.

ANTIQUES

Antique Marketplace. More than 50 vendors spread out over nearly 20,000 square feet. Lose yourself in the vintage linens, lunchboxes, posters and postcards, and sparkling rhinestone jewelry scattered among the antique chests of drawers, cabinets, and tables. ⊠*5350 Burnet Rd., North Austin* ☎*512/452–1000.*

Austin Antique Mall. This 30,000-square-foot mall boasts 100-plus dealers selling everything from antique paperweights to a giant wooden hammer from a carnival's strength-testing game. ⊠*8822 McCann Dr., North Austin* ☎*512/459–5900* ⊕*www.antiquetexas.com.*

BOOKSTORES

Curio Corner Books. Parents and children come here to peruse quality used cookbooks, children's books, and Texan titles. ⊠*5915 Burnet Rd., North Austin* ☎*512/371–0201* ⊕*www.curiocornerbooks.com.*

Hart of Austin Antiquarian Books. Beguiling bibliophiles with its selection of rare and out-of-print books (such as 104 volumes of Bell's *British Poets* dating from 1700 to about 1810), this place also brims with maps, botanical prints, early illustrated books, leather-bound sets, and decorative bindings. ⊠*5806 Burnet Rd., North Austin* ☎*512/477–7755* ⊕*www.abebooks.com.*

BOUTIQUES

Envie Boutique. Find elegant to whimsical women's fashions from such designers as Beth Bowley, Lewis Cho, and Rachel Pally, along with pj's, baby clothes, and small gift items at this little wooden-floor stone house near the corner of 49th Street and Burnet Road (across from the Omelettry restaurant). The dresses tend to be pricey, but watch for sales. ⊠*4901 Woodrow Ave., North Austin* ☎*512/371–1336* ⊕*www.envieboutique.com.*

Kismet. You don't have to be twentysomething to wear much of what's on sale in this friendly, nonintimidating boutique in the Rosedale neighborhood. One room of this two-room boutique run by a mother-and-daughter team carries new, modern attire; the other room contains vintage clothing (with some good deals), shoes, and many shiny purses. There's a full line of GloMinerals makeup and other skin products, along with scents and costume jewelry. ⊠*4410 Medical Pkwy., North Austin* ☎*512/374–1119.*

Lotus Boutique. Jennifer Brown, a former costume-and-art person for Austin moviemakers like Robert Rodriguez, opened this cheerful, bright space in the Rosedale neighborhood in 2007. Her hip, discerning sensibility leans to well-made items like Escama Studio purses crocheted from pull-tabs; Virgin, Saints, and Angels belt buckles from San

Miguel de Allende, Mexico; jeans from Paris-based purveyor Notify; and other fine clothes, accessories, and scents to delight the eye, nose, and fingertips. ⊠*4410 Burnet Rd., North Austin* ☎*512/454–9700.*

MARKETS

⏱ **Central Market.** This upscale, foodie-friendly offshoot of the giant Texas-★ based H-E-B supermarket chain is a few years older than its competitor down Lamar Boulevard, Whole Foods, but no less popular (expect big weekend crowds). It's equally serious about the cheeses, wine, beer, meat, and deli products it purveys, but compared to Whole Foods it seems more like a place real people go to shop (rather than gawk). It's a great spot to grab prepared foods on the run (like the good multicourse brown-bagged Dinners for Two for $14), or join the weekday lunch crowds at the in-house café, where an outdoor patio pleases kids and where various bands play Friday through Sunday evenings. Flag down an on-staff "foodie" (yes, that's the official job title) if you have any questions. The market is in the Central Park Shopping Center, which also houses a number of chic craft galleries, boutiques, and gift shops. There's a newer branch of Central Market in far South Austin's Westgate area. ⊠*4001 N. Lamar Blvd., North Austin* ☎*512/206–1000* ⊠*4477 S. Lamar Blvd., North Austin* ☎*512/899–4300* ⊕*www. centralmarket.com.*

THRIFT STORES

Top Drawer Thrift. Run by Project Transitions (an organization providing hospice, housing, and support to HIV/AIDS patients) as a funding source, this large store is fun and funky as all thrift shops should be. Go for posters, vintage costume jewelry, bric-a-brac, even used computer and stereo components. As you'd expect, everything is dirt cheap. Every fourth Tuesday from 7 to 10 PM, Top Drawer hosts a Moonlight Madness sale with live music and all clothing marked down 50%. ⊠*4902 Burnet Rd., North Austin* ☎*512/454–5161* ⊕*www.topdrawer thrift.org.*

NORTHWEST AUSTIN

If at first glance Northwest Austin seems to you like an endless succession of malls and superstores, you're not alone—after all, this is the 'burbs, where family comes first and home improvement right after. But hey, you're reading this page because you want to shop, right? And in a shop-centered land like this, and in a consumer culture like this, you're bound to find some place in this area that strikes your fancy. Read on, intrepid shopper.

MALLS & DEPARTMENT STORES

Arboretum at Great Hills. No longer considered the premier outdoor mall for well-heeled Austinites, the Arboretum lost some of its luster after the Domain opened. But Pottery Barn, Restoration Hardware, the Cheesecake Factory, Barnes & Noble, and the Sharper Image remain (for now), and the neighboring Renaissance Hotel is still doing booming business. The adjoining 95 acres of tree-studded parkland (for which the center is named) make this a lovely place to while away an hour—or three. Don't miss the life-size marble cow sculptures. ✉ *10000 Research Blvd., at Great Hills Dr. and Capitol of Texas Hwy., Northwest Austin* ☎ *512/338–4437.*

Austin Chinatown Center. This modern, 750,000-square-foot open-air mall is almost completely occupied by Asian businesses (mainly Chinese and Vietnamese), including restaurants, a travel agency, and retail outlets selling clothing, jewelry, and videos. The mall's cornerstone is the 55,000-square-foot MT (My Thanh) Supermarket, which stocks all manner of Asian foods and related items. Dining standouts include First Chinese BBQ and Pho Saigon; though a bit short on atmosphere, both eateries deliver well-prepared, simply presented lunch plates and noodle-based soups at easy-to-digest prices. ✉ *10901 N. Lamar Blvd., Northwest Austin* ⊕ *www.chinatownaustin.com* ◷ *Center is open daily, but some stores close 1 day a wk* ☎ *No phone.*

The Domain. A postmodern vision of an affluent downtown district, the Domain is home to Neiman Marcus, Tiffany & Co., the Apple Store, and other name-brand shops that cater to the platinum-card set. Those on more-modest budgets should check out kitchenware emporium Sur La Table, Macy's, and the large, cheerful Borders. Some complain that there's very little Austin-specific about the open-air Domain, but it's a pleasant place to spend a few hours (if only to gawk at the pricey goods in the windows). Domain II, the complex's second shopping area, is slated to open toward the end of 2009, nearly doubling the Domain's space. ✉ *11410 Century Oaks Terr., along North MoPac (Loop 1) between Braker La. and Burnet Rd., near the North Austin IBM campus, Northwest Austin* ☎ *512/795–4230* ⊕ *www.simon.com.*

2ND STREET DISTRICT

One of Austin's newest neighborhoods, this showcase downtown area around City Hall is tiny—only about 2 blocks deep by 3½ blocks wide—and still doesn't seem quite real, but it's an admittedly beguiling place to stroll among the boutiques, home-furnishings stores, and bistros among a young, happening, and beautiful downtown crowd. Incidentally, the entire district is managed (and much is owned) by AMLI, a large Chicago-based development firm.

BOUTIQUES

Peyton's Place. This modest-size gem of a boutique on the edge of the district is notable for its affordable prices and friendly staff. Whether you're a hip, young, and swingin' gal in the city or just, well, hip, it's worth checking out its black jeans, little black dresses, red silk thingies, and other accessories and shoes. During the January clearances, some items get discounted by up to 75%. ✉ *215 Lavaca St., 2nd Street District* ☎ *512/477–5224* ⊕ *www.peytonsplaceaustin.com.*

SOUTH AUSTIN

South Congress (⊠ *S. Congress Ave. from Lady Bird Lake [formerly Town Lake] to Oltorf St.*), or SoCo as locals call it, reflects South Austin's dual passions: bohemian counterculture and recycled style. You'll find truckloads of funky furniture and vintage collectibles, folk art, herbs, natural-fiber clothing, costumes, toys, cowboy boots, and Mexican imports amid a scattering of see-and-be-seen cafés and restored motor courts. The wildly colorful and imaginative storefronts on a few of the blocks (you'll know them when you see them) are natural photo ops. Many stores on this wide boulevard open after 11 AM and stay open late. On the first Thursday of each month about 50 merchants here stay open until 10 PM, and special events create a street-party vibe. SoCo is the poster street for a freewheeling neighborhood that's as much a state of mind as a zip code.

BOOTS & WESTERN WEAR

Allens Boots. A South Congress landmark for decades, Allens is impossible to miss: just look for the huge red boot above the door. Set amid trendy, touristy SoCo, Allens is anything but. More than a dozen brands of cowboy boots (including Durango, Frye, Justin, Lucchese, Sendra, and Tony Lama) are displayed on rows upon rows of shelves, along with other Western wear. If you're a newcomer to the boot world, study Allens's Web site before your visit for some basics on proper fit. A second store is located north of Austin in Round Rock. ⊠ *1522 S. Congress Ave., South Austin* ☎ *512/447–1413* ⊠ *1051 S. I–35 (just off I–35 to the north at the Round Rock exit), Round Rock* ☎ *512/310–7600* ⊕ *www.allensboots.com.*

IMPORTS

Mi Casa Gallery. Perhaps Austin's premier outlet for quality and unusual Mexican arts and crafts, Mi Casa goes far beyond your usual Mexican-imports souvenir shop. On-site are contemporary paintings and sculpture, painted furniture, religious art, copperware, ceramics, and much more. It's a great place to shop for gifts for folks back home. ⊠ *1700 S. Congress Ave., South Austin* ☎ *512/707–9797* ⊕ *www.micasa gallery.com.*

Fodor'sChoice **Tesoros Trading Co.** The buyers for this large, independently owned
★ world-market store comb the planet for colorful and unusual examples of folk art. Chinese gongs, Nepalese jewelry, Vietnamese hand-painted bamboo curtains, Turkish textiles, and lots of Mexican items (including *milagros,* postcards, and rather tacky calendars) are just a few of the goodies stashed away in this delightful place. ⊠ *1500 S. Congress Ave., South Austin* ☎ *512/479–8377* ⊕ *www.tesoros.com.*

WEST AUSTIN

The main neighborhood in West Austin is the **West End,** which is centered on West 6th Street, from west of North Lamar Boulevard to West Lynn Street. In a town where thrill-seeking college students compose one-tenth of the population, the West End is a grown-up neighborhood. Long-standing merchants sell art, antiques, and collectibles from shops housed in cottages and storefronts built in the 1930s and 1940s. They've been joined by a rash of newcomers, housed in the multistory buildings springing up on street corners once occupied by car dealerships. Good cafés and restaurants added to the mix make the West End one of Austin's most delightful neighborhoods to stroll through for an hour, or an afternoon.

ANTIQUES

Fortney's Artful Home Furnishings. The aisles and every other inch of Brad Fortney's store (a two-story 1927 brick building that was originally a grocery) are jam-packed with '50s barware, a host of old walking sticks, washbasins, and tons of other intriguing furniture and furnishings. A back room is filled with metal Lone Stars and Western furniture, and the courtyard is home to a host of large bronze sculptures for the garden. ✉1116 W. 6th St., West Austin ☎512/495–6505.

GALLERIES

★ **Artworks.** When you absolutely have to have that $195 Elizabethan-style garnet-topaz-and-crystal letter opener with matching magnifying glass, this is where you can get it. This large, modern space offers contemporary art, custom framing, and art restoration; but it's the large selection of knockout contemporary art glass of the highest quality (including huge pieces of Murano glass) that really sets apart this gallery. Founded in 1985, it also carries exceptional crafts from throughout the world, plus small bronzes and exquisite stemware. ✉1214 W. 6th St., West Austin ☎512/472–1550 ⊕www.artworksaustin.com ⊗Closed Sun.

OUTSIDE AUSTIN

Founded in the 1850s and known in Western lore as the site of an infamous 1878 shootout between Texas Rangers and stagecoach/train robber Sam Bass (Bass lost, and is buried here), the prosperous city of Round Rock, 19 mi north of downtown Austin, is today best known as the home base of computer manufacturer Dell Inc. To Austinites, if Round Rock isn't where they work, it's a place to drive to in order to see baseball (at the Dell Diamond, home of the Round Rock Express; ⇨ *Sports & the Outdoors*), or to do some serious shopping.

IKEA. When this well-known, extremely-big-box Swedish home furnishings retailer opened in November 2006, it sent shivers throughout Austin's retail furniture establishment. The 250,000-square-foot outlet is located about 22 mi north of downtown Austin, just off I–35. Set aside at least two hours to wander through the store (you have to follow certain paths to get from one end to the other). IKEA also has a decent and very low-price café, where you can get one of the best cups of coffee in town for less than a buck. ✉1 IKEA Way, Round Rock ☎512/828–4532 ⊕www.ikea.com.

Round Rock Premium Outlets You should be able to find just about anything you're looking for at this 125-store complex straddling the east side of I–35 northbound. Designer fashions, sportswear, and shoes are particularly strong; also here are leather goods, housewares, children's clothing, and more. ✉ *4401 N. I–35, Round Rock* ☎ *512/863–6688.*

SPORTS & THE OUTDOORS

With its lakes, abundant greenbelts and parks, and miles of hike-and-bike trails—not to mention year-round mild and mostly sunny weather (searingly hot summers and occasional gully washers aside)—Austin and its surroundings are made for outdoor enthusiasts and weekend athletes of all ages and abilities. Whether you live to run marathons, climb rocks, or just stroll through a wildflower garden, Austin's got you covered.

Although the city lacks major-league pro sports teams, fervor for UT's football team, a perennial collegiate top contender, fills the gap to such an extent that many Austinites avoid driving downtown on UT home game days, when thousands of faithful who "bleed orange" are visibly (and audibly) out and about. The team won the national championship in 2005 (the fourth in Longhorns history, and its first since 1970). UT's baseball team also won the collegiate title that year, its sixth overall since 1949. As for other spectator sports, Austin is home to minor-league basketball, hockey, and arena football teams, and nearby Round Rock hosts the Express Triple-A baseball team.

Just outside Austin, opportunities for prime fishing, hunting, and lakeside activities are abundant. Outdoor types might consider outfitting themselves for a Central Texas excursion at Cabela's in Buda, a full-service retail store about 15 mi south of Austin en route to San Antonio.

ANNUAL SPORTING EVENTS

AT&T Austin Marathon & Half-Marathon. Attracting international competition, the mid-February race starts and finishes downtown, winding both south and north of Lady Bird Lake. ☎ *512/478–4265* ⊕ *www. attaustinmarathon.com.*

Clyde Littlefield Texas Relays. One of the top track-and-field events in the United States, the Texas Relays are held in early April at Mike A. Myers Stadium at the University of Texas. The Relays, founded in 1925, attract about 5,000 of the best athletes in Texas (and elsewhere) on the high-school, collegiate, and professional levels. Tickets can be purchased about a month prior to the competition. ☎ *512/471–3333* ⊕ *www.texasboxoffice.com for tickets,* ⊕ *www.texassports.com for general information.*

Red Eye Regatta. Every January 1 since 1976, the Austin Yacht Club starts the year off with this popular sailboat race on Lake Travis (about a half hour from downtown Austin). ☎ *512/266–1336* ⊕ *www.austin yachtclub.net.*

Republic of Texas Biker Rally. Every June, tens of thousands of bikers invade Austin for three days of partying, camping, talking shop, and browsing vendors' wares. Based at the Travis County Expo Center just east of the city, the event includes a huge Friday-evening motorcycle parade from the Expo Center to Congress Avenue with much of Austin looking on, and much partying ensuing (both during and afterward) among bikers and spectators alike on 6th Street. There are also free concerts by local musicians Thursday through Saturday at the Expo Center rally grounds. On its more than 300 acres, the Expo Center provides special lots for RV and tent camping. Other bikers also stay in off-site RV lots and, of course, in hotels. On-site facilities include hot and cold showers, food service, a first-aid station, and a FedEx/UPS drop site. ☎ *512/252–9768* ⊕ *www.rotrally.com.*

☺ **Star of Texas Fair & Rodeo.** Did you come to Texas to see some real cowboy stuff? Austin puts on its hat and boots at this very popular perennial affair. The event, held at the Travis County Expo Center, typically runs from the last day of February through the first half of March. It includes an indoor rodeo, a livestock and horse show, various Texas-style cook-offs, and a carnival. Entertainment ranges from name acts like Willie Nelson, George Jones, and Styx to more than 40 local bands. Proceeds go toward scholarships and youth-education programs. ☎ *512/919–3000 for information, 512/477–6060 for tickets* ⊕ *www.staroftexas.org.*

Statesman Capitol 10K. Held in late March, this is Texas's largest foot-race, with as many participants as meters (10,000). It is sponsored by the *Austin American-Statesman* newspaper ☎ *512/445–3598* ⊕ *www. attaustinmarathon.com.*

PARKS & NATURAL AREAS

Austin has more than 200 parks within the city limits. Amenities in the parks range from playgrounds, swimming pools, and skate parks (the city's first was established at Maybel Davis District Park in South Austin) to artwork and historic sites, such as Umlauf Sculpture Garden at Zilker Park and Treaty Oak Square in northwest Austin.

DOWNTOWN

Austin Nature and Science Center. Adjacent to the Zilker Botanical Gardens *(⇨ Zilker Park, below),* this complex has an 80-acre preserve trail, interactive exhibits in the Discovery Lab that teach about the ecology of the Austin area, and animal exhibits focusing on subjects such as bees and birds of prey. ✉ *301 Nature Center Dr., Downtown* ☎ *512/327–8180* ⊕ *www.ci.austin.tx.us/ansc* ✉ *Suggested donation of $2 per adult and $1 per child* ☉ *Mon.–Sat. 9–5, Sun. noon–5.*

NORTH AUSTIN

Mt. Bonnell. Rising to a height of 785 feet, Mt. Bonnell offers the best views of Austin. Stop by during the day for a glimpse of the sweeping panorama of rolling hills, the Colorado River and the 360 Bridge, and the downtown skyline in the distance. It's an easy climb up from a parking area near the road (more of a diversion than a serious hike); you'll find students, lovers, families, picnickers and just plain old tourists here. ⊠*Mount Bonnell Rd. off E. 35th St., North Austin* ☎*817/265–7721 or 800/433–5374* ☜*Free* ☉*Daily dawn–dusk.*

WEST AUSTIN/ZILKER PARK

☺ **Zilker Park.** The former site of temporary Franciscan missions in 1730 and a former American Indian gathering place is now Austin's everyday backyard park. The 351-acre site along the shores of Lady Bird Lake includes Barton Springs Pool (⇨*Swimming, below*), numerous gardens, a meditation trail, and a Swedish log cabin dating from the 1840s. Canoe rentals are available for the hour or day (⊕*www.zilker*

boats.com). In March the park hosts a kite festival (2008 saw the 80th edition). During spring months, concerts are held in the park's Beverly S. Sheffield Zilker Hillside Theater, a natural outdoor amphitheater beneath a grove of century-old pecan trees; in July and August, musicals and plays take over. Umlauf Sculpture Garden & Museum, at the park's southern end, displays 130 or more works by sculptor and former UT art professor Charles Umlauf. Art workshops for both kids and adults are occasionally offered. ⊠*2201 Barton Springs Rd., West Austin* ☎*512/974–6700 Parks Dept., 512/477–5335 theater, 512/445–5582 museum* ⊕*www.ci.austin.tx.us/zilker* ☜*Main park f, museum $3.50, parking $3 per vehicle* ☉*Park: daily dawn–dusk. Museum: Wed.–Fri. 10–4:30, weekends 1–4:30.*

WEST LAKE

Barton Creek Greenbelt. This park follows the contour of Barton Creek and the canyon it created west along a 7.9-mi area from Zilker Park to west of Loop 360. It has a trail for hiking and biking, plus swimming holes when the creek is full (very rain-dependent, it's usually in spring and fall). ⊠*Access points: Zilker Park, Loop 360, Twin Falls, and Scottish Woods Trail Falls (near the intersection of MoPac and Loop 360), and Scottish Woods Trail (at the trail's northern border off Loop 360)* ☎*512/499–6700 or 512/472–1267* ☜*Free* ☉*Daily 5 AM–10 PM.*

☺ **Wild Basin Wilderness Preserve.** Stunning contrasting views of the Hill
★ Country and the Austin skyline make it worth the trip to this area near the 360 Bridge. You can wander along 227 acres of walking trails (there are 10 different ones); guided tours are offered on weekends. The cool folks at Wild Basin offer numerous outdoor-oriented classes, nighttime stargazing sessions, even concerts by well-known touring

2

musicians. ⌧*805 N. Capitol of Texas Hwy., West Lake* ☎*512/327–7622* ⊕*www.wildbasin.org* ⌧*$3 suggested donation, $4 guided hikes (weekends and by reservation only)* ⊗*Park: daily dawn–dusk; office: daily 9–4; gift shop: Tues.–Sun. 9–4.*

SOUTH AUSTIN

Lady Bird Johnson Wildflower Center. This 43-acre complex, founded in 1982 by Lady Bird Johnson and actress Helen Hayes, has extensive plantings of native Texas wildflowers that bloom year-round (although spring is an especially attractive time). The grounds include a visitor center, nature trail, observation tower, elaborate stone terraces, and flower-filled meadows. ⌧*4801 LaCrosse, South Austin Ave.* ☎*512/292–4100* ⊕*www.wildflower.org* ⌧*$7* ⊗*Tues.–Sun. 9–5:30.*

OUTSIDE AUSTIN

McKinney Falls State Park. This 744-acre state park is 13 mi southeast of downtown Austin. Per the name, the park has two waterfalls (visitors should exercise extreme caution near the water, as people have drowned here). A 4.5-mi nature trail is used for hiking and biking. Other popular activities in the park are fishing, picnicking, camping, and wildlife-viewing (including bird-watching and sightings of white-tailed deer, raccoons, squirrels, and armadillos). ⌧*5808 McKinney Falls Pkwy., off U.S. 183* ☎*512/243–1643* ⊕*www.tpwd.state.tx.us/spdest/findadest/parks/mckinney_falls* ⌧*$2* ⊗*Daily dawn–dusk.*

PARTICIPANT SPORTS

BICYCLING

As you might expect, Lance Armstrong's home base is a great bicycling town. The scenic back roads offer gently rolling hills and tempting diversions—from tucked-away waterfalls to country antiques emporia to barbecue joints. **Loop 360** provides a grueling workout, while the **hike-and-bike trail** around Lady Bird Lake is more leisurely. And the **Lance Armstrong Bikeway**, opening in 2008, runs east-to-west on a dedicated route through downtown. The path uses a combination of off-street concrete trails, on-street striped bike lanes, and on-street signed bike routes.

The Veloway. This 3.1-mi paved asphalt loop winding through Slaughter Creek Metropolitan Park is reserved exclusively for bicyclists and rollerbladers. Riders always travel in a one-way clockwise direction. It's off the beaten path in far southwest Austin, not far from the Lady Bird Johnson Wildflower Center. There are no facilities except for a water fountain that sometimes doesn't work. ⌧*4103 Slaughter La., South Austin* ☎*512/974–6700* ⊕*www.veloway.com.*

OUTFITTER

Bicycle Sport Shop (⌧*517 S. Lamar* ☎*512/477–3472* ⌧*10947 Research Blvd., Northwest Austin* ☎*512/345–7460* ⊕*www.bicyclesportshop.com*) rents bikes and helmets daily, year-round.

BOATING

⇨*Zilker Park under Parks & Natural Areas.*

Lance Armstrong: His Uphill Battles

Once upon a time, in the world of cycling, Lance Armstrong was always near the top, but could never quite get there—especially when it came to the Tour de France, the sport's premier event. And then he got cancer. The rest is history: seven straight yellow jerseys from the Tour, the most ever. Now retired from the cycling world, he barnstorms the planet on behalf of cancer research. The yellow "LIVESTRONG" bands that his foundation sold adorn celebrity wrists and started a cottage industry of silicone bracelets. But more than anything, Armstrong used sheer will and his bicycle to give hope to millions of people with cancer. His foundation has raised more than $150 million, which to Armstrong might mean even more than his seven Tour de France victories.

—Lisa Miller

DOWNTOWN & CAPITOL AREA

Capital Cruises. From March through October, this downtown-based company offers nightly bat-watching cruises from an electric paddle-wheel boat, along with sightseeing, dinner, and lunch cruises on Lady Bird Lake. Cruise prices vary, but start at $8. Charters are available. The company also rents canoes, pedal boats, and kayaks beginning at $10 an hour, and Duffy electric launches (seating up to 10) beginning at $45 an hour. ⊠*208 Barton Springs Rd., Downtown & Capitol Area* ☎*512/480–9264* ⊕*www.capitalcruises.com.*

Lone Star Riverboat. This double-decker paddlewheel riverboat sails every evening for hour-long bat-watching cruises March through October, and every weekend for 1½-hour sightseeing cruises. Tours are $8 or $9. ⊠*Docked on the south shore of Lady Bird Lake between the Hyatt hotel and S. 1st St. Bridge, Downtown & Capitol Area* ☎*512/327-1388* ⊕*www.lonestarriverboat.com.*

WEST AUSTIN

Daybreak Boat Rentals & Golf Park. On Lake Travis, Daybreak rents pontoons, ski boats, and waverunners, plus a party boat. Hourly prices begin at $60 for pontoons, $70 for ski boats, and $135 for a party boat (including captain). Ask about discounts for longer rentals. ⊠*5171 Hi-Line, West Austin* ☎*512/266–2176* ⊕*www.daybreakboatrentals.com.*

LAKE TRAVIS

Lakeway Marina. Adjacent to the Lakeway Resort and Spa (⇨ *Where to Stay*), this marina on Lake Travis rents ski boats, pontoon boats, and waverunners. Hourly rates begin at $75 for pontoon boats and waverunners, $80 for ski boats; ask about discounts for longer rentals. Also available are fishing guides, beginning at $225 for two people for four hours. The marina is open daily. ⊠*103A Lakeway Dr., West Austin, Lake Travis* ☎*512/261–7511* ⊕*www.lwmarina.biz.*

BATTY AUSTIN

The world's largest urban bat colony—750,000 Mexican free-tailed bats—hangs out beneath Austin's Congress Avenue Bridge from April through October. Once considered a nuisance, they're now prized as a tourist attraction and municipal symbol. Visitors and locals alike flock downtown to claim a spot before dusk and watch the tiny (and rather smelly) winged critters make their dramatic appearance against the setting sun.

The best viewing spots are from the hike-and-bike trail by the bridge, or from the patio of Shoreline Grill, adjacent to the Four Seasons hotel (⇨ Where to Eat). If you're staying lakeside at the Four Seasons or Radisson hotel (⇨ Where to Stay), there are excellent vantage points from some rooms and public spaces, as well as from T.G.I. Friday's at the Radisson. Watching the bats from the lake aboard a paddle-wheel cruise ship (⇨ Boating) is a classy way to go. For a real budget option, there are the pedestrian walkways on both sides of the bridge itself, but arrive early (as much as an hour ahead) in peak season, as it gets crowded; many bring a light folding chair and refreshments and settle in for the duration.

GOLF

WEST AUSTIN

Barton Creek Resort & Spa. This resort is associated with four private courses, including two of the top-ranked courses in Texas, Fazio Foothills and Fazio Canyons. Unfortunately, you either have to be a member or a hotel guest (⇨ Where to Stay) to play here. Greens fees vary widely by season, day of the week, and time of day, but for resort guests the Fazio Canyons and Fazio Foothills courses (both more than 7,100 yards) run from $80 (twilight) to $250 per person, including a forecaddie (but not gratuity). The 18-hole, par-71 Crenshaw Cliffside course runs from $60 to $180 (forecaddie not required) and the 18-hole, par-71 Palmer Lakeside course from $45 to $155 (forecaddie not required). Various golf packages are also available throughout the year; check the Web site for details. ⊠8212 Barton Club Dr., West Austin ☎512/329–4000 or 800/336–6158 ⊕www.bartoncreek.com/golf.

Lions Municipal Golf Course. The likes of Ben Crenshaw, Tom Kite, and Ben Hogan are among those who have played at this affordable 6,001-yard, par-71 public course in West Austin. It was originally built by the Lions Club in 1928 and taken over by the city six years later. It is open daily, dawn to dusk. Greens fees run $7–$20. Cart fees are $22. ⊠2901 Enfield Rd., West Austin ☎512/477–6963 ⊕www.ci.austin.tx.us/parks/lions.htm.

EAST AUSTIN

Bluebonnet Hill Golf Club. The 18-hole, par-72 course here emphasizes speedy play at reasonable rates. Instruction is offered. Greens fees are $10–$28 walking, $17–$37 with cart, plus tax. It's open daily, dawn to dusk. ⊠9100 Decker La., East Austin ☎512/272–4228 ⊕www.bluebonnethillgolf.com.

NORTHEAST AUSTIN

Harvey Penick Golf Campus. Named for a legendary local golf instructor, Harvey Penick opened in 2005 in Northeast Austin as a "First Tee" course for the specific purpose of teaching golf to young people (though golfers of all ages and abilities can play). The 112-acre, 9-hole, par-30, PGA Tour–designed course is next door to the East Communities YMCA. Lessons are

GOLF LINGO

A **forecaddie** (also spelled forecaddy) makes suggestions on shots, and help keep the game from delays by running ahead of a golfing foursome to perform such tasks as finding stray balls and raking traps. A forecaddie does not carry any of the players' clubs.

offered. There's also a driving range and short course. Greens fees are $12 for 9 holes, $18 for 18 holes. Youth pay less. Cart fees are $8.75 for 9 holes, and $13.50 for 18 holes. It's open daily 7–7. ⊠*5501 Ed Bluestein Blvd., Northeast Austin* ☎*512/926–1100.*

HORSEBACK RIDING

NORTHWEST AUSTIN

Cornerstone Farm. This 40-acre farm, in business since 1993, offers lessons, leasing, sales, and training of horses. All ages and abilities are accepted. ⊠*6734 Spicewood Springs Rd., Northwest Austin* ☎*512/349–7433* ⊙*Daily 8–8.*

SOUTH AUSTIN

Austin Equestrian Center. A full-service horseback-riding center, the Equestrian Center provides boarding, leasing, lessons, and guided group trail rides through the Onion Creek greenbelt. ⊠*8601 Bluff Springs Rd., South Austin* ☎*512/233–6700* ⊕*www.austinequestriancenter.com* ⊙*Daily 9–8; call for appointment.*

Bear Creek Stables These stables 13 mi south of downtown Austin offer riding lessons in both Western and English style, along with boarding and children's camps. ⊠*13017 Bob Johnson Rd., Manchaca* ☎*512/282–0250* ⊕*www.bearcreekstables.com* ⊙*Daily 9–5; call for appointment.*

ROCK CLIMBING

Austin Rock Gym. Serious about climbing? With two locations, Austin Rock Gym offers indoor rock climbing for all ages, along with outdoor classes and private lessons. ⊠*4401 Freidrich La., South Austin* ☎*512/416–9299* ⊠*$13 day pass (plus $25 belay safety course required for first-time climbers)* ⊙*Mon.–Thurs. 3–10, Fri. noon–10, Sat. 10–10, Sun. 10–7* ⊠*8300 N. Lamar, Suite B102, Northwest Austin* ☎*512/416–9299* ⊙*Weekdays noon–10, Sat. 10–10, Sun. 10–7* ⊕*www.austinrockgym.com.*

Austin's Park. Besides a nearly 25-foot-tall indoor rock-climbing wall, this amusement center 15 mi north of downtown Austin features laser tag, go-carts, miniature golf, bumper boats, batting cages, a video arcade, and other primo diversions for the under-15 set. Admission includes an all-you-can-eat buffet. Children 40–57 inches tall pay $15.95; children under 40 inches are admitted free. ⊠*16231 N. I–35,*

Pflugerville ☎*512/670–9600* ⊕*www.austinspark.com* ✉*$21.95 (but only $14.95 on Tues.; some weekend specials also available)* ☉ *Weekdays 3–10, weekends 11–11.*

SPELUNKING

☾ **Inner Space Cavern.** This cavern 24 mi north of Austin was discovered in 1963 and opened to the public three years later. Visitors access the entrance via cable car and can choose from two trails, one that is 0.75 mi and another that's 1.2 mi. Tours vary in length (and price), from just a little over an hour to nearly four hours. The temperature is a year-round 72°. The three- to four-hour tour is for ages 13 and older only. On Saturday, reservations are required and groups can be no larger than four. ■ TIP→ Sometimes there are $1 coupons on the Web site. ⊠*4200 S. I–35, Georgetown* ☎*512/931–2283* ⊕*www.innerspace. com* ✉*$15–$100 depending on tour* ☉ *Mid-May–early Sept., daily 9–6; early Sept.–mid-May, weekdays 9–4, weekends 10–5.*

SWIMMING

☾ **Barton Springs Pool.** When those summer days get hotter than a potter's
★ furnace, dip into Zilker Park's 300-yard-long, spring-fed swimming pool, a favorite with locals. The clear springs produce from 12 million to 90 million gallons in any 24-hour period, with the water always a cool 66° to 70°. ⊠*2201 Barton Springs Rd., Zilker Park, West Austin* ☎*512/476–9044* ⊕*www.ci.austin.tx.us/parks/bartonsprings.htm* ✉*Free Nov.–Mar., $3 rest of yr* ☉ *Hrs vary. Closed 3 wks in Feb. and Mar. for spring cleaning.*

☾ **Deep Eddy Pool.** The oldest swimming pool in Texas (1916), this former
★ natural swimming hole near the Colorado River was the centerpiece of an early-20th-century resort and was purchased and restored by the Works Progress Administration in the mid-'30s. In recent years, the Friends of Deep Eddy, a volunteer community group, led a successful effort to fully restore the long-closed 1936 bathhouse, which reopened in June 2007. ⊠*401 Deep Eddy Dr., West Austin* ☎*512/472–8546* ⊕*www.deepeddy.org* ✉*Free* ☉ *Hrs vary.*

SPECTATOR SPORTS

BASEBALL

Round Rock Express. Next to UT football, Austin's most popular spectator sport may be the Round Rock Express baseball team, an AAA affiliate of the Houston Astros. The Express (owned by a group led by Hall of Fame pitcher Nolan Ryan) began in 2000 as an AA team, and moved up to AAA in 2005. It plays 72 home games from April through September at the Dell Diamond, an extremely pleasant place to pass a few hours, no matter who's winning. The open-air stadium seats about 8,600 with room for more in an outfield grass berm area. No ticket costs more than $12 (as of 2008), and it's hard to find a bad seat in this very fan-friendly (and family-friendly) ballpark. ⊠*3400 E. Palm Valley Blvd., Round Rock* ☎*512/255–2255* ⊕*www.round rockexpress.com.*

BASKETBALL

The Austin Toros. Formerly the Columbus (Georgia) Riverdragons, the Toros, a team in the NBA's Development League, or "D-League," was rebranded when it moved to Austin in 2005. Affiliated with (and owned by) the San Antonio Spurs, the Toros play home games November through April at the Austin Convention Center. ✉*7800 Shoal Creek Blvd., Suite 115W, Downtown & Capitol Area* ☎*512/236–8333* ⊕*www.nba.com/dleague/austin.*

FOOTBALL

The Austin Wranglers. This arena football expansion team began play in 2004, and moved down from the AFL to af2 (the minor leagues) beginning in the 2008 season. The team plays from April to July. Home games are at UT's Frank Erwin Center. ✉*1701 Red River St., University of Texas* ☎*512/339–3939* ⊕*www.austinwranglers.com.*

HOCKEY

The Austin Ice Bats. This minor-league hockey team plays at the Chaparral Ice Arena (near Pflugerville) from October through March. The team logo is a very cool visual of a shrieking, flying bat wielding a hockey stick; buy a jersey and wow 'em back home. ✉*14200 N. IH–35, Pflugerville* ☎*512/927–7825* ⊕*www.icebats.com.*

ARTS & ENTERTAINMENT

Even when Austin was a backwater burg, it enjoyed a modicum of culture thanks to the University of Texas. The city's current culture vultures are still indebted to the construction-crazed university for its state-of-the-art concert halls like the Bass, which can accommodate grand symphonic, operatic, and theatrical performances. But in a town as creatively charged as Austin, the venues are virtually limitless, from hillsides in parks to the pavement of the Congress Avenue Bridge and from dark, smoky clubs to Victorian Gothic cathedrals.

Numerous traveling and homegrown bands play nightly in the city's music venues, many of which are clustered around downtown's 6th Street, between Red River Street and Congress Avenue. Although not as famous as Bourbon Street in New Orleans, 6th Street has an entertaining mix of comedy clubs, blues bars, electronica, and dance clubs. It's also the site of two "Old Pecan Street" outdoor fairs, held in May and September, with live bands, food vendors, and craftspeople.

College students are a large presence on 6th, but the Warehouse District around 4th Street and the newer 2nd Street District (which runs between San Antonio Street and Congress Avenue for two blocks north of the river) cater to a more-mature crowd looking for good food and great drinks. South Congress also has a lively scene, especially on the first Thursday of each month, when vendors set up booths with art, jewelry, and a variety of other creations all along the street. The shops stay open late, and bands perform live along the streets. (Warning: parking during "First Thursdays" is a challenge. Expect to park many blocks back and walk.)

Austin's cultural scene is getting a face-lift with the opening of three major arts-related venues. The $14.7-million renovation of the Bass Concert Hall at the University of Texas Performing Arts Center (UT PAC) is set to be completed by late 2008; it will feature a five-story atrium; new seating, flooring, and lighting; better acoustics; and a restaurant. The first phase of the Mexican-American Cultural Center (MACC), on Lady Bird Lake at River Street, opened in September 2007; the MACC will eventually offer 126,000 square feet for exhibits, performances, private events, and classes. And the Joe R. and Teresa Lozano Long Center for the Performing Arts, also on Lady Bird Lake, opened in March 2008 as part of a 54-acre cultural park.

DID YOU KNOW? The Austin City Limits Festival was inspired by the hit PBS show "Austin City Limits," a homegrown Public Television show that has run for more than 30 years and is known as the longest-running concert music program in the country. Taped in a small studio at KLRU, the Austin PBS affiliate on UT Campus, this acclaimed show hosts a wide range of country, rock, blues, jazz, and folk musicians. Legends Stevie Ray Vaughan, Johnny Cash, and Ray Charles once graced this tiny stage as did Buena Vista Social Club, Tracy Chapman, and Lyle Lovett.

To find out who's playing where, pick up the *Austin Chronicle* (a free alternative weekly) or "XLent," a Thursday supplement to the *Austin American Statesman.* Most of the larger venues in Austin sell tickets through **Front Gate Tickets** (☎*512/389–0315* ⊕*www.fronttickets.com*). But **AusTix** (☎*512/474–8497* ⊕*www.austix.com*) is a good resource for theater as well as smaller dance and music performances. Meanwhile, **GetTix** (☎*866/443–8849* ⊕*www.gettix.net*) is a smaller purveyor of advance tickets in Austin, but sells for popular venues such as La Zona Rosa, Austin Music Hall, and Emo's.

PERFORMING ARTS

DANCE & THEATER

The Long Center for the Performing Arts. The opera scene is alive and well in Austin with the help of this expansive venue along the shores of Lady Bird Lake. With much anticipation from the city of Austin, the Joe R. and Teresa Lozano Long Center opened its doors in the spring of 2008, playing host to a wide variety of performing arts groups. It also serves as the permanent home to: **Austin Symphony Orchestra** (☎*512/476–6064* ⊕*www.austinsymphony.org*); **Austin Lyric Opera** (☎*512/472–5927* ⊕*www.austinlyricopera.org*), Austin's premiere opera company putting on three productions a year for the past 20 years; and **Ballet Austin** (☎*512/476–2163* ⊕*www.balletaustin.org*). The Long Center for the Performing Arts also houses a wing for community arts education programs. ⊠*701 W. Riverside Dr., South Austin* ☎*512/482–0800* ⊕*www.thelongcenter.org.*

Paramount Theatre. A restored downtown vaudeville house and movie palace, this gorgeous 1915 theater presents musicals and plays by touring

Festivals with a Beat

In the self-proclaimed Live Music Capital of the world, it's needless to say the two largest festivals in town are all about music.

SEPTEMBER

Austin City Limits Music Festival. Austinites love any excuse to party outside, especially when music is involved. This unofficial farewell-to-summer shindig takes over Zilker Park for three days in late September. Fans come to hear 130 international, national, and local bands on eight stages. Performers have included the likes of Bob Dylan, Coldplay, Tom Petty, Bjork, the White Stripes, Sheryl Crow, Lucinda Williams, Steve Earle, and the Indigo Girls. ✉ *2100 Barton Springs Rd., West Austin/Zilker Park* ☎ *512/389–0315* ⊕ *www.aclfestival. com* ✎ *$50–$120.*

MARCH

South by Southwest. The grand-daddy of all music fests arrives in early spring. Usually shortened to SXSW, this event's festivals and conferences combine to form a huge music, film, and interactive extravaganza. In addition to all the fans, SXSW brings a fleet of hundreds of hopeful musicians, producers, and record-

Rock, country, folk, hip-hop, jazz, fusion... whatever your preferred music genre, you'll find it in Austin.

label execs to Austin to perform and network. It's such a take-over-the-city event that many Austin families evacuate town to some far-off spring break destination. Hotel rooms are scarce, restaurants and bars are packed, and everything from SXSW VIPs to plain, music-loving plebeians mix and mingle in expectation of finding "the next big thing." ■ TIP → **First-time participants should know that it pays to be organized in terms of the bands you want to see since SXSW happens all over town.** ✉ *Throughout Austin* ☎ *512/467–7979* ⊕ *www.sxsw.com* ✎ *$130–$175.*

theater companies and hosts concerts by well-known jazz, folk, and rock artists, along with the occasional stand-up comedian. ✉ *713 Congress Ave., Downtown & Capitol Area* ☎ *512/472–5470* ⊕ *www.austin theatre.org.*

Zachary Scott Theatre. Local theater thrives at this center named for an Austin native who was successful in 1930s Hollywood. ✉ *1510 Toomey Rd., South Austin* ☎ *512/476–0541* ⊕ *www.zachscott.com.*

Zilker Theatre Productions. Bring a blanket and picnic basket and enjoy a Broadway-inspired musical under the warm Texas sky. The summer-only shows are pay-as-you-wish admission. ✉ *2201 Barton Springs Rd., West Austin/Zilker Park* ☎ *512/479–9491* ⊕ *www.zilker.org.*

FILM

Alamo Drafthouse. Only in Austin will you find the original concept for this theater experience, where dinner, a movie, and a bucket of beer all happen in one place. At one of the many locations throughout town, moviegoers can order burgers, pizza, and the Drafthouse's famous fried pickles while sitting down to enjoy box-office hits, classics, or indie films. Be warned: you may never want to watch a movie any other way. Open year-round. ✉️ *320 E. 6th St., Downtown* ☎️ *512/476–1320* 🌐 *www.drafthouse.com.*

Dobie Theatre. When you're searching for the latest in indie films, the Dobie never fails to accommodate. Located on the artsy UT campus, the small theaters are crammed with students and film fanatics here for the latest in artistic film. ✉️ *2025 Guadalupe St., University of Texas* ☎️ *512/472–FILM (3456)* 🌐 *www.landmarktheatres.com/market/austin/dobietheatre.htm.*

Paramount Theatre. In summer, movie lovers escape the heat at this historic theater for the Summer Classic Film Series, featuring time-honored films from *Gone with the Wind* to *The Wizard of Oz.* ✉️ *713 Congress Ave.,Downtown* ☎️ *512/472–5470* 🌐 *www.austintheatre.org.*

MUSIC VENUES

Austin Music Hall. Having recently reopened from a modernizing face-lift in late 2007, the Austin Music Hall offers marquee bands a midsize venue to avoid arena staging yet still pack in a lively Austin crowd. Some of the first performers to grace the new stage included Van Morrison, Marilyn Manson, and the Cure. ✉️ *208 Nueces, Downtown & Capitol Area* ☎️ *512/263–4146* 🌐 *www.austinmusichall.com.*

The Backyard. On the western outskirts of town, the Austin Music Hall's sister venue, open from March through October, features an outdoor stage beneath a grove of oak trees. Willie Nelson kicks off the season each year, and a wide variety of performers from Lyle Lovett and David Gray to the String Cheese Incident and Sheryl Crow keeps the crowds coming. Just on the other side of the Backyard, the smaller adjoining venue, the **The Glenn** (☎️ *512/263–4146* 🌐 *www.theglennaustin.net*), has soft grass and hillside seating for enjoying more mellow acoustic and singer-songwriter acts. ✉️ *13101 Hwy. 71W, West Austin/Zilker Park* ☎️ *512/263–4146* 🌐 *www.thebackyard.net.*

Frank Erwin Center. When music events call for a big arena setting, it's held here, the largest venue in Austin. Also home to the University of Texas's Longhorn ladies' and men's basketball teams, the venue has played host to the likes of Eric Clapton, U2, the Dixie Chicks, and Hannah Montana. ✉️ *1701 Red River, University of Texas* ☎️ *512/471-7744* 🌐 *www.uterwincenter.com.*

La Zona Rosa. Just a block or two from the Austin Music Hall, this music venue hosts a rather eclectic mix of bands from the international rock acts Gomez and Arcade Fire to the Rastafarian sounds of the Wailers. ✉️ *612 W. 4th St., Downtown & Capitol Area* ☎️ *512/263–4146* 🌐 *www.lazonarosa.com.*

Artist Spotlight: Daryl Howard

Of all the cities in Texas, Austin is probably most known for its artistic edge. It's got the music-nightlife hotbed of 6th Street, the left-leaning University of Texas, and the city motto, "Keep Austin Weird"—all things that draw some artistic souls. But artist Daryl Howard isn't here (at least not primarily) for any of those urban enticements. Howard thrives in South Austin's rural setting, where she lives and works on a 50-acre ranch, complete with longhorns in the pasture and a creek running along the property.

Daryl Howard with her *One Single Tree Is Enough . . . to Keep Next to My Heart* woodblock print, created in 2007.

"This is where I get my energy," she says. "This is what feeds my soul."

The 59-year-old artist works partly in wood-block prints, which she learned how to create in Tokyo, using handmade brushes, watercolors, and damp mulberry paper so the colors bleed into the fibers of the paper to produce an image with real depth. She carves a separate piece of wood for each color in the print and then prints from light to dark. Each wood-block print is part of a limited-edition using the same blocks; but at the same time, each print is unique, because Howard accents each one by painting gold—real gold—onto it. "It adds an element of change to the piece," she says.

The other portion of her time is spent on collages, made from mixed media such as kimono fabric, gold, rubies, and other metals. A sort of sophisticated cut-and-paste procedure, it allows her to use a different part of her brain: unlike the block prints, which are carefully planned out, the collages are free form. "It just happens as I do it. I never have sketches," she says.

Her name carries weight with art collectors across the country, and her work can be seen in private collections (such as the San Antonio Marriott Hotel on the River Walk and the Detroit Westin Renaissance Hotel) and at occasional special museum exhibitions. Locally, she participates each December in Austin's Armadillo Christmas Bazaar. At one time she was in 43 galleries, but now, in general, her clients come to her.

She travels around the world, but where she most loves spending her time is at her ranch, where she lives with her lawyer husband, Owen. "I live in heaven," she says. "I live in Austin."

Howard's studio is open by appointment only (call ☎ *512/288–4744*). For more information on Howard, including samples of her work, see ⊕ *www. darylhoward.com.*

—Debbie Harmsen

Saxon Pub. If you can get past this pub's low ceilings, sticky beer-stained floors, and dark, small, and crowded room, then you'll find a phenomenal music experience. Bands play every night; usually from the local rock and blues scene. This is a small Austin classic with Shiner Bock on tap and a well-worn pool table that draws regulars from all over the city. ✉*1320 S. Lamar, South Austin* ☎*512/448-2552* ⊕*www.thesaxonpub.com.*

> **SAVE ON ENTERTAINMENT**
>
> If you'll be in Austin awhile, consider investing in the Austin edition of the Entertainment coupon book (⊕ *www.entertainment.com*). The about-$25 booklet is filled with discounts for many popular visitor attractions, amusement parks, sports teams, restaurants, car-rental companies, and more.

University of Texas Performing Arts Center. There's no end to the types of performances you can catch at this performing arts center that's home to six venues throughout the university campus: Bass Concert Hall, Hogg Memorial Auditorium, Bates Recital Hall, B. Iden Payne Theatre, McCollough Theatre, and Oscar B. Brockett Theatre. **UTPAC** hosts everything from chamber orchestras to alternative rock bands, African dance, and Russian ballet. ✉*2350 Robert Deadman, University of Texas* ☎*512/471-7539* ⊕*www.utpac.org.*

NIGHTLIFE

To say Austin's night scene is dominated by live music is an understatement. In fact, it's hard to fully distinguish bar from club from live-music venue as they tend to all blend together. Bands will play anywhere people will listen, and that's pretty much everywhere. It's one of the reasons the club scene in Austin is fairly small in comparison to music venues and bars. Depending on where you are in town, activity tends to bubble up in two waves: the social and professional, happy-hour faction; and the music-loving nightlife crowd. If visiting Austin for a short time, check out some of the classic venues such as Antone's, the Continental Club, and Stubb's.

The swank bar above Lamberts fancy barbecue restaurant also features some amazing jazz and blues performers. And be sure to grab a cold brew at Johnny Cash–inspired Mean-Eyed Cat or a martini at the Hollywood-esque Belmont, and sample the delectable cheese plate with a glass of wine on the patio of the Hotel San Jose.

BARS

WAREHOUSE DISTRICT

With its wide, windswept avenues and unfinished-looking buildings—offering a good contrast to the contained and somewhat urban-yuppie 2nd Street District—Austin's Warehouse District really is filled with brick-walled converted warehouses (and seemingly endless construction). It's where Austin wets its whistle at myriad bars, lounges, and slick restaurants, then gets down at a hopping nightclub.

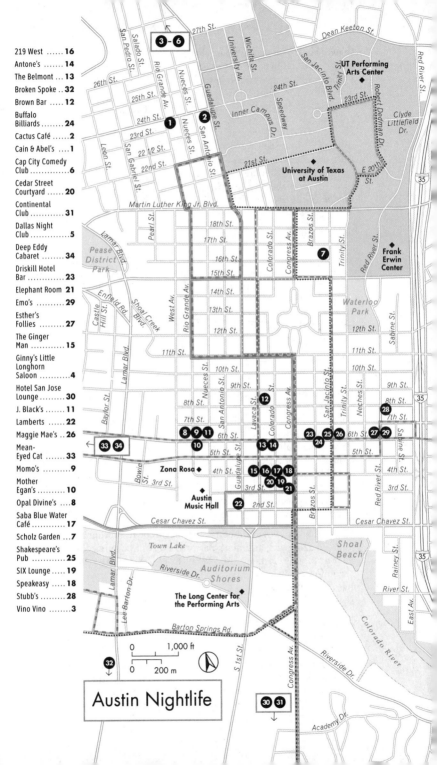

Austin Nightlife

★ **Ginger Man.** For one of Austin's larger selections of beers on tap, brew connoisseurs head to this watering hole, where the long bar serves up more than 70 draft beer varieties and almost double the number of bottled beers from all over the world. ✉ *304 W. 4th St., Downtown & Capitol Area* ☎ *512/473–8801* ⊕ *www.austin.gingermanpub.com.*

Saba Blue Water Café. The blue glowing fountain along the back wall draws the chic thirtysomethings to this Caribbean-island-meets-contemporary-martini-bar like moths to a flame. Stop in for happy hour with specials featuring apple-ginger martinis, lemongrass margaritas, and blue Caraçao Saba coladas, and a flavorful menu of small plates including crunchy plantain-crusted shrimp and creamy spinach con queso. ✉ *208 W. 4th St., Downtown & Capitol Area* ☎ *512/478–7222* ⊕ *www.sabacafe.com.*

★ **SIX Lounge.** Want to take in the see-and-be-seen crowd? Though there are a few hot spots around town, the SIX Lounge certainly provides an attractive glam scene. The warm lighting, exposed brick walls, and hardwood accents give this place a sexy urban-chic appeal, and the rooftop lounge provides amazing views of downtown and the Warehouse District at night. ✉ *117 W. 4th St., Downtown & Capitol Area* ☎ *512/472–6662* ⊕ *www.sixlounge.com.*

219 West. The dark and sophisticated lounge here remains cool and mellow in the early evening, when downtown professionals stop in for a post-work drink. But things heat up with a glitzy, albeit fairly young, crowd when the DJ arrives with bass-thumping music later in the night. ✉ *219 W. 4th St., Downtown & Capitol Area* ☎ *512/474–2194* ⊕ *www.219west.com.*

6TH STREET

Buffalo Billiards. Come here if you're looking for the perfect place to sink an eight ball in the corner pocket. With a floor full of pool tables, the only thing you'll have to worry about is waiting for one to open up. But the foosball and air hockey tables can keep you occupied while you sip a cold brew. ✉ *201 E. 6th St., Downtown & Capitol Area* ☎ *512/479–7665* ⊕ *www.buffalobilliards.com/austin.*

Maggie Mae's. This is one of 6th Street's longest-running bars, which says a lot, considering the turnover is pretty high in this district. Maggie Mae's is touristy and features mainly cover bands; you'll usually find a good crowd and a great beer selection. ✉ *323 E. 6th St., Downtown & Capitol Area* ☎ *512/478–1997* ⊕ *www.maggiemaesaustin.com.*

Shakespeare's Pub. Boasting the pomp of the Warehouse District without the circumstance, is a popular spot for Austin regulars looking for a relaxed spot to catch up with friends. Excellent beer selection and friendly waitstaff are an added bonus. But be ready for a dramatic change in atmosphere after 10 PM—less-laid-back local patrons, more-rambunctious late-night cruisers. ✉ *314 E. 6th St., Downtown & Capitol Area* ☎ *512/472–1666.*

WEST 6TH STREET

J. Black's. The dark-leather couches and chairs arranged in small group-ings throughout the sleek lounge make for an old Vegas "Rat Pack" environment. It's the type of place you'd expect to find Dean Martin curled up with a cigar in the corner. A classy cocktail menu and upscale small-plate menu make for a swanky place to intimately share a few drinks with friends. ✉ *600 W. 6th St., Downtown & Capitol Area* ☎ *512/477–8550.*

For a bit of good Irish craic with a local feel, **Mother Egan's** fits the bill with Irish and British beers on tap, old-style pub booths, and a clas-sic menu of authentic pub grub. Try the fried Snickers bar—it's a little piece of heaven. This family-owned pub plays host to Tuesday-night trivia quizzes and even offers prizes for the sharpest tools in the shed. ✉ *715 W. 6th St., Downtown & Capitol Area, Austin* ☎ *512/477–3308* ⊕ *www.motheregansirishpub.com.*

Opal Divine's. People love this bar for its laid-back atmosphere, wide-open patios, extensive beer selection, and the crispy chicken-tender basket. The dog-friendly environment makes it a nice place to bring your canine companions and enjoy weekend live music. ✉ *700 W. 6th St., Down-town & Capitol Area* ☎ *512/477–3308* ⊕ *www.opaldivines.com.*

AROUND AUSTIN

Brown Bar. When the legislature is in session, this is where the lawmak-ers, Capitol staff, and lobbyists stop in for a quick break. Housed in the historic Brown Building, the small, yet cool environment features a Turkish marble bar that glows a deep amber from lighting beneath it. ✉ *201 W. 8th St., Downtown & Capitol Area* ☎ *512/480–8330* ⊕ *www.thebrownbar.com.*

Cain & Able's. College students looking for the campus experience need to head to where you're likely to find brothers or sisters from the UT chapter of your fraternity or sorority. Walking distance from most anything on campus, this popular beer joint makes a safe option for non-designated drivers. ✉ *2313 Rio Grande St., University of Texas* ☎ *512/476–3201.*

Deep Eddy Cabaret. Gone are the smoke-filled rooms of Austin clubs and bars. If you haven't noticed, there's a smoking ban in this town and it couldn't have happened to a nicer place. A favorite dive for the Lady Bird Lake and Deep Eddy locals, there was a time when you could cut the cigarette smoke in this pool hall with a knife. Now it's abuzz most nights of the week with thirty- and fortysomethings looking to escape the downtown hype. ✉ *2315 Lake Austin Blvd., West Austin* ☎ *512/472–0961.*

★ **Driskill Hotel Bar.** The old-fashioned bar at the Driskill is where history is made. Rich carpeting and wood-trimmed walls, cowhide-finished and leather couches, plush green bar chairs, and the spectacular stained-glass dome in the center of the room saw some of President Lyndon B.

Johnson and Lady Bird Johnson's first dates as a couple. An excellent wine, beer, and cocktail list make cozying up in this classic Austin spot even more appealing. ✉ *604 Brazos St., Downtown & Capitol Area* ☎ *512/474–2214* ⊕ *www.driskillhotel.com.*

Ginny's Little Longhorn Saloon. Looking for an authentic honky-tonk dive experience? Ginny's is an Austin favorite, though from the looks of the rather dull exterior, you may not believe us. We never said it would be glamorous, but the beer is cold and the service is friendly. Local music legend Dale Watson often takes the tiny stage here, and the cast of regulars at this honored saloon is too good to miss. ✉ *5434 Burnet Rd., North Austin/Hyde Park* ☎ *512/458–1813* ⊕ *www.ginnyslittle longhorn.com.*

Fodor's Choice
★
Hotel San Jose Lounge. It may be the hippest hotel in town, but the San Jose is also home to one of the best wine bars in the city. On nice days, grab a patio seat, order a reasonably priced bottle of wine and the city-renowned cheese plate—we promise, you won't regret it. ✉ *1316 S. Congress Ave., South Austin* ☎ *512/477–3308* ⊕ *www.sanjosehotel.com.*

Mean-Eyed Cat. Soon to be overshadowed by a towering condo project, this little shack of a bar owes its name to the Man in Black. It may look more like a lean-to, but this little dive is an Austin cult favorite, with worn barn-wood walls covered with tattered Johnny Cash memorabilia, a shabby-chic patio with a random assortment of tables and chairs, and a very impressive beer selection. ✉ *1621 W. 5th St., Downtown & Capitol Area* ☎ *512/472–6326* ⊕ *www.themeaneyedcat.com.*

Scholz Garten. When not caught up in tailgating parties for the University of Texas Longhorns, sports fans are often living it up in the historic hall here. In continuous operation since 1866, the little beer joint that could is the oldest operating business in Austin, not to mention in the entire state! If you're not a Longhorns fan, Scholz's proximity to the Bob Bullock Texas State History Museum makes for a great stop after taking in some of the state's history. ✉ *1607 San Jacinto, Downtown & Capitol Area* ☎ *512/474–1958* ⊕ *www.scholzgarten.net.*

Vino Vino. Nestled in the hip Hyde Park neighborhood, Vino Vino serves a not-so-ordinary variety of wines—many of which are by the glass. Everything from Alsatian crémant (sparkling wine) to obscure Argentinian reds graces the perpetually evolving menu. The sleek amber-wood floors and bar give a warmth to this wine bar/market. Be sure to try a cheese plate or the flavorful pear, spinach, and goat-cheese salad. ✉ *4119 Guadalupe, North Austin/Hyde Park* ☎ *512/465–9282* ⊕ *www.vinovinotx.com.*

CAFÉS & COFFEEHOUSES
Caffé Medici. For quite possibly the best coffee in Austin, this little Clarksville coffeehouse draws quite a crowd for quick business meetings and weekend socializing. Here baristas pull exquisite shots for espresso drinks and even leave creative designs in latte and cappuccino

foam. ⊠*1101 W. Lynn, Downtown & the Capitol* ☏*512/524–5049* ⊕*www.caffemedici.com.*

Jo's Coffee. Though its sister location in the 2nd Street District attracts a more shi-shi crowd, the original Jo's on South Congress is where you're likely to pat the head of your neighbor's dog, catch the latest gossip on the Austin music scene, or even rub shoulders with the latest celebrity in town. Oh, and the coffee is fantastic, too. The morning rush hour is intense, yet somehow cool and lively. There's limited seating, and it's outside-only, so come early on a Saturday and bring a good read. ⊠*1300 S. Congress Ave., South Austin* ☏*512/444–3800* ⊠*242 W. 2nd St., 2nd St. & Warehouse District, Downtown & Capitol Area* ☏*512/469–9003* ⊕*www.joscoffee.com.*

Mozart's Coffee Roasters. Austinites frequent Mozart's on nice days to enjoy great coffee, indulgent baked goods, and the expansive, multitier deck overlooking Lake Austin. Live music on weekends is an added bonus. ⊠*3825 Lake Austin Blvd., Downtown & Capitol Area* ☏*512/477–2900* ⊕*www.mozartscoffee.com.*

★ **Ruta Maya Coffee House.** Grabbing a coffee at Ruta Maya is about as authentically Austin as it gets. After all, this is coffee with a cause. All beans are directly imported from a co-op of farmers in Chiapas, Mexico, who in turn receive support from the shop for sustainable farming. Most people just love the coffee and community feel. ⊠*3601 S. Congress Ave., South Austin* ☏*512/707–9637* ⊕*www.rutamaya.net.*

Spider House Patio Bar & Café. Truth be told, this is actually a full-service bar and café, but you'll find that the eclectic collection of patio furniture and cozy arrangement of old couches and overstuffed chairs inside make this near-campus joint a perfect coffee-shop escape for studying or catching up with friends. ⊠*2908 Fruth St., University of Texas* ☏*512/480–9562* ⊕*www.spiderhousecafe.com.*

CLUBS & DANCE HALLS

The Belmont. The coolest club in this very cool city? We're not absolutely sure, but a prime contender is the Belmont. Inside it feels like the swingin' '60s, Vegas style, with dark green banquettes and gold-on-black accents everywhere. Personable bartenders mix swanky cocktails, Frank and Dean are on the speakers, and Austin's beautiful people hang out on the breezy second-floor patio. During happy hour, appetizers are half price. Watch out for weekend crowds. ⊠*305 W. 6th St., Downtown & Capitol Area* ☏*512/457–0300* ⊕*www.thebelmont austin.com.*

Broken Spoke. Some of the town's most distinctive clubs are removed from the 6th Street scene. If live country music and dancing are your thing, two-step down to this venerable spot, where the old Texas lives (and dances) on. ⊠*3201 S. Lamar Blvd., South Austin* ☏*512/442–6189* ⊕*www.brokenspokeaustintx.com.*

Dallas Night Club. For mainstream country-and-western music and dance, this is the place to be. It's a jaunt north from the downtown scene, but you will get some serious two-stepping in here, and even a

CLOSE UP

Willie Nelson: Always on Our Mind

Willie Nelson in a suit? Nah, and legions of fans are thankful that he and tradition went their separate ways.

Willie was a musical kid, but he didn't turn it into work until after a stint in the Air Force and a year at Baylor University. Now it's all music with a huge helping of social activism.

He founded Farm Aid in the '80s. Then in 1990, the IRS came calling, and to pay the $16.7 million tax tab, Nelson released *The IRS Tapes: Who'll Buy My Memories*. The debt was settled by 1993, but he and the authorities were hardly finished. 1994 saw fresh troubles just off a Central Texas highway after officers found a marijuana joint in his ashtray.

Five wives, nine children, a guitar named Trigger, and 116 albums later, Nelson remains the iconoclast.

—Lisa Miller

line dance or two—if that's your kind of thing. ⊠*7113 Burnet Rd., North Austin/Hyde Park* ☎*512/452–2801.*

Speakeasy. In keeping with the old 1920s speakeasies, you have to gain entrance to this swanky club through the alley. The main room has that '20s vibe and features nightly live music from jazz, Latin, and big-band genres. This is the place to show off swing and Latin dance moves! For a fantastic view of the city, climb about 60 stairs to the Rooftop bar and catch a glimpse of the ever-growing Austin skyline. ⊠*412D Congress Ave.,* 2nd *St. & Warehouse District, Downtown & Capitol Area* ☎*512/476–8017* ⊕*www.speakeasyaustin.com.*

COMEDY CLUBS

Cap City Comedy Club. If you find yourself in North Austin, Cap City packs quite a punch with its stand-up comedian series. ⊠*8120 Research Blvd., No. 100, North Austin/Hyde Park* ☎*512/467–2333* ⊕*www.capcitycomedy.com.*

Esther's Follies. There's really one place in downtown Austin known for its rip-roaring comedy shows. Esther's has kept Austin rolling with laughter for more than 25 years. Situated in the heart of the entertaining 6th Street District, it's the perfect place to take in an evening of satire and parody. ⊠*525 E. 6th St., Downtown & Capitol Area* ☎*512/320–0553* ⊕*www.esthersfollies.com.*

LIVE MUSIC

Antone's. This is a local musical institution that books legendary blues and funk acts. Guiding spirit Clifford Antone, a blues fan's blues fan, passed away in May 2006, but his legacy lives on at the club he founded. ⊠*213 W. 5th St.,* 2nd *Sreet. & Warehouse District , Downtown & Capitol Area* ☎*512/320–8424 recording, 512/263–4146 information* ⊕*www.antones.net.*

Fodor's Choice ★ **Cactus Café.** For an intimate live-music experience unmatched by any other venue in Austin, head to this café on the UT campus and get in line for tickets. Texas singer-songwriter legends such as Lyle Lovett,

Robert Earle King, Patty Griffin, and Austin-renowned Bob Schneider have graced this tiny stage since the 1970s. It doesn't get much better than this. ⊠ *Texas Union, UT Campus, University of Texas* ☏ *512/475–6515* ⊕ *www.utexas.edu/txunion/ae/cactus.*

Cedar Street Courtyard. Squeezed between some of the Warehouse District's glam-filled bars, sounds from the open outdoor stage lure a bold and very beautiful crowd with jazzy, big-band, and swing music. Every night is a swinging time at the courtyard—just don't plan on lingering on the sidewalk too long without paying a cover. Bands do need to eat, after all. ⊠ *208 W. 4th St., 2nd St. & Warehouse District, Downtown & Capitol Area* ☏ *512/495–9669* ⊕ *www.cedarstreetaustin.com.*

Fodor'sChoice   **Continental Club.** Rustic, quirky, and no bigger than your parents' base-
★   ment, this smoky, no-frills club is one of Austin's signature entertainment spaces. The club hosts a variety of live acts but specializes in country-tinged rock and honky-tonkin'. Try to catch a performance by Heybale, a quintet of local pros that includes Redd Volkaert and Earl Poole Ball. ⊠ *1315 S. Congress Ave., South Austin* ☏ *512/441–2444* ⊕ *www.continentalclub.com/Austin.html.*

★   **Elephant Room.** Jazz fanatics hold court at the basement locale here, where serious jazz plays long into the night all week long. Named one of the top 10 jazz venues in the United States by the famed Wynton Marsalis, this longstanding Austin venue is what gives this town its Live Music Capital status. ⊠ *315 Congress Ave., Downtown & Capitol Area* ☏ *512/473–2279.*

Emo's. The thick sea of people swarming the indoor and outdoor stages may seem overwhelming at first, but you'll soon find it's the best way to take in one of Austin's most colorful night scenes. Not interested in fighting the crowd? Take a seat in the slightly less crowded beer garden. Three to four bands of the alternative, hard rock, heavy metal, or punk persuasion play this dark and hard-edged venue every night. It's not for the faint at heart. ⊠ *603 Red River, Downtown & Capitol Area* ☏ *512/477–3667* ⊕ *www.emosaustin.com.*

★   **Lamberts.** Barbecue fans will love the fancy spin on traditional Texas cuisine at this 2nd Street District hot spot, but the jazz and blues wailing from the upstairs bar are not to be missed. Strong, Southern-inspired cocktails served at simple heavy wood tables add to the dark and jazzy room, where some of Austin's up-and-coming jazz musicians take the spotlight. ⊠ *401 W. 2nd St., 2nd St. & Warehouse District, Downtown & Capitol Area* ☏ *512/494–1500* ⊕ *www.lambertsaustin.com.*

Momo's. Although heralded as a prime live music venue, what makes Momo's stand apart from other music facilities is the long and distinguished list of Austin performers who frequent the stage of this seven-year-old venue that has quickly gained legend status. With free parking and a cover charge that goes directly to the band, this is the place to get your fill of Austin tunes. ⊠ *618 W. 6th St., Downtown & Capitol Area* ☏ *512/479–8848* ⊕ *www.momosclub.com.*

Fodor's Choice **Stubb's.** You know you're in Austin when the smell of smoky barbecue
★ wafts throughout the venue as a top-billed band prepares to take the
outdoor stage. It's not heaven, it's Stubb's, a true Austin live-music
icon. If you're in town long enough and want to revive your spiritual side, take in a session of the Sunday gospel hour where a sizable buffet brunch awaits along with a soulful performance of gospel
music. ⌂ *801 Red River, Downtown & Capitol Area* ☎ *512/480–8341*
⊕ *www.stubbsaustin.com.*

WHERE TO EAT

Apart from on tourist- and student-heavy 6th Street, Austin's restaurant scene is geared to local tastes and is arguably more diverse than
the celebrated music scene, which is concentrated within a few narrowly defined genres. Though Mexican, Tex-Mex, and barbecue are
the default cuisines, everything from Brazilian to Pacific Rim fusion has
made headway here, and there are strong vegetarian and natural-food
followers. Austinites, in fact, have some of the most-adventurous and
educated palates in Texas.

To find the best barbecue, local consensus tends to be that you've got
to head out of town to Lockhart, Luling, or Llano, in the Hill Country.
Nevertheless, there are several fine options within the city limits, the
bulk of them simple places where your meat is sliced and placed uncer-
emoniously on the plate (or even on wax paper), with pickles, onions,
and jalapeño slices, and you eat at picnic tables, using paper towels off
the roll as napkins.

In some places the music and food share nearly equal billing, like
Threadgill's, whose massive chicken-fried steak is as much of a draw
as the well-known blues and rock acts on stage, and Stubb's Bar-B-Q,
which hosts a popular gospel brunch on Sunday and is a major player
on the club scene.

Finer dining has exploded in Austin, and upscale continental—especially Central European (the area was settled by Germans and Czechs)—
and New American establishments offer traditional fare and inventive
dishes with Southwestern touches. Some of the best restaurants in town
are in well-heeled hotels like the Driskill and the Four Seasons.

Austin is a casual city, and the dress code is almost always "come as
you are"; a few restaurants require a jacket for men. Tips are generally 15% to 20%. Smoking is prohibited in most restaurants and bars
within Travis County, which includes Austin.

DEALS & DISCOUNTS
Around midyear, many of Austin's best restaurants participate in Restaurant Week, when prix-fixe menus are offered for a low price, with
some of the proceeds earmarked for charity.

DINING WITH KIDS

Austin has plenty of families with young children and plenty of restaurants that work well for them. Burger joint Phil's Icehouse (✉ *5620 Burnet Rd., North Austin*) is a moms' favorite for its kid-friendly menu, play area for ages 3–12, and occasional live music or movies for kids in summer. Luby's is a Texas-based chain with five Austin locations serving affordable Southern food. The staff sees that young children (and their parents) are taken care of and kids eat free with the purchase of an adult meal Wednesday evenings and all day Saturday. Chuy's, Serranos Café & Cantina, and Romano's Macaroni Grill, chains with several Austin locations, are well attuned to children's needs. Restaurants in this chapter that are especially good for kids are marked with duckies.

WHAT IT COSTS					
	¢	$	$$	$$$	$$$$
Restaurants	under $8	$8–$12	$13–$20	$21–$30	over $30

Restaurant prices are per person for a main course at dinner.

DOWNTOWN & CAPITOL AREA

CONTINENTAL
$$–$$$
★

✕**Bess Bistro.** In the restored cellar of a 1918 brick building on the more-sedate end of 6th is this casually chic boîte owned by actress Sandra Bullock. (But if you come here to gawk at celebs, you'll likely leave disappointed.) Bess wins out with an eclectic mix of European and Southern American comfort food, including an artful *croque monsieur*: country ham, béchamel, and Gruyère piled atop sourdough toast, served with crisp, thin fries. Other popular entrées include shepherd's pie, grilled wild salmon on toasted herb spaetzle, and porcini-crusted halibut. Bullock designed the interior, which suggests an early-20th-century artists' sanctum, with framed French ads, exposed brick pillars, some half clad in quilted red leather. The staff is quietly efficient. Sunday brunch is served, and the bistro is open until the small hours. ✉ *500 W. 6th St., Downtown & Capitol Area* ☎ *512/477–2377* ⌂ *Reservations not accepted* ▤ *AE, D, MC, V.*

BURGER
¢–$

✕**Casino el Camino.** Slumming on 6th? This two-story club with a pleasant patio out back is the place to chow down. Put in your order at the kitchen window at the back of the bar, then return in 20 minutes for your grilled chicken-breast sandwich (with barbecue sauce, melted cheese, and sautéed peppers and onions), quarter-pound hot dogs, or the best and certainly biggest burgers in town, made from ¾ pound of Angus beef. If you have an especially daring palate, opt for the Amarillo burger, with roasted serrano chilies, jalapeño jack cheese, and cilantro mayo. The chicken wings are great, but be forewarned: the "medium" wings would be most other places' "atomic hot," so have plenty of liquid refreshment at hand. ✉ *517 E. 6th St., Downtown & Capitol Area* ☎ *512/469–9330* ⌂ *Reservations not accepted* ▤ *MC, V.*

WHERE SHOULD I DINE IN AUSTIN?

	Neighborhood Vibe	Pros	Cons
Downtown & Capitol Area	Premier New American and continental restaurants are here, along with wine bars, barbecue joints, and hip, upscale enclaves (especially west of Congress).	Hip and fun bistros, sophisticated nightlife, great upscale dining, something for nearly every taste.	Crowded, expensive, filled with tourists in season.
East Austin	Long a center for Austin's working-class Latinos and African-Americans, the area east of I-35 has Italian and Peruvian eateries amid auto-body shops and Mexican restaurants.	Great Mexican restaurants waiting to be discovered—at least, by you; eateries near airport great when you have a plane to catch.	Not the most attractive (or safest) neighborhoods; not the place to dine if you want to experience Austin.
North Austin	It's one of the best neighborhoods for various ethnic cuisines, including Asian and Middle Eastern.	Meet the locals in this low-key, low-pretension area; some good diners and ethnic eateries.	Clogged with traffic most of the time, sprawling, ugly, easy to get lost in.
Northwest Austin	Highways lead to seemingly endless shopping malls, most of them upscale, with fashionable restaurants to match. This is also the land of chain restaurants.	Family-friendly, some of Austin's best shopping, a natural stopping point on your way to Lake Travis.	Don't you have suburbs just like this at home?
2nd Street & Warehouse District	A mix of cool-but-friendly bistros lie between the lake and 3rd Street, and San Antonio and Congress. To the north, the Warehouse District has pubs, clubs, and casual places for post-collegians.	Great pubs and fun clubs, cutting-edge urban diversions, no car required.	Self-conscious hipitude can get a bit precious at times; some of the Warehouse District is a bit grungy.
South Austin	Still largely middle-class, and definitely individualistic, to some residents this area of South Congress (with its exhibitionistic painted facades) and Lamar is the last redoubt of Old Weird Austin. Here you find hippies, quirky stores, and veggie, Mexican, and barbecue restaurants.	Entertaining and unique center of "weird" Austin, great shops and Tex-Mex plates.	If hippies get on your nerves, don't bother.
Zilker Park	Barton Springs Road has several sprawling, ultracasual barbecue and hamburger joints, where the laid-back Austin lifestyle asserts itself to the fullest.	Great place to go native and surrender to Austin's casual, hip vibe; a morning swim, an afternoon barbecue platter—what else is there?	Parking can be a problem.

BEST BETS FOR AUSTIN DINING

As a foodie center, Austin delights palates daily with the inventions of a new wave of bright young chefs as well as with tried-and-true Mexican and barbecue. Below are some of our favorite restaurants in terms of style, cuisine type, and price points.

Fodor's Choice ★

Castle Hill Café, $$–$$$, Downtown & Capitol Area

Driskill Grill, $$$$, Downtown & Capitol Area

Enoteca Vespaio, $–$$, South Austin

Hudson's on the Bend, $$$$, Lake Travis

Jasper's, $$$–$$$$, North Austin

Lamberts, $$–$$$$, Downtown & Capitol Area

Salt Lick, ¢–$$, Driftwood

Uchi, $$–$$$$, South Austin

By Price

¢

Casino el Camino, Downtown & Capitol Area

El Mesón Taquería, East Austin

Flip Happy Crepes, Zilker Park

Hut's, Downtown & Capitol Area

$

Asia Cafe, Northwest Austin

Curra's Grill, South Austin

Hoover's, Northwest Austin, University of Texas

Hyde Park Bar and Grill, Hyde Park, South Austin

Iron Works Barbecue, Downtown & Capitol Area

$$

Bess Bistro, Downtown & Capitol Area

Castle Hill Café, Downtown & Capitol Area

European Bistro, Pflugerville

Lamberts, Downtown & Capitol Area

Primizie, East Austin

$$$

Estância Churrascaria, South Austin

Fonda San Miguel, North Austin

Mansion at Judges' Hill, University of Texas

$$$$

Driskill Grill, Downtown & Capitol Area

Hudson's on the Bend, Lake Travis

Jasper's, North Austin

Shoreline Grill, Downtown & Capitol Area

TRIO at the Four Seasons, Downtown and Capitol Area

By Cuisine

BARBECUE

Iron Works Barbecue, $–$$, Downtown & Capitol Area

Lamberts, $$–$$$$, Downtown & Capitol Area

Rudy's BBQ, ¢–$, Northwest Austin, Lake Travis, University of Texas, West Lake

The Salt Lick, ¢–$$, Driftwood

CONTINENTAL

Jeffrey's, $$–$$$$, Downtown & Capitol Area

Louie's 106, $$–$$$$, Downtown & Capitol Area

Mansion at Judges' Hill, $$–$$$$, University of Texas

Shoreline Grill, $$–$$$$, Downtown & Capitol Area

2

MEXICAN & TEX-MEX

Curra's Grill, $–$$, South Austin

El Azteca, ¢–$, East Austin

El Mesón Taquería, ¢, East Austin

Fonda San Miguel, $$–$$$$, North Austin

Juan in a Million, ¢–$, East Austin

Matt's Famous El Rancho, ¢–$$, South Austin

NEW AMERICAN

Castle Hill Café, $$–$$$, Downtown & Capitol Area

Driskill Grill, $$$$, Downtown & Capitol Area

Hudson's on the Bend, $$$$, Lake Travis

Jasper's, $$$–$$$$, North Austin

Lamberts, $$–$$$$, Downtown & Capitol Area

Zoot, $$–$$$$, Downtown & Capitol Area

By Experience

KID-FRIENDLY

County Line, $–$$$, West Austin, West Lake

Curra's Grill, $–$$, South Austin

Flip Happy Crepes, ¢–$, Zilker Park

Hoover's, $–$$, Northwest Austin, University of Texas

Hut's, ¢–$, Downtown & Capitol Area

Rudy's BBQ, ¢–$, Northwest Austin, Lake Travis, West Lake

Shady Grove, ¢–$$, Zilker Park

BEST BANG FOR YOUR BUCK

Asia Cafe, ¢–$, Northwest Austin

Casino el Camino, ¢–$, Downtown & Capitol Area

Dog and Duck Pub, ¢–$, Downtown & Capitol Area

Flip Happy Crepes, ¢–$, Zilker Park

Hoover's, $–$$, Northwest Austin, University of Texas

Juan in a Million, ¢–$, East Austin

Magnolia Cafe, ¢–$$, Downtown & Capitol Area, South Austin

DINING ALFRESCO

County Line, $–$$$, West Austin, West Lake

Flip Happy Crepes, ¢–$, Zilker Park

Iron Works Barbecue, $–$$, Downtown & Capitol Area

The Oasis–Lake Travis, $–$$, Lake Travis

The Salt Lick, ¢–$$, Driftwood

Shady Grove, ¢–$$, Zilker Park

YOUNG & HAPPENING

Bess Bistro, $$–$$$, Downtown & Capitol Area

Casino el Camino, ¢–$, Downtown & Capitol Area

Jasper's, $$$–$$$$, North Austin

Lamberts, $$–$$$$, Downtown & Capitol Area **Primizie, $–$$**, East Austin

SHORT ON ATMOSPHERE, LONG ON GOOD, CHEAP EATS

Asia Cafe, ¢–$, Northwest Austin

Casino el Camino, ¢–$, Downtown & Capitol Area

Curra's Grill, $–$$, South Austin

Juan in a Million, ¢–$, East Austin

Red Cap Chick, ¢–$$, South Austin

ROMANCE

Driskill Grill, $$$$, Downtown & Capitol Area

Fonda San Miguel, $$–$$$$, North Austin

Hudson's on the Bend, $$$$, Lake Travis

Jasper's, $$$–$$$$, North Austin

Jeffrey's, $$–$$$$, Downtown & Capitol Area

Joe DiMaggio's Italian Chophouse, $$–$$$$, North Austin

Mansion at Judges' Hill, $$–$$$$, University of Texas

Truluck's, $$$–$$$$, Downtown & Capitol Area, Northwest Austin

NEW
AMERICAN
$$–$$$
Fodor'sChoice
★

✕**Castle Hill Café.** This cheery, upscale downtown hangout rarely disappoints, which is why it's been an Austin mainstay since 1986. Here you'll find great tortilla soup, imaginative salads, and eclectic entrées such as grilled Indian lamb loin with Makhani cream and cauliflower-ginger relish. The menu usually changes every two to four weeks. A wine-and-beer bar was added in 2007. ⊠ *1101 W. 5th St., Downtown & Capitol Area* ☎ *512/476–0728* ⊟ *AE, D, MC, V* ⊗ *Closed Sun.*

FRENCH
$$–$$$

✕**Chez Nous.** Austin's first French bistro manages to maintain its quiet and cozy atmosphere despite its location mere feet from raucous 6th Street. Simple dishes from the French playbook make appearances on the reasonably priced menu, and the fixed-price option is a bargain. Start with the house-made pâté du jour or escargot, then treat yourself to carefully prepared duck. The casual bistro atmosphere encourages long meals and romantic glances, so pace yourself accordingly. ⊠ *510 Neches St., Downtown & Capitol Area* ☎ *512/473–2413* ⊟ *AE, DC, MC, V* ⊗ *Closed Mon. No lunch weekends.*

AMERICAN
¢–$

✕**Dog and Duck Pub.** This casual Texas spin on the British pub pours more than 30 varieties of beer, about half of them on tap. The menu is wholly pub grub: burgers, fried appetizers, and—in a nod across the pond—bangers and mash. There's a large outdoor patio and outdoor tables where students, political types, and businessmen while away the evenings. ⊠ *406 W. 17th St., Downtown & Capitol Area* ☎ *512/479–0598* ⊟ *AE, DC, MC, V.*

NEW
AMERICAN
$$$$
Fodor'sChoice
★

✕**Driskill Grill.** Dominated by shiny, dark paneling and etched glass, this would-be cattle baron's club inside the Driskill Hotel recalls the palatial restaurants of the 19th century (on a more-intimate scale)—until you look at the menu. Executive Chef Josh Watkins takes tasteful liberties with the meat-and-potatoes format by integrating world-cuisine influences. Entrées include hot smoked Bandera quail, pistachio-crusted sea scallops, and pan-roasted duck breast. Nightly piano music adds to the charming ambience. ⊠ *604 Brazos St., Downtown & Capitol Area* ☎ *512/391–7162* ⊟ *AE, D, DC, MC, V.*

SOUTHERN
$$–$$$$

✕**Gumbo's.** Billing itself as a Louisiana-style café, Gumbo's occupies a spiffy split-level space in the art deco Brown Building downtown. The busy kitchen, which opens to the main dining area, prepares everything from fried seafood po'boys to more-complex contemporary Cajun and Creole entrées. Try the tilapia George (pan-sautéed, topped with blue-crab meat and served over herb beurre blanc) or blackened beef tenderloin with a red wine reduction. The comfortable room balances a high-ceiling main floor with more intimate nooks and booths. ⊠ *710 Colorado St., Downtown & Capitol Area* ☎ *512/480–8053* ⊟ *AE, D, DC, MC, V* ⊗ *No lunch weekends.*

BURGER
¢–$
☺

✕**Hut's.** Locals consistently choose Hut's for the best-burger award in *Austin Chronicle* restaurant polls. Part of the mystique may be the *American Graffiti*–like atmosphere: the joint is a local institution that began in 1939. It's been in its present location since 1969, and old license plates, vintage ads, and UT memorabilia are everywhere. Huge, juicy burgers come in about 25 varieties, and the gigantic onion rings are crunchy and addictive. It's hard not to surrender to the experience. Vegetarians can request substitute patties—this is Austin, after all. ✉ *807 W. 6th St., Downtown & Capitol Area* ☎*512/472–0693* 🍽*D, MC, V.*

BARBECUE ✕**Iron Works Barbecue.** From its creek-side perch in the shadow of the
$-$$ Austin Convention Center, this spot caters to name-tagged conference
★ attendees, construction workers, and thoroughly starched office work-
ers alike. Dependable house specialties include pepper-crusted smoked
pork loin, tender brisket, and Flintstones-size beef ribs (the junior rib
plate will satisfy all but the hugest of appetites). Wrought-iron grills,
forged here when the building was an ironworks, hang from the rafters.
It's a charming and authentic slice of Texas—maybe not the best barbecue joint within city limits, but definitely in the top five. There's also
a decent salad bar. ✉ *100 Red River St., Downtown & Capitol Area*
☎*512/478–4855* 🍽*AE, DC, MC, V* ⊘ *Closed Sun.*

CONTINENTAL ✕**Jeffrey's.** Executive chef Alma Alcocer holds court at this fine-dining
$$-$$$$ institution in the historic Clarksville area downtown, where the menu
★ of "contemporary Texas cuisine" changes regularly. Expect complex
dishes that combine Latin and Southwestern flavors with standbys
from more-continental traditions. Start with crispy oysters on yucca
chips with habanero-honey aioli, then move on to the balsamic duck
and shrimp with baby vegetables, apples, and Roquefort cheese for an
entrée. The sophisticated wine list is carefully selected. Cozy alcoves,
a romantic atmosphere, and consistently attentive service make for a
memorable evening. ✉ *1204 W. Lynn St., Downtown & Capitol Area*
☎*512/477–5584* 🍽*AE, D, DC, MC, V* ⊘ *No lunch.*

NEW ✕**Lamberts.** On an up-and-coming block near City Hall, Lamberts
AMERICAN draws businessmen, Web types, trenchermen, and foodies for its "fancy
$$-$$$$ barbecue," aka stylish twists on Texas classics. You know this isn't
Fodor'sChoice your father's barbecue joint when you hear Belle & Sebastian on the
★ speakers instead of LeAnn Rimes or Merle Haggard. Chimay beer is
available *on draft*, and the Frito pie costs $10 and contains goat cheese.
Appetizers range from Asian-style crispy wild-boar ribs to broiled gulf
oysters with apple-smoked bacon. Desserts, like lemon chess pie with
blueberry sauce, are tangy sweet and satisfying. They even make a
decent cappuccino. Service is competent and cheerful. The restaurant is
housed in a historic two-story 1873 brick building; the front room has
whitewashed brick, green leatherette '60s banquettes, and a bar serving
top single-malt Scotches. The second floor has a bar with a few tables
and a stage where bands play the nights away. ✉ *401 W. 2nd St.* 2nd *St.
& Warehouse District, Downtown & Capitol Area* ☎*512/494–1500*
🍽*AE, D, DC, MC, V.*

CONTINENTAL ✕**Louie's 106.** Crisp white tablecloths, gleaming black-and-white tiled
$$-$$$$ floors, and wrought-iron balconies suggest the 1940s at this dressy
but convivial downtown bistro. Louie's bills itself as a "Mediterranean
grill and tapas bar" and serves traditional and not-so-traditional Span-
ish-style small bites such as fried olives with Romesco sauce, Moroc-
can barbecue shrimp, ravioli empanadas, and soups like gazpacho
Andaluz, topped with lumps of rich crabmeat. Entrées show a wider
range of cultural influences, with dishes like seafood risotto, pump-
kinseed-crusted salmon, and maple-glazed rotisserie-roasted duck with
wild rice and caramelized green apple chutney. The stylish bar is an

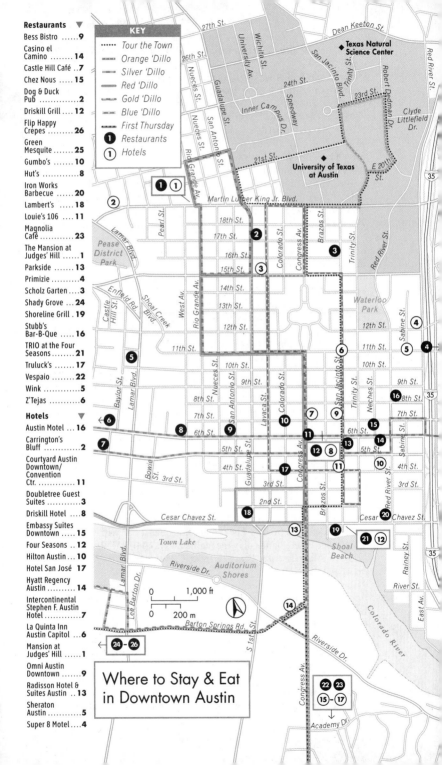

Restaurants ▼

Bess Bistro **9**

Casino el
Camino **14**

Castle Hill Café .**7**

Chez Nous **15**

Dog & Duck
Pub **2**

Driskill Grill **12**

Flip Happy
Crepes **26**

Green
Mesquite **25**

Gumbo's **10**

Hut's **8**

Iron Works
Barbecue ...**20**

Lambert's **18**

Louie's 106 ....**11**

Magnolia
Café **23**

The Mansion at
Judges' Hill **1**

Parkside **13**

Primizie **4**

Scholz Garten **3**

Shady Grove ...**24**

Shoreline Grill .**19**

Stubb's
Bar-B-Que **16**

TRIO at the Four
Seasons **21**

Truluck's **17**

Vespaio **22**

Wink **5**

Z'Tejas **6**

Hotels ▼

Austin Motel ...**16**

Carrington's
Bluff **2**

Courtyard Austin
Downtown/
Convention
Ctr. **11**

Doubletree Guest
Suites **3**

Driskill Hotel **8**

Embassy Suites
Downtown ...**15**

Four Seasons ..**12**

Hilton Austin ...**10**

Hotel San José ...**17**

Hyatt Regency
Austin **14**

Intercontinental
Stephen F. Austin
Hotel **7**

La Quinta Inn
Austin Capitol ...**6**

Mansion at
Judges' Hill **1**

Omni Austin
Downtown **9**

Radisson Hotel &
Suites Austin ..**13**

Sheraton
Austin **5**

Super 8 Motel **4**

KEY

```
······· Tour the Town
▨▨▨ Orange 'Dillo
▨▨▨ Silver 'Dillo
▨▨▨ Red 'Dillo
▨▨▨ Gold 'Dillo
✕✕✕ Blue 'Dillo
▬▬▬ First Thursday
① Restaurants
① Hotels
```

Where to Stay & Eat in Downtown Austin

2

attractive place to indulge in the Iberian tradition of a late-afternoon tapas break. ⊠*106 E. 6th St., Downtown & Capitol Area* ☎*512/476–1997* ⊟*AE, D, DC, MC, V* ⊗*No lunch weekends.*

NEW AMERICAN $$

✕**Parkside.** The bustling array of bars and nightclubs that lines Austin's famed 6th Street welcomes a new upscale restaurant for urban-chic and late-night diners. Parkside's austere, cavernous interior features exposed brick walls and long black cables dangling single lightbulbs above each table. Celebrated Austin chef Shawn Cirkiel has created a menu as simple as the restaurant's decor, but more than delivers on taste with fresh oysters and ceviche-style offerings from the raw bar, as well as bistro entrées including steak and fries, and roasted chicken. Fried oysters with a garlicky aioli make for a great start. The savory grilled lamb served with tangy roasted peppers is perfectly prepared and surprisingly un-gamey. Buttery snapper arrives sashimi-style with piquant lime and chili accents. For dessert, order the homemade doughnuts, which arrive warm and sugar-dusted in a plain paper sack. ⊠*301 E. 6th St., Downtown & Capitol Area* ☎*512/474–9898* ⊕*www.parkside-austin.com* ⊟*AE, D, MC, V.*

ECLECTIC ¢–$

✕**Scholz Garten.** Established in 1866, this beer garden and dining room is a local favorite and a longtime hangout for Austin's Democratic politicos. In addition to standard American fare, the menu includes barbecue platters, burgers, chicken-fried steak, and some German dishes like Wiener schnitzel, jägerschnitzel, and bratwurst. Sides include German potato salad, red cabbage, sauerkraut, and peach cobbler. There's a good selection of local and international beers, including German selections from Franziskaner, Paulaner, Spaten, and Aventinus. ⊠*1607 San Jacinto Blvd., Downtown & Capitol Area* ☎*512/474–1958* ⊟*AE, D, DC, MC, V.*

CONTINENTAL $$–$$$$ ★

✕**Shoreline Grill.** Just steps from the Four Seasons hotel, this upscale lakeside restaurant has one of Austin's most intimate terraces (a fine place to watch sunset bat flight). Chef Dan Haverty presents nightly seafood variations that might include seared sea scallops with pistachio–goat cheese polenta, or roasted salmon served with a cashew crust and orange-Dijon butter. Meat lovers enjoy robust Texas platters like chicken-fried venison with mashed potatoes and green chili gravy, and ancho-cured half rack of lamb with roasted sweet potato and amontillado demi-glace. Inside, floor-to-ceiling windows provide a commanding view of Lady Bird Lake (formerly Town Lake). For a real taste of Texas, try the huge chicken-fried steak (served at lunch only); it's one of the best versions you'll find. ⊠*98 San Jacinto Blvd., Downtown & Capitol Area,* ☎*512/477–3300* ⊟*AE, D, DC, MC, V* ⊗*No lunch weekends.*

BARBECUE $–$$

✕**Stubb's Bar-B-Que.** This downtown 6th Street–area institution, which traces its roots to a legendary Lubbock barbecue joint founded in 1968 by the late C. B. "Stubb" Stubblefield, is known as much for music as food. Stubb's hosts an always-crowded Sunday gospel brunch (book ahead), and big-name and lesser-known local and touring acts including Willie Nelson, Johnny Cash, Joan Jett, and the White Stripes have played the outdoor stage. To many local barbecue mavens, the hickory-smoked choices—beef brisket, pork loin, pork ribs, sausage, chicken and turkey breast—are average, but the sides, like spinach with cheese and serrano peppers, are delicious. Salads, sandwiches, and homemade desserts complete the menu, and there's a full bar. Stubb's also markets a popular line of barbecue sauces and rubs. The venue, an old stone building with wooden floors and tables, suits the fare to a T. ⊠*801 Red River St., Downtown & Capitol Area* ☎*512/480–8341* ▭*AE, D, MC, V.*

NEW
AMERICAN
$$–$$$$
★

✕**TRIO at the Four Seasons.** Steak, seafood, and wine are the three focal points (thus the name) of this sophisticated, sun-washed oasis. Executive chef Elmar Prambs, a fixture at the Four Seasons since 1987, opened TRIO in 2007. The menus, which change weekly, are planned by inventive chef de cuisine Todd Duplechan, who emphasizes freshness—all the seafood is fresh (some shipped overnight; some brought in that day from the gulf), including Dover sole from Denmark—and produce and other ingredients sourced locally wherever possible. Prime-quality steaks range from an 8-ounce filet mignon to a 22-ounce bone-in cowboy steak (a rib-eye cut). Diners rave about inventive appetizers like "bacon and egg" made with pork belly and an egg that's poached, breaded in *panko* (Japanese flaky bread crumbs), then deep-fried, and squid *a la plancha* (lightly seared). An outstanding wine list is overseen by an in-house sommelier. No detail has been overlooked. Breakfast is served daily. TRIO is worth a visit even if you're staying far from the hotel. ⊠*98 San Jacinto Blvd., Downtown & Capitol Area* ☎*512/685–8300* ▭*AE, D, MC, V.*

NEW
AMERICAN
$$$
★

✕**Wink.** Tucked away from Lamar near 12th Street, this petite, sleek restaurant is as dedicated to excellence in service and artful delicious dishes as it is to fresh, quality ingredients from local purveyors. Portions are equally as petite as the contemporary dining room, but somehow you never leave hungry. We suggest putting your trust in chef Eric Poltzer's tasting menu. Each course brings a surprising mix of flavors from bison carpaccio with goat cheese and tomato relish to duck confit with baby yams and wilted greens. The wine list is carefully selected, with an array of varietals from around the world. We were particularly impressed with a rare Alsatian crémant (sparkling wine). ⊠*1014 N. Lamar, Downtown & Capitol Area* ☎*512/482–8868* ▭*AE, D, MC, V* ⊙*No lunch.*

MEXICAN
$–$$$

✕**Z'Tejas.** This stylish Southwestern fusion outpost started in downtown Austin and currently has 10 locations in Texas and 5 in other Western states. (In addition to the original, there's another Austin branch at the Arboretum mall.) Z'Tejas is popular for its upscale yet unpretentious vibe and imaginative, attractively presented dishes at fair prices. Try the smoked-chicken chile relleno, a poblano stuffed with chicken, chopped pecans, apricots, jack cheese, and raisins, served with green-chili mole and roasted tomato cream. Appetizers are outstanding, particularly the grilled shrimp and guacamole tostada bites: herb-and-pumpkin-seed tostada rounds topped with pesto-grilled shrimp, fresh guacamole, and a dash of chipotle. Peak hours can be noisy. ⊠*1110 W. 6th St., Downtown & Capitol Area* ☎*512/478–5355* ⊠*9400-A Arboretum Blvd., Northwest Austin* ☎*512/346–3506* ⊠*10525 W. Parmer La., Northwest Austin* ☎*512/388–7772* ▭*AE, D, MC, V.*

TEXAS BARBECUE

Deciphering the politics of barbecue is difficult in Texas. All Texans are in agreement that barbecue is indeed the "national cuisine" of the Lone Star State, but preparation and presentation are anything but consistent. In fact, depending on where you are in Texas, the proper method for smoking and serving brisket, ribs (pork or beef), and sausage—the bedrocks of 'cue—is a big, meaty bone of contention.

The true origin of Texas barbecue is hard to pinpoint. What *is* clear are the three primary influences on what Texans religiously consume. In East Texas, there are clear overtones of classic Southern-style barbecue: hickory smoked for many, many hours; basted frequently with a tomato-based sweet "sop"; and served with the meat practically falling off the bone. German and Czech influences prevail in Central Texas, where meat is rubbed with spices that create a thick crust, then smoked over indirect heat from oak or pecan for long periods of time and served with slices of white bread, onion, and pickles. The cowboy/West Texas style of barbecue involves smoking over direct heat from mesquite wood, which gives the meat a somewhat bitter (yet satisfying) taste.

Another issue is "wet" vs. "dry." In Central and West Texas, dry rubs are used to produce a nice crust and tender-but-firm meat. In some circles, dry barbecue is served with a side of barbecue sauce—usually a thin and spicy liquid. In East Texas, barbecue is wet, and in South Texas, the meat is basted with thick, molasses-like sauces that are eventually reduced to a glorious, gooey glaze.

Like religion and politics, Texans take their barbecue seriously. If you bring up the conversation of the best style of barbecue or the best purveyors, expect to have your particular definition of barbecue questioned—so know where you stand on the matter.

And although we cannot do the genre justice by simply skimming the surface with a short list of the state's best 'cue joints, *some* legends are indisputable. The Hill Country's Lockhart is *the* destination for barbecue, where Kreutz's and Smitty's reside. Mason claims the *true* Cooper's original barbecue (as opposed to Llano's same-name-different-style Cooper's), and Salt Lick in South Austin (technically in Driftwood) is always a big hit. But this is a big state, so you can scout out plenty of fantastic places—write in and let us know what you find!

Cooper's Pit Bar-B-Q (⊠ *Hwy. 87 S., Mason* ☎ *325/347–6897* or *800/513–6963* ⊟*MC, V*). **Kreutz's Market** (⊠*619 N. Colorado St., Lockhart* ☎*512/398–2361* ⊟*No credit cards* ☉ *Closed Sun.*). **Louie Mueller** (⊠*206 W. 2nd St., Taylor* ☎*512/352–6206* ⊟*MC, V* ☉ *Closed Sun.*). **Salt Lick** (⊠*18001 FM 1826, 5 mi northeast of Wimberley, Driftwood* ☎ *512/858–4959* ⊟*No credit cards*). **Smitty's Market** (⊠*208 S. Commerce St., Lockhart* ☎*512/398–9344* ⊟*No credit cards*).

–by Jessica Norman Dupuy

NEW
AMERICAN
$$–$$$$

✕**Zoot.** One of central Austin's house-to-restaurant conversions, Zoot focuses on fresh, local ingredients and specializes in smaller but perfectionist-oriented plates. It's not cheap, but Zoot has a core of devoted foodie fans. The creations of chef-owners Stewart Scruggs and Mark Paul (who also own the upscale American bistro Wink on North Lamar) range from wood-grilled venison with honey glazed root vegetables, braised greens, and juniper reduction to smoked salmon salad with Texas squash galette and 20-year-old balsamic vinegar. Menus change seasonally. Understated decor, impeccable service, and one of Austin's best-stocked wine cellars contribute to Zoot's stellar reputation. Two five-course tasting menus (one is vegetarian) are available, in addition to à la carte items. ⊠*509 Hearn St., Downtown & Capitol Area* ☎*512/477–6535* ⊟*AE, D, DC, MC, V* ☉*No lunch.*

EAST AUSTIN

MEXICAN
¢–$

✕**El Azteca.** This old-school family restaurant, now run by the second generation, has been around since 1963 in the heart of bustling, working-class East Austin, and draws local Latinos and downtown workers alike. The decor is a decades-old accretion of Mexican and American kitsch, and great tacky posters featuring half-naked Aztec warriors, swooning women, and volcano goddesses. The servers are no-nonsense, even brusque. You dine at red Naugahyde booths with wood-tone Formica tables with steel-frame chairs, but you're here for expertly rendered Tex-Mex and Mexican platters. The house specialty is *cabrito,* or kid goat, which, at $11.95, is the most expensive dish on the menu, served with guacamole salad, beans *a la charra* (in a smoky broth), and salsa. The cabrito is served in a pile of small chops on the bone; it's lean and just the right side of gamey, and slightly sweet with a hint of baked apple. There's a covered patio with outdoor tables as well. ⊠*2600 E. 7th St., East Austin* ☎*512/477–4701* ⌦*Reservations not accepted* ⊟*MC, V.*

MEXICAN
¢

✕**El Mesón Taquería.** Although it's called a taquería, El Mesón, housed in a picture-perfect orange-hue wooden building in an industrial neighborhood near the airport, is not just another Tex-Mex fast-food joint. The menu is sparked by traditional dishes from Mexico's interior, such as *cochinita pibil* (marinated pork cooked in banana leaves with achiote), a Yucatecan dish; *pipian,* chicken cooked in a pumpkin-seed sauce; and *al pastor,* grilled cubes of pork with pineapple, onion, and cilantro. Vegetarians can try *calabacitas* (sautéed zucchini, onions, and corn with cilantro, finished with freshly chopped tomatoes and spices). Locals consider it worth the trip. Portions are quite generous. ⊠*5808 Burleson Rd., East Austin* ☎*512/416–0749* ⊟*No credit cards* ☉*No dinner.*

MEXICAN
¢–$

✕**Juan in a Million.** The not-so-secret weapon of this classic East Austin breakfast spot is its owner and namesake, local legend Juan Meza, who has run his modest eatery since 1981 and still greets every diner with a bone-crushing handshake and a smile. Juan's strong community spirit is catching, but the simple, filling, and reliably good fare will start your day off right on its own. The Don Juan taco (a massive mound of eggs, potato, bacon, and cheese) is the true East Austin breakfast of champions; *machacado con huevo* (shredded dried beef scrambled with eggs), *migas* (eggs scrambled with torn corn tortillas, onions, chili peppers, cheese, and spices), and huevos rancheros are also above average. A variety of inexpensive Tex-Mex and Mexican specialties is served at lunch. ⊠ *2300 E. Cesar Chavez St., East Austin* ☎ *512/472–3872* ⌖ *Reservations not accepted* ⊟ *AE, D, MC, V.*

ITALIAN
$-$$
★
✕ **Primizie.** Opened in mid-2007, this hip-and-modern, foodie-friendly *osteria* (simple Italian-bistro-style restaurant) on a rapidly gentrifying central East Austin block is a magnet for young techies and creative types. Co-owner Mark Spedale is a native Sicilian, though the menu hews more toward northern Italian. Salads, pizzas, and entrées are all fresh and inventive in their simplicity. The pastas and gnocchi are reliable favorites, and bread and pastries are made in-house. Lunch is ordered at the counter, at dinner there's table service, and half-price appetizers are available during happy hour (4–7 weekdays). Try the *bistecca alla griglia,* savory grilled marinated sirloin steak with potato, arugula, garlic, caramelized onion, and melted Gorgonzola butter. A good selection of Italian, American, and French wines is available by the glass or bottle, and pastries are made in-house. On our last visit, the only imperfect note was slightly burned espresso. ⊠ *1000 E. 11th St., East Austin* ☎ *512/236–0088* ⊟ *MC, V.*

LAKE TRAVIS

NEW
AMERICAN
$$$$
Fodor's Choice
★
✕ **Hudson's on the Bend.** About 20 mi outside downtown in a beautifully restored and landscaped stone ranch house overlooking a bend in the road near Lake Travis, Hudson's has been the place to dine on wild game in Austin since 1984. Owner/chef Jeff Blank and executive chef Robert Rhoades are kings of imaginative, gutsy cuisine, serving serve up exotic, unique, seasonal dishes such as pistachio-crusted diamondback rattlesnake cakes with chipotle cream sauce, venison prosciutto–wrapped seared sea scallops topped with sturgeon caviar, wild boar three ways—scaloppine, sausage, and *taquito* (a thin, rolled and fried enchilada)—and espresso-, chocolate-, and chili-rubbed smoked elk backstrap (loin cut) topped with crab. Despite the hefty price tag, Hudson's is a fun, unpretentious place. There's an extensive wine list, including half bottles. Six-course tasting menus are available ($140, or $200 with wine). ⊠ *3509 Ranch Rd. 620 N, Lake Travis* ☎ *512/266–1369* ⊟ *AE, D, DC, MC, V* ☾ *No lunch.*

AMERICAN
$-$$
☻
✕ **Oasis–Lake Travis.** A 2005 fire destroyed most of the wooden outdoor deck seating that made the cliff-side Oasis–Lake Travis such a draw, but the Austin institution has been rebuilt and reemerged with perhaps even more spirit; some consider the food much improved as well. Scenic views make this a popular spot for sunset dinners—sometimes too popular, as weekend crowds can be overwhelming in nice weather. If you can, try to get one of the tables overlooking Lake Travis (arrive early). The menu includes shrimp, burgers, fajitas, and margaritas. ⊠ *6550 Comanche Trail, Lake Travis* ☎ *512/266–2442* ⊟ *AE, D, MC, V.*

Where to Stay & Eat in Greater Austin

2

KEY

● Restaurants

① Hotels

NORTH AUSTIN

MEXICAN
$$–$$$$

✕ **Fonda San Miguel.** This celebrated villa-style North Loop spot combines sophisticated ambience with a seasonal menu of authentic Mexican classics. Start with quesadillas layered with poblano, chicken, or mushrooms; or go light with ceviche Veracruzano (with chilies, onion, tomato, and spices). Continue with a multilayered dish like the *ancho relleno* San Miguel—a roasted pepper stuffed with chicken, capers, raisins, and olives and topped with cilantro cream—or try the *pollo pibil,* chicken baked in a banana leaf. Shrimp dishes are extraordinary. Yes, most of it is pricey for what you get, but we feel the lovely, romantic atmosphere makes up for it. The extravagant Sunday brunch is the quintessential upscale Austin weekend breakfast. ⊠ *2330 W. North Loop Blvd., North Austin* ☎ *512/459–4121* ▭ *AE, D, DC, MC, V* ⊗ *No lunch.*

NEW
AMERICAN
$$$–$$$$
Fodor'sChoice
★

✕ **Jasper's.** Executives and upscale tourists alike are drawn to this handsome, 9,000-square-foot eatery for its "gourmet backyard cuisine"—that's how owner and celebrated chef Kent Rathbun describes his Texas-based chain. This branch is in the chichi Domain right across from Joe DiMaggio's. Seafood features prominently in the inventive menu— the star is Allen Brothers dry-aged prime steak, served with a choice of six sauces. Entrées, from a tender grilled flatiron steak with portobello whipped potatoes to a Cajun grilled redfish sandwich, are attractively plated and well conceived. If you want to go upscale on a tight budget, try the pizza-size three-cheese focaccia with caramelized shallots and portobellos for $10. In 2007 the *Austin Chronicle* called Jasper's fried chicken, with its perfectly crispy skin, the best in town (it's served only at lunch on weekends). Servers are attentive, but not overly familiar. Decor is midtown-Manhattan modern. ⊠ *The Domain shopping center, 11506 Century Oaks Terr., North Austin* ☎ *512/834–4111* ▭ *AE, DC, MC, V.*

STEAKHOUSE/
ITALIAN
$$–$$$$

✕ **Joe DiMaggio's Italian Chophouse.** The designers of this impressive, larger-than-life establishment (the second branch of a nascent chain that began in San Francisco in 2006) have spared no expense to re-create a 1954 lavish, romantic-yet-masculine supper club, complete with polished floors, plush leather booths, wide marble bar, black-and-white decor with splashes of red, and photos of Joe and Marilyn everywhere (never mind that their marriage only lasted nine months). Fritto misto, pepper-crusted beef carpaccio, and wood-fired mussels appeal as appetizers. Pastas and pizzas—the Pizza Uovo, for example, topped with sopressata sausage and a runny egg (slightly undercooked but otherwise tasty)—get mixed reviews from diners. Steaks are the main event, from an 8-ounce filet mignon to a 24-ounce porterhouse. The house has a good selection of cocktails and sizable appetizers, $5 apiece, at a daily happy hour (3–6 PM). ⊠ *The Domain shopping center, 11410 Century Oaks Terr., North Austin* ☎ *512/835–5633* ▭ *AE, DC, MC, V.*

ITALIAN
¢–$
★

✕ **Mandola's Italian Market.** Mandola's is the closest you'll get to Italy without leaving Austin. Houston restaurateur, winemaker, cooking-show host, and cookbook author Damian Mandola (cofounder of the Carrabba's Italian Grill restaurant chain) opened this throwback "neighborhood grocery store" and the attached café in 2006 in the

2

equally new Triangle apartment complex just north of Central Market. Mandola gets it right with house-made sausage, mozzarella, artisanal breads, cakes, and cookies. They serve up panini, soups, salads, and antipasti, and daily fresh ravioli specials. The pastas, the very decent southern Italian-style pizza, the vegetarian sandwich, and the pignoli cookies are especially good, and the coffees deliver. The staff is friendly and well trained, and the atmosphere is welcoming. You can also purchase wine from Mandola's winery out in Driftwood, 28 mi southwest. ⊠ *4700 W. Guadalupe St., North Austin* ☎ *512/419–9700* 🖃 *AE, D, DC, MC, V.*

VIETNAMESE
¢–$

✕ **Pho Saigon.** One of the brightest spots of the new Chinatown Center on North Lamar, this friendly noodle house lacks atmosphere but serves up especially tasty bowls of its signature item, *pho*, a traditional Vietnamese noodle soup that comes in variations with beef, chicken, seafood, or tofu. The small portion should be big enough for almost anyone. They have decent vermicelli dishes, too. ⊠ *10901 N. Lamar Blvd., North Austin* ☎ *512/821–1022* 🖃 *MC, V.*

SEAFOOD
¢–$$

✕ **Quality Seafood.** Airport Boulevard isn't just a road to the airport—it's one of Austin's great working-class commercial arteries, and this combination seafood market and casual eatery is one of its gems. Serving the landlocked city's freshest seafood (fresh off the plane, if not the boat), Quality traces its history back to 1938 and has been at this address since 1970. Prices are low, preparation is straightforward, and blackboard specials include regional and Cajun favorites like gumbo, catfish beignets, and inventive twists like crawfish tamales. A large central oyster bar serves up appealing po'boys, steamed mussels, seafood tacos, and a platters with catfish, cod, salmon, shrimp, or rainbow trout—grilled, blackened, or fried as best suits the fish. A half dozen oysters on the half shell is just $4.99, but the counterman is honest enough to steer you away if he feels they're not up to snuff. Wine is available by the glass and beer by the bottle. Wi-Fi is free. ⊠ *5621 Airport Blvd., North Austin* ☎ *512/454–5827* 🖃 *AE, D, DC, MC, V* ⊙ *Closed Sun.*

MEXICAN
¢–$$

✕ **Santa Rita Tex-Mex Cantina.** This self-consciously hip spot in the 26 Doors shopping center serves traditional platters with a twist. The lunch crowd enjoys the laid-back patio, and the dinner crowd digs the huge portions. The grilled tilapia taco plate with lime avocado sauce, and the shrimp with chipotle cream sauce are two highlights; salsa and *pico de gallo* (finely chopped fresh tomato, onion, and chilies) are expertly assembled. Decoration is equally original: one wall is covered with old wooden shoe forms, another has gilt-framed portraits of Mexican heroes and a few other intruders, like Columbus and Eleanor Roosevelt. Add friendly, capable service to the mix, and you see why everyone keeps coming back. ⊠ *1206 W.t 38th St., North Austin* ☎ *512/419–7482* 🖃 *MC, V.*

NORTHWEST AUSTIN

CHINESE
¢–$

✕ **Asia Cafe.** In the back of the Asia Market food store in a run-down strip mall in far northwest Austin, this unassuming, bare-bones spot gets raves from local foodies as Austin's most authentic Szechuan cuisine. Bypass the standard Chinese options for palate-tingling winners like the Asia Eggplant (in a spicy sauce), Chicken Delight (aka kou shui ji, bone-in, chilled chicken slices in a spicy sauce), and the best Spicy Fish in town. They employ Szechuan peppercorns and fiery red oil liberally, so be prepared. Takeout is available, and a Chinese breakfast is served Saturday mornings. ⊠ *8650 Spicewood Springs Rd., Suite 115, Northwest Austin* ☏ *512/331–5780* ▭ *MC, V.*

SOUTHERN ✕ **Hoover's.** In recent years local chef Hoover Alexander has created one
$–$$ of Austin's best comfort-food oases, blending mama's home cooking,
☾ diner short-order specials, Tex-Mex favorites, and Cajun influences.
★ The self-styled "Smoke, Fire & Ice House" is known for its large portions, and the chefs aren't shy with the spices, either. The huge, flavorful chicken-fried steak puts most others to shame (even Threadgill's). The moist, flavorful fried chicken, smoked boudin sausage, and jalapeño creamed spinach are additional standouts; extravagant, New Orleans–influenced breakfasts are worth a trip. We've never had room to try the pies, but we hear they're pretty good, too. ⊠ *2002 Manor Rd., University of Texas* ☏ *512/479–5006* ⊠ *13376 Research Blvd., Northwest Austin* ☏ *512/335–0300* ▭ *AE, D, MC, V.*

BARBECUE ✕ **Rudy's BBQ.** Many local barbecue snobs turn up their noses at Rudy's
¢–$ because it's a chain (albeit Texas-based) with hokey decor, but plenty
☾ of Austinites count this as their "go-to" choice for brisket, ribs, or sausage. Takeout is brisk, but many a diner chows down at the vinyl-covered picnic tables. Three kinds of brisket—regular, extra moist, and extra lean—are cooked with a dry spice over wood fired with oak (not mesquite). Go for the extra moist unless you're watching your waist. The peppery "sause" (available bottled) is added at the table. Aside from brisket, there are pork and baby back ribs, pork loin, prime rib (not worth the extra cost, we think), and even turkey breast. Sides are uniformly good, especially the creamed corn, which has a cult following. ⊠ *11570 Research Blvd., Northwest Austin* ☏ *512/418–9898* ⊠ *2451 Capital of Texas Hwy. S, West Lake* ☏ *512/329–5554* ⊠ *7709 FM 620, Lake Travis* ☏ *512/250–8002* ⌔ *Reservations not accepted* ▭ *MC, V.*

SEAFOOD ✕ **Truluck's.** Pricey-but-excellent fish, shellfish, and steak are served in
$$$–$$$$ handsome surroundings that suggest a businessmen's yacht club at Truluck's, part of an upscale chain with restaurants in Texas and Florida. The specialty here is stone crab: the company owns a fleet of crab boats and its own fisheries in Florida. Every Monday is all-you-can-eat Jonah crab claw night, but you can get them any day of the week at the downtown and Northwest (near the Arboretum) locations. Alaskan king crab is also expertly rendered, if expensive. Try the "superlump" crabcake appetizer, the hot-and-crunchy trout over citrus aioli sauce with a mango-jalapeño puree, the Thai-chili scallops, and any of the steaks. Service is professional; the Northwest location is so dimly lighted that waiters regularly lend out flashlights so you can read the menu. Both locations have elegant bars, with occasional live piano music. ⊠ *401 Colorado St., Downtown & Capitol Area* ☏ *512/482–9000* ⊠ *10225 Research Blvd., Northwest Austin* ☏ *512/794–8300* ▭ *AE, D, DC, MC, V.*

PFLUGERVILLE

EASTERN
EUROPEAN
$$–$$$

✗ **European Bistro.** The service here can be scatterbrained (though things have been improving), but occasional lapses are forgiven, since this two-story Central European restaurant in Central Texas is a charmer—an authentic slice of the Old World in downtown Pflugerville, about 15 mi north of Austin. Co-owner Anni Zovek is a true champion of her native Hungarian cuisine, and a delightful hostess. Her sister Piroska whips up some of the most decadent desserts this side of Vienna, and the unusual soups, such as sour cherry, are also worth trying. Main courses of chicken paprika, panfried catfish, and all manner of schnitzels and wursts are reliable comfort food. The restaurant also serves Czech, Russian, Polish, and Armenian specialties. Hungarian, German, and Romanian wines are available, as are Czech and German beers. ⊠*111 E. Main St., Pflugerville* ☎*512/835–1919* 🖃*AE, D, DC, MC, V* ⊙*Closed Mon. No lunch Tues.–Thurs.*

SOUTH AUSTIN

BARBECUE
$–$$$
☾

✗ **County Line.** Part of a local chain, County Line has a few too many amenities to be considered a classic Central Texas barbecue joint. Chairs instead of bargain-basement picnic setups, little loaves of multigrain bread on tables, and functional air-conditioning make things downright civilized. But families, older couples, and anyone seeking a reasonably civilized traditional meal in bucolic surroundings enjoy the specialty slow-smoked ribs—huge slabs of beef and tender pork. The lakeside branch on FM 2222 is particularly picturesque. ⊠*6500 W. Bee Cave Rd., West Lake* ☎*512/327–1742* ⊠*5204 FM 2222, West Austin* ☎*512/346–3664* 🖃*AE, D, DC, MC, V.*

MEXICAN
$–$$
☾

✗ **Curra's Grill.** If you're looking for authentic Mexican food at an affordable price (read: cheaper than Fonda San Miguel), Curra's is your best bet. Both locations, south and northwest of center, are casual. *Cochinita pibil* (marinated pork cooked in banana leaves) is as moist, tender, and flavorful as it ought to be; the shrimp and fajitas are a cut above most Austin establishments. Outstanding brunch entrées are served all day—you might want to sample the enchiladas Chiapas (in a poblano cream sauce) or the enchiladas Curras, filled with melted Monterey Jack cheese and covered with *carne guisada* (flank steak in a tomato, onion, and pepper sauce with herbs and spices). ⊠*614 E. Oltorf St., South Austin* ☎*512/444–0012* 🖃*MC, V.*

ITALIAN
$–$$
Fodor'sChoice
★

✗ **Enoteca Vespaio.** Vespaio's kid sister has quickly harnessed the lion's share of popularity on South Congress. Known for its tantalizing antipasti counter filled with delectable charcuterie, pâtés, cheeses, and salads, this more-casual café has an authentic trattoria feel complete with brightly colored Italian countryside tablecloths. Sink your fork into a bowl of plump gnocchi bathed in garlicky tomato-arrabiata sauce, or nibble on a slice of classic Margherita pizza studded with garden-fresh basil. Juicy hanger steak and crispy french fries (bistecca con patate fritte) leave you wanting more, but don't fill up on dinner; the dessert case is home to some phenomenal treats—the crème puff is about as close to Paris as you can get. Pastries for breakfast or lunch on the patio are alone worth the visit. ⊠*1610 S. Congress, South Austin* ☎*512/441–7672* ▭*AE, D, MC, V* ☺*Sun. brunch only 10–3.*

BRAZILIAN   ✕**Estância Churrascaria.** This all-you-can-eat Brazilian steak house
$$$ owned by Brazilian expats opened in 2007 and quickly became a popu-
lar addition to Austin's dining scene. In an attractive limestone building
with post-and-beam ceilings, Estância has a prix-fixe menu for lunch
and dinner that covers everything except drinks and dessert. Start with
the large salad bar, but leave room for the 11 different grilled meats
that gaucho-costumed servers carve from skewers tableside. These
include *picanha* (rump steak), beef and pork ribs, filet mignon, New
Zealand leg of lamb, linguica (seasoned sausage), and chicken. It keeps
coming as long as you display the green card on your table. The wine
list has some 250 labels. It's a bit out of the way, just off Highway
290 in the Sunset Valley area of South Austin (about 8 mi southwest
of downtown), but worth the trip. ⊠*4894 Hwy. 290W, South Austin*
☎*512/892–1225* ▭*AE, D, MC, V.*

AMERICAN   ✕**Hyde Park Bar and Grill.** With its simple, eclectic menu focusing on
$–$$ comfort foods and more than ample portions, it's no wonder that
this welcoming neighborhood hangout has kept the locals coming in
since 1982. Both the original restaurant on Duval Street and the newer
South Austin location decorate the walls with original paintings (for
sale) by local artists, and maintain an easygoing atmosphere for both
the shorts-and-T-shirt crowd and dressier factions. The variations on
simple fare run from generous salads and sandwiches to steaks and
grilled seafood. Platter-size chicken-fried steak and delicately breaded
and peppered fries are house favorites. Service is friendly and very competent. Weekend brunch is busiest—look for the hungry crowd milling
around the towering fork-in-the-road sculpture outside. Area parking
is limited. ⊠*4206 Duval St., Hyde Park* ☎*512/458–3168* ⊠*4521
West Gate Blvd., South Austin* ☎*512/899–2700* ⌂*Reservations not
accepted* ▭*AE, D, DC, MC, V.*

AMERICAN   ✕**Magnolia Cafe.** This locally beloved restaurant serves a full comple-
¢–$$ ment of the simple breakfast/brunch foods that Austinites tend to crave
☺   at all hours. The typical selection of sandwiches, omelets, salads, and
desserts is supplemented by seven enchilada options and hearty hash-
brown dishes enhanced with cheese, bacon, and other ingredients. Try
the Love Migas (eggs scrambled with crisp tortilla chips and fresh salsa,
spiked with garlic-serrano butter and served with black beans) for a
savory treat. Breakfast, including stellar plate-filling pancakes—but-
termilk, whole wheat, cornmeal, or richly luscious gingerbread—is
available 24/7. Service is always friendly. ⊠*2304 Lake Austin Blvd.,
Downtown & Capitol Area* ☎*512/478–8645* ⊠*1920 S. Congress
Ave., South Austin* ☎*512/445–0000* ⌂*Reservations not accepted*
▭*AE, DC, MC, V.*

MEXICAN   ✕**Matt's Famous El Rancho.** Opened by the Martinez family in 1952, this
¢–$$ South Austin landmark does old-school Tex-Mex extremely well, and
☺   you'll hear few complaints from diners. Combination dinners are many
and varied, with all the usual standbys: enchiladas, tamales, crispy
tacos, and more. Diehards swear by the chiles rellenos and old-fashioned tacos. The expansive dining room can get noisy at peak hours,

but the large outdoor patio is pleasant in good weather. Be sure to strike up a conversation with the staff—some employees have worked here for decades. ⊠*2613 S. Lamar Blvd., South Austin* ☎*512/462–9333* ☐*AE, D, DC, MC, V* ✆*Closed Tues.*

FAST FOOD ✕**Red Cap Chick.** We're recommending this tiny (seven-table) fast-food
¢–$$ joint for one reason: Korean hot pepper chicken. Not necessarily similar to the versions on offer at New York's Korean fried-chicken stands, let alone Korea's, these are large chunks of bone-in chicken, breaded and fried, with a slightly spicy, sticky crust. It suggests a variant on General Tso's chicken, and it's perfect party food. Red Cap also sells more-conventional fried chicken, and huge servings of fried okra for next to nothing. ⊠*2510 S. Congress, South Austin* ☎*512/416–1134* ☐*MC, V.*

BARBECUE ✕**Salt Lick.** When Texans argue about the relative merits of barbecue
¢–$$ joints, the Salt Lick usually winds up at or near the top of the heap.
Fodor's Choice Getting here entails a 30-minute drive southwest of Austin, but diners
★ who make the trek are rewarded with finger-licking-good ribs, beef, chicken, turkey, and sausage slow-cooked over an open pit and accompanied by a tangy sauce (unusual for central Texas) and the usual sides. Slaw is fresh and crisp, not smothered in mayo. If you can manage it, top your meal off with peach cobbler or pecan pie. The area is dry, alcohol-wise, so if you want anything stronger than Dr Pepper, bring it with you. It's cash-only, but there's an on-site ATM. **Salt Lick 360** (⊠*3801 N. Capital of Texas Hwy., West Lake* ☎*512/328–4957*), in town, is a fancier offshoot of the original barbecue joint. ⊠*18300 Farm-to-Market Rd. 1826, Driftwood* ☎*512/894–3117* ☐*No credit cards.*

JAPANESE ✕**Uchi.** You've heard the term "extreme sports"? Uchi is "extreme
$$–$$$$ sushi." Respectful of traditional sushi and sashimi methods—but not
Fodor's Choice limited by them—this standout sushi bar (a consistent critical and pop-
★ ular favorite) starts with superfresh ingredients. After that, anything goes, including touches of the South or south-of-the-border: yellowtail with ponzu sauce and sliced chilies, tempura-style fried green tomatoes, or seared monkfish cheeks with Vietnamese caramel, Belgian endive, roasted red grapes, and cilantro; unusual salsas enliven most any dish. You can make a tapas-style meal from the cold and hot "tastings" menu. If you sit at the sushi bar you can watch the enthusiastic kitchen staff at work. Attentive, knowledgeable service seals the deal. ⊠*801 S. Lamar Blvd., South Austin* ☎*512/916–4808* ☐*AE, MC, V* ✆*Closed Mon.–Wed. No lunch.*

ITALIAN ✕**Vespaio.** This buzzing Italian bistro on South Congress consistently
$$–$$$$ attracts Austin's bold and beautiful. Patrons crowd the narrow, warmly
★ lighted bar while waiting for a table in the small, tawny-hue dining room. Noshing on the gratis white-bean puree doused with a shot of basil-infused olive oil makes perusing the menu of delicate handmade pastas, thin wood-fired pizzas, and robust northern Italian-inspired entrées an even greater treat. Chef specials change daily, including soul-warming risottos of the day—the last bowl we tried included braised veal cheek and earthy wild mushrooms. Smoky grilled prawns wrapped in crispy prosciutto and served with warm suppli (fried risotto balls) never disappoints, nor does the savory veal scaloppine wrapped with

sage, prosciutto, and wilted spinach. Desserts change daily, but are worth the indulgence. ⊠ *1610 S. Congress, South Austin* ☎ *512/441–6100* ⊟ *AE, D, MC, V* ⊘ *No lunch* ⬙ *Reservations not accepted Fri.–Sat.*

UNIVERSITY OF TEXAS

CONTINENTAL **✕ Mansion at Judges' Hill.** One of the most romantic places in town is
$$–$$$$ this intimate, dimly lighted dining room in a boutique hotel in a cen-
★ tury-old mansion near the UT campus. Chandeliers hang from the ceiling, and portraits of cabaret singers line the walls. The first-course lobster beignets with avocado, roasted tomato, and corn sauce have a crusty exterior and a creamy, delicately spiced center. The duck confit quesadillas with smoked Gouda, provolone, forest mushrooms, and a tomatillo salsa are subtly complex. Seasonal entrées include petite beef medallions with a trio of sauces that reveal new flavors with each bite, and a 16-ounce rib-eye steak with potato mousseline, lemon-scented broccolini, and a béarnaise sauce. Save room for large, well-conceived desserts like caramelized s'mores with almond ice cream. Glitches in the prompt and considerate service are rare. Breakfast is served daily. ⊠ *1900 Rio Grande St., University of Texas* ☎ *512/495–1857* ⊟ *AE, D, DC, MC, V* ⊘ *No lunch Mon.–Sat.*

BARBECUE **✕ Ruby's BBQ.** On a busy corner of the Drag (UT's commercial strip),
¢–$$ this nuevo barbecue joint—which many locals consider among the best in town—has a deep list of menu options not found at old-school pits. The beef is trumpeted as all natural and hormone-free, but perhaps more important, it's tender, tasty, and perfectly juicy. Side dishes are vegetarian-friendly: two kinds of beans (black and BBQ), a couple of slaw options, potato salad, home fries, and collard greens. Also on the menu are garden salads and a few Cajun dishes. There are daily chalkboard specials. ⊠ *512 W. 29th St., University of Texas* ☎ *512/477–1651* ⬙ *Reservations not accepted* ⊟ *MC, V.*

ZILKER PARK

FRENCH **✕ Flip Happy Crepes.** More than just a restaurant, Flip Happy is the
¢–$ dream-made-real of Andrea Day Boykin and Nessa Higgins, who are
☺ doing their share to "keep Austin weird," serving up French-inspired
★ crepes out of a 1966-vintage silver trailer on a tree-sheltered side street in South Austin. The crepes are supermoist, salty-spicy, flavorful, and substantial (just one makes a good-size lunch). Chicken, mushrooms, goat cheese, shredded pork, and smoked salmon are typical ingredients, and the team also whips up sweet crepes and Saturday breakfast. It's just a fun place to grab a bite and sit with some of the happiest, in-the-know diners in town at a motley assortment of mismatched tables and chairs. Short hours are the main drawback: Flip Happy is generally open 10–2:30 Wednesday–Friday and 9–3 Saturday, but check the Web site for changes. Dinner is sometimes served on Saturday in warm weather. ⊠ *400 Jessie St., Zilker Park* ☎ *512/552–9034* ⊟ *No credit cards* ⊘ *Closed Sun.–Tues. No dinner.*

BARBECUE ✕**Green Mesquite.** It doesn't get much more Austin than this joint on
$ hippie-barbecue row by Barton Springs Pool. From the green-and-white
☼ striped awning to the checkerboard floor, this place oozes an ultraca-
sual, irreverent 21st-century vibe popular with hipsters of all ages and
singles about town. As a sign says, they've been "horrifying vegetarians
since 1988." Besides nicely priced standard barbecue platters and sides,
they do chicken-fried steak, catfish, and some Cajun dishes (though the
jambalaya we tried was oddly soupy). Soft herbed garlic butter served
with the bread is a nice touch. Pies are available, too. ✉*1400 Barton
Springs Rd., Zilker Park* ☎*512/479–0485* ▭*AE, D, DC, MC, V.*

AMERICAN ✕**Shady Grove.** If any one restaurant defines the laid-back, somewhat
¢–$$ goofy Austin aesthetic, it's probably Shady Grove. On any clear day,
☼ expect the stone patio here to be packed with folks fighting the heat
with schooner-size frozen margaritas. Visitors to Barton Springs Pool
frequent this state park–theme establishment for its funky vibe, high-
profile music events, and huge servings of simple fare. Burgers and hot
dogs are big movers here, as are the vegetarian "hippie sandwiches"
(roasted eggplant and grilled vegetables) and impossibly large salads.
On summer evenings the patio becomes a dine-in theater, as vintage
movies are projected onto an outdoor screen. ✉*1624 Barton Springs
Rd., Zilker Park* ☎*512/474–9991* ✑*Reservations not accepted* ▭*AE,
D, DC, MC, V.*

SOUTHERN ✕**Threadgill's.** Locals take their out-of-town guests to this local legend
$–$$ for "real Texas food." Kenneth Threadgill opened the original loca-
★ tion on North Lamar in 1933 as a gas station that soon evolved into
a honky-tonk that drew local musicians, including a pre-fame Janis
Joplin in the early '60s. Today, Threadgill's is a friendly restaurant
with cleaned-up Texas charm, and the main attraction is the massive
chicken-fried steak, followed by homemade cobbler and ice cream.
Some other mains may disappoint, though veggie sides are satisfying. Live music happens regularly at both locations. The atmosphere
is a bit hokey, but Threadgill's has earned it. ✉*6416 N. Lamar Blvd.,
North Austin* ☎*512/451–5440* ✉*301 W. Riverside Dr., Zilker Park*
☎*512/472–9304* ▭*AE, D, MC, V.*

WHERE TO STAY

Finding a place to stay in Austin isn't hard. Finding a place with personality is harder. Downtown, ample brand-name high-rises offer anony-
mous luxury, but despite Austin's history and capital status there are
only a few stately, historic hotels. The I–35 corridor is a logjam of chain
motels ranging from pleasant to horrid, catering largely to travelers
with limited expectations. In the tech-centered Northwest, it's hard to
drive any distance without passing an all-suites executive lodging.

Fortunately, things are improving. A good number of the hotels we list
have benefited from extensive renovations between 2006 and 2008,
and Austin is such a competitive market that many managers feel com-
pelled to provide the latest and greatest, whether it's flat-screen TVs,
radios with iPod docking stations, or ultracomfy beds. This being Austin, free, public Wi-Fi is near-ubiquitous.

Downtown, the Driskill and the Intercontinental Stephen F. Austin are two grandes dames that still shine. A couple of old motor courts on South Congress have been rediscovered and refitted, capturing Austin's bohemian charms. In the business district, there are plans to build a 1,000-room Marriott convention-center hotel (to be completed in 2011), ruffling a few local feathers in the process. On the other end of the spectrum are several well-run bed-and-breakfasts in historic homes.

Conventions and university events can pack the city at any time, but you'll especially need to plan ahead during a University of Texas football home game, South by Southwest in March, the Austin City Limits festival in September, or legislative sessions (held in odd-numbered years). At slower times many hotels have deep discounts. Keep in mind that parking at downtown hotels can add over $20 a day to your bill. In general, only hotels near Austin–Bergstrom International Airport have free airport shuttles.

WHAT IT COSTS					
	¢	$	$$	$$$	$$$$
Hotels	under $50	$50–$100	$101–$150	$151–$200	over $200

Hotel prices are per night for two people in a standard double room in high season, excluding service charges and Austin's 15% hotel tax.

DOWNTOWN & CAPITOL AREA

$$–$$$
Fodor'sChoice
★

Carrington's Bluff. Pine-covered arbors, a gazebo, and a tree-shaded, gently sloping lawn frame this B&B in a two-story, five-room 1877 dairy farm and adjoining 1920 three-room "Writers' Cottage" on a quiet residential street seven blocks from UT. Phoebe Williams is a genial hostess who works to accommodate specific needs. The cottage is filled with well-chosen period antiques; the only anachronisms are bedside clock radios and cable TVs. **Pros:** One of the most charming and personality-filled historic B&Bs in Austin, close to UT and a mile from downtown, convenient to bus routes. **Cons:** No pool, spa, or other luxury-hotel gewgaws; a bit hard to find, especially at night. ⌧*1900 David St., Downtown & Capitol Area,* ☎*512/479–0638 or 888/290–6090* ⊕*www.carringtonsbluff.com* ⌁*8 rooms* ⌂*In-room: no phone, Wi-Fi. In-hotel: no elevator, laundry facilities, public Wi-Fi, parking (no fee), some pets allowed, no-smoking rooms* ▤*AE, D, MC, V* ⍟*BP* .

$$$–$$$$

Courtyard Austin Downtown/Convention Center. Comfortable if unmemorable, this Courtyard is quite up to the brand standard and well maintained. You can't get more central to downtown Austin; the Convention Center is a short walk away, as is everything else in the business district. The staff is professional and helpful. **Pros:** Above-average business-oriented hotel, very central. **Con:** Lacks personality. ⌧*300 E. 4th St., Downtown & Capitol Area,* ☎*512/236–8008* ⊕*www.marriott.com* ⌁*270 rooms* ⌂*In-room: dial-up. In-hotel: room service, bar, pool,*

WHERE SHOULD I STAY IN AUSTIN?

	Neighborhood Vibe	Pros	Cons
Downtown & Capitol Area	Austin's vibrant downtown is growing into a place with a "real" big-city feel, yet retaining touches of the overgrown village it used to be. Close to most tourist attractions, it's ideal for first-time visitors and many business travelers.	Where the action is, in terms of business and restaurants and clubs; compact and pedestrian-friendly; good public transport.	Rooms tend to be either expensive or seedy, overnight parking pricey, daytime traffic heavy.
Lake Travis	Known for water sports, upmarket resorts, and casual restaurants, parts of the Lake Travis area have an almost Mediterranean look. Leisure travelers, conventioneers, and business groups frequent the hotels.	Luxurious resorts, pretty lake and surrounds, relaxed air, peaceful and untouristy.	Nearly 20 mi from the city; few, if any budget options; a car is a necessity.
Near the Airport	The roads leading to Austin–Bergstrom International Airport pass mainly through drab, working-class commercial and industrial strips of greater or lesser density. Business travelers and flight crews fill most hotels.	Unsurprisingly, convenient to airport; cheap and good Mexican eats nearby.	Properties are about 10 mi from downtown; most hotels uninteresting chains; surrounding areas generic and not pedestrian-friendly; a good stretch of Highway 71 is a seedy zone.
North Austin	Hotels and motels line the I–35 corridor for miles on both sides, attracting mainly transient business travelers and some families on weekends. You'll need a car to get around and you should choose your hotel with care, as some areas verge on unsafe.	Easy access to the highway and downtown, some hotels off I–35 are surprisingly characterful and pleasantly quirky.	The I–35 corridor is noisy and traffic-clogged night and day; some areas feel unsafe.
Northwest Austin	Hotels in this sprawling suburban area filled with large upscale malls and superstores are focused on business travelers and families on a budget. There are some worthwhile shops and restaurants, though you'll have to do a bit of research to find them.	Staff well tuned to needs of business travelers, comparatively good value, tons of malls and big-box stores close by.	Spread-out and generic suburban area; lodgings have little personality; not pedestrian-friendly.
South Austin	Hotels here come in all types and sizes and are relatively close to both downtown and the airport. Some areas are not pedestrian-friendly. The touristy, "fun" areas are nearer to the river.	Excellent business hotels at significant discounts compared to downtown counterparts, South Congress is hotel nirvana if you're looking for artsy and unusual.	Some hotel staff and managers are lax or overly casual; areas below Highway 290 are far from interesting neighborhoods.

2

BEST BETS FOR AUSTIN LODGING

For all the big hotel chains' efforts at standardization, any lodging's quality still depends largely on the manager and staff at an individual location. Since Austin is a desirable place to live, it draws many of the hospitality industry's best. We've chosen some especially well-run places below.

Fodor's Choice ★

Carrington's Bluff, $$–$$$, Downtown & Capitol Area

Doubletree Guest Suites, $$$–$$$$, Downtown & Capitol Area

Driskill Hotel, $$$$, Downtown & Capitol Area

Four Seasons, $$$$, Downtown & Capitol Area

Hyatt Place, $$$–$$$$, North Austin

Mansion at Judges' Hill, $$–$$$$, Downtown & Capitol Area

By Price

$

Austin Motel, South Austin

Days Inn University, Downtown & Capitol Area

$$

Carrington's Bluff, Downtown & Capitol Area

Habitat Suites, North Austin

Wyndham Garden Hotel–Austin, South Austin

$$$

Hotel San José, South Austin

Hyatt Place, North Austin

Lakeway Resort and Spa, Lake Travis

Mansion at Judges' Hill, Downtown & Capitol Area

Radisson Hotel & Suites Austin, Downtown & Capitol Area

$$$$

Barton Creek Resort & Spa, West Lake

Doubletree Guest Suites, Downtown & Capitol Area

Driskill Hotel, Downtown & Capitol Area

Four Seasons, Downtown & Capitol Area

By Type

B&B

Carrington's Bluff, $$–$$$, Downtown & Capitol Area

Woodburn House, $$, Downtown & Capitol Area

BOUTIQUE HOTEL

Habitat Suites, North Austin

Mansion at Judges' Hill, Downtown & Capitol Area

LARGE HOTEL

Crowne Plaza, $–$$$, North Austin

Four Seasons, $$$$, Downtown & Capitol Area

Hilton Austin, $$$$, Downtown & Capitol Area

Hilton Austin Airport, $$$$, Near the Airport

Omni Austin Hotel at Southpark, $$–$$$$, South Austin

Renaissance Austin Hotel, $$$$, Northwest Austin

Sheraton Austin, $$–$$$$, Downtown & Capitol Area

RESORT

Barton Creek Resort & Spa, $$$$, West Lake

Lakeway Resort and Spa, Lake Travis

By Location

CAPITOL AREA

Doubletree Guest Suites, $$$–$$$$, Downtown & Capitol Area

Doubletree Club Austin–University Area, $$–$$$, Downtown & Capitol Area

Mansion at Judges' Hill, $$$–$$$$, Downtown & Capitol Area

NEAR SHOPPING

Courtyard Austin NW/Arboretum, $$–$$$, Northwest Austin

Hilton Garden Inn Austin NW/Arboretum, $$–$$$, Northwest Austin

NEAR OUTDOOR ACTIVITIES

Embassy Suites Downtown, $$$–$$$$, Downtown & Capitol Area

Holiday Inn Lake Austin–Town Lake, $$$–$$$$, Downtown & Capitol Area

Hyatt Regency Austin, $$$$, Downtown & Capitol Area

SOUTH AUSTIN

Austin Motel, South Austin

Hotel San José, South Austin

Omni Austin Hotel at Southpark, $$–$$$$, South Austin

By Experience

FAMILY-FRIENDLY

Barton Creek Resort & Spa, $$$$, West Lake

Habitat Suites Hotel, $$–$$$, North Austin

Hawthorn Suites Austin Central, $$–$$$, North Austin

Lakeway Resort and Spa, $$$–$$$$, Lake Travis

Omni Austin Hotel at Southpark, $$–$$$$, South Austin

HISTORIC

Carrington's Bluff, $$–$$$, Downtown & Capitol Area

Driskill Hotel, $$$$, Downtown & Capitol Area

InterContinental Stephen F. Austin Hotel, $$$$, Downtown & Capitol Area

Mansion at Judges' Hill, $$–$$$$, Downtown & Capitol Area

MOST CHARMING

Carrington's Bluff, $$–$$$, Downtown & Capitol Area

Mansion at Judges' Hill, $$–$$$$, Downtown & Capitol Area

Woodburn House, $$, Downtown & Capitol Area

GREAT VIEWS

Barton Creek Resort & Spa, $$$$, West Lake

Doubletree Guest Suites, $$$–$$$$, Downtown & Capitol Area

Four Seasons, $$$$, Downtown & Capitol Area

Holiday Inn Austin–Town Lake, $$$–$$$$, Downtown & Capitol Area

Lakeway Resort and Spa, $$$–$$$$, Lake Travis

Omni Austin Hotel at Southpark, $$–$$$$, South Austin

gym, laundry facilities, laundry service, concierge, executive floor, no-smoking rooms ⊟AE, D, DC, MC, V.

$ 🏨**Days Inn University.** In 2007 and 2008, new owners replaced worn furniture and carpets in hopes of repairing the image of this onetime run-down fleabag. On I–35, across from St. David's Medical Center and near UT, highway noise can be a problem, but the price is right and rooms have microwaves and free Wi-Fi and HBO, and there's free Internet, faxing, and printing off the lobby. Downtown is a $5–$7 cab ride away. Star Seeds Cafe, next door, is a classic 24-hour Austin hipster-slacker dive, though the food is mediocre at best. **Pros:** Good value, close to UT. **Cons:** Ever-present highway noise once you step outside your door (though most rooms are quiet enough with the door closed), area not walkable. ✉*3105 I–35N, Downtown & Capitol Area,* ☎*512/478–1631* ⊕*www.daysinnaustintexas.com* 🛏*63 rooms* ⌂*In-room: safe, refrigerator, Wi-Fi. In-hotel: pool, no elevator, laundry facilities, public Wi-Fi* ⊟*AE, D, DC, MC, V* ⦿*CP.*

$$–$$$$ 🏨**Doubletree Club Austin–University Area.** Business travelers, large groups, and visiting sports teams keep this medium-size hostelry off I–35 near UT (and next to a historic cemetery) humming. Rooms were substantially renovated in 2007 and 2008. There's a nicely landscaped, if smallish, outdoor pool. A Denny's next door is so convenient it should qualify as an in-house restaurant. **Pros:** Recent renovations, close to UT. **Con:** A car is a necessity. ✉*1617 I–35N, Downtown & Capitol Area,* ☎*512/479–4000* ⊕*www.doubletreehotels.com* 🛏*152 rooms* ⌂*In-room: refrigerator (some), Wi-Fi. In-hotel: restaurant, room service, bar, pool, gym, laundry service, parking (fee), no-smoking rooms* ⊟*AE, D, DC, MC, V.*

$$$–$$$$ 🏨**Doubletree Guest Suites.** One of the best-managed hotels in the city,
Fodor'sChoice the all-suites Doubletree has a staff that anticipates your every need.
★ Business travelers, sports teams, and families frequent the downtown high-rise. The capitol—visible from many of the rooms, spectacularly so from upper-story balconies—is only a few minutes' walk away. Most of the classically decorated suites have one bedroom and two TVs; some have two bedrooms, two baths, and three TVs; four are penthouses. Each has a small kitchen with a full-size refrigerator and dishwasher. A free shuttle takes you anywhere within a 2-mi radius. Smoking is only allowed on the third floor. **Pros:** Superbly run, above-average ambience. **Cons:** Can be crowded, busy area, fee for parking. ✉*303 W. 15th St., Downtown & Capitol Area,* ☎*512/478–7000 or 800/222–8733* ⊕*www.doubletreehotels.com* 🛏*188 suites* ⌂*In-room: kitchen, refrigerator, Wi-Fi. In-hotel: restaurant, room service, bar, pool, gym, laundry facilities, laundry service, parking (fee), some pets allowed, no-smoking rooms* ⊟*AE, D, DC, MC, V.*

$$$$ 🏨**Driskill Hotel.** Built in 1886 and impeccably restored, the Driskill is a
Fodor'sChoice beautiful public space created when people relished mingling in grand
★ settings. The lobby is highlighted by vaulted ceilings, decorative columns, and chandeliers. The entire effect is old-fashioned luxury, and Texas to the core. Each room is unique: walls are decorated with old photos, postcards, lace, and bric-a-brac scoured from local antiques shops. Ceilings are higher in rooms in the historic wing than in the

newer tower wing (which dates merely to 1930) and bathrooms are old-fashioned and spotless. The Driskill Grill *(⇨ Where to Eat)* and semicasual 1886 Café & Bakery are both worth a visit. The elegant bar, with frequent live piano music, has long attracted Austin's movers and shakers. The hotel is widely reported to be haunted. **Pros:** Flawless restoration, historic, lots of personality. **Cons:** No pool, immediate neighborhood is an unattractive city block. ⊠*604 Brazos St., Downtown & Capitol Area,* ☎*512/474–5911 or 800/252–9367* ⊕*www. driskillhotel.com* ➷*176 rooms, 13 suites* ⚟*In-room: Ethernet, Wi-Fi. In-hotel: restaurant, room service, bar, gym, parking (no fee)* ⊟*AE, D, DC, MC, V.*

$$$–$$$$ ⊞ **Embassy Suites Downtown.** This central all-suites hotel is across the street from the Lady Bird Lake hiking and biking trail, 4 blocks from the Convention Center, and 10 blocks from the state capitol. Rooms look out onto an interior atrium lobby with a 550-gallon aquarium. The standard two-room suites have two televisions, a microwave, and a refrigerator; rates include evening cocktails. In addition to a pool and exercise room, there's a sauna and hot tub. The property is remaining open while it undergoes a complete renovation, expected to be completed in 2009. **Pros:** Attractive, well run, close to airport. **Con:** Under renovation until 2009. ⊠*300 S. Congress Ave., Downtown & Capitol Area,* ☎*512/469–9000 or 800/362–2779* ⊕*www.embassysuites. com* ➷*262 rooms* ⚟*In-room: refrigerator, Wi-Fi. In-hotel: restaurant, room service, bar, pool, gym, laundry facilities, laundry service, parking (no fee)* ⊟*AE, D, DC, MC, V* �aBP.*

$$$$ ⊞ **Four Seasons.** You get what you pay for in superior service and amenities at this elegant hotel on beautifully manicured grounds overlooking Lady Bird Lake. Rooms are average size, but stylish. Beds with goose-down pillows and comforters, flat-screen plasma TVs, and iPod docking stations are standard. Some rooms have terraces, and upper-floor units have impressive views. Extras include a lending library of Texas literature and in-room martini bars. The hotel has an attractive outdoor saltwater pool, an indoor pool, and a whirlpool, as well as a modern fitness center and a gorgeous spa, installed during extensive 2007 renovations. There are two business centers. Smoking is relegated to one floor. **Pros:** Beautiful, with resort feel; central downtown location. **Cons:** Expensive, parking among priciest in town. ⊠*98 San Jacinto Blvd., Downtown & Capitol Area,* ☎*512/478–4500 or 800/332–3442* ⊕*www.fourseasons.com* ➷*291 rooms* ⚟*In-room: safe, DVD, Ethernet, Wi-Fi. In-hotel: 2 restaurants, room service, bar, pool, gym, spa, laundry service, concierge, public Wi-Fi, parking (fee), some pets allowed, no-smoking rooms* ⊟*AE, DC, MC, V.*

FodorsChoice ★ *(left margin, next to Four Seasons)*

$$$$ ⊞ **Hilton Austin.** Austin's largest hotel rises 26 stories over one of downtown's quieter blocks, next to small Brush Park (home to the O. Henry house). But the Hilton is defined by its proximity to the colossal Austin Convention Center, and this is *the* conventioneers' hostelry. It has two proper restaurants, plus a coffee shop and business center, and Austin's second-largest outdoor pool (heated). Standard rooms have two full beds or one king and a leather loveseat; the latter configuration seems roomier. Room safes accommodate a laptop. The entire eighth floor

is a 16,000-square-foot health club with a steam room and sauna, and a gym with great views of UT's stadium. **Pros:** Downtown location, easy drive to airport. **Cons:** Huge, rather impersonal. ✉ *500 E. 4th St., Downtown & Capitol Area,* ☎ *512/482–8000* ⊕ *www.hilton.com* ⤳ *775 rooms, 25 suites* ⌂ *In-room: safe, Ethernet, Wi-Fi. In-hotel: 3 restaurants, room service, bar, pool, gym, spa, laundry service, concierge, public Wi-Fi, parking (fee), no-smoking rooms* ▭ *AE, D, DC, MC, V.*

$$$–$$$$ ⊡ **Holiday Inn Austin–Town Lake.** Comfortable rooms are paired with remarkable vistas in every direction at this two-tower complex rising 11 and 14 stories on the north shore of Lady Bird Lake. The sixth-floor heated outdoor swimming pool affords a lake view (and a continuous soundtrack of I–35 traffic). A hike-and-bike trail is just outside the back door, and the Congress Avenue Bridge is a 15-minute walk away. Extensive 2007–2008 renovations resulted in bicycle, kayak, and Segway rentals, and a 12-seat movie theater. The rooms—with two double beds or one king—have subdued, contemporary decor, firm mattresses, a refrigerator and microwave, free Wi-Fi, and some pull-out sofas. A modest, sunny gym overlooks the pool and lake. **Pros:** Nicely renovated older hotel, friendly staff, adjacent lakeside trail. **Cons:** Busy highway just outside, rooms on lower floors noisier, immediate neighborhood not very interesting. ✉ *20 I–35N, Downtown & Capitol Area,* ☎ *512/472–8211* ⊕ *www.holiday-inn.com* ⤳ *320 rooms* ⌂ *In-room: refrigerator, Wi-Fi. In-hotel: restaurant, room service, bar, pool, gym, bicycles, laundry facilities, laundry service, concierge, airport shuttle, parking (no fee), no-smoking rooms* ▭ *AE, D, DC, MC, V.*

$$$$ ⊡ **Hyatt Regency Austin.** On Lady Bird Lake near Auditorium Shores, the
★   hotel has great views of the water and downtown skyline. The huge, skylit lobby, with tons of native stone and a central atrium rising 17 stories, oozes rugged sophistication. Rooms, which were upgraded in 2006, have 32-inch flat-panel TVs and luxe bathrooms. Business meetings and banquets keep the Hyatt hopping year-round. **Pros:** Attractive, luxurious, well equipped and well staffed for meetings. **Con:** Some find it too slick and corporate. ✉ *208 Barton Springs Rd., Downtown & Capitol Area,* ☎ *512/477–1234* ⊕ *www.hyatt.com* ⤳ *448 rooms* ⌂ *In-room: Ethernet, Wi-Fi. In-hotel: restaurant, room service, bar, pool, parking (fee)* ▭ *AE, D, DC, MC, V.*

$$$$ ⊡ **InterContinental Stephen F. Austin Hotel.** This historic 1924 hotel
★   reopened in 2000, after a 12-year vacancy, following a top-to-bottom renovation, including restoration of many original architectural features. The location is ideal: one block from 6th Street, four blocks from the capitol, and next door to the historic Paramount Theater. Rooms are dressed in dark woods, and the decor is sparked with understated nods to Texas, like the Lone Star emblem on the headboards—all in all they are a bit bland apart from the opulent bathrooms with marble vanities. At the end of the day, relax at the terrace bar, whose balcony overlooks Congress Avenue and the capitol, or at Roaring Fork, a critically praised Western bistro and saloon. **Pros:** Well run, centrally located, historic. **Cons:** Some rooms rather small, pricey valet parking. ✉ *701 Congress Ave., Downtown & Capitol Area,* ☎ *512/457–8800 or 800/327–0200* ⊕ *www.austin.intercontinental.com* ⤳ *189 rooms,*

2

16 suites ☼ *In-room: safe, Ethernet. In-hotel: 2 restaurants, room service, bar, pool, gym, laundry service, concierge, executive floor, parking (fee)* ☰ *AE, D, DC, MC, V.*

$$ 🖭 **La Quinta Inn Austin Capitol.** If you can forgo the froufrou, you can save a bundle at this well-maintained property with a million-dollar location. The rooms, last renovated in 2007, are modestly sized—ask for a corner king if you want extra space. The outdoor pool is on a windy patio: good for a quick dip, and not much more. This is not the place to come during UT Longhorn home football weekends if you want a good night's sleep. **Pros:** Centrally located, friendly staff, free breakfast buffet. **Cons:** Parking is valet only, some rooms (and patrons) can be noisy. ☒ *300 E. 11th St., Downtown & Capitol Area,* ☎ *512/476–1166 or 800/531–5900* ⊕ *www.lq.com* ⬳ *145 rooms, 5 suites* ☼ *In-room: refrigerator (some), Ethernet. In-hotel: pool, gym, laundry service, public Wi-Fi, parking (fee), some pets allowed, no-smoking rooms* ☰ *AE, D, DC, MC, V* ⑩ *CP.*

$$–$$$$
Fodor's Choice
★
🖭 **Mansion at Judges' Hill.** History and modern amenities come together in this exquisite boutique hotel near the southern edge of UT's main campus. The Goodall Wooten house, a Texas Historic Landmark completed in 1900, was of fairly simple design until 1910, when the owners remodeled it into a grand Classical Revival mansion. All rooms have high-speed Internet connections, and there's twice-daily maid service. Little touches—his and hers bathrobes, extra pillows, and beautiful bathrooms (in the more-expensive wing)—make the difference. There's also an exceptional, fine-dining restaurant, a handsome bar, and occasional cabaret performances in the second-floor banquet hall. **Pros:** Beautifully restored, historic, perfect for romantic getaways, attentive staff. **Cons:** Parking somewhat limited, no pool. ☒ *1900 Rio Grande St., Downtown & Capitol Area,* ☎ *512/495–1800 or 800/311–1619* ⊕ *www.mansionatjudgeshill.com* ⬳ *48 rooms* ☼ *In-room: Ethernet. In-hotel: restaurant, concierge* ☰ *AE, D, DC, MC, V.*

$$$$ 🖭 **Omni Austin Downtown.** Your introduction to this bustling, business-oriented hotel is a soaring, granite-and-glass atrium lobby. From atrium-view rooms you can spy on diners and scurrying businesspeople below. Exterior rooms have balconies and city vistas (on upper floors). The decor neither inspires nor offends. Most of the suites were once condos and have full kitchens, washers and dryers, and walk-in closets. Some rooms have whirlpool baths, and there's an outdoor swimming pool on the roof. At breakfast, the eggs are cage-free, the bagels are shipped from New York. Service is professional, if on the cool side. **Pros:** Central location, everything for the business traveler. **Con:** Can feel impersonal. ☒ *700 San Jacinto St., Downtown & Capitol Area,* ☎ *512/476–3700* ⊕ *www.omnihotels.com* ⬳ *375 rooms* ☼ *In-room: Wi-Fi. In-hotel: restaurant, room service, bar, pool, gym, spa, laundry service, concierge, executive floor, parking (fee), no-smoking rooms* ☰ *AE, D, DC, MC, V.*

$$$–$$$$ 🖭 **Radisson Hotel & Suites Austin.** This informal riverside hotel has an attractive outdoor pool patio with prime views of Lady Bird Lake and Congress Avenue Bridge sunset bat flights. Many of the East Tower's large two-room suites have gorgeous views of the lake or downtown.

Standard rooms are spacious, and all rooms have beds with Sleep Number mattresses. A T.G.I. Friday's and a Starbucks are on-site. The business district, the hike-and-bike trail, 6th Street, and the Warehouse District are each a short stroll away. **Pros:** Reliable downtown choice, friendly and responsive staff. **Cons:** May be better values nearby, pricey parking. ⊠*111 E. Cesar Chavez St., Downtown & Capitol Area,* ☎*512/478–9611* ⊕*www.radisson.com* ⏍*413 rooms* ⏍*In-room: Ethernet, Wi-Fi. In-hotel: restaurant, room service, bar, pool, gym, laundry service, concierge, executive floor, public Wi-Fi, airport shuttle, parking (fee), no-smoking rooms* ▤*AE, D, DC, MC, V.*

$$–$$$$ 🏨 **Sheraton Austin.** A convenient downtown location, a friendly, responsive staff, and rooms that were renovated in 2007 are three reasons to choose the Sheraton on your next business trip. This 16-story hotel appeals primarily to road warriors looking for little more than a comfortable bed, a 27-inch flat-screen plasma TV, a bite to eat, a business center, and a quick exit (via neighboring I–35) to the next town. Some rooms have Capitol or downtown views, which is just about the only variable in the uniform accommodations, which are pleasant but rather small for the price. There's a decent fitness center. The ground-floor restaurant is stylish, if overpriced; the lobby bar serves drink and bistro fare; and there's an in-house coffee emporium. **Pros:** Central location, business-friendly. **Cons:** Not family-friendly; some complaints of subpar service, housekeeping, and noise. ⊠*701 E. 11th St., Downtown & Capitol Area,* ☎*512/478–1111* ⊕*www.starwoodhotels.com/sheraton* ⏍*365 rooms, 4 suites* ⏍*In-room: refrigerator (some), Ethernet, Wi-Fi. In-hotel: restaurant, room service, bar, pools, gym, laundry facilities, laundry service, concierge, executive floors, public Wi-Fi, some pets allowed, no-smoking rooms* ▤*AE, D, DC, MC, V.*

$–$$ 🏨 **Super 8 Motel.** For basic, reasonably priced lodging close to downtown, you could do worse than this basic two-story brick motel just off I–35 northbound. There's a clean outdoor pool, and a good view of downtown from the second floor. Be sure to request a room away from highway noise. Rooms have slightly worn carpet and older refrigerators and microwaves, and there are no no-smoking floors (only no-smoking rooms), but for these prices it's hard to complain. An employee cautions to beware of "party people." Ask for a quieter room, especially during UT home games and SXSW. **Pros:** Price, proximity to downtown. **Cons:** Can be noisy, not scenic. ⊠*1201 I–35N, Downtown & Capitol Area,* ☎*512/472–8331* ⊕*www.super8.com* ⏍*60 rooms, 5 suites* ⏍*In-room: refrigerator (some), Ethernet. In-hotel: pool, laundry facilities, some pets allowed, no-smoking rooms* ▤*AE, D, DC, MC, V.*

$$ 🏨 **Woodburn House.** Built in 1909, Hyde Park's only B&B—listed in the National Register of Historic Places—is a simply and tastefully decorated three-story home with a mix of antiques and newer furniture. Large wraparound porches and mature pecan trees add to the charm. Owners Kristen and Noel De La Rosa can provide a self-guided walking tour of Austin's historic Hyde Park area. The large room in an adjoining detached carriage house has a kitchenette, big-screen TV, and hot tub. Some good restaurants are within walking distance. There's free in-room Wi-Fi, and the entire house is no-smoking. **Pros:** Well-maintained and historic, charming neighborhood, close to public transport, 1 mi from UT and 2 mi from downtown. **Con:** Only suites have TVs. ✉4401 Ave. D, Downtown & Capitol Area, ☎512/458–4335 or 888/690–9763 ⊕www.woodburnhouse.com ⥲4 rooms, 2 suites ⚐In-room: No TV (some), Wi-Fi. In-hotel: no elevator, parking (no fee), no kids under 12, no-smoking rooms ⏇CP ⊟AE, MC, V.

2

LAKE TRAVIS

$$$–$$$$ 🞖**Lakeway Resort and Spa.** On a finger of land surrounded on three sides by Lake Travis, this sprawling, handsome resort housed in low-rise stone buildings is about 20 mi from downtown. The property has all you'd expect from a large conference center and resort, including a full-service, state-of-the-art spa, built in 2007, and a tiered infinity-edge outdoor pool. Many recreational opportunities are available on the lake and adjacent marina, from sunset cruises to watercraft rentals, and four golf courses are nearby. Rooms (all no-smoking) are tasteful, mocha-hued, and modern, with contemporary art and plush beds. Most rooms have lakeside views and balconies. The upscale Travis Restaurant offers largely steaks and seafood (some diners have noted glaring service glitches). **Pros:** Gorgeous resort hotel in peaceful lakeside location, many high-end amenities. **Cons:** Not convenient to downtown, some may find the ambience stuffy. ✉101 Lakeway Dr., Lake Travis, ☎512/261–6600 or 800/525–3929 ⊕www.lakeway.dolce.com ⥲166 rooms, 2 suites ⚐In-room: Wi-Fi, Ethernet. In-hotel: 2 restaurants, bar, room service, golf courses, tennis court, pools, gym, spa, children's programs (ages 4–12), laundry service, public Internet, public Wi-Fi, airport shuttle, parking (no fee), no-smoking rooms ⊟AE, D, DC, MC, V.

NEAR THE AIRPORT

$$$$ 🞖**Hilton Austin Airport.** On the grounds of the Austin–Bergstrom International Airport, this circular building was built in the late '60s as a U.S. Air Force base (known as "the donut") and reopened as a hotel in 2001. The atrium is like a Texan starship, with a dome soaring above three balconied floors, and limestone pillars surrounding a central bar area. Rooms overlook the atrium or the large outdoor pool and hot tub with adjacent above-average fitness center. Rooms have well-padded beds, two-cup coffeemakers, and Crabtree & Evelyn toiletries. A touch screen near the front desk allows you to pay bills, check out, and even print airline boarding passes, and a free shuttle runs to and from airport terminals. Ample meeting space and four ballrooms mean many events and conferences. The hotel is smoke free. **Pros:** Attractive, well run, business oriented, close to airport. **Cons:** Isolated from areas beyond the airport. ✉9515 Hotel Dr., near the airport, ☎512/385–6767 ⊕www.austinairport.hilton.com ⥲251 rooms, 11 suites ⚐In-room: refrigerator (some), Ethernet. In-hotel: restaurant, room service, bar, pool, gym, laundry facilities, laundry service, concierge, public Wi-Fi, airport shuttle, parking (fee), no-smoking rooms ⊟AE, D, DC, MC, V.

$$ ⬚ **La Quinta Inn & Suites Austin Airport.** Popular with flight crews on layovers, this standout among nearby lodging choices is 3 mi from Austin–Bergstrom International Airport (there's a free shuttle), and was totally renovated in 2007. Two-story lobby-atrium windows open onto a heated courtyard pool and nicely landscaped grounds. Rooms are modern, with light-wood furnishings. King-bed rooms have 42-inch flat-screen TVs, an ergonomic office chair, and a desk running the length of the wall. Some rooms have microwaves. Several decent casual eateries are a few minutes' drive away. **Pros:** Good value, friendly staff, convenient to airport. **Con:** Removed from downtown and any sights. ✉️ *7625 E. Ben White Blvd., South Austin,* 🕾 *512/386–6800* ⊕ *www. lq.com* ⬚*129 rooms, 13 suites* ⬚ *In-room: refrigerator, Ethernet. In-hotel: pool, gym, laundry facilities, laundry service, public Wi-Fi, airport shuttle, parking (no fee), some pets allowed, no-smoking rooms* ▤*AE, D, DC, MC, V* ⑩*BP.*

NORTH AUSTIN

$–$$$ ⬚ **Crowne Plaza.** A mall and shopping plaza are 2 mi from this seven-
★   story hotel continually bustling with conventions and meetings; downtown is 4–5 mi away. Prime rib and similar fare is served in the restaurant, but there are several decent places to eat nearby. Complimentary vans shuttle you within a 3-mi radius. Rooms have plush, comfy beds. One extra is a Sleep Advantage packet with a calming CD, sleep tips, eye mask, ear plugs, and lavender linen spray. **Pros:** Full-service hotel with responsive staff, modern amenities. **Cons:** Large and impersonal, lots of conventions and big groups. ✉️ *6121 I–35N, North Austin,* 🕾 *512/323–5466* ⊕ *www.crowneplaza.com* ⬚*280 rooms, 13 suites* ⬚ *In-room: refrigerator, Ethernet, Wi-Fi. In-hotel: restaurant, room service, bar, pool, laundry facilities, concierge, executive floor, public Internet, public Wi-Fi* ▤*AE, D, DC, MC, V.*

$$–$$$$ ⬚ **Doubletree.** This 1983-vintage hotel turns its back on the rat race of nearby I–35 and transports guests to a surprisingly convincing Spanish colonial world. Huge, arched windows in the lobby open onto a landscaped and terraced courtyard, with pool and hot tub enclosed by six floors of arched walkways. Rooms are spanking clean, spacious, and decorated with plush, high-quality gold-and-cream fabrics, linens, and carpets. Bathrooms are large, with granite sinks. The free local shuttle transports you within a 1-mi radius. **Pros:** Charming, pseudo-grand-hotel atmosphere; close (but not too close) to highway. **Cons:** Few decent restaurants within walking distance; fee for parking, unusual for this area. ✉️ *6505 I–35N, North Austin,* 🕾 *512/454–3737* ⊕ *www. doubletreehotels.com* ⬚*322 rooms, 28 suites* ⬚ *In-room: refrigerator (some), Wi-Fi. In-hotel: restaurant, room service, bar, pool, gym, laundry service, parking (fee), no-smoking rooms* ▤*AE, D, DC, MC, V.*

$$ ⬚ **Drury Inn.** A mall and several chain restaurants are within walking distance of this four-story hotel, which was renovated in 2007 but retains an outdated, though clean, look. Rooms are a bit cramped, but have a refrigerator and microwave. Bargain prices and good service are the Drury's assets, and it is popular with state employees and visiting collegiate sports teams. It's less than 5 mi from downtown and 12 mi from the airport. The hotel bar is only open 5:30–7 PM. **Pros:** Good value, friendly, family-run. **Cons:** Small, unattractive rooms; access difficult during rush hour. ✉ *6711 I–35N, North Austin,* ☎ *512/467–9500* ⊕ *www.druryhotels.com* ⇨ *224 rooms* ⌂ *In-room: refrigerator, Ethernet, Wi-Fi. In-hotel: bar, pool, gym, laundry facilities, laundry service, public Wi-Fi, parking (no fee), some pets allowed, no-smoking rooms* ☰ *AE, D, DC, MC, V* ⚭ *CP.*

$$–$$$ **Embassy Suites Austin–Central.** One of the busiest intersections in town (U.S. 290 and I–35) is an unlikely location for pseudo-south-of-the-border charm. Hiding behind a deceptively boring exterior is a Disney-esque version of a Mexican village: meandering paths, a zocalo (central square) with a gazebo, lots of plants, park benches, and street lamps, and a carp-filled creek. French doors open onto this surreal scene from every perfectly standardized room. Extensive renovations were completed in early 2008. Rooms have mini-refrigerators and there's a complimentary business center. **Pros:** Atrium is pure eye candy, excellent highway access to downtown and malls. **Cons:** Little within walking distance, some may find decor tacky, rooms dimly lighted. ✉ *5901 N. I–35, North Austin,* ☎ *512/454–8004* ⊕ *www.embassysuitesaustinnorth. com* ⇨ *250 suites* ⌂ *In-room: refrigerator, Wi-Fi. In-hotel: restaurant, room service, bar, pool, gym, laundry facilities, laundry service, parking (no fee), no-smoking rooms* ☰ *AE, D, DC, MC, V* ⚭ *BP.*

$$–$$$ **Habitat Suites Hotel.** Native flowering plants, organic vegetable gar-
★   dens, and fruit-bearing trees surround this environmentally friendly lodging. A member of the Green Hotels Association, it has won an impressive number of awards for sustainability. The beautifully land-scaped pool is sanitized with a salt generator instead of chlorine, the rooms are cleaned with nontoxic products, and the breakfast buffet includes macrobiotic selections. The apartment-like suites are light-filled and roomy, with vaulted ceilings and open kitchens; most have fireplaces. Two-bedroom suites have two stories. Highland Mall, a major shopping center, is just across the road. There's a business center. **Pros:** Ecoconscious, attractive landscaping, peaceful, hospitable staff. **Cons:** Poor-quality furniture, small TVs, can be hard to find. ✉ *500 E. Highland Mall Blvd., North Austin,* ☎ *512/467–6000 or 800/535–4663* ⊕ *www.habitatsuites.com* ⇨ *96 suites* ⌂ *In-room: Wi-Fi. In-hotel: pool, no elevator, laundry facilities, laundry service, parking (no fee), no-smoking rooms* ☰ *AE, D, DC, MC, V* ⚭ *CP.*

$–$$ **Hampton Inn Austin North.** Far more welcoming inside than the ugly facade would indicate, this basic hostelry near the junction of I–35 and U.S. 183 is near several malls and 6 mi from downtown Austin. Rooms are clean, with comfy beds, a small table, and a few extras like a lumbar pillow and lap desk. The small heated outdoor pool is accompanied by constant highway noise. The staff is friendly. There's free Wi-Fi throughout the hotel. **Pros:** Decent free breakfast buffet with good coffee, free local calls, well maintained. **Cons:** Next to a very busy highway, no restaurants within walking distance. ✉ *7619 I–35N, North Austin,* ☎ *512/452–3300* ⊕ *www.hamptoninn.com* ⇨ *121 rooms* ⌂ *In-room: refrigerator (some), Wi-Fi. In-hotel: pool, laundry service, public Wi-Fi, parking (no fee)* ☰ *AE, D, DC, MC, V* ⚭ *CP.*

\$\$–\$\$\$ 🏨 **Hawthorn Suites Austin Central.** This quiet, landscaped, apartment-like property is usually booked during the week with corporate clients, but opens up on weekends. All of the large suites have full kitchens, fireplaces, and enclosed patios or balconies. Two-bedroom suites have a second story, up steep stairs. Breakfast is served in a room with a huge fireplace and circular stained-glass window. A complimentary Monday–Thursday light dinner buffet, a basketball court, and 96-channel cable service are notable extras. Highland Mall is a minute away, and Pappadeaux Seafood Kitchen is next door. **Pros:** Convenient to downtown, frequent discounts, old-pro staffers. **Con:** Boring in-room decor. ✉*935 La Posada Dr. N, North Austin,* ☎*512/459–3335 or 800/527–1133* ⊕*www.hawthorn.com* ⤶*69 suites* ⚒*In-room: Ethernet (some). In-hotel: pool, gym, no elevator, laundry facilities, laundry service, parking (no fee), no-smoking rooms* ▤*AE, D, DC, MC, V* ⫿*BP.*

\$–\$\$ 🏨 **Howard Johnson Plaza Hotel & Conference Center.** This eccentric Southwest version of HoJo's was built in 1972 at what is now one of the city's busiest intersections, but has weathered the years reasonably well; guest rooms were last renovated in 2007. It attracts mainly business travelers and is 4 mi from downtown. "Business king" rooms are larger. Ask for a room away from traffic noise. **Pros:** Good value, pleasant inner courtyard, close to the highway. **Cons:** On one of the noisiest corners in Austin, prone to traffic jams at nearly any hour, public spaces not inviting. ✉*7800 I–35N, North Austin,* ☎*512/836–8520* ⊕*www.hojoplazaaustin.com* ⤶*60 rooms, 5 suites* ⚒*In-room: safe, refrigerator, Ethernet, Wi-Fi. In-hotel: pool, gym, laundry facilities, laundry service, public Wi-Fi, some pets allowed, no-smoking rooms* ▤*AE, D, DC, MC, V* ⫿*BP.*

\$\$\$–\$\$\$\$
Fodor'sChoice
★
🏨 **Hyatt Place.** Set back from the roar of I–35, this handsome five-floor hotel built in 2007 isn't the usual forgettable off-ramp inn. The stylish, postmodern lobby has a breakfast/sandwich bar serving Starbucks drinks, bacon and eggs, sandwiches, beer, and wine most of the day. Crisp and contemporary rooms have Asian-influenced touches like a screen separating the lounge area from the bedroom; all have pull-out sofas, kitchenettes, and ergonomic office chairs. The 42-inch flat-screen TVs have input ports for hooking up electronic devices like DVD players, gaming systems, and computers. Several okay restaurants are nearby. There's a business center. **Pros:** Attractive and up-to-date; friendly, young, customer-oriented staffers. **Cons:** Removed from downtown, can be hard to access during rush hour. ✉*7522 N. I–35, North Austin,* ☎*512/323–2121* ⊕*www.hyatt.com* ⤶*120 rooms* ⚒*In-room: Ethernet, Wi-Fi. In-hotel: restaurant, bar, pool, gym, laundry service, parking (no fee)* ▤*AE, D, DC, MC, V.*

\$\$ 🏨 **SpringHill Suites Austin North.** This mid-range lodging near the intersection of I–35 (southbound) and Parmer Lane may look like it's in the middle of exurban nowheresville, but outside of rush hour it's really not far from downtown or tech valley, and there's a large shopping center just across I–35. Rooms are serviceable and inoffensive, and include kitchenettes. Major renovations are planned in 2008; call ahead to avoid walking into a construction zone. All rooms are no-smoking. **Pros:** Great highway access, efficient staff. **Cons:** Feels remote, views of highways and shopping centers, style is cookie-cutter corporate. ⊠*12520 I–35N, North Austin,* ☎*512/833–8100* ⊕*www.marriott. com/ausne* ⌑*60 rooms, 5 suites* ⌂*In-room: refrigerator, Ethernet. In-hotel: pool, gym, laundry facilities, laundry service, public Wi-Fi, no-smoking rooms* ⊟*AE, D, DC, MC, V.*

NORTHWEST AUSTIN

$–$$ ⊡**Candlewood Suites.** One of several such plain-Jane hotels along a popular executive-lodging strip near the upscale Gateway shopping center, Candlewood has studio- and one-bedroom suites that are simply but comfortably furnished with a firm bed (vintage 2007), recliner, fully stocked kitchen, desk, spacious closet, and a decent bathroom. Larger suites have an extra sofa, second TV, and conference table. Welcome extras include free broadband, free laundry machines, and a video and CD library. **Pros:** Good value; friendly staff; close to upscale mall with multiplex, good restaurants, and shops. **Cons:** Lacks pool, housekeeping weekly only, removed from downtown. ⊠*9701 Stonelake Blvd., Northwest Austin,* ☎*512/338–1611* ⊕*www.candlewoodsuites.com* ⌑*125 suites* ⌂*In-room: kitchen, Ethernet, DVD, VCR. In-hotel: laundry facilities, laundry service, parking (no fee), some pets allowed, no-smoking rooms* ⊟*AE, D, DC, MC, V.*

$$–$$$ ⊡**Courtyard Austin Northwest/Arboretum.** Rooms are well kept, if ultimately forgettable, in this business-centric hotel close to Highway 183 and the Gateway shopping center. Pillow-top mattresses and flat-screen TVs are legacies of a 2008 renovation; rooms also have large desks and free Wi-Fi. The young staff is endearingly goofy. There's a decent indoor pool and hot tub, and a lobby honor bar (wine and beer only). Some rooms have microwaves. All rooms are nonsmoking. **Pros:** Good value, well maintained, convenient to highways and good restaurants and shops. **Cons:** Rooms lack character, surrounded by massive commercial district, some staff appear inexperienced. ⊠*9409 Stonelake Blvd., Northwest Austin,* ☎*512/502–8100* ⊕*www.marriott.com* ⌑*102 rooms* ⌂*In-room: Wi-Fi. In-hotel: restaurant, room service, pool, gym, laundry facilities, laundry service, concierge, public Wi-Fi, parking (no fee), no-smoking rooms* ⊟*AE, D, DC, MC, V.*

$$$–$$$$ ⊡**Embassy Suites Austin–Arboretum.** Amid a dense cluster of similar business-oriented lodgings in the Northwest/Arboretum area, this hotel is a class act, and its lobby is the fairest on Stonelake Boulevard: marble floors buffed daily to a high gloss, a central atrium surrounding six floors of balconies rising to a skylight, and live swans in an indoor pond. There's a heated indoor pool and hot tub. Each suite has a kitchenette with a refrigerator and microwave, and a separate living area and bedroom. The many freebies include Wi-Fi in the lobby, a business center with copier and printer, faxes (via the front desk), a shuttle within 3 mi, breakfast, and happy hour from 5:30 to 7:30 PM. **Pros:** Close to restaurants and shops, good amenities for businesspeople. **Cons:** No views to speak of, busy front desk, removed from downtown attractions. ⊠*9505 Stonelake Blvd., Northwest Austin,* ☎*512/372–8771* ⊕*www.embassysuites.com* ⌑*150 rooms* ⌂*In-room: refrigerator, Ethernet, Wi-Fi. In-hotel: restaurant, room service, bar, pool, gym,*

laundry service, concierge, parking (no fee), no-smoking rooms ⊟*AE, D, DC, MC, V* ⊚|*BP.*

$$–$$$ 🏨 **Hilton Garden Inn Austin NW/Arboretum.** Business travelers and some
★ short-term leisure travelers patronize this five-story hotel in suburban, shopaholic Northwest Austin. Room renovations were completed in early 2008. Set back from the busy highway, the hotel is quiet, and parking is ample. A ground-floor business center provides free Internet and local faxes. There's an indoor pool. Rooms, with contemporary decor, have a mini-refrigerator, microwave, coffeemaker, flat-panel TV, and a bed or beds with Sleep Number mattresses. Large, filling breakfasts (but no other meals) are served in the sun-washed front lobby and adjacent outdoor patio. Rudy's barbecue joint, a good local chain, is on the opposite side of U.S. 183. **Pros:** Well maintained, attentive staff, business center. **Cons:** Few good restaurants in immediate vicinity, far from downtown, not scenic. ⊠*11617 Research Blvd., Northwest Austin,* ☎*512/241–1600* ⊕*www.hiltongardeninn.com* ⨝*138 rooms, including 8 deluxe.* ⌂*In-room: refrigerator, Wi-Fi. In-hotel: restaurant, pool, gym, laundry facilities, no-smoking rooms* ⊟*AE, D, DC, MC, V.*

$$$$ 🏨 **Renaissance Austin Hotel.** The enormous, skylit lobby of this hotel—connected to the upscale Arboretum shopping center—is an eccentric mix of Victorian-style street lamps, crystal chandeliers, and giant mobiles. Rooms, on the other hand, are soothingly traditional, and the front doors of most open onto the atrium. Some on upper floors have great views of the surrounding parkland, with the downtown skyline in the distance. You couldn't spend the night any closer to Restoration Hardware, Banana Republic, or any of the mall's other specialty shops. There's also an indoor pool with whirlpool, and the decent-size health club has a good assortment of cycles, treadmills, and free weights. The restaurant overlooks a 95-acre park. All rooms are no-smoking. **Pros:** Luxurious, quiet rooms, nice pool and health club. **Cons:** Removed from downtown, pricey in high season. ⊠*9721 Arboretum Blvd., Northwest Austin,* ☎*512/343–2626* ⊕*www.renaissancehotels.com* ⨝*492 rooms, 58 executive rooms, 29 suites* ⌂*In-room: Wi-Fi. In-hotel: restaurant, room service, bars, pools, gym, laundry service, concierge, executive floor, public Internet* ⊟*AE, D, DC, MC, V.*

SOUTH AUSTIN

$–$$ 🏨 **Austin Motel.** What used to be a fading 1938 motor court is now a
★ fun and funky motel. On the hopping South Congress stretch of trendy restaurants, clubs, and shops, this crash pad is a favorite with musicians and artsy folk, who hang by the pool and hot tub, with whimsical concrete statuary for company. Imaginative rooms range from sedate to outrageous and from a diminutive all-white room to palatial pool-view rooms. The '70s-style Flamingo Room is decked out with shag pillows and blue, pink, and turquoise leatherette chairs. The staff aims to please. **Pros:** Fun, hopping neighborhood; friendly staff; hip and artistic. **Con:** Not for those who prefer their lodgings new and with an excess of amenities. ⊠*1220 S. Congress Ave., South Austin,* ☎*512/441–1157* ⊕*www.austinmotel.com* ⨝*39 rooms, 2 suites*

♿ *In-room: refrigerator. In-hotel: restaurant, pool, no elevator, laundry facilities, parking (no fee)* ⊟*AE, D, DC, MC, V.*

$$ 🏨 **Hampton Inn Austin South.** Rooms may be basic, but they're also spanking clean and reasonably priced. You do get a few perks, such as cable, free hot breakfast buffet, local calls, free Wi-Fi, and a free airport shuttle. The rooms, updated from 2005 through 2007, are pleasant enough, with decent beds (one king- or two full-size beds per room) and granite bathroom sinks; some rooms have microwaves. The lobby has a single-user business center with free services. The hotel is about 3.5 mi from downtown and 5 mi from the airport. Only the second floor has smoking rooms. **Pros:** Clean, decently run, free breakfast. **Cons:** Area not pedestrian-friendly, away from downtown. ⊠*4141 Governors Row, South Austin,* 📞*512/442–4040* 🌐*www.hamptoninn. com* ↦*123 rooms* ♿*In-room: refrigerator (some), Wi-Fi. In-hotel: pool, gym, laundry facilities, parking (no fee), no-smoking rooms* ⊟*AE, D, DC, MC, V* 🄁*BP.*

$$$–$$$$ 🏨 **Hotel San José.** This quaint-but-hip stand of 1936 bungalows, in
★ the middle of the action on South Congress, was transformed from a derelict motor court into a warren of rooms and suites done up in South Austin chic: a modern, minimalist style adorned with balconies, patios, and tropical vegetation. Rooms have concrete floors, flat-screen TVs, and pine furniture created by a Marfa, Texas, artist. Butterfly chairs abound inside and out. The pool is small (and could be cleaner) but pretty, and there's no on-site restaurant but ever-hip Jo's Coffee Shop is just across the parking lot, and many good eateries are a brief stroll away. At this writing the owners are planning to build 15 new units. **Pro:** Epitome of South Austin cool and the antidote to antiseptic motels everywhere. **Con:** Not for those who don't appreciate Zen-style simplicity. ⊠*1316 S. Congress Ave., South Austin,* 📞*512/444–7322* 🌐*www.sanjosehotel.com* ↦*40 rooms* ♿*In-room: Ethernet. In-hotel: bar, pool, no elevator, laundry service, parking (no fee), no-smoking rooms* ⊟*AE, DC, MC, V.*

$$–$$$$ 🏨 **Omni Austin Hotel at Southpark.** This elegant 14-story hotel towers
★ near the tangled intersection of I–35 and U.S. 290. It earns high marks for value, but feels removed from the city though it's only about 3 mi from downtown. The regularly renovated property has a resort air, with a semicircular fountain out front; a huge marbled lobby; an outsize indoor-outdoor heated pool; a large exercise room, whirlpool, and sauna; and a modest-size spa. Rooms are decorated with classic restraint, which some might find stuffy or old-fashioned. (For a larger room without breaking the bank, request a corner king.) Upper floors have unobstructed views from the downtown skyline to the airport tower. A city bus stop is within walking distance; a free shuttle makes the 5-mi trip to the airport. **Pros:** Far better value than comparable hotels downtown, customer-oriented staff. **Cons:** Arguably corporate and stuffy, immediate neighborhood is a major highway intersection. ⊠*4140 Governors Row, South Austin,* 📞*512/448–2222 or 800/THE–OMNI* 🌐*www.omnihotels.com* ↦*306 rooms, 7 suites* ♿*In-room: refrigerator (some), Ethernet, Wi-Fi. In-hotel: restaurant, room service, bars, pool, gym, children's programs (ages 2–12), laundry service, concierge, airport shuttle, no-smoking rooms* ⊟*AE, D, DC, MC, V.*

$$–$$$ 🏨 **Wyndham Garden Hotel–Austin.** This five-story hotel 3 mi south of downtown is an impressive sight from the highway, with its stone-and-whitewashed-yellow facade with "lone stars" everywhere. The big-as-Texas motif continues into the contemporary lobby with oversize leather sofas and large portraits of local musicians. Rooms, renovated in 2007, have pale yellow walls, one king or two full beds (in doubles), granite bathroom sinks, and free Wi-Fi. Most guests rave about the friendly, professional staff. An airport shuttle is free, and the screen by the front desk displays arrivals and departures at the international airport. Executive rooms have a leather club chair, a 42-inch flat-screen TV, and a separate shower and tub. **Pros:** Good value, exceptionally well designed, excellent service. **Con:** You'll need a car. ⊠ *3401 I–35S, South Austin,* ☎ *512/448–2444* ⊕ *www.wyndham.com* ➫ *190 rooms, 20 suites* ⚷ *In-room: refrigerator (some), Wi-Fi. In-hotel: restaurant, room service, bar, pool, gym, laundry facilities, laundry service, executive floor, airport shuttle, parking (no fee), some pets allowed, no-smoking rooms* ⊟ *AE, D, DC, MC, V.*

WEST LAKE

$$$$ 🏨 **Barton Creek Resort & Spa.** Fortune 1000 execs and groups galore
★   flock to this resort on 4,000 acres of prime Hill Country acreage in a tony area west of Austin. Among the many top-resort amenities are four championship golf courses (two rated among Texas's best), 11 tennis courts, a spa with salon services, and a huge fitness center. Major 2007 and 2008 renovations considerably improved formerly dowdy interiors, but old-money luxury remains the theme. Standard rooms have one king- or two queen-size beds, 1½ baths, a radio with iPod docking station, a 42-inch flat-screen TV, and a well-stocked minibar. Many have panoramic views of the countryside. Downtown is a 15-minute drive outside of rush hour. All rooms are nonsmoking. **Pros:** Luxurious, gorgeous views, great golf courses. **Cons:** Expensive, fees for extras like bottled water. ⊠ *8212 Barton Club Dr., West Lake,* ☎ *512/329–4000 or 800/336–6158* ⊕ *www.bartoncreek.com* ➫ *285 rooms, 18 suites* ⚷ *In-room: safe, Ethernet, Wi-Fi. In-hotel: 3 restaurants, bars, golf courses, tennis courts, pools, gym, spa, children's programs (ages 6 months–8 yrs), laundry service, concierge, public Wi-Fi, airport shuttle, parking (no fee), no-smoking rooms* ⊟ *AE, D, MC, V.*

AUSTIN ESSENTIALS

Research prices, get travel advice, and book your trip at fodors.com.

TRANSPORTATION

BY AIR

If you have to be stuck in an airport, it might as well be Austin–Bergstrom International Airport (ABIA). Neither tiny nor overwhelmingly large, it's modern, easy to navigate, and reasonably user-friendly. It even frequently has live music, with area musicians playing concerts on stages at two airport taverns—quite appropriate for the "live-music capital." The concourse's restaurants have a decidedly local slant, with branches of the Salt Lick, Matt's El Rancho, and Waterloo Ice House, to give travelers their first taste (or in some cases, farewell taste) of barbecue and Tex-Mex, Austin style. Wi-Fi is available (for a fee), and PowerPort stations offer plugs for laptops and chargers, laptop rentals, and printing.

Also, despite its medium-city size, Austin has direct flights to major cities, so you don't necessarily have to fly to or from Austin by first stopping in Houston or Dallas–Fort Worth. Airlines fly nonstop from ABIA to 37 cities outside Texas, including New York (Delta, JetBlue, Continental), Los Angeles (American, Southwest), Chicago (American, Southwest, United), and Minneapolis/St. Paul (Northwest).

Within Texas itself, Southwest Airlines flies to Austin from six cities: Dallas, El Paso, Harlingen, Houston, Lubbock, and Midland/Odessa; American flies from Austin to Dallas; Continental goes to Houston.

ABIA, which is about 11 mi southeast of downtown Austin, is well served by rental-car agencies. However, if you need a vehicle, you might consider taking a taxi or SuperShuttle to your hotel and then renting a car at a regular city location to avoid special airport taxes and surcharges, which can be considerable (for example, taxes on car rentals at the airport can top 25%, while those from nonairport locations tend to be closer to 15%).

The local branch of the national SuperShuttle airport shuttle chain is found at ABIA's ground level (same level as baggage claim). Some cab companies allow for online reservations (although there's no need to reserve a cab to wait for you at the airport; plenty of them should be around). A shared SuperShuttle ride to the airport from a downtown or South Austin hotel will cost $12.75 per person plus tip; add $5 for the Arboretum area. This compares to $20–$25 plus tip for a cab ride between the airport and a downtown-area hotel.

Airport Information Austin–Bergstrom International Airport (⊠ 3600 Presidential Blvd., Austin ☎ 512/530–2242 ⊕ www.ci.austin.tx.us/austinairport).

Airport Shuttle SuperShuttle (☎ 512/258–3826 ⊕ www.supershuttle.net).

Taxis Austin Cab (☎ 512/478–2222 ⊕ www.austincab.com). **Lone Star Cab Co.** (☎ 512/836–4900 ⊕ www.lonestarcabaustin.com). **Yellow Cab** (☎ 512/452–9999 ⊕ www.yellowcabaustin.com).

BY BUS

Greyhound's main Austin terminal, which never closes, is in central north Austin near the intersection of FM 2222 and I–35, a block or so from Highland Mall. There are frequent departures to Houston (the trip takes 3 to 3½ hours) and Dallas (averaging 3¾ hours) and many other cities large and small throughout Texas.

Capital Metro, Austin's municipal bus service (full name: Capital Metropolitan Transportation Authority), thoroughly covers the entire Austin metro area, from Leander in the far suburban north to points southwest of the airport. Cap Metro runs frequent service to and from ABIA and four downtown locations. Its Web site has comprehensive schedules and maps (the full version of which will probably confuse first-time users with its incredible complexity).

The free 'Dillo (short for armadillo) trolleys run downtown along five routes, from Deep Eddy Pool (just west of MoPac) in the west to Pleasant Valley Road in East Austin, and north–south from the University of Texas to the northern end of South Congress.

Bus & Trolley Information Capital Metro (⊠ *2910 E. 5th St., Austin* ☎ *512/389-7400* ⊕ *www.capmetro.org*). **'Dillo Trolleys** (⊕ *www.capmetro.org/riding/down-town_trollies.asp* ☎ *512/389–7400*). **Greyhound Bus Lines** (⊠ *916 E. Koenig La., Austin* ☎ *512/458–4463* ⊕ *www.greyhound.com*).

BY CAR

Although Greater Austin stretches well beyond these boundaries, most consider the downtown core to be bordered on the west by two highways running in a roughly north–south direction: MoPac (Loop 1) to the west, and I–35 to the east. Other major arteries are Highway 183, which snakes north from the airport (well east of I–35), crossing I–35 and MoPac in North Austin, and continuing to the northwest suburbs; and Loop 360 (Capital of Texas Highway), which runs from the Arboretum area in the northwest, through the upscale West Lake area, crosses MoPac and becomes Highway 71 (aka Ben White Boulevard), running through South Austin to Austin's airport (ABIA).

In addition to the major roads, drivers can choose from a number of local roads to travel relatively smoothly within Austin, notably mighty Lamar Boulevard, which runs south from Ben White all the way up to Parmer Lane and I–35 in the far north. Many major roads run in an east–west direction: in general, you'll find a good horizontal artery every 5 to 10 blocks.

If you don't expect to travel outside downtown, there is no need to have a car at all. By relying on shoe leather and the extensive public bus-and-trolley system (the free 'Dillo trolleys and the regular Capital Metro bus lines) in the central core *(⇨ By Bus)*, you'll avoid getting lost, plus save on unnecessary parking charges at your hotel.

If you need to rent a vehicle, it's cheaper to do so from a nonairport location. *(⇨ Texas Essentials at the back of the book for national rental companies' contact information.)*

BY TRAIN

Austin sits at the midpoint of Amtrak's Texas Eagle line, which snakes from Chicago through Illinois, Missouri, Arkansas, Texas, New Mexico, and Arizona before ending up in Los Angeles. Trains depart from Dallas daily at noon, arriving in Austin at 7 PM and then traveling on to San Antonio, with a 10:25 PM arrival time—a nearly 3½-hour journey that by car you could do in half the time. As is common in much of the United States, cargo gets priority over people on the rail lines, so you may find yourself sitting in a stopped train watching freight trains go by.

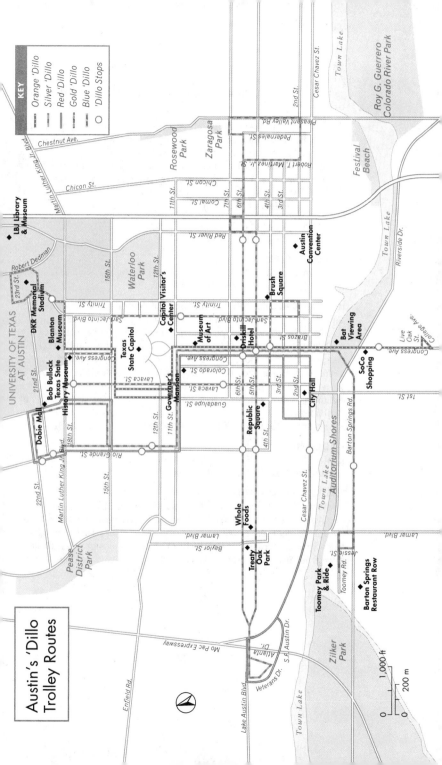

Austin's 'Dillo Trolley Routes

KEY

- Orange 'Dillo
- Silver 'Dillo
- Red 'Dillo
- Gold 'Dillo
- Blue 'Dillo
- ○ 'Dillo Stops

UNIVERSITY OF TEXAS AT AUSTIN

DKR Memorial Stadium
Blanton Museum
Bob Bullock Texas State History Museum
Dobie Mall
Texas State Capitol
Governor's Mansion
Capitol Visitor's Center
Museum of Art
Driskill Hotel
Republic Square
City Hall
Whole Foods
Treaty Oak Park
SoCo Shopping
Bat Viewing Area
Austin Convention Center
Brush Square
LBJ Library & Museum
Toomey Park & Ride
Barton Springs Restaurant Row

Pease District Park
Waterloo Park
Rosewood Park
Zaragosa Park
Festival Beach
Roy G. Guerrero Colorado River Park
Zilker Park
Auditorium Shores

Town Lake
Town Lake
Town Lake
Town Lake

Chestnut Ave.
Chicon St.
Martin Luther King Jr. Blvd.
11th St.
Robert T. Martinez Jr. St.
Pleasant Valley Rd.
Cesar Chavez St.
Pedernales St.
2nd St.
3rd St.
4th St.
6th St.
7th St.
Comal St.
Chicon St.
Red River St.
Riverside Dr.
Robert Dedman
23rd St.
15th St.
12th St.
Trinity St.
San Jacinto Blvd.
Congress Ave.
Brazos St.
Trinity St.
San Jacinto Blvd.
Lavaca St.
Congress Ave.
Colorado St.
5th St.
6th St.
3rd St.
2nd St.
Barton Springs Rd.
Live Oak St.
College Ave.
Congress Ave.
1st St.
4th St.
Guadalupe St.
Rio Grande St.
11th St.
12th St.
15th St.
18th St.
21st St.
22nd St.
Martin Luther King Jr. Blvd.
Lamar Blvd.
Baylor St.
Cesar Chavez St.
Lamar Blvd.
Jessie St.
Toomey Rd.
Mo Pac Expressway
Atlanta Dr.
S.F. Austin Dr.
Veterans Dr.
Lake Austin Blvd.
Enfield Rd.

0   1,000 ft
0   200 m

Austin's Amtrak station is located conveniently downtown near the intersection of 3rd and Lamar, on the north bank of Lady Bird Lake. Although there are many shops within walking distance, there's little to the station itself other than a ticket counter and waiting room. The ticket office is open weekdays, 7:30 AM to 9:30 PM.

As for local rail travel, although voters narrowly defeated a light-rail proposal at the ballot box in 2000, a Cap Metro Leander–to–downtown commuter rail service using existing lines is set to begin in the fall of 2008, and Austin's progressive mayor, Will Wynn, is pushing hard for a modern, rapid urban streetcar system. However, most of the powers that be in Texas have focused in recent years solely on building ever-larger, longer and more-intrusive highways and toll roads.

Information Amtrak (✉ *250 N. Lamar Blvd., Austin* ☎ *512/476–5684* ⊕ *www.amtrak.com*).

EMERGENCIES
In an emergency, dial 911. Each of the following medical facilities has an emergency room open 24 hours a day.

Hospitals Dell Children's Medical Center of Central Texas (✉ *4900 Mueller Blvd., Austin* ☎ *512/324–0000*). **People's Community Clinic** (✉ *2909 N. I–35, Austin* ☎ *512/478–4939* ⊕ *www.pcclinic.org*). **Seton Medical Center Austin** (✉ *1201 W. 38th St., Austin* ☎ *512/324–1000*). **Seton Northwest Hospital** (✉ *11113 Research Blvd., Austin* ☎ *512/324–6000*). **Seton Southwest Hospital** (✉ *7900 FM 1826, Austin* ☎ *512/324–9000*). **St. David's Medical Center** (✉ *919 E. 32nd St., Austin* ☎ *512/476–7111* ⊕ *www.stdavids.com*). **St. David's North Austin Medical Center** (✉ *12221 N. MoPac Expwy., Austin* ☎ *512/901–1000*). **St. David's South Austin Hospital** (✉ *901 W. Ben White Blvd., Austin* ☎ *512/447–2211*).**University Medical Center at Brackenridge** (✉ *601 E. 15th St., Austin* ☎ *512/324–7000*).

LODGING
Contact Austin Hotel & Lodging Association (✉ *12407 N. MoPac Expwy., Austin* ☎ *512/296–7492* ⊕ *www.austinhotelassn.org*).

VISITOR INFORMATION
Contacts Austin Convention and Visitors Bureau (✉ *301 Congress Ave., Suite 200, Austin* ☎ *866/GO–AUSTIN [462–7846]* ⊕ *www.austintexas.org*). **Austin Visitor Center** (✉ *209 E. 6th St., Austin* ☎ *866/GO–AUSTIN [462–7846]* ⊕ *www.austintexas.org/visitors/center*). **Greater Austin Chamber of Commerce** (✉ *210 Barton Springs Rd., Suite 400, Austin* ☎ *512/478–9383* ⊕ *www.austin-chamber.org*).

The Hill Country

WORD OF MOUTH

"Fredericksburg makes a good home base for see-ing wineries, visiting other Hill Country towns and there are many restaurants and shopping in the town itself. It is touristy but very charming."

—ilovetulips

By Jessica
Norman
Dupuy

YOU CAN'T GO MANY PLACES in Texas without seeing or hearing the phrase "Texas is a State of Mind." If Texas is indeed a state of mind, the Hill Country is the reason why.

The region is etched with dramatic slopes of rocky terrain, wide-open vistas displaying an endless horizon of blue sky, and roads that go on forever. Countless creeks and old cedar posts wrapped in rusty barbed wire meander through mesquite-filled pastures; in spring, blooming bluebonnets and other wildflowers transform the rough-hewn landscape.

The Hill Country's defining feature is, of course, the hills. (The lovely lakes and rivers are a close second, though.) Geographically, the area comprises the lower region of the Edwards Plateau, which rises from 750 feet to 2,700 feet in some places and is covered primarily by a thin, limestone-based soil that reveals solid, limestone rock just beneath. The calcite-rich limestone formations create perfect environments for the many freshwater springs and extensive caverns that spot the region. The rugged soil sustains grass for cattle, and weeds and tree foliage for sheep and goats, thus making the area a ranching hub and one of the nation's leading Angora goat and mohair-producing regions. The region is also home to the Llano Basin, a stretch of land that lies at the junction of the Llano and Colorado rivers and features outcroppings of granite.

The Hill Country is a retreat for businesspeople from Austin, and even Houston, who trade in their Armani and city sights for Levis and ranch life each weekend at their second homes (and later their retirement homes). It's also been growing in popularity with Winter Texans, who are passing through en route to the Rio Grande Valley at Texas's tip. Tourists make up the third wave of visitors, flying into San Antonio or Austin and driving up for a day or weekend trip. They're drawn by the chance to play in the lakes, travel the Texas Wine Trail, sample fruit at roadside farm stands, and become short-term cowpokes at one of the local dude ranches.

EXPLORING THE HILL COUNTRY

The Hill Country encompasses the region west and southwest of Austin and north of San Antonio. The distance between these two gateway cities is 60 mi. Interstate 35 marks the eastern border, while San Antonio's State Loop 1604 notes the southern limit. The northern border is ambiguous, but generally includes everything south of Lake Buchanan and along Highway 29. The western border is also open to interpretation, but is best followed along U.S. 83 from Junction to Uvalde.

Along the many winding roads of these boundaries are the fabled music towns of Luckenbach and Gruene, the tourist draws of Fredericksburg, Marble Falls, and Boerne, and a few best-kept secrets sprinkled in between: Comfort, Mason, and Wimberley, to name a few.

Fredericksburg is the number-one tourist draw, so we start our coverage there. It's also easily accessed from both Austin and San Antonio.

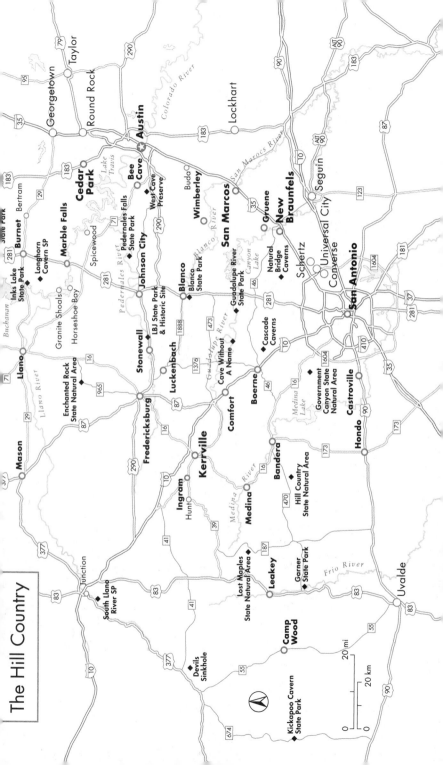

The Hill Country

20 mi

20 km

ABOUT THE RESTAURANTS

The Hill Country is an extension of the great eating opportunities—the amazing Tex-Mex and barbecue—of San Antonio and Austin, with the addition of heavy German influences. Fredericksburg certainly corners the market for relatively authentic German fare, but Boerne, Comfort, New Braunfels, and everywhere in between serve decent schnitzel and wurst. Barbecue bests are spread all over: the Salt Lick in Driftwood, Cooper's in Llano, and Cooper's in Mason (it's not a chain; they just happen to have the same name), and Rudy's Country Store in a number of locations between Austin and San Antonio, and in Leon Springs.

On the Hill Country backroads you're not going to get a whole lot of haute cuisine delivered by celebrity chefs, but you'd be surprised at some of the fine dining experiences you can have here. Two upscale restaurants to try in Fredericksburg are August E's and Rebecca's Table. For a special Tex-Mex treat, head to Mason for the handmade gorditas from the family-run Santo's Taqueria y Cantina.

Most places are casual in the Hill Country. You may want to don your Sunday best for a few places, but you really don't need to. Boots and jeans are formal enough for the average restaurant, especially for men. You'll see plenty of local women wearing "country-chic" clothing, such as embroidered, tailored blazers, or swishy broomstick skirts—with boots, of course. In the summer heat you'll see many patrons wearing just about anything that keeps them cool, flip-flops and tank tops included.

Though the attire may not be formal, Texans tend to be formal in their mannerisms. Gentlemen really do hold the door open for ladies, and most of them in the small towns still stand on ceremony when a lady enters the room, especially if they're acquainted.

Don't expect to dine too late into the evenings. With the exception of a few live-music bars and venues, most restaurants and cafés are finished serving by 9 or 10, especially during the week. It's a trademark of the Hill Country that the stars that shine so brightly in the heart of Texas should be enjoyed in peace and quiet.

ABOUT THE HOTELS

There are plenty of chain hotels speckled throughout the region, particularly in Fredericksburg and Marble Falls, but you're missing out on the local flavor if you don't try or (at least investigate) the many bed-and-breakfasts, guesthouses, ranches, and small resorts in the area—it's the absolute best way to get a feel for the culture. From historic and authentically restored guesthouses such as Palo Alto Creek and Austin Street Retreat in Fredericksburg and the Gamel House in Mason to the plush mini-resort luxury of Escondida Resort in Medina and River Rock Ranch in Comfort, to even retro-country at the Roadrunner Inn in Fredericksburg, there truly is something for everyone here.

Before deciding on the place that's right for you, it's important to make a few distinctions. Bed-and-breakfasts and guesthouses are not the same thing, no matter how close they may be in appearance. B&Bs

PLANNING YOUR TRIP

WHEN TO GO

There really isn't a bad time to visit the Hill Country. Winters are mild, with days averaging 50°. Summers are undeniably the high season, albeit extremely warm in July and August, with temperatures averaging about 85°–90° (but many days above 100°). Sunny, stiflingly hot days keep visitors in constant search of cool activities that usually involve water.

The summer heat doesn't really break until late October (sometimes even later). But once the weather cools, the Hill Country comes alive with food and wine festivals, such as New Braunfels's Wurstfest and Fredericksburg's Oktoberfest, both of which deliver plenty of beer, German sausage, and good times. October is also Texas Wine Month, with many of the Hill Country wineries offering tastings and special events.

Though late winter can be cold and seemingly desolate, the festive holiday season transforms the small towns into Dickens-like portraits of Christmas carolers, building facades with flickering lights, and main-street parades. Fly-fishers usually find fantastic winter action in any of the 100 stocked lakes and rivers for trophy rainbow trout.

By early March, outdoor enthusiasts are ready to head into the wild for cool fresh mornings at a campsite, hiking Enchanted Rock, and cycling the back roads. It's also the season for wildflowers. Brilliant red Indian paintbrushes, yellow brown-eyed Susan's, and the state's famed bluebonnets flourish in fields along the road. It's a sight to behold, and one deeply cherished by Texans statewide.

GETTING THERE & AROUND

The Hill Country is the land of the open road. The best, and really the *only* way to access the Hill Country is by car—or by motorcycle, which is an increasingly popular method.

You can access the region from I-35 or I-10, coming from the north and south or east and west, respectively. The gateway cities are Austin and San Antonio (Austin is technically even part of the Hill Country). These two cites are about 60 mi from each other on I-35. Between these two hubs on the interstate lie New Braunfels, Gruene, and San Marcos. Running north and south through the Hill Country is Highway 281, which intersects with I-10 West and San Antonio, and can be reached from Austin via Highway 71 or U.S. Highway 290, the latter traversing the region from east to west.

The most direct, and economical way to reach the Hill Country by air is to come into either San Antonio or Austin, though there is also a small airport at Del Rio. From San Antonio International Airport, take Highway 281 north for about 90 mi to go through Blanco, Johnson City, Marble Falls, and Burnet, or cut across on State Loop 1604 heading west to I-10 West and you'll go through Boerne, Comfort, Kerrville, and can then easily make your way to Bandera and Medina, or Fredericksburg and Mason. From Austin Bergstrom Airport, take Highway 290 west to Highway 281 to get to most of the Hill Country towns.

HILL COUNTRY TOP 5

■ **Fredericksburg:** An afternoon on this favorite town's Main Street will likely net a collection of shopping bags, a hearty German meal, and a few samplings of German beer and Texas wine.

■ **Scenic Drives:** Some of the most spectacular views can be experienced from the seat of a car, or the back of a Harley, if you prefer. Though most of the land along the roadside is private, you will not be hampered from enjoying many a breathtaking vista from the endless roads traversing the region.

■ **Gruene:** It may only be the size of an average city block or two, but this little town packs quite a punch.

Live-music fans must pay homage to the famed Gruene Hall and catch an evening show. Be sure to grab a burger, cold beer, and the sunset on the Guadalupe River at the Gristmill before hitting the hall.

■ **Enchanted Rock State Park:** Who wouldn't be curious about scaling the face of a massive pink rock protruding to an elevation of 1,825 feet? Camping, hiking, and rock climbing are also popular attractions at this legendary state park.

■ **Wine:** Set out on a journey down the Texas Wine Trail and taste for yourself why some wine critics see a robust and full-bodied future for Hill Country wine.

invite you to join your hosts and sometimes other guests for breakfast each morning. Guesthouses do not. Although you may receive a generous basket of muffins or other breakfast breads from the occasional guesthouse manager, you will more likely need to fend for yourself. When looking at reservation agencies such as the Gästehaus Schmidt in Fredericksburg, or Boerne Reservations, be sure to confirm which accommodation you are choosing. You may like the personalized touch and communal atmosphere of a B&B, or you may prefer the greater privacy afforded by a guesthouse.

WHAT IT COSTS					
	¢	$	$$	$$$	$$$$
Restaurants	under $8	$8–$12	$13–$20	$21–$30	over $30
Hotels	under $50	$50–$100	$101–$150	$151–$200	over $200
Camping	under $10	$10–$17	$18–$35	$36–$50	over $50

Restaurant prices are per person for a main course at dinner. Hotel prices are per night for two people in a standard double room in high season, excluding taxes (8.25%) and service charges. Camping prices are for a standard (no hookups, pit toilets, fire grates, picnic tables) campsite per night.

FREDERICKSBURG AREA

It was once a secret weekend getaway for Texans-in-the-know, but someone in the late 1990s let the cat out of the bag, and Fredericksburg is now a destination hot spot featured in the likes of *Travel & Leisure*, *Gourmet*, and *National Geographic*. Those who love this little slice of

Bavarian culture have warmly deemed it the "Aspen" of Texas. Those who wish the best-kept secret in the state had been kept exactly that, echo the sentiments of renowned Texas travel writer Suzy Banks, who once referred to the town as "Touristenburg."

Regardless of which side of the fence you sit on, the truth is that it's hard not to love the town where you can shop a day on Main Street and still not see everything, or spend a day touring the Texas Wine Trail in town and the vicinity, or a morning or afternoon hiking Enchanted Rock, and then unwind at night in one of 300 guesthouses or B&Bs, after, of course, you've savored a schnitzel or beer stein at a German restaurant. Area attractions include LBJ and Pedernales state park. Among the townships nearby are Stonewall, Luckenbach, and Johnson City.

FREDERICKSBURG

78 mi west of Austin via U.S. Hwy. 290, 70 mi north of San Antonio via I–10 and U.S. Hwy. 87.

Fredericksburg is a heavily German-influenced town. The city square is called Marketplatz, there's a "willkommen" sign hanging from every shop door, and the main B&B booking organization is called Gästehaus Schmidt. It's Oktoberfest year-round in this hot little town, and everyone's invited!

Named for Prince Friedrich of Prussia, Friedrichburg (now Fredericksburg) was established in 1846 by Baron Ottfried Hans von Meusebach (better known as John O. Meusebach in Texas). It was the second main settlement, after New Braunfels, from the Society for the Protection of German Immigrants in Texas, or Adelsverein. This organization of German nobles brokered land in Texas to increase German emigration. Meusebach also managed to broker a peace treaty with the Comanche Indians that prevented raids and helped promote trade in the area (to this day, it is the only American Indian treaty not broken in the state). Cattle and agriculture eventually became the primary sustainable commerce in the city as it grew through the Civil War and moved into the 20th century.

In addition to the town's German roots, something else to keep in mind: Fredericksburg is primarily a weekend destination. Locals enjoy the influx of visitors, but they also say their favorite days are Sunday and Monday because people pack up and leave, meaning that for a short while it feels like a small town again. If you want that experience, visit during the week, particularly in fall or winter.

WHAT TO SEE

Most of the sights are on Main Street and the side streets in between Washington and Milam. Parking is easy to find on the side streets if it's not a holiday weekend. To tour the wineries, hike Enchanted Rock, view Mexican free-tailed bats at the Old Tunnel Wildlife Management area, or pick fresh peaches right off the tree, you'll have to leave the town center, but not more than a few miles.

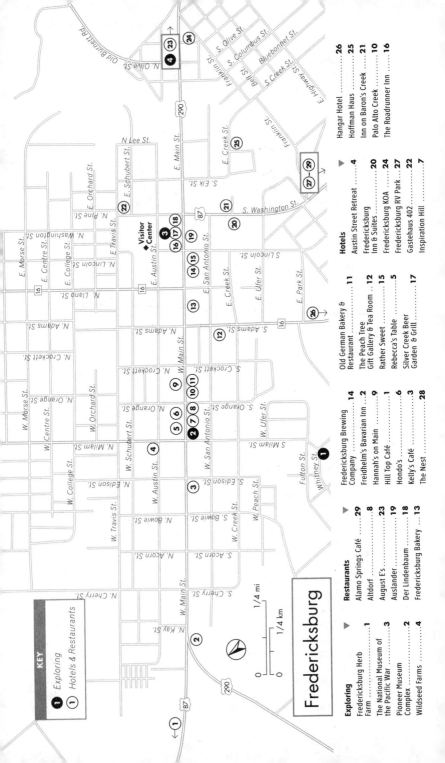

Fredericksburg

KEY

- 1 Exploring
- 1 Hotels & Restaurants

IF YOU LIKE

THE OUTDOORS

In the Hill Country, there's no shortage of things to do for those who love spending time outdoors in adventurous, caloric-burning ways. Rock climb at Enchanted Rock State Park, cliff dive at the Devil's Water Hole at Inks Lake, and get vertical in four-wheel drive vehicles at Katemcy Rocks near Mason. Or water ski the Highland Lakes and at the Texas Ski Ranch in New Braunfels, where you can trick ski and motor cross. Want something a bit tamer and on terra firma? Opt for cycling the scenic loop from Kerrville to Comfort.

Rated one of the top 100 fly-fishing streams in America, the Guadalupe River below the Canyon Lake dam flows with copious amounts of bass and bluegills; On rare occasions anglers may even bring in the beautiful Rio Grande perch, a dark gray perch dotted with brilliant sapphire spots. Farther west, in Mason County, the Llano River is a natural and pure environment for native species. Some of the river is wade-able, but a kayak or canoe is advised.

Bird lovers are also drawn to the Hill Country's great outdoors. Those looking to check a few native and migratory species off their "life list" should venture out to Lost Maples and Pedernales state parks, or try a kayak trip down the Llano River from Mason County, where a variety species—herons, hawks, and flycatchers among them—can be seen.

If going underground is more your thing, there are a number of caves to choose from in the Hill Country, including the Eckert James River Cave outside Mason and the Old Tunnel Wildlife Management Area near Fredericksburg.

FOOD

Though you can find anything from thick, juicy burgers to elegantly pan-seared escolar, the predominant cuisine in many of the Hill Country towns (especially in Fredericksburg, New Braunfels, and Boerne) is German. It's pretty standard fare, including a variety of wursts—knackwurst, bratwurst, bockwurst—sauerkraut, warm German potato salad, and of course, schnitzel. Meat lovers will also find happiness delivered from large pit-smokers in the form of brisket, sausage, smoked-turkey, and ribs. Texas barbecue has quite a reputation in the Hill Country, particularly from Cooper's in Llano and the Salt Lick in Driftwood (just south of Austin). Tex-Mex permeates the region as well, particularly the closer you get to San Antonio. ■ TIP→ Those not familiar with this locally treasured type of food should go easy on hot salsas, but indulge in cheesy enchiladas and sizzling fajitas.

MUSIC

It's impossible to escape the strong musical influence of this region, and how the different cultures have influenced each other. For instance, the cheerful tones of the accordion, originally popular in German polka-style music, are now frequently used in the widely popular Mexican-influenced Tejano music. More prevalent in the Hill Country are the soulful and often humorous chords strummed by Texas singer-songwriters. From Gruene Hall to Luckenbach and the honky-tonk bars of Bandera, poets such as Robert Earl Keen, Bruce and Charlie Robison, Lyle Lovett, the Dixie Chicks, and Willie Nelson have all taken center stage at one venue or another.

❶ Fredericksburg Herb Farm. Just a short jaunt from downtown is a magical
★ little herb farm churning out an endless variety of fresh herbs; serving
guests culinary creations inspired by an edible garden; offering blissful
relaxation in a cozy B&B and spa; and creating a vast array of heavenly
scented candles, toiletries, cooking oils, and herbal cooking rubs and
marinades. One of the gardens is artfully designed in the shape of a
star with an old windmill in the center. Each arm of the star represents
herbs for specific purposes—medicinal, cosmetic, culinary, crafting, or
ornamental. ⊠*405 Whitney St.* ☎*830/997–8615* ⊕*www.herb-farm.
com* ⊘*Mon.–Thurs. 9:30–5:30, Fri. and Sat. 9:30–9, Sun. noon–4.*

❸ The National Museum of the Pacific War. Dedicated solely to telling the
Fodor's Choice story of the Pacific battles of World War II, this museum is the only one
★ of its kind in the nation, and is a popular attraction for history buffs
and the mildly curious alike. Originally the museum was the Admiral Nimitz Museum, named after Admiral Chester W. Nimitz, who is
famed for successfully halting the Japanese advances after the attack
on Pearl Harbor. His leadership in the Pacific wars afforded the United
States victories over such skirmishes as the battles of the Coral Sea,
Midway, and the Solomon Islands Campaign. Today the museum has
grown to include the George Bush Gallery, Plaza of Presidents, Veterans' Walk of Honor, Japanese Garden of Peace, Pacific Combat Zone,
and Center for Pacific War Studies. In its more than 45,000 square feet
of exhibit space the museum exhibits both Allied and Japanese air-
planes, tanks, and guns among its numerous displays. ⊠*328 E. Main
St.* ☎*830/997–4379* ⊕*www.nimitz-museum.org* ⊠*$7* ⊘*Daily 9–5.*

❷ Pioneer Museum Complex. Those looking to dig a little deeper into the
history of this area may find a few answers at the Pioneer Museum
Complex and its second branch, the **Vereins Kirche Museum** (⊠*Main
St. in Market Sq.* ☎*830/997–7832*), a reproduction of an eight-sided
church that was Fredericksburg's first public building. Both museums
include permanent exhibits with collections of woodworking tools, tex-
tile pieces, furniture, paintings, and a number of domestic artifacts from
the area. The collection of historic buildings at the Pioneer Museum
includes an 1849 pioneer log home and store, an old First Methodist Church, and a smokehouse. Also on the premises stands a typical
19th-century "Sunday house." Sunday houses catered to farmers and
their families who traveled long distances to attend church services
and had to stay the night. With the advent of the automobile, such
accommodations became obsolete. ⊠*309 W. Main St.* ☎*830/990–
8441* ⊕*www.pioneermuseum.com* ⊠*$4 Pioneer Museum, $1 Vereins
Kirche Museum* ⊘*Mon.–Sat. 10–5, Sun. 1–5.*

**NEED A
BREAK?**
Known for a number of sweet delicacies, including creamy Danishes and
sausage kolaches, **Fredericksburg Bakery** (⊠*141 E. Main St.* ☎*830/997–
3254* ☰*AE, D, MC, V)* whips up affordable flaky German pretzels coated with
pecans and a sugary frosting, keeping customers coming back for more.

❹ Wildseed Farms. If you're heading west on Highway 290 to Fredericksburg from Johnson City, you'll inevitably note a large, expansive spread
of land flush with vibrant colors. (You may see less of this color in the

JUST PEACHY

When driving in and even near Fredericksburg in summer, you can almost smell the fresh, sweet aroma of peaches all around. The Fredericksburg–Stonewall area is known as the Peach Capital of Texas. More than one-third of the state's peach production happens in this area. The sandy soils and cool (but not too cold) winter climate create ideal conditions for peach production.

The process of pruning the orchards, managing the ripening process, and harvesting is a year-round affair, and one that is well worth the work when peach season comes around. (Depending on the weather, the season can begin as early as the beginning of May and end as late as August.) Some farms will even let you grab a crate and pick your own

peaches off the tree. Here are a few peachy places we recommend:

Burg's Corner (⊠ *15194 U.S. 290 E* ☎ *800/694–2772* ⊕ *www.burgs corner.com*).

Fisher & Weiser's Das Peach Haus (⊠ *1406 S. U.S. 87* ☎ *800/880–8526* ⊕ *www.jelly.com*) is also a phenomenal stop for specialty jellies and preserves.

Hill Country Fruit Council (⊠ *1684 Gelleman La.* ☎ *830/644–2341* ⊕ *www.texaspeaches.com*).

Itz's Fredericksburg Peaches (⊠ *235½ E. Main St.*) is simply a peach stand on the road, but don't miss it!

Whitworth Orchards (⊠ *339 Jenschke La.* ☎ *830/997–4796*).

late fall and winter months, but the expansive fields are still hard to miss.) You're looking at the largest working wildflower farm in the country. Owner John Thomas created Wildseed Farms in 1983 in an effort to share the Hill Country's bounty with all who visited. The farm has more than 200 acres under cultivation and produces 88 varieties of wildflower seeds. You can walk the meadows, step into the live butterfly house, and purchase packets of wildflower seeds. ⊠ *100 Legacy Dr.* ☎ *830/990–1393* ⊕ *www.wildseedfarms.com* ☉ *Sun.–Thurs. 9:30–5, Fri. and Sat. 9:30–5:30.*

SPORTS & THE OUTDOORS

Old Tunnel Wildlife Management Area. Hardly worth deeming a state park, this small piece of land (just 16 acres) is managed by the Texas Parks and Wildlife Department. However, it has a particular draw: bats. From April to October this old abandoned railroad tunnel is home to more than 3 million Mexican free-tailed bats. If you want to view them, arrive at the tunnel just before sunset, when the bats begin emerging in fleets of thousands for their evening hunt. You can view the bats seven nights a week, but may want to opt for an evening Thursday through Sunday, when interesting educational presentations are given on-site. After the bat viewing, head to the Alamo Springs Café just down the road (⇨ *Where to Eat*) for one of the best burgers in the Hill Country. ⊠ *102 E. San Antonio, 0.5 mi east of Fredericksburg,* ✥ *take Old San Antonio Rd. south for about 10.5 mi. The Old Tunnel WMA is located on the left at the top of the hill* ☎ *866/978–2287* ⊕ *www.tpwd.state.tx.us* 🎟 *Free* ☉ *Daily dawn–dusk.*

NIGHTLIFE

During the week most things seem to close up by about 9 or 10 o'clock. But on the weekend a number of the beer gardens open their stages for live music. Among the best bets for Texas bands playing everything from rockabilly to the blues are **Hondo's** (*312 W. Main St.*, ⇨ *Where to Eat*) and the **Silver Creek Beer Garden and Grill** (*310 W. Main St.*, ⇨ *Where to Eat*), which also hosts an open

> ## FLASH FLOOD NEWS FLASH!
>
> Flash flooding is a common phenomenon among the rivers in the Texas Hill Country. If visiting any of the regions' rivers and you notice the water levels beginning to rise, leave immediately. Visitors to state rivers are advised to be aware of weather conditions.

mike once a week to anyone who wants to belt a tune. Those looking for a little more sophistication in an evening may enjoy the lounge at **house.wine.** (⊠ *327 E. Main St.* ☎ *830/997–2665*). A home-furnishings store at the front of the building and a high-end wine bar in back, it serves more than 750 bottles from around the world.

SHOPPING

Main Street is deceiving. It has what seems like a simple few blocks of shops and restaurants, but serious shoppers, beware. It's possible to spend a whole day here and still not get to everything. Part of the reason is that distractions run high: there's a coffee shop, bakery, or wine-tasting room every few doors along the thoroughfare. Shops are open daily unless noted otherwise. Most are open from 10 to 5 Monday through Saturday, and noon to 5 on Sunday.

CLOTHING

Country-chic fashion is defined at the **Haberdashery** (⊠ *203 E. Main St.* ☎ *830/990–2462*), where women with a flair for sassy style with unmistakable Western inspiration will find a clothing treasure trove. Also selling clothes, **Root** (⊠ *306 E. Main St.* ☎ *830/997–1844*) has a little something for everyone's fashion tastes. Fashion-forward frocks and clothes are found at **Zertz** (⊠ *108-2 E. Main St.* ☎ *830/990–8900*).

HOME ACCESSORIES

Homestead and Friends (⊠ *230 E. Main St.* ☎ *830/997–5551*) shows impeccable taste in its refined-rustic home styles selection. Tucked away from Main Street, **Jabberwocky** (⊠ *105 N. Llano St.* ☎ *830/997–7071*) offers unique gifts, trendy clothes, and a wide array of linens. Custom-made and original iron pieces of high-end home furnishings are found at **Phil Jackson's Granite & Iron Store** (⊠ *206 E. Main St.* ☎ *866/353–0152*). **Red** (⊠ *218 W. Main St.* ☎ *830/990–0700*) is just the place for contemporary furniture and home accents as well as funky gifts and jewelry.A taste of Provence and Tuscany awaits shoppers at **Villa Texas** (⊠ *234 W. Main St.* ☎ *830/997–1068*), where the herb of choice is lavender and comes in everything from soaps to lotions. French-inspired home accents also abound here.

PET GOODS

Even man's best friend has a dedicated spot at **Dogologie** (⊠*148B E. Main St.* ☎*830/997–5855*) with more flashy beds, toys, treats, and accessories than a pup can wag its tail at.

WHERE TO EAT

Though you may find a recognizable difference in culinary offerings from one region of Germany to another, the pretty standard fare includes a variety of wursts—knackwurst, bratwurst, bockwurst—sauerkraut, warm German potato salad, and of course, schnitzel.

CAFE ✕**Alamo Springs Cafe.** At this spot near the Old Tunnel Wildlife Man-
¢–$ agement Area you can dig into one of the best burgers in the region
★ here. The more-adventuresome eaters order theirs with the jalepeño-cheese bun—it's really not as spicy as it sounds. If you're here in peach season, your Alamo Springs experience isn't complete without a serving of homemade peach crisp—ask for a scoop of Blue Bell Homemade Vanilla ice cream on top. ⊠*107 Alamo Rd.* ☎*830/990–8004* ▭*AE, D, MC, V.*

GERMAN ✕**Altdorf.** Although there's usually a long line for lunch here, it's worth
$–$$ waiting. The food is fantastic, especially the juicy Reuben sandwiches on toasty pumpernickel. ⊠*301 W. Main St.* ☎*830/997–7865* ▭*AE, D, MC, V.*

AMERICAN ✕**August E's.** At this polished, fine-dining establishment chef-owner Leu
$$$–$$$$ Savanh offers a constantly evolving seasonal menu—and schnitzel is
Fodor'sChoice *not* on the menu. He also adds a subtle hint of his Thai background
★ to such dishes as the New Zealand lamb with balsamic honey-glaze, and a cloudlike fillet of Hawaiian escolar pan-seared and served with a tempura-fried lobster tail, baby bok choy, and mascarpone whipped potatoes. August E's is the only place in town for sushi and sake. Desserts are homemade by co-owner Dawn Savanh. ⊠*203 E. San Antonio* ☎*830/997–1585* ▭*AE, D, MC, V.*

GERMAN ✕**Auslander.** With its authentic German architecture, the Auslander
$–$$ draws quite a crowd for lunch and dinner. This popular dining attraction offers more of a Munich *biergarten* feel than a fine-dining experience. For more than 20 years it has been one of the town's most popular beer gardens, and you're bound to find a few things to your liking—we recommend the Texa-schnitzel, a bold concoction featuring a hand-breaded pork loin cutlet prepared schnitzel-style, smothered with Tex-Mex ranchero (tomato-chili) sauce and melted Monterey Jack cheese. ⊠*323 E. Main St.* ☎*830/997–7714* ▭*AE, D, MC, V.*

GERMAN ✕**Der Lindenbaum.** The menu at this family-owned restaurant fea-
$$–$$$ tures dishes directly from the Rhineland (bordering the Alsace Lorraine region between Germany and France). It has, of course, standard schnitzel, but the sauerbraten (a Rhineland sweet-and-sour version of roast beef) and *Hühner-frikassee* (chicken fricassee with mushroom sauce) are among the favorite house specialties. ⊠*213 E. Main St.* ☎*830/997–9126* ▭*AE, D, MC, V.*

GERMAN ✕**Fredericksburg Brewing Company.** Serving a variety of homemade Ger-
$–$$ man-style brews from the large copper beer tanks accenting the far wall, the brewery is a popular nightspot for both locals and visitors. The German food is all well prepared, but the Texas-size chicken-fried

steak is no slouch either. ⊠*245 E. Main St.* ☎*830/997–1646* ⊟*AE, D, MC, V.*

GERMAN
$$–$$$$

✕**Freidhelm's Bavarian Inn.** Driving to the end of town to try this Haufbraü-Haus-meets-Disneyland restaurant is certainly a trip, in more ways than one. Schnitzel is available in more versions than you can count on one hand, and the beer selection is impressive. ⊠*905 W. Main St.* ☎*830/997–6300* ⊟*AE, D, MC, V.*

AMERICAN
$$$–$$$$
Fodor'sChoice
★

✕**Hannah's on Main.** Friendly service is everything at this fine-dining establishment. Hannah is the bubbly red-headed daughter of Dean and Kim Brenner, who escaped a fast-paced Dallas life to raise their family in a more-relaxed environment—someone forgot to tell them that serving breakfast, lunch, and dinner to a increasingly selective dining crowd is hardly a life of leisure. But they sure make it look easy. Everything on the menu is superbly prepared. New Zealand lamb rubbed with a fresh-herb-and-Dijon-mustard crust has rich and bold taste without being too gamey. Seasonal desserts such as the molten butterscotch cake are not to be missed. ⊠*232 W. Main St.* ☎*830/990–1037* ⊟*AE, D, MC, V* ☉*Closed Sun. and Mon. No dinner Tues.–Thurs.*

AMERICAN
$$–$$$

✕**Hill Top Cafe.** Ten miles north of town, this hilltop dive is in the middle of nowhere. But it's a beautiful trip to nowhere—just ask all the weekend motorcycle cruisers. All menu conventions are thrown out the window. How else would you explain the Athens–meets–New Orleans dishes? On weekends the best bet is to grab a few appetizers, a bottle of wine, and sit back for a little live music. The *kefalotiri saganaki* (a flavorful Greek cheese flambé) and a Cajun-style avocado stuffed with blue crab are fantastic starts. The chicken-fried steak is a safe bet, but snapper *pontchartrain* (in a white-wine sauce with mushroom and crab) is a decadent adventure. ⊠*10661 U.S. Hwy. 87* ☎*830/997–8922* ⊟*AE, D, MC, V.*

BARBECUE
¢–$$
★

✕**Hondo's.** Named for John Russell "Hondo" Crouch, self-proclaimed mayor of Luckenbach, this local dive is becoming something of a legend in itself. If the live music and Texas country decor aren't entertaining enough, the menu certainly is. From the "What's David Smokin' Plate" of finger-lickin' fabulous barbecue to the "Supa Chalupa Salad," everything about this place radiates good old-fashioned fun. The half-pound donut burgers, made in the shape of a donut, are excellent, especially the "Blue Ribbon Barbecue Bacon Burger." ⊠*312 W. Main St.* ☎*830/997–1633* ⊟*AE, D, MC, V.*

SEAFOOD/
MEXICAN
$–$$

✕**Kelly's Café.** Just on the tail end of Main Street, Kelly's is a perfect escape from the weekend mayhem released on all of the other central restaurants. The crab cakes made with thick chunks of fresh crab and served with a sweet-and-spicy papaya sauce are wildly popular. Having spent many years in New Mexico, chef Kelly Rogers's specialty is the blue corn chicken enchiladas. Served with either smoky red chili sauce or a piquant tomatillo green sauce, these cheesy tortilla rolls make for a satisfying experience. ⊠*505 W. Main St.* ☎*830/997–8593* ⊟*AE, D, MC, V.*

AMERICAN
$$–$$$

✕**The Nest.** Tucked away in a little historic house off Washington Street, the Nest is a nice option for a special occasion. It's probably the best value for fine dining in town. The seasonal menu by chef John Wilkinson, a Culinary Institute of America graduate, might include a perfectly prepared Black Angus fillet with a rich bordelaise sauce or plump pan-seared sea scallops served with a citrus-tasting chipotle-lime hollandaise. Enjoy a taste of the Hill Country with a scoop of homemade lavender ice cream. ⊠*607 S. Washington St.* ☎*830/990–8383* ⊟*D, MC, V.*

GERMAN ✕**Old German Bakery & Restaurant.** Though it's also open for lunch, most
¢ locals flock here for a hearty breakfast where a variety of sweet pastries and potato pancakes with applesauce abound. The sausage rolls are pretty tasty, too. ⊠*225 W. Main St.* ☎*830/997–9084* ⊟*AE, D, MC, V* ⊗*No dinner.*

AMERICAN ✕**Peach Tree Gift Gallery and Tea Room.** The gift shop came first, but
$ since 1984 Cynthia Pedregon has wowed crowds with her homemade soups, sandwiches, and daily quiches. Portions are hearty, but to get a sampling of as much as possible, opt for the Sandwich Sampler, which comes with a quarter sandwich each of tangy chicken salad, fresh tuna salad, perky jalepeño-pimento cheese, and a cup of the soup of the day. Pedregon's cookbooks are prized staples in Hill Country kitchens. ⊠*210 S. Adams St.* ☎*830/997–9527* ⊟*AE, D, MC, V.*

AMERICAN ✕**Rather Sweet.** From Main Street, between Llano and Lincoln streets,
¢–$ make your way down a stone path to one of the town's most celebrated
★ treats. This bakery run by chef Rebecca Rather (who runs Rebecca's Table for dinner) serves some of the most decadent baked goods around. Simple oatmeal–chocolate chip cookies taste like heaven, and mammoth chocolate cakes blanketed in buttercream frosting beckon from behind the dessert case. Homemade soups and cold and hot sandwiches are worth a try, too. ⊠*249 Main St.* ☎*830/990–0498* ⊟*AE, D, MC, V* ⊗*Closed Sun. and Mon. No dinner.*

AMERICAN ✕**Rebecca's Table.** Chef Rebecca Rather's outpost of "fine, farm-fresh
$$$–$$$$ cuisine" is giving the Main Street dining scene a run for its money. The dining room balances rustic and contemporary elements, with exposed limestone walls and dark-stained wood floors and beams. The short menu is driven by what Rather finds daily at Texas-based markets. The thick-cut Niman Ranch pork chop with chunky apple-pear chutney is a happy layering of textures and flavor. Also great are the Kobe beef sliders—miniburgers topped with caramelized onions and Dijon mayonnaise. Be sure to finish with one of Rather's signature desserts; the sticky toffee pudding is worth every sweet and gooey calorie. The excellent, diverse wine list includes a few Hill Country bottles. ⊠*342 W. Main St.* ☎*830/997–5100* ⊟*AE, D, V, MC* ⊗*Closed Sun. and Mon. No lunch.*

GERMAN ✕**Silver Creek Beer Garden and Grill.** Though lacking a German name, the
$–$$$ Silver Creek shouldn't be overlooked if you're seeking cuisine from the motherland. With an abundance of outdoor dining, regular live music, and an extensive beer selection, this place is a spring and summer favorite. All menu items are served with a side of sweet and vinegary German potato salad. ⊠*310 E. Main St.* ☎*803/990–4949* ⊟*AE, D, MC, V.*

WHERE TO STAY

Serving Fredericksburg for more than 20 years, the **Gästehaus Schmidt** (✉*231 W. Main St., 78624* ☎ *830/997–5612 or 866/427–8374* ⊕*www. fbglodging.com*) is the place to consult when seeking the perfect B&B or guesthouse. This booking operation manages more than a third of the 300-plus accommodations in the town, but it's also a great resource to turn to for local travel advice.

$$ **Austin Street Retreat.** One of the most popular downtown guesthouses, the Austin Street Retreat offers five elegantly appointed private suites, each featuring the original Fachwerk log-cabin and limestone architecture used by original Fredericksburg settlers. You're in the heart of the town here, but once you enter the compound you'll likely feel like you're approaching a cabin in the woods. Get directions and reservations through Gästehaus Schmidt *(⇨above).* **Pros:** Very authentic in the preservation; beds are large and comfortable; bathrooms are all spacious and welcoming, with oversize tubs. **Cons:** Two-night minimum can be inconvenient; Victorian accents are tasteful, but may be a little too historic for some. ✉*408 W. Austin St.,* ☎*830/997–5612 or 866/427–8374* ⊕*www.austinstreetretreat.com* ⤳*5 suites* ⌂*In-room: refrigerator, kitchen (some)* ▤*AE, D, MC, V.*

$–$$ **Fredericksburg Inn & Suites.** Just a couple of blocks off Main Street and nestled on the banks of Baron's Creek, this no-frills, straightforward inn offers clean, comfortable rooms, refreshing pools, and a quiet respite from the hustle and bustle of the main thoroughfare. **Pros:** Close to Main Street, pleasant view of Baron's Creek. **Cons:** Staff can be somewhat cold and unhelpful, some rooms cleaner than others, water pressure is weak for showers and toilets. ✉*201 S. Washington St.,* ☎*830/446–0202 or 830/997–0202* ⊕*www.fredericksburg-inn.com* ⤳*94 rooms, 10 suites* ⌂*In-room: refrigerator, Ethernet, dial-up, Wi-Fi. In-hotel: pools, gym, public Internet, public Wi-Fi, parking (no fee), some pets allowed, no-smoking rooms* ▤*AE, MC, V* ⎥⎢*CP.*

$$ **Gastehaus 402.** Experience Fredericksburg in luxurious style here, ★ where Central Texas–renowned interior designer and owner Jennifer Eggleston has added her personal touch to every detail. This loftlike cottage mixes contemporary country style with a touch of urban flair. A relaxing private patio invites guests to relax and unwind. A bit small, this guest cottage is the perfect place for a romantic retreat or a getaway for one. **Pros:** Decor is fresh, inviting, and comfortable; large pillow-top bed makes it easy for lingering in the mornings; easy walk to Main Street. **Con:** Not ideal for children due to high-end decor. ✉*402 E. Schubert,* ☎*888/991–6749* ⊕*www.fredericksburg-lodging.com/ Gastehaus-402* ⤳*1 cottage* ⌂*In-room: kitchen, refrigerator, DVD, VCR . In-hotel: no-smoking rooms* ▤*AE, D, MC, V* ⎥⎢*CP.*

$$–$$$ **Hangar Hotel.** This fun (yet not overdone) hotel was built to look like ★ a 1940s airplane hangar. Stepping into the lobby is like entering an old black-and-white movie—you almost expect to see Humphrey Bogart puffing on a stogie. The lobby experience extends all the way to the 50 uniform rooms designed meticulously with mahogany accents and club chairs upholstered in bomber-jacket leather. At the foot of each plush king-size bed is a neatly folded Army-green wool blanket bearing the

Hangar Hotel logo. **Pro:** $10 discounts for military and seniors. **Cons:** Not many activity options on-site or nearby, and not an easy location to find. ⊠ *155 Airport Rd.,* ☏ *830/997–9990* ⊕ *www.hangarhotel. com* ☞ *50 rooms* ⌂ *In-room: refrigerator, Wi-Fi. In-hotel: restaurant, bar, public Wi-Fi, parking (no fee), no-smoking rooms* ▭ *AE, MC, V* ✶|◎|*CP.*

$$–$$$$ 🖼 **Hoffman Haus.** Stepping onto this beautiful property spotted with
★ historic cabins and private courtyards with glowing fire pits, you won't believe Main Street is just a stone's throw away. The main lodge is a renovated 1850s barn, with an inviting library and formal dining room in the far part of the building. Rooms are elegantly decorated with individual styles, from rustic Texas to French countryside. A lovely spa is on-site, but the full experience of the Hoffman Haus is in joining one of the terrific cooking classes offered by chef-owner Leslie Washburne ($65 per person). **Pros:** Close to Main Street yet private and peaceful; excellent, comfortable beds; breakfasts are hot, filling, and delicious—and delivered right to your room. **Cons:** Not ideal for children; difficult to relax if a big event, such as a wedding, is going on in the main lodge. ⊠ *608 E. Creek St.,* ☏ *830/997–6739* ⊕ *www. hoffmanhaus.com* ☞ *8 rooms, 4 suites, 1 cabin (sleeps 6)* ⌂ *In-room: no phone, kitchen, refrigerator, DVD (some), VCR (some), Wi-Fi. In-hotel: spa, no elevator, some pets allowed, no-smoking rooms* ▭ *AE, MC, V* ✶|◎|*BP.*

$$$ 🖼 **Inn on Baron's Creek.** Looking for a more-traditional hotel atmosphere and want to stay close to town? This locally owned operation fits the bill; it's just a couple of blocks from downtown and offers a feel unique to Fredericksburg. The staff is very friendly and happy to help give tips and advice on the best things to do around town. Four of the suites are extended-stay and include kitchen facilities. **Pros:** Spacious, clean rooms; friendly, helpful staff. **Cons:** Not the quaint experience you'd find in guesthouses or B&Bs, some residual noise when bands play at the nearby Auslander restaurant. ⊠ *308 S. Washington St.,* ☏ *830/990–9202 or 866/990–0202* ⊕ *www.innonbaronscreek.com* ☞ *90 suites* ⌂ *In-room: refrigerator, DVD (available upon request), Ethernet, Wi-Fi. In-hotel: pool, gym, spa, laundry facilities, public Wi-Fi, parking (no fee), no-smoking rooms* ▭ *AE, D, MC, V* ✶|◎|*BP.*

$$$ 🖼 **Inspiration Hill.** If you're looking for a retreat from town with mag-
★ nificent views of the Hill Country, look no further than Inspiration Hill. The home presents a contemporary style with a rustic flair. The designers aimed to bring the Hill Country indoors. You can enjoy the views from the screened porch, which even has a gas fireplace for cold evenings. Each bedroom has plush linens and private bath—the master bath has a river-rock shower and hot tub. The best part is the privacy; you rent the entire home. Pricing is based on the number of bedrooms used, so it's possible for couples to enjoy a quiet getaway by themselves. **Pros:** Beautiful escape for a group of friends or family, with lots of privacy; well-equipped kitchen; excellent views. **Con:** A bit far from downtown. ⊠ *1063 Luckenbach–Cain City Rd.,* ☏ *830/997–5612 or 866/427–8374* ⊕ *www.fbglodging.com* ☞ *3 rooms* ⌂ *In-room: kitchen, refrigerator, DVD, Ethernet. In-hotel: public Wi-Fi, no kids under 12, no-smoking rooms* ▭ *AE, D, MC, V.*

$$$–$$$$ 🏠 **Palo Alto Creek.** Just a few miles outside Fredericksburg and nestled along the shady Palo Alto Creek, this property has the original 1875 buildings built by German immigrant Karl Itz. They've been updated with modern amenities, yet they're perfect for fans of the outdoors. Choose from the main Itz House, which sleeps eight, or opt for the quainter Log Cabin, Barn, or Hideaway cabin, complete with a screened-in porch. Children are not allowed to stay in certain rooms. A breakfast of fresh pastries is delivered to your door each morning. Get directions and reserve through Gästehaus Schmidt *(⇨above)*. **Pros:** A perfect nature escape with glimpses of deer and a view of the creek, each cabin offers utmost privacy, in-room massage therapist option is an added bonus. **Con:** A bit far from downtown, not ideal for children. ✉*Palo Alto La.,* ☎ *830/997–5612 or 866/427–8374* ⊕*www.palo altocreekfarm.com* ⮐*6 rooms* ♿*In-room: kitchen, refrigerator, DVD (some), VCR (some). In-hotel: parking (no fee), no kids, no-smoking rooms* ▤*AE, D, MC, V* �|O�|*CP.*

$$–$$$ 🏠 **Roadrunner Inn.** Not all B&Bs are stuffed with Victorian decor and
★   period pieces. In fact, Fredericksburg has recently welcomed a few urban-minded accommodations offering a more-contemporary environment. The Roadrunner Inn is composed of three little loftlike rooms perched above the Root clothing store on Main Street. Bright, fresh colors and lush green tropical plants create a nouveau-Miami feel. From robin's-egg blue and canary-yellow dishes mounted on the wall to lime-green–and–white accent pillows resting on the 1970s sectional couch, everything screams "we're retro, but we're still Texas-friendly." Kitchens are stocked with juice, milk, tea, coffee, and cereal. Fresh fruit and breakfast pastries are brought to your room each morning. **Pros:** Clean rooms and beautiful bathrooms, proximity to Main Street is hard to beat, complimentary Cheerios a plus. **Cons:** Might be too trendy for some, Main Street–facing rooms get street noise. ✉*306 E. Main St.,* ☎*830/997–1844* ⊕*www.theroadrunnerinn.com* ⮐*3 rooms* ♿*In-room: no phone, kitchen, refrigerator, Ethernet. In-hotel: no elevator, no-smoking rooms* ▤*AE, D, MC, V* �|O�|*CP.*

CAMPING

$$–$$$$ ⛺ **Fredericksburg KOA.** Though you're a few miles from town, this RV site is happily situated in a beautiful rural area. Both Fredericksburg and Luckenbach are just a few minutes away. Wi-Fi is available, as is a modem dataport. **Pros:** Quiet and spacious camping area, seasonal pool. **Cons:** Need a car to drive to downtown area, not all sites are well shaded. ✉*5681 U.S. 290 E,* ☎*830/997–4796* ⊕*www.koa.com/ where/tx/43153* ⮐*89 sites (most pull-through)* ♿*Flush toilets, showers, full hookups, drinking water, dump station, swimming pool, Wi-Fi* ▤*AE, D, MC, V.*

$$ ⛺ **Fredericksburg RV Park.** Fairly close to downtown, this hospitable RV Park offers nice amenities and friendly service from staff. Laundry and private bath facilities are conveniently on-site. Wi-Fi is available as is cable TV. **Pros:** Close to downtown, clean facilities, nice recreational room. **Con:** Campsites are close together. ✉*305 E. Highway St.* ☎*830/990–9582* ⊕*www.fredericksburgtexasrvpark.com* ⮐*100*

pull-through RV sites ♿ Flush toilets, showers, full hookups, drinking water, dump station, guest laundry, Wi-Fi 🖃 AE, D, MC, V.

ENCHANTED ROCK STATE NATURAL AREA

16 mi north of Fredericksburg via RR 965.

★ Protruding from the earth in the form of a large pink dome, Enchanted Rock looks like something from another planet. This granite formation rises 1,825 feet—the second-largest in the nation, after Georgia's Stone Mountain—and its bald vastness can be seen from miles away. Today the massive batholith is part of the 624-acre Enchanted Rock State Park and one of the most popular destinations in the Hill Country region. Once considered to have spiritual powers by the Tonkawa tribe, the rock is traversed day in and day out by those curious about its mysterious occurrence. The park is perfect for day hikers, most of whom can't wait to scale the summit—it's a steep climb to the top. The rock also yields a number of faces to test the skills of technical rock climbers. But even if you're not into rock climbing, the park is a perfect spot for camping, picnicking, and hiking. Arrive early; park officials close the park to protect the resources once parking lots reach capacity. Amenities include restrooms, an interpretive center, and campgrounds (⇨ *Where to Stay*). ⊠ *16710 RR 965* ☎ *325/247–3903* ⊕ *www.tpwd.state.tx.us* 💲 *$6.*

WHERE TO STAY

CAMPING

$ ⛺ **Enchanted Rock State Natural Area.** Backpackers can opt for either the closed-in surface tent sites or one of the three primitive camping areas 1 to 2 mi from the trails. Either way, your access to good hiking trails, rock faces to scale, and magnificent views of the great granite dome are everywhere you go. Reservations are strongly recommended in spring (when the area is flush with wildflowers), early summer, and late fall. **Pros:** Primitive sites are picturesque and private, excellent access to trails from all campsites. **Cons:** Close-in surface sites are close together with little to no privacy, summer camping can be stiflingly hot. ⊠ *Enchanted Rock State Natural Area* ☎ *325/247–3903 or 800/792–1112* ⊕ *www.tpwd.state.tx.us* 🛏 *60 tent sites* ♿ *Flush toilets (some), dump station, fire pits, picnic tables.* 🖃 *AE, D, MC, V.*

LUCKENBACH

10 mi from Fredericksburg via Hwy. 290 and RR 1376.

Fodor's Choice Luckenbach isn't just some fabled Texas town romanticized by classic
★ country singers Willie Nelson and Waylon Jennings. In fact it's hardly a town at all, but more a cul-de-sac at the end of a country road. Luckenbach is an attitude. It's a place to which Texas songwriters and music lovers from Nacogdoches to El Paso dream of traveling to pay homage to Texas music legends. Of course, if you blink while driving south on Ranch Road 1376 from Highway 290 West, you just might miss it. Aside from the general store, post office, rows of picnic tables, and ample parking for the many daily visitors, there's not much else here.

CLOSE UP

Texas Chili

There's no denying that chili is part of the stick-to-your-ribs heart and soul of Texas cuisine. After all it *is* the official dish of Texas. When the weather turns cool in fall, Crock-Pots are fired up to make heaping servings of the thick, spicy stew to be enjoyed by the bowl beside the fire—or over a heaping pile of Fritos, garnished with shredded cheddar cheese and diced onions, at high school football games (the legendary Frito Pie).

The question is: what defines an authentic bowl of "Texas red?" The simple answer is small chunks of sirloin (or coarsely ground meat) simmered with crushed chilies (or chili powder), garlic, and cumin. From there, myriad additions—possibilities include tomato, onion, venison, and the ever-controversial beans (family feuds have erupted over whether or not to include the protein-packed legume)—can lead to millions of different tasty end results.

Texas chili recipes are such a hot topic that they've spawned competitive cook-offs, a trend that's caught on nationwide. The granddaddy of chili cook-offs is in the tiny West Texas town of Terlingua, where hundreds of established cooks take their best shot at the annual title over a four-day competition each year. (If you look at the distinguished list of winners, you'll find that most of them are Texans.)

Though officially established in 1849 by German immigrants, it wasn't until 1970, when John Russell "Hondo" Crouch purchased the town—with a population of just three at the time—and created what soon became a legendary dance hall, that it became famous. The legend began when Texas singer-songwriter Jerry Jeff Walker recorded his album "Viva Terlingua!" at the dance hall in 1973. Four years later the town was memorialized by Willie Nelson and Waylon Jennings in the famed song "Luckenbach, Texas (Back to the Basics of Love)."

During Crouch's reign as the self-proclaimed town mayor, he coined the famous phrase "Everybody's Somebody in Luckenbach," a motto still heard today.

Whether you're a fan of country music or not, you haven't officially been to Luckenbach without grabbing an ice-cold brew, listening to whoever may be strumming the guitar on stage, and picking up a souvenir bumper sticker for the road.

JOHNSON CITY

30 mi east of Fredericksburg and 30 mi west of Austin on Hwy. 290; 25 mi south of Marble Falls and 60 mi north of San Antonio on Hwy. 281.

Johnson City is often described as a great place to stop on the way to somewhere else. Aside from its proximity to some of the Hill Country's main towns, Johnson City is probably most famous as the home of President Lyndon Baines Johnson—though the president is not the town's namesake.

The town was actually founded in the late 1870s by James Polk Johnson, a second cousin to the former U.S. president. It was established as the county seat for Blanco County, but the town experienced little growth economically. LBJ may have first brought notoriety to the area in the 1930s, when the former president was a junior congressman from Texas. He was the first to lobby for full electric power to the area, and in a 1959 letter wrote, "I think of all the things I have ever done, nothing has ever given me as much satisfaction as bringing power to the Hill Country of Texas."

Johnson's wife, "Lady Bird" Johnson, was known for her passion to beautify cities across the country. During her time as First Lady, she pioneered the Highway Beautification Act to clean up national highways. Her inspiration came from the abundant Texas wildflowers that flourished along Hill Country highways each spring.

Following his presidency, LBJ offered his family ranch to the United States as a National Historical Park. It is preserved as a peaceful spot about 14 mi west of Johnson City, near Stonewall.

WHAT TO SEE

Exotic Resort Zoo. Wild animals—from goats, deer, and kangaroos to buffalo, zebras, and oryx—eat right out of your hand when you take a safari tour of this 137-acre wildlife park. When you purchase your ticket, be sure to buy the pellets so you have something to give the animals. ⊠*235 Zoo Trail, 4 mi north of Johnson City on Hwy. 281* ☎*830/868–4357* ⊕*www.zooexotics.com* ☜*petting zoo $6, zoo and tour $11, bucket of feed $6* ⊗*Daily 9–6 (last tour leaves at 5).*

Lyndon Baines Johnson National Historical Park. History buffs will enjoy wandering through the rooms of LBJ's boyhood home in Johnson City, where every effort has been made to restore the home to its 1920s appearance. ⊠*100 Ladybird La.* ☎*830/868–7128* ⊕*www.nps.gov/lyjo* ☜*$6* ⊗*Daily.*

Lyndon B. Johnson State Park and the LBJ Ranch. It's easy to feel confused, but the state park and the national park are technically separate entities that operate in conjunction with each other. The national park includes Johnson's boyhood home in Johnson City proper, while the state park is confined to the property 14 mi west of town. You're welcome to drive around the state park, but to get the best historical experience it's best to take the 1½-hour bus tour ($6), which departs from the State Park Visitor Center in Stonewall. The bus ride takes you on a guided tour of the ranch, and afterward you can hike the many park trails, fish the Pedernales River, picnic, and even take a dip in the pool in summer. ⊠*Hwy. 290 E. at Park Rd. 52, Stonewall* ☎*830/644–2252* ⊕*www.tpwd.state.tx.us* ☜*Free* ⊗*Daily, tours 10–4.*

OFF THE BEATEN PATH

Pedernales Falls State Park. With cool aquamarine pools created from the picturesque Pedernales River shaded by towering cypress trees, this park brings a respite from the glaring sun on hot summer days, especially if you're here to partake of one of its water-based activities like swimming and tubing. If you're here to burn calories with a long trek, you've also come to the right place. Hikers and mountain bikers can embark on 19.8 mi of trails, with an additional 14 mi of backpacking trails (hiking only). Fishing, bird-watching, picnicking, and camping are also popular here. Park facilities include picnic sites, restrooms (some with showers), a trailer dump station, and campsites (some with water and electricity, others that are primitive and must be hiked to, with a 2-mi or longer hike). No pets are allowed at the park. ⊠*2585 Park Rd. 6026y* ☎*800/792–1112* ⊕*www.tpwd.state.tx.us* ☒*$5* ☉*Daily dawn–dusk.*

WHERE TO EAT

SOUTHERN

¢–$$

✕**Silver K Cafe.** Though you may only be passing through Johnson City, try to do it on an empty stomach and make a stop at the Silver K. The mashed potatoes alone are worth it, and the fried-chicken is no ordinary affair: it's served in a gooey yet crunchy honey-pecan sauce. The Hill Country photography and Western paintings mixed with the Silver K's diner personality make you feel like you are in someone's home for dinner. ⊠*209 E. Main St.* ☎*830/868–2911* ☲*AE, D, MC, V.*

NORTH & NORTHWEST OF SAN ANTONIO

CASTROVILLE

15 mi west of San Antonio via U.S. 90.

This small town west of San Antonio, in the Medina River valley, is known as the "Little Alsace of Texas." The town's deep French roots began with founder Henri Castro, who first came to Texas in 1842.

FUN
FESTIVAL

Every August the town celebrates the St. Louis Day Church Festival (☎*830/931–2826***), beginning with a mass in St. Louis Catholic Church, and including a picnic, silent auction, barbecued beef and Alsatian-style sausage dinner, rides and games, performances by popular bands and dance groups, and more. The event began in the mid-1800s in honor of the feast day of Louis IX of France (St. Louis). It draws guests from across the state, country, and world.**

WHAT TO SEE

Moye Retreat Center. The Sisters of Divine Providence, an order from France, were the first residents of this 1873 convent. Later it was used as a school and today ministers to people from many walks of life. The tiny original **St. Louis Catholic Church** (⊠*Houston Sq.* ☎*830/538–3142* ☒*Free* ☉*Daily 9–5*) stands on the grounds. You can hear a recorded account of the history of this 1868 Gothic-style church. ⊠*U.S. 90 W* ☎*830/931–2233* ☒*Free* ☉*Tues.–Fri. 8:30–5.*

EN
ROUTE

Medina Lake. More than 5,500 acres of water welcome boaters and swimmers at this lake between Castroville and Bandera. From Castroville, take Highway 471 north about 15 mi to FM 1283; head west to Park Road 37, then southwest to the lake.

SCENIC DRIVES

Some of the most spectacular views can be experienced from the seat of a car, or the back of a Harley, if you prefer. Though most of the land along the roadside is private, you can still enjoy the breathtaking vistas the Hill Country has to offer from the endless roads that traverse the land. ■ TIP➜ **Be sure you have a full tank of gas before venturing out on any of these drives, and also have a good map on hand.**

At the top of the list is Ranch Road 337 from **Medina to Vanderpool**. Along this road, you'll cross the cool crystal waters of the Medina River, scale some of the higher hilltops in the region with majestic views, and encounter some of the most-remote reaches of the area. You won't find much in the way of civilization, but you will get a feel for what early settlers must have felt when falling in love with this land at first sight. End this picturesque drive with a few hours at Lost Maples State Natural Area by heading north on Ranch Road 187.

There is a more-direct route from **Kerrville and Bandera** with Highway 173, but the longer route on Highway 16 offers a more-worthwhile experience, winding passages, and steep climbs—take precautions if you're prone to motion sickness. The hypnotic meandering of the Medina River, lined with bald cypress trees that seem to raise their ancient branches to the westward setting sun, will keep your interests peaked.

For an all-day drive with lots of ups and downs and panoramic scenery, go from **Fredericksburg to Leakey**. From Fredericksburg follow Highway 16 to Kerrville and then switch to Highway 173 going south to Camp Verde and then west on Ranch Road 337 to Medina. Alternatively, if you're adventurous and okay with potentially getting lost, instead of continuing all the way from Fredericksburg to Kerrville on Highway 16, turn left off the highway at Old Kerr Highway/Center Point Road (it's a very small road; so drive slowly so you don't miss it). Old Kerr Highway turns into Bear Creek Road and then Center Point Road—when you get to the fork with Whiskey Canyon Ranch Road, hang a right. You're on the backroads now and you'll be driving by lots of ranches. As you follow this winding road around you'll sneak up from behind on the southeastern side of Kerrville. When you pass by I–10, you want to take Highway 27/Ranch Road 2771 west toward Camp Verde and Medina.

Whichever route you take to get to Medina, from there follow Ranch Road 337 to Vanderpool, with a stop at Lost Maples State Natural Area to stretch your legs, and, if it's fall, to see the changing colors. Continue on to Leakey. From there you can take U.S. 83 north and then Highway 39 back over to Kerrville. The trip highlights lots of hills, striking mountain scenery, and pockets of vistas that capture the rocks' layers. Locals call the area along the route from Medina to Leakey "the Switzerland of Texas."

In the Highland Lakes area, Highway 29 from **Mason to Llano** boasts some of the most beautiful panoramas of rugged hill country in the region with dramatic granite outcrops that burst from the landscape in pink, speckled domes.

BANDERA

52 mi northwest of San Antonio via Hwy. 16, 24 mi west of Boerne via Hwy. 46, 26 mi south of Kerrville via Hwy. 16/173.

Dust off your chaps, loosen your saddle cinch, and stay a while. In Bandera the mythic tales of rodeos, ranches, and the "cowboy way" are all true. Not only will you see beat-up boots, worn Wrangler jeans, and more than a few cowboy hats, you may even catch a glimpse of one of the local ranch hands riding his horse to the general store on Main Street. After all, this isn't considered the cowboy capital of the world for nothing. Open rodeos take place twice weekly from Memorial Day through Labor Day, and you can't drive any direction outside town without passing a dude ranch (⇨ *The Dude Ranch Experience box*).

This tiny ink spot on the Texas map was originally established in 1853 as a sawmill town based solely on the cypress trees along the Medina River. Throughout much of the late 1800s, both German and Polish settlers made their home here. After the Civil War the town boomed with cattle drives on the Great Western Cattle Trail (which paralleled the Chisolm Trail between Texas and Kansas). But the rugged terrain slowed things down, as railroads couldn't find passages through the hills and most roads weren't even paved until the 1950s.

DID YOU KNOW?

Ranches that host guests are known as "dude" ranches because dude was how Westerners referred to Easterners, especially those from major cities. The word came from New York slang in the 1880s.

WHAT TO SEE

Frontier Times Museum. The collection here is truly eclectic. Hand-built in 1933 by Hough LeStourgeon from stones gathered from the region, this popular tourist stop teems with oddities and relics—take for instance the two-headed goat or the mummified cow fetus. ✉ *510 13th St.* ☎ *830/796–3864* ⊕ *www.frontiertimesmuseum.com* ✉ *$5* ⊗ *Mon.–Sat. 10–4:30.*

Hill Country State Natural Area. With more than 5,300 acres of rolling hills, spring-fed creeks, and thick patches of live oaks, this natural park is a slice of backcountry paradise. Adventurers seeking an avenue for primitive camping, mountain biking, backpacking, limited fishing, and even horseback riding will find happiness here. ■TIP➔ **The park is primitive. You'll need to bring your own water, and you'll need to pack out what you bring in.** ✉ *10600 Bandera Creek Rd.* ☎ *830/796–4413* ✉ *$6 ($3 extra for primitive campsite)* ⊗ *Feb.–Nov., daily; Dec and Jan., Fri.–Sun.*

NIGHTLIFE

For such a small town, Bandera certainly offers a lively night scene—at least, if you're into gritty bars, live Texas-style country music, and an occasional turn on the dance floor.

Tucked into a line of stores on Main Street, it may be easy to miss **Arkey Blue's Silver Dollar** (✉ *308 Main St.* ☎ *830/796–8826*) during the day. But at night it turns into a beacon calling all cowboys and bikers

The Dude Ranch Experience

Bandera's Cowboy Capital title not only stems from the long-standing cattle ranches in the area, but from all the visitors who pony up the cash for a bit of the cowboy life for themselves, albeit a bit cushier than the real thing in some cases.

The dude ranch experience allows families or individuals (sometimes even a group of women on a girlfriends getaway) to catch a glimpse or what it means to live and work on the open range. Most ranches pride themselves on combining a rustic, outdoorsy, and sometimes primitive environment with today's modern amenities. Depending on the ranch, guests may be able to take daily horseback rides, learn about the area's natural history, watch wranglers barrel race and rope cattle (and sometimes participate), take evening hayrides, and sit around the campfire roasting marshmallows and listening to cowboys sing old trail songs. You don't have to worry about throwing a lasso your first time out, and horseback-riding instruction is available for all levels of experience.

These *City Slickers*–type adventures began with one enterprising couple back in 1920. Ebenezer and Kate Ross of 1901 Buck Ranch decided to open their property on San Julian Creek, just outside Bandera, to guests from Houston who were looking for a change of pace. Before long, other established ranches began opening their gates to those curious about a Western style of living. With the influx of these seasonal wannabe cowhands, Bandera became famous for its resortlike camps, rodeos, cowboy bars, and restaurants to compliment these newly appointed guest ranches. (Before this, small rodeos and live-

Help with the chores on a ranch vacation.

stock shows took place in a lot of the different areas in the Hill Country, but centered primarily around trade through much of the early 1900s, not as much for show as they are today.)

Many of these dude ranches have changed in appearance since the early 1900s. Although early ranches were bare-bones, offering room for only a few families, and usually serving not-so-gourmet cuisine, many have added such amenities as rustic cabins or high-end guest accommodations, dining lodges serving old-fashioned Southern dishes with modern twists, cable TV, Wi-Fi, an on-site masseur, and golf courses.

Most ranches operate their guest programs from early spring to late fall, providing all-inclusive packages with meals and daily horseback rides included. Prices vary, but average $125 to $150 per person per night.

⇨ *Where to Stay for recommended dude ranches in Bandera.*

to throw back a cold one and forget their sorrows. The truly honky-tonk **11th Street Cowboy Bar** (⊠*307 11th St.* ☏*830/796–4849*), with its outdoor patio and music stage, is crammed with locals. Be ready to look the part in some Wranglers and boots, and if you're a woman, be prepared to get pulled onto the dance floor for a little boot scootin'.

WHERE TO EAT

TEX-MEX
$–$$

✕ **Full Moon Cafe.** Looking for lunch fare other than chicken-fried steak, barbecue, or Tex-Mex? The Full Moon Cafe is for you. A Houston couple took ownership of this pleasant Main Street venue in 2004 with the intent of offering slightly more-sophisticated cuisine with a healthful edge. Pasta salad, for example, is spiced up with a zesty lime-cayenne dressing, adding quite a kick to the average rotini mix. The chicken-and-broccoli sunflower salad is also worth a try. Don't leave without a slice of moist pineapple cake. The best dinner menu of the week is offered on Friday. ⊠*204 Main St.* ☏*830/460–8434* ⊟*D, MC, V* ⊘*No dinner Sat.–Thurs.*

BARBECUE
¢–$

✕ **The Grotto.** You have to leave Main Street to find this seemingly suspect hole-in-the-wall with mint-green walls and plywood tables. Don't let the retro '50s with an urban flair look fool you; this may be one of the best meals you have in town. The pulled-pork sandwich is a mouth-watering concoction of slow-roasted pork shoulder in a hoisin–Shiner Bock (dark Texas ale) marinade. Served on grilled ciabatta with a spicy apple-raspberry chutney, it adds new dimensions to Texas barbecue. ⊠*907 13th St., at the corner of Sycamore* ☏*830/796–9555* ⊟*AE, D, MC, V* ⊘ *Closed Sun. and Mon. No dinner Tues.–Wed.*

AMERICAN/
TEX-MEX
¢–$

✕ **O.S.T Restaurant.** This is John Wayne country, and patrons of the O.S.T. (Old Spanish Trail) don't let you forget it. There's a whole wall covered with the Duke's photos and memorabilia. Authentic Tex-Mex and hearty American plates are served, including a Texas-size chicken-fried steak that flaps over the lip of the plate. When in doubt, order whatever the locals are having. ⊠*305 Main St.* ☏*830/796–3836* ⊟*MC, V.*

WHERE TO STAY

DUDE RANCHES

$$
☉

🏨 **Dixie Dude Ranch.** One of Bandera's oldest dude ranches, the Dixie opened its doors to guests in 1937. Cabins and cottages are available for large parties, as are individual rooms in the rustic bunkhouse and main lodge. Though decor is laced with Western kitsch, rooms all include the modern amenity that combats the Texas heat—namely, air-conditioning. Be sure to get the full cowboy experience on the overnight trail ride, with cookouts, swimming, and cowboy serenades. Meals are served family-style in the dining lodge. Rates include two horseback rides per day. **Pros:** Overnight trail-ride package, on-site masseur, excellent for children. **Cons:** Some of the modern amenities are somewhat dated, two-night minimum. ✛*9 mi southwest of Bandera on FM 1077. The ranch is 7 mi west down 1077 on the right* ☏*Box 548, 78003* ☏*830/796–7771 or 800/375–9255* ⊕*www.dixie duderanch.com* ⇆*20 rooms* ⌂*In-room: no TV, Wi-Fi. In-hotel: pool, public Wi-Fi, no-smoking rooms* ⊟*AE, D, MC, V* ⅋*AI.*

$$$$ 🏨 **Flying L Guest Ranch.** Though it's been around since 1946, the Flying ☾ L is anything but stuck in the past. Guests can horseback ride, go on hayrides, and enjoy nightly s'mores roasting, as is the case with most dude ranches, but this expansive 772-acre property also has an 18-hole golf course, a water park and lounging pool, and an entire kids' activity program. Accommodations range in size from stand-alone villas with room for 13 to smaller condolike suites that sleep four to six. All have a gas fireplace and cozy bedding. **Pros:** Well-appointed condos including washer/dryer, variety of activities to choose from. **Cons:** Home-sites built up around the golf course take away from the resort feel, thin walls make things audible between condos. ✉ *566 Flying L Dr.,* ✛ *from Bandera, take Hwy. 173 south; the ranch is approximately 1 mi from town at the intersection of Wharton Dock Rd.* ☎ *800/292–5134* ⊕ *www.flyingl.com* ⇆ *23 rooms, 36 suites* ⚑ *In-room: kitchen, refrigerator, dial-up. In-hotel: 3 restaurants, pools, golf course, tennis court, concierge, public Wi-Fi* ▭ *AE, D, MC, V* ⑩ *AI.*

$$ 🏨 **Mayan Ranch.** Each morning here begins with OJ and coffee delivered to your split-timber-and-riverstone cabin. You can relax the day away or join the ranch crew for two daily horseback rides, swimming, fishing, tubing on the Medina River, and even lessons in the Texas two-step. Rates include two horseback rides per day. Children's programs are offered in summer (June to August). **Pros:** Access to the Medina River, fun and friendly staff. **Cons:** Some rooms not as well maintained as others, activities are set each day, meal times in the dining room are the only chance to eat. ✛ *From the courthouse square on Main St. take Pecan St. down to 6th, turn right on 6th, and cross the Medina River* ✉ *350 Mayan RR,* ☎ *830/796–3312* ⊕ *www.mayanranch.com* ⇆ *36 rooms, 21 cabins* ⚑ *In-room: no phone, refrigerator (some), no TV. In-hotel: restaurant, bar, tennis court, pool, children's program (ages 3–6), laundry facilities, public Wi-Fi, airport shuttle* ▭ *AE, D, MC, V* ⑩ *AI.*

MEDINA

14 mi west of Bandera via Hwy. 16.

If you like the remote feel of Bandera, head farther west on Highway 16 to Medina, a quiet treasure along the namesake river. Apple growing became a large part of this tiny town's industry in the late 1980s thanks to pioneer farmer Baxter Adams, who started the town's first apple orchard. Today Medina is known as the Apple Capital of Texas. The bounty can best be tasted in the form of a 5-pound pie at **Bit O' Honey Bakery** (☎ *830/589–7434*)., moving in 2008 from Highway 16 to a Main Street location. A few shops sell sundry gifts and homemade apple jellies and spreads, and the **Old Timer** gas station at the junction of Ranch Road 337 is a good place for catching local gossip at an old picnic table.

WHERE TO STAY

$$$$
Fodor'sChoice
★

Escondida Resort. Spanish for "hidden," Escondida is a pristine, luxe Mexican-style villa nestled amid cowboy country. The small resort and spa is the creation of property host Christy Carnes and Texas television personality Bob Philips. In their stately manor, each guest room is outfitted with elegant hardwood and iron furniture and subtle Mexican tile accents. Some rooms include gas fireplaces. Don't leave without a trip to the spa—you won't be sorry! **Pros:** Beautiful surroundings and private accommodations, on-site chef, library and living rooms in main portion of the villa. **Cons:** Two-hour drive from either San Antonio or Austin, palatial bathrooms lack large bathtubs. ⌧*23670 Hwy. 16 N,* ☎*888/589–7507* ⊕*www.escondidaresort.com* ⤢*10 rooms* ♿*In-room: safe, refrigerator, DVD, VCR, Ethernet, Wi-Fi. In-hotel: pool, gym, spa, no elevator, public Wi-Fi, some pets allowed, no kids under 21, no-smoking rooms* ▭*AE, D, MC, V* ⭘*AP.*

LOST MAPLES STATE PARK

39 mi west of Bandera via FM 337.

Once you get to Medina, you're slowly slipping further from civilization and into the Western frontier. But if you can get comfortable with that idea, travel a little farther west towards Vanderpool on Ranch Road 337 and then north on Farm Road 187 to Lost Maples State Park. You'll find yourself on arguably one of the most breathtaking drives in the state.

If you're here in fall, you'll likely be joined by a few thousand other travelers trying to catch one of the few patches of Texas land where you can actually witness a change in season. At Lost Maples, the fall foliage often rivals that of the Colorado golden aspens or the magnificent shades of Vermont and New Hampshire maples.

■TIP➔ Arrive early; the park only allows 250 cars; note that visitors pack the place during October and November weekends.

Other times of year you'll have the park almost to yourself. Even in the stark grayness of winter, Lost Maples is lovely. Stroll the Maple Trail amid the towering trees to see rough-hewn limestone canyons, serene creeks, and emerald pools.

⌧*Lost Maples State Park, 37221 FM Rd. 187* ☎*830/966–3413* ⊕*www.tpwd.state.tx.us* ▭*$5* ⭘*Daily.*

BOERNE

31 mi northwest of San Antonio via I–10.

Just a few years ago Boerne was a quiet little town with a smattering of shops and small-town restaurants. Even though it had easy access to San Antonio (just 30 minutes' drive away), Boerne flew under the radar while Fredericksburg boomed. But in recent years a whole slew of big-city Texans looking for the good life have descended upon Boerne, buying ranches in the hills, or retiring to the many high-end developments that have popped up along Highways 16 and 46. The result is a revitalized downtown district with a number of new restaurants—though still few accommodations—and a passel of new shops along Main Street. Even so, you won't find the shopping hordes here that you might in Fredericksburg.

Now that it's on the map, Boerne has begun attracting a crowd from the San Antonio area looking for a little "Hill Country action." Weekends in December are particularly festive. From the lighting of the town tree to an evening of Charles Dickens–inspired carolers, Boerne knows how to get people in the holiday spirit.

Originally settled in the 1840s by the same group of German "Free thinkers" that set up communities in nearby Comfort and surrounding areas, Boerne (pronounced burr-knee) grew steadily along the banks of Cibolo Creek. The town bears remnants of its German heritage around every corner, including the bilingual German-style street signs along the *Hauptstrasse* (Main Street).

WHAT TO SEE

Cascade Caverns. Take a half-mile tour past awe-inspiring limestone formations, deep caverns, stalactites, and stalagmites; you may even catch a glimpse of the endangered Cascade Caverns salamander. Watch for the impressive 100-foot waterfall spilling into a black pool at the end of the tour. ⊠226 *Cascade Caverns Rd. (I–10 W, Exit 543)* ☎830/755–2400 ⊕*www.cascadecaverns.com* ☞$11 ☉*Daily 10–5.*

Cave Without a Name. That's not a typo; the cave officially has no name—or rather, not having a name is part of its name. The story goes that in 1939, the owner of the cave, James Horne, held a public contest to name the cave. A young boy, upon visiting the cave commented that the geologic site was too beautiful to name and won the contest with the suggestion that it be called Cave Without a Name. Similar to the other living limestone caverns in the region, the cave has magnificent stalactite and stalagmite formations and calcite deposits. ⊠325 *Kreutzberg Rd., 12 mi from Boerne* ☎ 830/537–4212 or 888/839–2283 ⊕*www.cavewithoutaname.com* ☞$14 ☉*Memorial Day–Labor Day, daily 9–6; Labor Day–Memorial Day, daily 10–5.*

NEED A BREAK?

If you need a quick caffeine fix, hit the Daily Grind at the **Boerne Grill** (⊠*143 S. Main St.* ☎*830/249–4677*). It's a relaxed place to read or sip a potent coffee, and the Friday-night steak nights at the adjoining Boerne Grill are not to be missed.

Cibolo Nature Center. Nature lovers will enjoy strolling the trails through this 100-acre park set aside for the conservation of natural grasslands, marshlands, and riverbeds. Educational outdoor workshops and camps are available for kids. ⊠140 *City Park Rd.* ☎830/249–4616 ⊕*www.cibolo.org* ☞*Free* ☉*Daily 8–dusk.*

OFF THE
BEATEN
PATH
Guadalupe River State Park. This park gives some of the best public access to the shady cypress tree–lined Guadalupe River, a great spot for kayaking, swimming, and fishing. Of course, hiking and camping are great here, too. In winter, fly-fishing fanatics have a top opportunity to land rainbow trout stocked here by the state each year. ⊠ *3350 Park Rd. 31, Spring Branch* ☎ *830/438–2656* ⊕ *www.tpwd.state.tx.us* ☉ *Daily 8 AM–10 PM.*

SHOPPING

Perhaps Boerne's greatest attraction is the growing number of shops popping up along Main Street. Shops are open daily unless noted otherwise.

ANTIQUES & ART

The **Iron Pigtail** (⊠ *470 S. Main St.* ☎ *830/249–8877*) has a unique collection of South American art and early Texas pottery and antiques. d1e2454Find Victorian jewelry and 19th-century furniture at **Simple Treasures** (⊠ *195 S. Main* ☎ *830/249–5454*).

CLOTHING & ACCESSORIES

Be sure to stop in **Celeste** (⊠ *140 S. Main St.* ☎ *830/249–9660*) for reasonably priced, stylish outfits. **Green Bull Jewelry** (ADDRESS ⊠ *325 S. Main St.* ☎ *830/249–7393* ☉ *Closed Sun.*) has hard-to-find jewelry by Jerry Gowen, and other one-of-a-kind pieces. Country meets bohemian on the racks of women's clothes at **Mon a Me** (⊠ *305 S. Main St.* ☎ *830/249–2525* ☉ *Closed Sun.*).

HOME FURNISHINGS

Ordering custom-designed, high-end furniture is a pleasurable experience at **Calamity Jane's** (⊠ *322 S. Main St.* ☎ *830/249–0081*), where owner Shawn Beach meticulously conjures up Texas Hill Country decor. Wander the three small houses and courtyard of **Good & Co.** (⊠ *248 S. Main St.* ☎ *830/249–6101*) for a variety of plush furniture and rustic home accents, such as iron chandeliers. With unique European new and vintage odds and ends, the **Rusty Bucket** (⊠ *195 S. Main St.* ☎ *830/249–2288* ☉ *Closed Mon.*) is the perfect place to find a housewarming gift or stylish home furnishings.

WHERE TO EAT

CAFE
¢–$$
★
✕ **Bear Moon Bakery.** On weekends you may find a line out the door at this town favorite, which serves up an extensive breakfast buffet with eggs, fruit, and fresh-baked muffins, pastries, and breads. The breakfast crowd arrives early for one of the few inside tables. Most patrons brave the long counter line for cinnamon rolls—bring an appetite, they're as big as a Frisbee! Locals swarm here for lunch as well. ⊠ *401 S. Main St.* ☎ *830/816–2327* ▭ *AE, D, MC, V* ☉ *Closed Mon. No dinner.*

AMERICAN
$–$$$$
✕ **The Creek.** Dining alongside Cibolo Creek in this historic house, while listening to the rhythmic turn of a water mill, is a treat. There's a nice array of steaks, fresh seafood, and wild game. We particularly liked the blue crab fingers lightly sautéed with lemon and wine and the soul-warming rich and hearty beef-potato soup. ⊠ *119 Staffel St.* ☎ *830/816–2005* ▭ *AE, D, MC, V* ☉ *Closed Mon.*

AMERICAN
$$–$$$
★

✕**Cypress Grille.** People-watching has never been so inviting. From the small bistro tables in front of the narrow wine bar you can sip a glass of wine and nibble on crisp crab cakes while watching the passersby. The dinner menu also has much to offer. Blackened sea scallops with andouille sausage has a nice Cajun twist. Salads are fairly sizable and not your plain-Jane variety. The Texas Cobb, for example, has spicy grilled shrimp and slices of grapefruit. ⊠ *170 S. Main St.* ☎*830/248–1353* ⊟*AE, D, MC, V* ⊘ *Closed Sun. and Mon.*

AMERICAN
$–$$$
★

✕**Limestone Grille.** Tucked around the back side of the stately Ye Kendall Inn, the Limestone Grille is one of the most-traditional fine restaurants in town. Low lighting and deep greens and earthy tones give the dining room a historical ambience that whispers "This is where Robert E. Lee would have dined." In fact, the Confederate general was a guest at this building's old stage-coach stop. Soups and salads are pretty straightforward with a few exciting surprises, namely the thick and hearty Texas chili served with delicious yucca-root fries. Take your time with the wine list; it's one of the most extensive in the entire region. ⊠ *128 W. Blanco* ☎*830/249–2138* ⊟*AE, D, MC, V.*

AMERICAN
$–$$$

✕**Po Po Family Restaurant.** You might rub your eyes here; more than 21,000 collector plates crowd this country-cooking café. When it first opened in 1929, Prohibition was still in full swing and countless bootleggers would sell moonshine in the parking lot. Now people come for the fried chicken and chicken-fried steak. The fried frog legs—yes, frog legs—are really good, too. Save room for a warm brownie sundae. ⊠ *829 FM 289, via the Welfare exit (No. 533) off I–10 W* ☎*830/537–4194* ⊟*AE, D, MC, V.*

WHERE TO STAY

$$ 🛏 **August House.** Deemed one of the oldest continuously running B&Bs in Boerne, this charming 1912 white cottage offers two rooms in the main house and a separate Garden House. Each room is decorated with old-fashioned Western and Texan style. Guests are served coffee, juice, and light snacks for their stay and receive breakfast coupons to the Bear Moon Bakery, Boerne's hot spot for fresh-baked pastries. Rooms are spacious and comfortable; the country decor is slightly overwhelming. **Pro:** Located only a couple of blocks from Main Street. **Con:** Small twin beds in the Cabin Room. ⊠ *109 W. Evergreen St.,* ☎*830/249–4964* ⊕*www.augusthousetexas.com* ⇆*3 rooms* ⬡*In-room: refrigerator. In-hotel: no-smoking rooms* ⊟*AE, D, MC, V* ⦿*CP.*

$$ 🛏 **Crescent Quarters.** Though it may seem a bit out of place in the Texas Hill Country, a little piece of the Crescent City sits prominently on Boerne's Main Street. The New Orleans–style second-floor balcony overlooks the entire city center and gives you the sudden sensation you've been transplanted to the French Quarter. The 11 rooms each feature a different theme varying from shabby chic and the Hill Country to Asian and, of course, New Orleans. The building is a new construction, and rooms are spacious and clean. Hardwood or stained-concrete floors are found in each room, as well as refrigerators and big, open bathrooms. After a day of wondering the town, the balcony is certainly a nice retreat for a glass of wine and a little relaxation. **Pros:** Perfect view of Main Street from balcony; friendly staff; spacious, clean rooms. **Cons:**

Room decor is slightly kitschy, outside access to rooms seems more like a motel. ⊠*170 S. Main St.,* ☎*830/249–8016* ⊕*www.crescent quarters.com* 🛏*9 rooms, 2 suites* ♿*In-room: Ethernet. In-hotel: no elevator, no-smoking rooms* ⊟*AE, D, MC, V* ❖*CP.*

$$$$ 🛏 **Paniolo Ranch.** You'll have to drive down a winding back road to reach this Hawaiian-named retreat, but once you see the beautiful rolling valley below this hilltop perch you'll be glad you made the trip. The property features four private cottages, each with a suite or two rooms as well as luxurious living spaces. The O'Hana House is the most private and has some of the best views of the ranch; it also has its own hot tub, ideal for stargazing before bed. **Pros:** Remote property is beautiful, on-site spa. **Cons:** Slightly difficult to find, prices are fairly high in comparison to other Hill Country accommodations. ⊠*1510 FM 473,* ☎*866/726–4656* ⊕*www.paniolranch.com* 🛏*4 cottages* ♿*In-room: kitchen (some), refrigerator, DVD, Ethernet. In-hotel: pool, gym, spa, public Wi-Fi, no kids* ⊟*AE, D, MC, V* ❖*CP.*

$$–$$$$ ✕🛏 **Ye Kendall Inn.** Built in 1859 as Boerne's stagecoach stop, the inn
★ is now a recognized state and national historic landmark. The main lodge of this 9-acre property features 22-inch-thick hand-cut limestone walls and airy porches giving an authentic Hill Country feel. Beyond the main house is a collection of fully restored cottages—there's even a chapel that serves as a bridal suite. Each of the rooms, suites, and cottages is uniquely decorated with vintage pieces as well as modern luxuries. **Pros:** Excellent location on river and near Main Street, nice spa and gym. **Cons:** Some rooms are slightly dusty and have an old, musty smell; breakfast is not included with the price of a room; front desk service isn't overly friendly. ⊠*128 W. Blanco,* ☎*830/249–2138 or 800/364–2138* ⊕*www.yekendallinn.com* 🛏*36 rooms, suites, and cottages* ♿*In-room: Wi-Fi. In-hotel: restaurant, bar, pool, gym, spa, public Wi-Fi, no-smoking rooms* ⊟*AE, D, MC, V.*

COMFORT

17 mi northwest of Boerne via I–10/U.S. 87.

At first glance, Comfort resembles a lot of quiet Hill Country towns. It has the standard Dairy Queen and a small main street with historic buildings and antiques shops. But Comfort, known as the start of the Texas Hill Country, seems to have a magic effect on the people who visit. You don't find the crowded sidewalks of Fredericksburg, Boerne, and Kerrville. Here, time slows to a crawl, and the friendly faces of locals on High Street, the town's main thoroughfare, make you want to pull up a chair and stay a while.

The laid-back mentality mirrors the mind-set of those who settled here in 1852 along the banks of the Cypress Creek. Unlike the austere German settlers of Fredericksburg, New Braunfels, and Boerne, Comfort was settled by Ernst Hermann Altgelt and a community of Germans known as the "Freethinkers," who fled political and religious oppression and lived a far less conservative life than did traditional Germans.

The community prospered in this new way of thinking until the outbreak of the Civil War. Although most Texans were pledging their oath to the Confederacy, the Freethinkers swore loyalty to the Union army. Fearful of threats from Confederate loyalists, much of the community fled toward the Mexican border for protection. Those who didn't, or didn't make it, met their doom: on August 10, 1862, 36 men were slaughtered in the Battle of Nueces. Today Comfort is home to one of only six flags across the country that fly at half-mast year-round in remembrance of the Union patriots.

3

WHAT TO SEE

Many of the buildings on High Street were constructed in the late 1800s by noted British architect Alfred Giles, and are listed on the National Register of Historic Places. These include the Comfort Common and the remnants of Ingenhuetts General Store, the longest continuously run operation in Comfort until a fire in 2006 destroyed much of it. Plans to rebuild not yet to been determined.

WHERE TO EAT

SOUTHERN
¢–$

✕**Double D.** Don't be put off by the no-frills atmosphere of this side-of-the-road joint. What it lacks in charm it more than makes up for with good home cooking. Notable menu options are the hand-battered chicken-fried steak with cream gravy and the thick-cut onion rings. The daily lunch buffets are a great deal at just $7.50. ✉ *1004 Front St.,* ☎ *830/995–2001* ▭ *AE, D, MC, V.*

STEAKHOUSE
$–$$

✕**814: A Texas Bistro.** Colorful, quilt-draped walls and a cool ceiling-fanned patio make this a comfortable spot no matter the weather. The menu changes with the season, but you might find an entrée such as a juicy grilled New York strip steak in a balsamic reduction or sautéed rainbow trout. The 814 Burger is a half pound of grilled bliss, and the thick-cut, crispy fries are worth every calorie. Leave room for the Kentucky bourbon–pecan pie if it's on the daily menu. ✉ *814 High St.,* ☎ *830/995–4990* ▭ *AE, D, MC, V* ☾ *Closed Mon. and Tues.*

ECLECTIC
$–$$$$

✕**Welfare Cafe.** A former post office now serves appetites in the middle of nowhere. There are some unusual dishes like mahimahi (a mild, white fish) with tomatillo sauce, but also plenty of German fare. Start with potato pancakes served with applesauce or sour cream. The schnitzel is fabulous, as is the rouladen—a tenderized beef fillet wrapped around dill pickle, ham, sauerkraut, and Swiss cheese. If it's warm outside, sit beneath the vined trellis and watch the resident goats and donkeys grazing nearby. Live music accompanies your meal on Thursday and Sunday. Reservations are strongly recommended. ✉ *223 Waring Welfare Rd.,* ☎ *830/537–3700* ▭ *AE, D, MC, V* ☾ *Closed Mon. and Tues.*

WHERE TO STAY

$–$$$

▦ **Comfort Common.** These B&B guest rooms are tangled in a labyrinth of antiques shops and private cabins; there are even a couple of donkeys in back. British architect Alfred Giles built the Common in 1880 as the Ingenhuett-Faust Hotel. Now it's divided into two areas: the earthy Altgelt room and the more-private Victorian Storyville cottage, a block away from the main building and decorated with monochromatic whites. Breakfast is served to you in your room. **Pros:** Beautiful antique decor, perfect location for Christmas in Comfort. **Cons:** Some of the accommodations are spread out, Storyville is a few blocks from the inn, heavy tourist traffic through the inn shops on weekends can feel intrusive. ⊠ *717 High St.,* ☏ *830/995–3030* ⊕ *www.comfort common.com* ↩ *6 rooms* ⌂ *In-room: kitchen (some), refrigerator, Wi-Fi. In-hotel: no kids under age 12, no-smoking rooms* ⊟ *AE, D, MC, V* ⦿ *BP.*

$–$$$ ⊞ **Meyer Bed and Breakfast.** Originally a stage stop for travelers preparing to cross the Guadalupe River for the Old Spanish Trail, the Meyer is beautifully situated along the banks of Cypress Creek and is also just a few blocks' walk from town shopping. Each room and suite displays a different theme, such as the era of jazz music or an African safari. ■ **TIP→** Be prepared to book here, and at most other hotels or bed-and-breakfasts, more than six months in advance if you're planning to spend Thanksgiving week here (the Saturday after Thanksgiving is "Christmas in Comfort," a huge draw with lots of activities in town. **Pros:** Excellent proximity to shops, riverfront location is serene and inviting. **Con:** Some of the newer rooms are spacious and clean, but aren't as atmospheric as the rooms in the more-historic buildings. ⊠ *845 High St.,* ☏ *830/995–6100* or *888/995–6100* ⊕ *www.meyerbedandbreakfast. com* ↩ *5 rooms, 22 suites* ⌂ *In-room: refrigerator (some), Wi-Fi. In-hotel: pool, public Wi-Fi, parking (no fee), no-smoking rooms* ⊟ *AE, D, MC, V* ⦿ *BP.*

$$$$ ⊞ **Riven Rock Ranch.** It's a bit off the beaten path, but if you can bear
Fodor's Choice   with a bend or two in the road, you'll find this Hill Country treasure.
★   Three ranch-style cottages and one late-1800s farmhouse have immaculate Texas-meets-French-countryside interiors, gas fireplaces, and beautiful views of the hills. The ranch also has a large meeting/entertaining hall that accommodates up to 150 people, and an intimate dining room that serves up to 50 guests for special events. Standing in the center of the property, a former water tower has been converted into an observation tower. **Pros:** Immaculate property with beautifully designed accommodations, afternoon refreshments are a nice bonus. **Cons:** Remote location makes visiting area towns a longer journey, fairly expensive compared to other Hill Country accommodations. ⊠ *390 Hermann Sons Rd.,* ☏ *830/995–4045* or *877/726–2490* ⊕ *www.rivenrockranch.com* ↩ *9 rooms* ⌂ *In-room: kitchen, DVD, Wi-Fi. In-hotel: pool, public Wi-Fi, no-smoking rooms* ⊟ *AE, D, MC, V* ⦿ *BP.*

SHOPPING

ANTIQUES & HOME DECOR

Note that several stores close Monday. Find classic American selections at **Antiques on High** (⊠ *641 High St.* ☏ *830/995–3662* ⦿ *Closed Mon.*). Browse the local artwork and artisan designs in **Antiquities, etc & Folk Art Gallery** (⊠ *702 High St.* ☏ *830/995–4190* ⦿ *Closed Mon.*) where you'll also find a variety of antique collectibles from jewelry to books. **Blackbird Antiques** (⊠ *724 High St.* ☏ *830/995–2550* ⦿ *Closed Mon.*) offers exquisite folk-art pieces as well as Victorian and copper antiques. The shops at the **Comfort Common** (⊠ *717 High St.* ☏ *830/995–3030*) stock all sorts of home accessories and unique trinkets. The **Heart Cottage** (✉ *510-A 7th St.* ☎ *830/995–5660* ☉ *Closed Mon.*) has a noteworthy gift shop with Hobo bags, Robeez children's items, and tasteful home accents.Browse beautiful Mexican and European primitives and handmade furniture at **Wilson Clements Antiques** (✉ *405 7th St.* ☎ *830/995–2000*).

KERRVILLE

67 mi northwest of San Antonio via I–10.

Years ago, Kerrville had the small-town appeal that draws thousands to Fredericksburg and Boerne. With the arrival of the railroad in the late 1800s this settlement of primarily shingle makers became a center for trade and commerce, bringing droves of urban refugees from all walks of life. Happily situated among some of the most dramatic bluffs and valleys in the Hill Country, with the Guadalupe River running through it, the town has some of the more-picturesque views in Texas. Now it's one of the biggest little cities in the region. With a population of more than 20,000, Kerrville has become the source for necessities that can't be found in the smaller towns.

DID YOU KNOW?

When Kerrville was settled in the early 1850s, it was called Brownsborough. The name was later changed to pay tribute to Texas Revolution major James Kerr. Though Kerr was originally from Kentucky, his tenure in the war of 1812 and as a major in the legendary Texas Rangers and Republic of Texas Army brought him great notoriety. His political activism during the early years of the Republic of Texas included negotiating peace before the Fredonian Rebellion and organizing a treaty with the Karankawa Indians. For his devotion to the Texas frontier, pioneer Joshua Brown, who originally settled the area, renamed the land after Major Kerr.

Despite its massive growth in the past few decades, Kerrville has a lot to offer those looking to catch a glimpse of the region. One of Texas's most-famed music festivals happens here each year. The Kerrville Folk Festival in late spring draws folk music fans from miles around to camp in fields beneath the stars and celebrate folk music for a few weeks. Kids enjoy the summer camps in the surrounding areas; families make camps of their own in the many Guadalupe River RV parks.

If you're coming to Kerrville to stock up on supplies, make it a day outing. After your errands in the morning, take the afternoon to wander around the Museum of Western Art, browse the Texas-celebrated sterling silver designs of **James Avery** (d2e4112 ✉ *145 Avery Rd.* ☎ *830/895–6800* ☉ *Closed Sun.*), and then enjoy a nice meal overlooking the Guadalupe River.

WHAT TO SEE

☉ **Museum of Western Art.** Dedicated to preserving the authenticity of Western American heritage, the museum not only showcases Western art from past and present artists, but also shares the rich history of the cowboys, American Indians, settlers, mountain men, and tradesmen through educational programs. Interactive seminars give youngsters a chance to build their own "home on the range" and see how difficult life was on the open frontier. ⊠ *1550 Bandera Hwy.* ☎ *830/896–2553* ⊕ *www.museumofwesternart.org* 🖾 *$5* ☉ *Tues.–Sat. 9–5, Sun. 1–5.*

WHERE TO EAT

STEAKHOUSE
$$–$$$

✕ **Cowboy Steakhouse.** Western paintings and the smoke-stained limestone hearth of the wood-burning fire create a homey life-on-the-ranch feel. Grilled on an open mesquite-fire, the steaks are excellent, especially the not-so-petit filet mignon wrapped with a crispy strip of bacon. Not a fan of red meat? Not to worry: the grilled salmon is exceptionally fresh and flavorful. All entrées come with the standard baked potato, or a cinnamon-and-brown-sugar-topped sweet potato—we suggest the latter. ⊠ *416 Main St.* ☎ *830/896–5688* ▭ *AE, D, MC, V* ☉ *Closed Sun. No lunch.*

TEX-MEX
¢–$$

✕ **Mamacita's.** In Kerrville, Mamacita's is as much a tradition as Frito pie at a high-school football games. Though billed as "authentic" Mexican food, we'd argue that it's more along the lines of standard Tex-Mex fare, and about as straightforward as you can get. Don't be alarmed by the borderline fluorescent-green salsa served up with the red salsa and chips. It's actually pretty good, though the recipe remains a well-kept secret. One of the best items on the menu is the beef fajita with grilled onions and all the fixin's (guacamole, sour cream, pico de gallo, and shredded cheese). There are also locations in Fredericksburg, San Marcos, and New Braunfels. ⊠ *215 Junction Hwy.* ☎ *830/895–2441* ▭ *AE, D, MC, V.*

CAFE
$–$$

✕ **Rails–A Café at the Depot.** Just off the railroad tracks is a cheery historic house with cream timber siding and red trim. Built in 1915, the house once served as a train depot but was transformed into a fantastic little restaurant offering a variety of homemade soups, salads, and hearty entrées. Daily lunch and dinner specials vary. Look for the spicy grilled-shrimp tostada with creamy chipotle sauce and the grilled venison burger. ⊠ *615 E. Schreiner St.* ☎ *830/257–3877* ▭ *AE, D, MC, V* ☉ *Closed Sun.*

ITALIAN
$$–$$$
★

✕ **River's Edge–A Tuscan Grille.** Try to get here before sunset, to watch the sky fade from orange to pink and purple over the Guadalupe River. It's a view you can have from almost any seat at this little Italian locale. Here every effort is made to create authentic Italian cuisine with a bit of a Texas flavor. Spark your appetite with a salad of Bibb lettuce, pear, candied walnuts, and goat cheese. The Bolognese dish, with sweet Italian sausage and creamy penne pasta, is a good standby; another favorite is the beef tips swimming in a Gorgonzola cream sauce. ⊠ *1011 Guadalupe St.* ☎ *830/895–1169* ▭ *AE, D, MC, V* ☉ *Closed Sun.*

WHERE TO STAY

$$–$$$

🖫 **Y.O. Ranch Resort Hotel.** You may be on one of the bustling main streets of Kerrville, but a stay at the Y.O. Ranch Resort is a little like a retreat to a star 1950s dude ranch. No, there aren't horses or hayrides, but the rooms are all decorated in a Western theme, with exposed limestone walls and old-fashioned fixtures and curtains. Almost every room has a set of mounted deer antlers, just in case you were beginning to forget you were in Texas. The main lobby flaunts the Lone Star State's attributes as well: it displays more than 40 full mounts of exotic game along the high limestone walls and a life-size sculpture of a cowboy on a bucking bronco. A special family suite includes a separate room with bunk beds for kids. **Pros:** Friendly and helpful staff, good for "old-fashioned" Texas feel, large and affordable rooms. **Cons:** Entire property could use some updating and remodeling, room decor is sparse and drab. ⊠ *2033 Sidney Baker,* ☎*830/257–4440* ⊕*www.yoresort.com* ⟿*200 rooms* ⌂*In-room: Wi-Fi. In-hotel: restaurant, bar, tennis court, public Wi-Fi, some pets allowed (with deposit), no-smoking rooms* ▤*AE, D, MC, V.*

> ### GETTING FOLKSY IN KERRVILLE
>
> The **Kerrville Folk Festival** (☎*830/257–7474* ⊕ *www.kerrvillefolkfestival.com*) is the oldest continuously running music festival of its kind in the country. It usually begins the Thursday before Memorial Day and runs 24/7 for 18 days straight, with performances by more than 100 singer-songwriters and their bands. Since 1972 the festival has grown to attract more than 30,000 guests. Among those who've graced the stages of this music celebration are Willie Nelson, Lyle Lovett, Mary Chapin Carpenter, and Robert Earl Keen.

CAMPING

$$–$$$ ⚠**Buckhorn Lake Resort.** The Buckhorn is a peaceful RV community just outside town. Those pulling in from a long haul will enjoy the clean and well-kept facilities. Of the many amenities included, guests will enjoy free cable TV featuring three full-length movies each evening, an on-site general store, a fairly large exercise facility, instant-on telephone hookups, and free Wi-Fi. The property has two swimming pools, fenced-in tennis courts, and scenic walking trails. Trash is picked up daily. **Pros:** Clean and spacious sites, convenient amenities, friendly staff. **Cons:** Sites are somewhat close together, not the most convenient location to town. ⊠*2885 Goat Creek Rd.* ☎*830/895–0007 or 800/568–6458* ⊕*www.buckhornlake.com* ⟿ *3 cottages, 133 RV sites* ⌂*Full hookups, showers, dump station, drinking water, guest laundry, showers, picnic tables, grills, electricity, general store, swimming (pool)* ▤*AE, D, MC, V.*

$$–$$$ ⚠**Guadalupe RV Resort.** Only a few minutes from downtown, this RV campsite is really a cream-of-the-crop experience. Along the banks of the Guadalupe River, this beautifully maintained property offers shaded, spread-out sites for big-rig pull-throughs and motor-home pull-ins, each with a concrete patio and picnic table. Fully furnished one- and two-bedroom cabins are also available to rent with a full kitchen and bathrooms. There are plenty of distractions, too: a game room with pool and Ping-Pong tables, three swimming pools, volleyball, basketball, and the on-site River Rock Saloon. **Pros:** Spacious campsites, nice landscaping, friendly staff. It's open year-round. **Cons:** Not all sites have river views, need a car to get to town. ⊠*2605 Junction Hwy. 27* ☎*830/367–5676 or 800/582–1916* ⊕*www.guadaluperiverrvresort.*

com ⤴*16 cabins, 202 sites* ⚠*Full hookups, dump station, drinking water, guest laundry, showers, picnic tables, general store, play area, pool, electricity, public telephone, Wi-Fi* ▭*AE, D, MC, V.*

$ ⚠**Quiet Valley Ranch.** Probably most noted for its stake in hosting the annual Kerrville Folk Festival, Quiet Valley Ranch is an idyllic plot of land 9 mi south of Kerrville. Covering more than 50 acres of rugged Hill Country terrain, half the property is dedicated to the areas used for the festival, while the other half is used for tent and RV camping. The camp itself is fairly primitive compared to some of the other RV parks in town. Quiet Valley is open year-round. **Pros:** Perfect location for enjoying the Kerrville Folk Festival, very laid-back and low-maintenance environment. **Cons:** Not as many amenities as RV sites, more suited for primitive camping. ⊠*3876 Medina Hwy.* ☎*830/257–3600* ⊕*www.qvranch.com* ⤴*28 RV/tent sites* ⚠*Full hookups, toilets, fire pits, grills, drinking water.* ▭*AE, D, MC, V.*

INGRAM

Just 7 mi west of Kerrville, along the picturesque Guadalupe River, lies the small town of Ingram, where you can find a thriving art community. There's a turnoff to the south just west of town but it's easy to miss! In 1958 the Hill Country Arts Foundation was established with an emphasis on providing cultural arts to the region. It offers both art classes and theater for professionals and amateurs. An afternoon visiting the studios or the main art gallery displaying rotating exhibits of regional, national, and international artists is a worthwhile experience.

THE ARTS

ART GALLERIES & SHOPS
In Ingram you have an opportunity to stop by—and shop—in the studios where artists are doing their work. Ingram's many art galleries are in Old Ingram, the older section of town off Texas Highways 39 and 27. If you're heading east into town on Highway 39, this little village is on your right, just before you get to the main town area. Drive slowly, because it's easy to miss. The arts village has about 20 merchants and a half dozen fine artists, including Clint Orms, belt-buckle maker of the stars. Most galleries are closed Monday (some shops will close also on Tuesday and Wednesday November through January). It's best to call ahead if you plan to visit.

Silversmith Clint Orms crafts one-of-a-kind Western belt buckles worth thousands of dollars at **Clint Orms Workshop & Store** (⊠*229–B Old Ingram Loop* ☎*830/367–7949* ⊕ *www.clintorms.com)* Fine artist Kathleen Cook lights up the canvas with her pastel paintings. Find her and her works at the **Kathleen Cook Art Gallery & Studio** (⊠*218 Old Ingram Loop* ☎*830/329–3046* ⊕ http://kathleencook.com).S.RDarrin Potter sculpts cypress wood at **River Wood Studio** (⊠*100 Old Ingram Loop* ☎*830/367–4142),* a studio inside the Copper Cactus (⊕ *www. thecoppercactus.com),* a larger studio and shop where Jay Chatfield builds rustic furniture and his wife, Sherri, makes jewelry. At **Steven Napper Fine Art** (⊠*217 Old Ingram Loop* ☎*830/367–7775* ⊕ *www.*

napperfineart.com) pastels are the medium of choice for longtime artist Steven Napper. Working in bronze, sculptor Tom Moss creates his art at the **Tom Moss Studio Gallery** (✉*229-D Old Ingram Loop* ☎*830/367–3430* ⊕*www.tommossstudio.com*) . Specializing in watercolor and also acrylic, artist Todd Winters sets up shop at the **Winters Gallery** (✉*214 Old Ingram Loop* ☎*830/285–1382* ⊕*www.wintersgallery.com*), where his works use dramatic colors and often focus in on one object.

PERFORMING ARTS A full lineup of plays is produced from the **Point Theater** (✉*120 Point Theatre Rd.* ☎*830/367–5121 or 800/459–4223* ⊕*www.hcaf.com*) in both indoor and outdoor venues.

BETWEEN SAN ANTONIO & AUSTIN

GRUENE

38 mi north of San Antonio via I–35.

Gruene is purely Texan. Ask many Central Texans if they've ever two-stepped in this little town and you'll see a nostalgic gleam in their eye. Just north of New Braunfels, Gruene stands as a pristine portrait of Texas history and is revered as a place of Texas legends. After all, the entire town has been added to the National Register of Historic Places, and many of the buildings hold a medallion from the Texas Historical Commission.

Settled in the late 1840s by German farmer Ernst Gruene and his sons, the town gained most of its prosperity from the family's cotton business. Gruene's second son, Henry D. Gruene, built a Victorian-style home that is now the iconic Gruene Mansion Inn. Then in the late 1870s he built the Guadalupe River–powered cotton gin, which now houses the famed Gristmill River Restaurant & Bar, and Guene Hall, a dance hall and saloon that served as *the* social venue for the community before becoming a live-music venue in the 1970s.

Though the attack of the boll weevil on cotton crops in the late 1920s and the hostile economic effects of the Depression all but shut down the little town, this Texas star rose again in the 1970s with the restorative support of Pat Molak and Mary Jane Nalley. The two poured their boundless energy into preserving the original turn-of-the-20th-century feel of the town.

ARTS & ENTERTAINMENT

DANCE HALL

★ What really puts Gruene on the Texas map is the legendary **Gruene Hall**, known as the oldest continuously operating dance hall in the entire state. Many famous musicians owe their success to performances on this fabled stage, including Willie Nelson, Lyle Lovett, George Strait, Garth Brooks, Jerry Lee Lewis, and the Dixie Chicks. A trip to Gruene isn't complete without a turn on the old hardwood floors of Gruene Hall. ✉*1281 Gruene Rd.* ☎*830/606–1281* ⊕*www.gruenehall.com.*

WHERE TO EAT

AMERICAN
¢–$$$

✕**Gristmill River Restaurant & Bar.** Dining at the Gristmill is as mandatory as shuffling your boots along the floors of Gruene Hall when visiting Gruene. On a sunny day, request a seat on the multitier deck that climbs the side of the cliff overlooking the Guadalupe River. Though you can find fabulous soups and salads, there's nothing quite like the Gristburger. The secret to this burger's success is the spicy chili con queso that oozes from the sides. ⊠*1287 Gruene Rd.* ☎*830/625–0684* ▭*AE, D, MC, V.*

AMERICAN
¢–$$$

✕**Gruene River Grill.** Behind the Gruene Mansion Inn, this riverside grill draws quite a crowd. People seem to frequent this locale for the famed rib eye pan-seared in butter and balsamic vinegar, but a cup of the creamy jalepeño corn chowder brimming with fresh crawfish tails makes a notable impact as well. ⊠*1259 Gruene Rd.* ☎*830/624–2300* ▭*AE, D, MC, V.*

WHERE TO STAY

$–$$$

🖫**Gruene Homestead Inn.** Just outside Gruene, and on the way to New Braunfels, it's hard to miss this cluster of historic farmhouses scattered along a rolling green. Choose from 21 uniquely decorated suites that reflect a historic late 1800s feel. Each room has its own Texas-theme style, such as the Bluebonnet Room. Included on this expansive 8-acre property is the newly popular **Tavern in the Gruene** (☎*830/608–0438* ⊕*www.taverninthegruene.com*), a live-music venue hosting a number of up-and-coming Texas artists. **Pros:** Rooms are impeccably clean and well maintained, and remain quiet despite music from the nearby Tavern in the Gruene; friendly and accommodating staff. **Cons:** Close range to a new housing development, which takes away from its quaintness; noise from frequent Harley-Davidsons passing on the main road is unavoidable; breakfast is good, yet simple. ⊠*832 Gruene Rd.,* ☎*800/238–5534* ⊕*www.gruenehomesteadinn.com* ⊃*21 rooms* △*In-room: refrigerator (some), Ethernet, Wi-Fi. In-hotel: pool, no-smoking rooms* ▭*AE, D, MC, V* ⦿*BP.*

$$$–$$$$

🖫**Gruene Mansion Inn.** If you can stay in Gruene for an evening or two, this is the place to do it. The main house is the original home of Henry Gruene, and owners Cecil and Judi Eager have painstakingly worked to restore everything to its original condition. The guest accommodations extend much farther than the main house, including a row of cabins with river views, a renovated corn crib, and a period-designed lodge in the middle of the expansive property. **Pros:** Riverfront rooms give a nice view, close to shopping and restaurants. **Cons:** Big shows at Gruene Hall can be heard in the rooms, not the ideal place for children. ⊠*1275 Gruene Rd.,* ☎*830/629–2641* ⊕*www.gruenemansioninn.com* ⊃*30 rooms* △*In-room: refrigerator, DVD (upon request), Wi-Fi. In-hotel: public Wi-Fi, parking (no fee), no-smoking rooms* ▭*MC, V* ⦿*BP.*

SHOPPING

The **Buck Pottery** (⊠*1296 Gruene Rd.* ☎*830/629–7975*) building hosts its own workshop, where customers can watch as some of the beautiful earthenware is created by the artists. Unique pieces from a number of local artists keep this family-run shop a main attraction. Grab a souvenir T-shirt, bumper sticker, or cap at **Cotton-Eyed Joe's** (✉*1608 Hunter Rd.* ☎*830/620–1995*). The aforementioned fanfare comes in a variety of styles and colors, and the shop is open until 9 or 10, even on Sunday. Those about to embark on a Hill Country wine tour may want to stop in at the **Grapevine** (✉*1612 Hunter Rd.* ☎*830/606–0093*) to get a sampling of what's ahead on the Hill Country Wine Trail.Antiques lovers should duck into the **Gruene Antique Company** (✉*1607 Hunter Rd.* ☎*830/629–7781*), where more than 8,000 square feet of antiques and collectibles await. It's open until 9 PM.If Gruene Hall is king of the town, the **Gruene General Store** (✉*1610 Hunter Rd.* ☎*830/629–6021*) is its queen. Parts of the building date to the 1850s; the soda fountain is a 1950s time warp. You can find all sorts of unusual Texas gifts, cards, and foods. The store closes by 6 PM Sunday.

NEW BRAUNFELS

6 mi from Gruene, 30 mi north of San Antonio, and 45 mi southwest of Austin via I–35.

With a name like New Braunfels, it's a safe bet that Germans had a great deal of influence in this town. And in fact, they did. New Braunfels was the first of the Adelsverein movement settlements in the 1840s to create secure land in Texas under the German flag. The town was founded by Prince Carl of Solms-Braunfels, the Commissioner General of the Adelsverein. In 1845 Prince Carl led hundreds of sea-lagged German settlers from Galveston to a plot of land north of San Antonio on the banks of the Comal River. The settlement would later be named for his hometown in Germany, Braunfels (pronounced *brawn-fells*). The settlement endured a shaky beginning with the outbreak of the Mexican-American War in 1846, wet seasons that produced great floods in the Comal and Guadalupe rivers, and an outbreak of cholera. But by 1850 the town was a thriving community boasting the title of the fourth-largest city in Texas.

It lies along the Balcones Fault, where the Hill Country meets rolling prairie land to the east, putting New Braunfels barely inside the realms of the Hill Country region. The fault line produced a string of artesian springs known as Comal Springs that create the Comal River. Stretching a mere 3 mi before flowing into the Gaudalupe River, the Comal is considered the shortest river in the world.

Whereas many Hill Country towns are frequented for the shopping, wine, romantic getaways, or pure beautiful scenery, New Braunfels is considered more of an activity town. People come to tube down the Guadalupe River and splash around at Schlitterbahn water-park, or to get a taste (literally) of the annual Wurstfest in late October and early November celebrating the town's German heritage.

WHAT TO SEE

Fodor'sChoice
★
Natural Bridge Caverns. Guides will take you on an incredible journey underground at the largest known cavern in Texas, which has a half mile of paved trails. View awe-inspiring rock formations that are

constantly changing and growing due to the dripping and flowing water. The brave of heart shouldn't miss the flashlight tour of the Jaremy Room, a 120-foot-deep chamber known for its soda straws and delicate formations. If you're claustrophobic, be aware that the underground chambers are connected by fairly narrow passageways. Next to the caverns you can go on a driving safari at the **Natural Bridge Wildlife Ranch** (⊠ *26515 Natural Bridge Caverns Rd.* ☎ *830/438–7400* ⊕ *www.wildliferanchtexas.com* ☒ *$15.50* ☉ *Memorial Day–Labor Day, daily 9–6:30; early Sept.–late May, daily 9–5*), which is home to white rhinos, antelope, kudus, and dozens of other exotic animals from around the world. ⊠ *26495 Natural Bridge Caverns Rd., I–35 Exit 175 (Natural Bridge Caverns Rd./FM 3009)* ☎ *210/651–6101* ⊕ *www. naturalbridgecaverns.com* ☒ *$16.95* ☉ *Daily; call for hrs.*

SPORTS & THE OUTDOORS

☾ **Schlitterbahn.** Thousands of sun-beaten travelers seek refuge from the Texas heat each year at this 65-acre water park with more than 40 rides and family activities spread over six theme areas. ⊠ *Off I–35, Exit 184 or 190B* ☎ *830/625–2351* ⊕ *www.schlitterbahn.com* ☒ *$36* ☉ *Late Apr.–mid-Sept.; call for hrs.*

FISHING & TUBING

The Guadalupe River runs from the western points of Kerr County and stretches down to the Gulf of Mexico through Victoria. The upper river near Kerrville and Boerne is a wide, meandering centerpiece to the Texas Hill Country shaded by pecan and cypress trees. Below Canyon Lake, the Guadalupe River serves as a major recreational spot. Whitewater rafting and kayaking are both popular, but the more-relaxed activity of tubing down the river trailing a cooler of beer is the main attraction in summer.

Below the Canyon Dam, the Gaudalupe is also considered one of the top 100 trout streams in the country. The state stocks the river with trout each winter, attracting anglers from miles around. While casting for beautiful rainbow and brown trout, you'll likely get a few hits from the native Guadalupe smallmouth bass (the state fish of Texas), large-mouth bass, and Rio Grande perch.

FISHING OUTFITTERS There are many reputable fishing guides in the area. For referrals and to stock up on fishing gear, visit **Gruene Outfitters** (⊠ *1629 Hunter Rd.* ☎ *830/625–4440*).

KAYAKING, RAFTING & TUBING OUTFIITTERS

River outfitters are easily found dotting the banks of the river where tubes, rafts, and kayaks can be rented for the day. A few to try: **Gruene River Co.** (⊠ *1404 Gruene Rd.* ☎ *830/625–2800*), **Rio Raft & Resort** (⊠ *14130 River Rd.* ☎ *830/964–3613*)**Rockin 'R' River Rides** (⊠ *1405 Gruene Rd.* ☎ *830/629–9999*).

SKIING

Texas Ski Ranch. For those looking for a little adventure, or who have teenagers along for the ride, the Texas Ski Ranch offers a great outlet for skiers and skateboarders. Most recognized for its cableway that pulls up to six skiers, wakeboarders, or kneeboarders at all levels around a lake, the 70-acre park also features a 15,000-square-foot skateboarding street-style course offering everything from ramps and rails to half-pipes. The park also has a challenging motocross track featuring a mix of flats, obstacles, and hills, but it is only open to members who pay an annual $425 fee. ✉ *Off I–35 in New Braunfels, between San Antonio and Austin, Exit 193 or 194* ☎*830/627–2843* ⊕*www. texasskiranch.com* ✉*$23–$36 (skiing, does not include rentals), $5 (skateboard course)* ⊗*Mar.–Sept., daily 9* AM*–dark (night rides available until midnight on Thurs.); Oct.–Feb., Fri.–Sun. 11–dark.*

WHERE TO EAT

STEAKHOUSE
$–$$$

✗**Gruene Onion Grill.** Don't be deterred by its strip-mall location. This little café serves up some amazing dishes, from thick and juicy burgers with crispy cracked-pepper fries to a savory pork tenderloin Wellington wrapped in a flaky pastry dough with mushroom confit and baked into a flavorful little package. Chef's features change daily, but this is one of the few places in New Braunfels that you're likely to find duck a l'orange on the menu, and, we must say, it's pretty good. ✉*1324 E. Common St.* ☎*830/629–2989* ▭*AE, D, MC, V.*

AMERICAN
$–$$
Fodor'sChoice
★

✗**Huisache Grille.** Hidden near the train tracks off San Antonio Street, the Huisache (pronounced *wee-satch*) is a must-stop. Consistently delivering fantastic soups, salads, sandwiches, and main dishes, there's a lot to love about this place, and the beautiful historic 1920s building only adds to the experience. For lunch the ham-and-Gouda sandwich with sweet caramelized onions offers a nice adult version of a grilled cheese. Pecan-crusted pork chops soar with a rich bourbon-butter sauce. ✉*303 W. San Antonio St.* ☎*830/620–9001* ▭*AE, D, MC, V.*

NEW
AMERICAN
$$–$$$$

✗**Liberty Bistro.** From the portraits of presidents along the walls to the cleverly named entrées—Freedom Filet, 49th State Wild Salmon Filet, Freedom of the Press Chicken—the patriotic theme is hard to miss at this upscale eatery. The *cabriqueso* is a fantastic starter of melted goat cheese mixed with jalepeño and cilantro pesto and spicy-sweet red piquillo peppers. In an effort to lessen the bistro's carbon footprint, owner Darren Scroggins has created a completely green kitchen free of gas cooking. ✉*200 N. Seguin St.* ☎*830/624–7876* ▭*AE, D, MC, V* ⊗*Closed Sun.*

WHERE TO STAY

$$$–$$$$

▥**Lamb's Rest Inn.** Getting a little rest is easy to do at this spot on the Guadalupe River. Expansive wooden decks surround live oaks and hammocks sway in the garden. The spacious rooms have comfortable beds and colorful accents. Warm chocolate-chip cookies tend to present themselves each afternoon. **Pros:** Rooms have an up-to-date look, tiered decks have wonderful river views, excellent staff. **Cons:** Small bathrooms in some rooms, over-the-top decor in some rooms. ✉*1385 Edwards Blvd.,* ☎*830/609–3932* ⊕*www.lambsrestinn.com* ⇖*4 rooms, 1 two-bedroom suite, 1 two-bedroom cottage* ⚥*In-room: refrigerator, Wi-Fi. In-hotel: public Wi-Fi, parking (no fee), no-smoking rooms* ▭*AE, D, MC, V* ⊗|*BP.*

3

SAN MARCOS

19 mi northeast New Braunfels and 30 mi south of Austin via I–35.

San Marcos is the largest town between Austin and San Antonio on I–35. It's home to former President Lyndon B. Johnson's alma mater, Texas State University, the crystal-clear Aquarena Springs that feed the San Marcos River, and the Southwestern Writers Collection at the Alkek Library. For the most part it's a college town, but most visitors to San Marcos buzz right by downtown and hit the state's best outlet-mall shopping at the Prime Outlet and the Tanger Outlet malls.

SHOPPING

For years, Texans anywhere within a 200-mi radius have flocked to the outlets for back-to-school, Christmas, and spring and summer shopping. During these times, patience and dumb luck finding a parking space are virtues. But really, the endless variety of shops at the two adjoining locations draws a steady crowd year-round. For either, take the Centerpoint Road exit off the interstate. **Prime Outlets San Marcos** (⊠*3939 I–35 S* ☏*512/396–2200 or 800/628–9465* ⊕*www.prime outlets.com*) is the sprawling mall on the north side of Centerpoint Road, and is host to such fashionable shops as Crate & Barrel, J. Crew, Pottery Barn, Giorgio Armani, and Gucci. The better part of a day can be spent strolling through the more than 130 stores. **Tanger Outlets San Marcos** (⊠*4015 I–35 S* ☏*512/396–7446 or 800/408–8424* ⊕*www.tangeroutlet.com*), on the southern side of Centerpoint Road, where more than 100 stores, from Old Navy to the Le Creuset kitchen store, await.

WHERE TO EAT

CAFE ✕**Root Cellar Café.** If you can spare the time, skip the chain restaurants
¢–$$ at the outlet malls and head to San Marcos's town square for lunch at this café and art gallery. The cheerful staff and bright, eclectic art–filled walls make for a very comfortable atmosphere. With choices like the zingy Holy Aioli sandwich of citrus-marinated chicken with cilantro aioli, lunch here beats any fast-food option at the mall. They serve breakfast until 4 PM. ⊠*215 N. LBJ,* ☏*830/392–5158* ▭*AE, D, MC, V* ☉*No dinner Sun.–Wed.*

WIMBERLEY

14 mi northwest of San Marcos via RR 12.

Wimberley's windy little roads, shady oak and cypress trees, and compact town square give it the feel of an English village. Established in 1848 with only a small trading post to its name, Wimberley's first industries were lumber and shingle making. The Blanco River and Cypress Creek, which run through the city, fueled the Wimberley Mill. But the Great Depression left the town stagnant with the exception of a few working ranches. The 1980s saw a revitalization in Wimberley as it began to gain notice as a retirement and artists community. Galleries and shops selling local artists' Hill Country creations, from oil paintings to crafts, are found throughout Wimberley Village Square.

NEED A BREAK?

Wimberley Pie Company. Tell anyone in Central Texas that you're heading for Wimberley and the first response you likely may hear: "Be sure to get some pie at the Wimberley Pie Company!" The dimly lighted glass case along the front of the shop is filled with fresh, vacuum-sealed pies ready to be picked up and taken to some lucky home, but you can also grab a slice from pies right out of the oven. The traditional cherry pie has a perfect balance of tart and sweet. ⊠ *13619 RR 12, just east of the town square* 🕾 *512/847–5588* 🗖 *No credit cards* 🕙 *Closed Mon., Tues., and major holidays.*

3

WHERE TO EAT

STEAK HOUSE
$$–$$$
★

✕ **Cedar Grove Steakhouse.** Texas-style elegance radiates through this contemporary steak house. An ambitious and well-executed menu makes this one of the best examples of Hill Country fine dining. The steaks here are excellent, particularly the 6-ounce Black Angus fillet wrapped in applewood-smoked bacon. Another favorite is the light, creamy white-chocolate cheesecake with flecks of fresh lavender. ⊠ *9595 RR 12, Suite 1, at the junction of RR 12 and FM 32* 🕾 *512/847–3113* 🗖 *AE, D, MC, V* 🕙 *Closed Mon.*

AMERICAN
¢–$

✕ **Ino'z.** Pronounced eye-nose, Ino'z offers the type of food you'd expect from a place called a "brew and chew"; it's either fried or at the very least mildly greasy. But that's not to say it's all bad. On a warm night, sitting on the expansive wood patio overlooking the Cypress Creek with a plate of cheesy nachos and a beer with friends can certainly take the edge off of a day. Ino'z "Okie" burger with grilled onions hits the spot as well. Thankfully it comes in manageable quarter-pound sizes or hefty half-pounds for the Texan in you. Wimberley is in a dry county, so ordering alcohol is legal only with a "club membership," which Ino'z will give you free; just ask your server. ⊠ *14004 RR 12* 🕾 *512/847–6060* 🗖 *MC, V.*

BARBECUE
$–$$
Fodor's Choice
★

✕ **The Salt Lick.** If you see smoke rising while driving along FM 1826, don't be alarmed. It's just a barbecue beacon calling you to the perpetually smoking pits, long picnic tables, and dance hall–style compound of the Salt Lick. On weekends, and particularly when the University of Texas Longhorns have a home game, this family-friendly hot spot on the edge of south Austin is tough to get into, but always worth the wait. You'll be joined by locals and travelers from miles around waiting to feast on perfectly smoked brisket, baby back ribs, vinegary German potato salad and coleslaw, and enough soft white bread to sop up a gallon of the secret sauce. Oh, and did we mention the sausage? Get some of that, too. You can order the all-you-can-eat, family-style option and share with friends. Though it may seem impossible to save room for homemade blackberry cobbler with Blue Bell homemade vanilla ice cream on top, we promise it is worth every calorie. If you're driving from the Hill Country back to the Austin airport, this makes a great lunch stop on the way. ⊠ *18001 FM 1826, Driftwood, 5 mi northeast of Wimberley* 🕾 *512/858–4959* 🗖 *No credit cards.*

CLOSE UP

Wines of the Hill Country

Newsflash: You don't have to go to Napa or the Saint Ynez Valley to sample good wine. Vintners across Texas are abuzz with hearty blends of wine that have started turning heads from wine spectators worldwide. Some of the most-talked-about wines originate in the Hill Country, straight from the region's arid limestone earth—the same type of soil you'd find in northwest Italy, southern Spain, and Provence.

The best time to come is in fall, when wine-related festivals are underway. These include the Fredericksburg Food & Wine Fest held at the end of October, the Gruene Music & Wine Fest held in the beginning of October, and the San Antonio New World Wine & Food Festival at the beginning of November. If you come in spring, you'll be treated to the splash of wildflowers (including the vibrant bluebonnets) along the roads and Austin's Texas Hill Country Wine and Food Festival in mid-March.

The Hill Country has been turning out wines since the 1970s. More than 20 wineries now dot the region and most are open daily year-round, providing tours and tastings (some are free, some are not). This is a great place for a wine-tasting road trip—but remember, those sips add up. Limit your tastes and drink water if you're driving.

At the top of the list is **Alamosa Wine Cellars** (✉ *677 CR 430, Bend* ☎ *325/628–3313* ⊕ *www.alamosawinecellars.com*). About 30 mi north of Llano, Alamosa is where winemaker Jim Johnson makes a superb Viognier, a bold and flavorful Syrah, and the celebrated "El Guapo," a tawny little Tempranillo blend with a horned frog

on the label that has been billed by many connoisseurs as a "revelation."

Happily situated on the sparkling waters of Lake Buchanon, **Fall Creek Vineyards** (✉ *1820 CR 222, Tow* ☎ *325/379–5361* ⊕ *www.fcv.com*) has been a prolific producer of such wines as its refreshing Chenin blanc and the award-winning red blend "Meritus."

The highest concentration of wineries is in the Fredericksburg area, in Fredericksburg as well as the townships of Sisterdale, Comfort, and Stonewall.

Enjoy live music with your wine on Saturday at the family-run **Torre Di Pietra** (✉ *10915 E. U.S. Hwy. 290, Fredericksburg* ☎ *830/644–2829* ⊕ *www.texashillcountrywine.com*). **Sister Creek Vineyards** (✉ *1142 Sisterdale Rd. [RR 1376], Sisterdale* ☎ *830/324–6704* ⊕ *www.sistercreekvineyards.com*) produces Muscat Canelli, an Italian wine, as well as traditional blends. **Comfort Cellars** (✉ *723 Front St., Comfort* ☎ *830/995–3274* ⊕ *www.comfortcellars.com*) reminds you you're in Texas with its hot jalepeño wine, which is mostly used in the kitchen rather than for drinking.

Just east of Fredericksburg, the sprawling estate of **Becker Vineyards** (✉ *464 Becker Farms Rd., Stonewall* ☎ *830/644–2681* ⊕ *www.beckervineyards.com*) has enchanting fields of lavender and a B&B in addition to the old stone barn where you can taste the fruity Reisling and smooth and rich Cabernet-Syrah blend. **Grape Creek Vineyards** (✉ *97 Vineyard La., Stonewall* ☎ *830/644–2710* ⊕ *www.grapecreek.com*) also has a B&B attached to the winery (children are not allowed).

Enjoy a tasting at Becker Vineyards, near Fredericksburg.

Other wineries in the Hill Country:

Bell Mountain Vineyards (⌧ *463 Bell Mountain Rd., Willow City* ☎ *830/685–3297* ⊕ *www.bell mountainwine.com).*

Driftwood Vineyards (⌧ *4001 Elder Hill Rd. [CR 170], Driftwood* ☎ *512/858–9667* ⊕ *www.driftwood vineyards.com).*

Dry Comal Creek (⌧ *1741 Herbein Rd., New Braunfels* ☎ *830/885–4121* ⊕ *www.drycomalcreek.com).*

Flat Creek Estate (⌧ *24912 Single- ton Bend E, Marble Falls* ☎ *512/267– 6310* ⊕ *www.flatcreekestate.com).*

Sandstone Cellars (⌧ *211 San Antonio St., Mason* ☎ *325/347–9463* ⊕ *www.sandstonecellarswinery.com).*

Off the beaten path—and out of the Hill Country—a couple of wineries in the Panhandle are also worth men- tioning. Lubbock's **Llano Estacado Winery** (⌧ *3426 E. FM 1585, Lubbock* ☎ *806/745–2258* ⊕ *www.llanowine.*

com), producing fairly consistent wines for the past 30 years, is prob- ably Texas's forerunner in the wine industry. Near Lubbock, **Cap*Rock Winery** (⌧ *408 E. Woodrow Rd., Lamesa* ☎ *806/863–2704* ⊕ *www. caprockwinery.com)* has been on the wine scene for some time; recently, however, Cap*Rock's winemaker Kim McPherson has taken the state by storm with his own label, McPherson Cellars, which focuses on Rhone-style wines. His signature Rhone-style Tre Colore has attracted a lot of atten- tion, and his Grenache-Mourverdre and Rosé of Syrah-Grenache blends are successful examples of growing grapes suited to the region.

Local visitors bureaus and gift shops stock the "Hill Country Wine Trail" (⊕ *www.texaswinetrail.com)* pamphlet with a handy map inside, and the "Texas Wine Country" brochure produced by the Texas Department of Agricul- ture (www.gotexanwine.org) shows a regional view of the different wineries.

WHERE TO STAY

$$–$$$$ 🔲 **Blair House Inn.** There's a lot to experience at this lovely little com-
★ pound. Unwind with a rejuvenating massage, take a dip in the refresh-
ing pool, or roll up your sleeves for one of the hands-on cooking classes.
Even if you just retreat to one of the cowboy-chic rooms, you'll still
find an amazing sense of release here. The Laredo Room in the Honey-
suckle Cottage is one of the nicest, with its subtle hints of Old Mexico
and large limestone fireplace. The romantic San Rafael Cottage is also
a great choice for its covered deck and its tin roof that sings a lullaby
when the rain blows through. Breakfast alone is nearly worth the price
of your stay. **Pros:** Beautiful grounds, comfortable rooms, excellent for
a private getaway. **Con:** Traffic noise from nearby RR 12. ⊠ *100 Spoke
Hill Rd.,* ☎ *877/549–5450* ⊕ *www.blairhouseinn.com* ↘ *4 rooms, 7
suites* ⌂ *In-room: refrigerator , DVD, Wi-Fi . In-hotel: pool, public
Wi-Fi* ⊟ *AE, D, MC, V* ⏍ *BP.*

$$–$$$$ 🔲 **Creekhaven Inn.** Though you're only a short walking distance from
Wimberley Village Square, the meandering dirt road to the inn makes
this feel like a true hideaway. Look for deer in the tree-framed meadows nearby. The sprawling main house is shaded by pecan trees and
wrapped in a series of wooden decks. Each guest room has a distinct
style, with different color schemes and handmade bedspreads. After a
good sleep on one of the pillow-top beds, be sure to stroll the grounds
along the creek or soak in the hot tub with a glass of wine. **Pros:**
Very friendly staff, clean rooms, beautiful grounds and landscaping.
Cons: Some rooms have less-attractive decor, some bathrooms are
small or awkwardly laid out. ⊠ *400 Mill Race La.,* ☎ *512/847–9344
or 800/827–1913* ⊕ *www.creekhaveninn.com* ↘ *14 rooms* ⊟ *AE, D,
MC, V* ⏍ *BP.*

$$$$ 🔲 **Inn Above Onion Creek.** Not 10 mi from Wimberley is a little week-
★ end escape set on a 100-acre plot with rolling hills and enchanting
vistas. You won't even have to leave the premises to forage for dinner.
Instead, a five-course meal is prepared each night and served family-
style to you and the other inn guests. (The inn does not serve alcohol,
but you're allowed to bring your own wine.) Rooms have romantic
fireplaces and views of the fiery Texas sunsets. The new spa is small,
but digs in with excellent Swedish and deep-tissue massage therapy.
Pro: Views of the Hill Country from the west-facing decks are spectacular. **Cons:** Beds aren't as comfortable as the rest of the accommodations, some rooms have much better views than others. ⊠ *4444 W. FM
150,* ☎ *512/268–1090* ⊕ *www.innaboveonioncreek.com* ↘ *7 rooms,
3 suites* ⌂ *In-room: kitchen (some), refrigerator (some), DVD (some),
VCR (some), Wi-Fi. In-hotel: pool, spa, bicycles, public Wi-Fi* ⊟ *AE,
D, MC, V* ⏍ *AP (dinner and breakfast).*

SHOPPING

Upon arriving in Wimberley, it soon becomes clear that the **Wimberley Village Square**—a virtual spiderweb at the crossroads of RR 12
and a number of small Wimberley streets—is the place for an afternoon of shopping. For that last-minute gift for a friend's new baby
or the kids back home, stop in at **Blue Bacon Toys** (⊠ *14011 RR 12*
☎ *512/847–2150*) for an extremely unusual assortment of children's

toys. The **Old Mill Store** (✉ *14100 RR 12* ☎ *512/847–3068*) has all the knickknacks of an old-fashioned trading post toward the front, but if you stroll to the back you'll find paintings, sculptures, and handmade furniture. Duck into the **River House** (✉ *104 Wimberley Sq.* ☎ *512/847–7009*) for an inspiring selection of home accessories. Take a detour to **Wimberley Glassworks** (✉ *6469 RR 12* ☎ *512/393–3316*), one of the art community's most-impressive contributors, to watch artisans blow and shape beautiful glass creations.

> **MARKET DAYS**
>
> From April to December, the first Saturday of each month brings a surge of bargain hunters to Wimberley for the famed Market Days. Excellent deals can be had at the 450 booths full of arts and crafts, furniture, and more. Gates open at 6 AM and close whenever vendors decide to pack up. ✉ *At Lions Field on RR 2325, 0.25 mi from the RR 12 junction.*

3

THE HIGHLAND LAKES

LAKE TRAVIS & LAKEWAY

Lake Travis, the fifth in the series of Highland Lakes fed by the Colorado River, is a refreshing playscape for the Austin and Lago Vista areas, with dramatic Hill Country slopes. When the sun sets on Lake Travis, some of the most brilliant views are enjoyed from the decks of hillside restaurants, where spectators applaud the visual pyrotechnics.

Along the southwest shores of the lake, the town of Lakeway is home to some of Austin's most celebrated golf courses, tennis centers, and boating operations. The 1970s retirement community Lakeway was little more than a quiet retreat for Austinites. Today, with new renovations to the more-than-30-year-old Lakeway Inn, countless upscale residential subdivisions, and myriad restaurants and shops that have popped up along the southern stretch of RR 620, the area is a thriving extension of the Austin-metro area.

SPORTS & THE OUTDOORS

☺ **Hamilton Pool Nature Preserve.** About 30 mi southwest of Austin off Highway 71 is a small nature preserve that is home to one of the Hill Country's most beautiful natural pools. The continuously flowing Hamilton Creek spills over an enormous limestone outcropping creating a beautiful 50-foot waterfall that gently plunges into the crystal waters of Hamilton Pool. It's particularly crowded on weekends. Parking is limited and controlled by the state, with a nominal fee for entry, so it's best to call ahead to see if spaces are available. ✉ *13 mi southwest on Hamilton Pool Rd. from Hwy. 71 W (about 20 mi from Lakeway)* ☎ *512/264–2740* ⊕ *www.co.travis.tx.us* 🎫 *$8 per vehicle* ⊙ *Daily 9–6*).

☺ **Pace Bend Park.** Explore some of Lake Travis's narrow coves and great limestone cliffs at Pace Bend Park. Here you'll experience spectacular sunsets over the lake. Visitors can hike and bike the rustic trails that lead to different lake and Hill Country views. Pace Bend Park is a favorite of college students who like to jump off the high cliff walls (up to 30 feet) into the water below. Be warned: the only way back up is to climb and varying lake levels make this a risky activity. ⊠ *12011 Pace Bend Rd.; from the intersection of RR 620 and Hwy. 71 take 71 west 11 mi to RR 2322 (Pace Bend Park Rd.); entrance is in 4.6 mi (about 20 mi from Lakeway)* ☏ *512/264–1482* ⊙ *Daily sunrise–9.*

BOATING

For much of the year, even in the cooler months, Lake Travis is alive with boats, water skis, and wakeboards. Public boat ramps are available in a number of different locations along the shores. Contact the marinas listed to get the nearest location.

To get a little piece of lake action, a few of the reputable boat outfitters include: **Hurst Harbor Marina** (⊠ *16405 Clara Van St.* ☏ *512/266–1800* ⊕ *www.hhmarina.biz* ⊙ *Daily 8–5 (May–Aug. until 7),* **Just For Fun Watercraft Rental** (⊠ *5973 Hiline Rd.* ☏ *512/266–9710* ⊕ *www.jff.net* ⊙ *Daily; call for times)* **Lakeway Marina** (⊠ *103-A Lakeway Dr.* ☏ *512/261–7511* ⊕ *www.lwmarina.biz* ⊙ *Daily 8–5; extended summer hrs 8–7)*

GOLF

Lakeway Golf Club. Two of Austin's most honored courses are in Lakeway. Both the Live Oak and Yaupon courses, which are part of the Lakeway Golf Club, have challenging rounds with rolling hills and tree-lined fairways. ⊠ *1 World of Tennis Sq.* ☏ *512/261–7200* ⊕ *www.lakewaygolfclub.com* ⊙ *Daily. Call for reservations.*

WHERE TO EAT

NEW AMERICAN
$$$$
Fodor'sChoice
★

✕ **Hudson's on the Bend.** Chase the sun west from Austin to where an unforgettable experience awaits in this refined little ranch house. This is the place for expertly crafted wild-game dishes such as pistachio-crusted rattlesnake cakes or rich pheasant-confit tamales with white chocolate–tomatillo sauce. In celebrated chef Jeff Blank's kitchen, the philosophy is "cooking fearlessly." Although the restaurant can accommodate families, the soft lighting and the conversation-inspiring art cater to an adult crowd. ⊠ *3509 RR 620, Austin* ☏ *512/266–1369* ▭ *AE, D, DC, MC, V* ⊙ *No lunch.*

AMERICAN
$–$$

✕ **The Oasis.** There are sunsets, and then there are sunsets at the Oasis. Here you can sit on one of the many wooden decks that scale the hillside of this Lake Travis hot spot with a frozen margarita and bid farewell to the day with one of the most spectacular sunsets in the state. The menu offers fairly standard American and Mexican fare, from burgers to enchiladas. Be sure to get there early; you won't be the only one with the bright idea to swing by. ⊠ *6550 Comanche Tr.* ☏ *512/266–2442* ⚑ *Reservations not accepted* ▭ *AE, D, MC, V.*

ITALIAN
$–$$$

✕ **Rocco's Grill.** Pronounced "Roh-coh" as opposed to "*Rock*-oh," this delightful restaurant owned by the local Piazza family has bright murals depicting family events and traditions in bold caricatures. The menu is primarily American-Italian, with personal touches from family recipes.

Try the salmon Allessondra, named for the owner's daughter: a salmon fillet with lump crabmeat and a bright lemon-caper butter sauce. The views of the rolling Lakeway Golf Course fairways are stunning ⊠*900 RR 620 S* ☎*512/263–8204* ⊟*AE, D, MC, V.*

TEX-MEX ✕**Rosie's Tamale House.** This little nondescript shack proclaiming
¢–$ "Rosie's Food To Go" in big black letters usually has a swarm of locals
★ each morning clamoring for their favorite breakfast tacos. For lunch, you can order takeout and sit at one of the picnic tables outside. But for a sit-down meal, head across the street to the official restaurant in a big red building where you can order Rosie's signature tamales or enchiladas. Famed Texas singer-songwriter Willie Nelson is a frequent-enough customer to have his very own dish, the Willie's Plate: a crispy beef taco, one cheese enchilada smothered in chili con carne, and a side of guacamole salad. There's no liquor license, so bring your own cooler of beer. ⊠*13436 W. Hwy. 71* ☎*512/263–5245* ⊟*No credit cards.*

WHERE TO STAY

$$$–$$$$ ⊞**The Crossings.** This spa and hotel, on a hilltop overlooking Lake Tra-
★ vis, is a luxurious camp for adults. The compound is spread out over several acres, with eco-minded architecture of native limestone and aluminum rooftops. Float in peace at the negative-edge pool; you'll feel like you're hovering over the lake. The guest rooms are contemporary and comfortable, free of distractions from the outside world (read: no television). **Pros:** Beautiful surroundings, spa with excellent massage therapists, healthy food. **Cons:** Difficult to get Internet access in rooms, spotty cell-phone service. ⊠*13500 FM 2769,* ☎*512/258–7243 or 877/944–3003* ⊕*www.thecrossingsaustin.com* ⇆*28 singles, 41 doubles, 25 bunkhouse rooms with twin bed, 1 four-bedroom cottage* ♿*In-room: refrigerator, Ethernet. In-hotel: restaurant, pool, spa, public Wi-Fi, airport shuttle* ⊟*D, MC, V* ⊠*BP.*

MARBLE FALLS

48 mi northwest Austin via Hwy. 71.

Only 45 minutes west of Austin, bustling Marble Falls has become a popular destination for a quick weekend getaway. Three lakes, Marble Falls, LBJ, and Buchanan, are the primary summer attractions here, but a number of other spots in and around town stand out, including the nearby Krause Springs, Quarry Mountain, and the renowned golf courses of Horseshoe Bay Resort.

Though the sides of Highway 281 running through town are littered with your typical retail stores, the town's 19th-century Main Street offers much in the way of gift, home-decor, and apparel shops, as well as excellent restaurants. And if you happen to be in the area around the holidays, Marble Falls is noted for having some of the most amazing Christmas lights along the lake.

Marble Falls is named for the natural falls formed by a shelf of limestone that runs diagonally across the Colorado River that flowed through the area. At the time, the water over the limestone created a bluish appearance that gave the impression of naturally occurring marble, for which the town was later named. However, visitors won't find marble here, and with the formation of the Highland Lakes, the falls are now completely under water and only visible on the rare occasions when the Lower Colorado River Authority lowers the lakes for repairs to the dam and boat docks.

Marble Falls has since gained fame for the amazing granite outcrops resulting from ancient formations in the Llano Basin, the most obvious marker being Granite Mountain, a monolith rising 866 feet above ground and spanning more than 180 acres. In the late 1800s, much of the economic growth of Marble Falls was due to the quarrying of this rock.

HIGHLAND LAKES

The Texas Highland Lakes are six lakes in the Hill Country region formed by several dams along the Colorado River. The dams were constructed in the 1930s and '40s to help provide flood control for the river, which used to flood severely. As a result, six lakes were created: Lake Buchanan, Inks Lake, Lake LBJ, Lake Marble Falls, Lake Travis, and Lake Austin. Though built for river control and to help generate hydroelectric power, the lakes now provide main attractions for the neighboring towns of Marble Falls, Horseshoe Bay, Burnet, Lakeway, and Austin.

DID YOU KNOW?
The entire Texas capitol building was constructed from granite quarried in Marble Falls. Other examples of the predominantly pink granite can be found in the construction of countless countertops of residential homes across the state.

WHAT TO SEE

Longhorn Caverns. Formed over thousands of years from water cutting and dissolving limestone bedrock, Longhorn Caverns is a fantastic example of Texas natural history. With a history of Comanche tribes seeking refuge in the caves and calcite-crystal beds, the caverns are a perfect destination for families interested in how the limestone caverns in the Hill Country were formed. ■TIP→ Be sure to wear rubber-soled shoes; it gets slippery down there! ⊠*Park Rd. 4, 6 mi west of Hwy. 281* ☏*830/598–2283 or 877/441–2283* ⊕*www.longhorncaverns.com* ☞*$12.99* ☉*Daily dawn–dusk.*

SPORTS & THE OUTDOORS

Krause Springs. If you need a little relief from the Texas heat, a trip here will certainly cool you off. Just a few miles east of Marble Falls in Spicewood, the springs are actually two separate swimming holes on a private ranch opened to the public. From Highway 71, splash through a low-water crossing and up to a hilltop bluff with hypnotic views of rolling grasslands, sprawling oak trees, and an undisturbed horizon. Park your car near the main house and stroll down a flight of outdoor stairs to the spring-fed pools. Be prepared for the biting chill as your toes hit the water. ⊠*404 Krause Springs* ☏*830/693–4181* ☞*$10* ☉*Daily 9–sundown.*

OUTFITTER

☺ **Cypress Valley Canopy Tours** (✉ *1223 Paleface RR, Spicewood* ☎ *512/264–8880* ⊕ *www.cypress valleycanopytours.com* 🍴 *$65– $125* ⊙ *Call for times*) zips you through the treetops to experience nature from a bird's eye view. Tucked away in a ravine lined with bald cypress trees, the Canopy Tour leads you along a maze of zip lines and sky bridges. For even more adventure, the Canopy Challenge is an additional longer—and more challenging—course with endurance high ropes obstacles. Bird-watchers may also enjoy the Sunrise Birding Tour, which is guided by a local biologist.

> **GRANITE MOUNTAIN**
>
> One of Marble Falls' economic foundations is Granite Mountain. The great granite dome rises 866 feet; its more than 180 acres of exposed granite serve as the largest granite quarry of its kind in the United States. Although visitors are not admitted to the quarry itself, you can get a great view of the mountain from J Street toward 2nd Street.

BOATING

Boating Lake Marble Falls and Lake LBJ. In the warmer months, if you want to know where the good time is, you'll have to get out on the water. Most of the recreational activity centers around Lake Marble Falls and Lake LBJ in spring, summer, and early fall. These two lakes are known for being more family-friendly than Austin's wilder Lakes Travis and Austin. **Lake LBJ Yacht Club and Marina** can assist in outfitting you and your crew with the perfect watercraft. ✉ *200 S. Wirtz Dam Rd.* ☎ *830/693–9172* ⊕ *www.lakelbjmarina.com.*

WHERE TO EAT

CAFE
¢–$$
★

✗ **Blue Bonnet Café.** Don't even think about coming to Marble Falls without taking a seat at this small-town diner. There's a sign above the hostess stand that says, "Eat some pie." We suggest you follow these directions. At least 10 different types of pie are made fresh daily. From mountainous meringue to creamy custards, the geniuses behind these sweet concoctions mean business. If you come between 2 and 5, you've made it for "Pie Happy Hour," when you can have a slice of pie and a cup of joe for $3! They also serve everything you'd find at an old-fashioned diner. ✉ *211 Hwy. 281* ☎ *830/693–2344* 🚫 *No credit cards.*

ECLECTIC
$$–$$$
Fodor's Choice
★

✗ **Café 909.** You may not be able to see it from Main Street, but we promise it's there. Tucked around the corner, this café with muted exposed-brick walls; a long, thin bar; and a cozy New York–size dining room offers a little bit of urban chic with relaxed Hill Country attitude. Chef-owner Mark Schmidt spikes familiar dishes with bold flavors. Take for instance the seared day-boat scallops with farruto (sort of like risotto), fiery horseradish, and crème fraîche. Be sure to end the meal with the frozen pistachio parfait with burnt honey caramel, which has won national attention. ✉ *909 2nd St.* ☎ *830/693–2126* 🚫 *AE, D, MC, V* ⊙ *Closed Mon. No lunch.*

AMERICAN
$–$$

✗ **Falls Bistro and Wine Cellar.** You may find it odd to see Asian decor in a tapas bar, but the mix of reds and blacks with bamboo plants somehow works. Be sure to bring a friend or two along to share these small plates. Try the scallops wrapped in crispy serrano ham; the roasted-corn cream sauce beneath these morsels is not to be missed. The duck tostadas are also a must. The wine list is reasonably priced and offers a good selection of international bottles. ⊠*202 Main St.* ☎*830/265–4580* ⊟*AE, D, MC, V* ⊘*Closed Mon.*

SOUTH-WESTERN

$$–$$$$

★

✕**Patton's On Main.** Chef Patton Robertson has brought haute cuisine to his hometown and created quite a buzz at this self-proclaimed "Texas fusion" restaurant. Look for beef tenderloin tacos with tangy guacamole, perfectly grilled salmon with caramelized shallots and a grapefruit-and-lemon-brown-butter sauce. The shrimp and grits, a classic Southern dish, has a vivid spiciness and perfect texture. ⊠*201 Main St.* ☎*830/693–8664* ⊟*AE, D, MC, V* ⊘*Closed Sun.*

STEAKHOUSE

$–$$$

✕**River City Grille.** On a nice evening, dining on the deck is the thing to do here. The views are amazing, and the food holds up its end of the bargain. The house specialty is a well-seasoned, juicy 12-ounce prime rib. Thankfully, they also serve an 8-ounce portion. The friendly waitstaff expertly coaxes people to order dessert, like warm carrot cake. ⊠*700 1st St.* ☎*830/798–9909* ⊟*AE, D, MC, V.*

WHERE TO STAY

$$

▦**Hampton Inn on the Lake.** Marble Falls may not have as many independent accommodations as the bustling tourist town of Fredericksburg, but the Hampton Inn on the Lake does its best to make your experience as unique to the Hill Country as possible. The staff is exceptionally friendly, and the facility has a spectacular view over the lake. Rooms feature plush, comfortable beds and are available with two queen beds or one king plus a fold-out couch. **Pros:** Lakeside rooms have fantastic views, great value. **Cons:** Staff is somewhat undertrained, cleaning service comes late. ⊠*704 1st St.,* ☎*830/798–1895* ⊕*www.marblefallshotel.com* ⌨*64 rooms* ⌕*In-room: refrigerator, Ethernet. In-hotel: pool, gym, laundry facilities, public Wi-Fi* ⊟*AE, D, MC, V* ⦿*AP.*

$$$

▦**The Moriah.** If you have a large group, and would like a little privacy, we suggest the Moriah, a small collection of three restored historic buildings on a picturesque 3-acre property with a private boat dock on Lake Marble Falls, just 8 mi from town. The large wooden porches offer spectacular views of the hills and the expansive backyard, which includes a full volleyball court, hammocks, and plenty of room to run around. The main timber-frame house has a large main room, a full kitchen, and an upstairs loft with two futons. Two 1850s timber cabins have a master room with comfortable king beds and a bunkroom with two sets of bunk beds. **Pros:** Perfect for a family reunion or a weekend getaway for friends, beautiful decor and amenities, feels like home. **Cons:** Not convenient to town, expensive for smaller groups. ⊠*1741 County Rd. 343,* ☎*650/321–9246* ⊕*www.historiccabins.com* ⌨*5 rooms (sleeps 16 total)* ⌕*In-room: kitchen, refrigerator, DVD. In-hotel: some pets allowed, no-smoking rooms* ⊟*MC, V* ⊘*Closed Thanksgiving wk.*

$$

▦**Wallace Guesthouse.** This stately manor just off Main Street opened in 1907 as the Bredt Hotel, and hosted guests for only 25¢! Today, the guesthouse offers guest suites fully decorated in vintage furniture and elegant fabrics. The rooms are reasonably spacious for a turn-of-the-

20th-century building. Each suite is named after one of the Highland Lakes. The staff is exceptionally friendly and happy to help with any questions about what to do in the area. **Pros:** Excellent access to Main Street shopping, friendly and helpful staff. **Cons:** Rooms are somewhat small, antique decor may be a little much for some. ⊠*910 3rd St.,* 🖀*830/798–9808* ⊕*www.thewallaceguesthouse.com* ↩*5 suites* ⚒*In-room: kitchen, refrigerator. In-hotel: no elevator, parking (no-fee), no-smoking rooms* ▤*AE, D, MC, V* ⟊◯*CP.*

SHOPPING

The best shopping in Marble Falls is on Main Street. Spend an after-noon strolling home-accent and interior shops such as Wisteria and Canyon Trails. The Square at Old Oak Village houses a number of fun shops, including **It's All About Me** (⊠*309 Main St.* 🖀*830/798–9191*), a children's specialty toy store; **Lucky Star** (⊠*309 Main St.* 🖀*830/693–6450*), with trendy apparel; the place for handmade cards and gifts, **Sakow Cards** (⊠*309 Main St.* 🖀*830/798–9191*) **Zoo La La** (⊠*309 Main St., No. 6* 🖀*830/693–0161*), a food and kitchen gift shop

Other notable shops not to miss include **Wisteria** (⊠*202 Main St.* 🖀*830/798–2477*), where you can find a beautiful selection of home decor and specialty gifts, and **Canyon Trails Furniture** (⊠*203 Main St.* 🖀*830/798–1041*)

HORSESHOE BAY

5 mi west of Marble Falls via FM 2147.

Adding to Marble Falls' tourist fame is the nearby resort town of Horseshoe Bay. Tucked into an immense cove on Lake LBJ, the resort began in the early 1970s and over the past few decades has added resi-dential subdivisions, lakefront condominiums, a yacht club, and world-class golf courses. In fact, Horseshoe Bay is home to some of the most renowned golf courses in the nation.

SPORTS & THE OUTDOORS

GOLF

Horseshoe Bay Resort Golf Courses. With three championship Trent Jones Sr.–designed courses and a future Jack Nicklaus golf course expected to open by 2009, the resort is a haven for those who love to spend their days on the green. The Ram Rock course (18 holes, par 71) has been deemed the "Challenger" course, offering some of the toughest fairways in the country. The Apple Rock course (18 holes, par 72) has racked up a number of awards and is known for its amazing scenery as it hugs Lake LBJ. The Slick Rock course (18 hole, par 72) and the Whitewater putting course are also favorite options. ⊠*101 Horseshoe Bay Blvd.* 🖀*830/598–2561 Slick Rock, 830/598–6561 Apple Rock, 830/598–6561 Ram Rock, 830/598–2591 Whitewater Putting Course* ⊕*www.hsbresort.com* 🖼*$110–$150* ◷*Daily dawn–dusk.*

TENNIS

Whitewater Tennis Center. Tennis fanatics will feel right at home here with 12 professional courts including 6 red clay courts, 4 hard courts, and 2 Pro-Grass courts. The new Andy Roddick Kids' Courts are the first in the United States to feature USTA cutting-edge, shorter, 60-foot courts to give children a training ground for learning the game more quickly. ⊠*101 Horseshoe Bay Blvd.* ☎*830/598–2591* ⊕*www.hsbresort.com* ☒*Free for guests of the Horseshoe Bay resort, $10 for visitors* ⊙*Call for reservations.*

YACHT CLUB

Horseshoe Bay Resort Marina. To get the full experience of a stay at Lake LBJ, be sure to reserve a boat from the marina and cruise the lake for an afternoon. A wide variety of watercraft is available for rent as well as ski and Jet Ski rentals. ⊠*101 Horseshoe Bay Blvd.* ☎*830/598-2591* ⊕*www.hsbresort.com* ☒*Call for pricing* ⊙*Call for reservations*

WHERE TO STAY

$$$$ 🏨**Horseshoe Bay Resort Marriott Hotel.** This isn't your typical Marriott
★   experience. The breathtaking views of Lake LBJ spreading its glimmering fingers should be your first clue. Every room overlooks a lush, tropical-meets-Texas landscape. Subdued earth-tone decor keeps the focus on the views. There's enough to keep you busy for days: access to three championship golf courses, a full-service spa, clay and hard-surface tennis courts. Though quiet in location, silence is easily broken if louder guests are returning to their rooms later at night. **Pros:** Excellent activities for kids, top golf and tennis options, comfortable rooms. **Cons:** Caters more to families, staff can be a bit too laid-back. ⊠*200 Hi Circle N, 78657* ☎*830/598–8600* ⊕*www.horseshoebay marriott.com* ☜*349 rooms, 64 one-bedroom and 29 two-bedroom condos* ⅁*In-room: refrigerator, Ethernet, Wi-Fi. In-hotel: gym, spa, pools, children's program (ages 4 and up), laundry facilities, airport shuttle and limousine service for Austin airport (reservation required, $55), some pets allowed* ▭*AE, D, MC, V.*

THE NORTHWEST QUADRANT

BURNET

13 mi north of Marble Falls via Hwy. 281.

During most of the year, Burnet is a sleepy little town best known as a stop for people heading south from the Dallas area or east from Llano. Visitors can stop at the town square for a quick stretch, or grab an old-fashioned drive-through burger at **Storm's** (⊠*700 N. Water St.* ☎*512/756–7143* ▭*AE, D, MC, V* ⊙*Closed Sun.)*

In late March through late April, the town comes alive with visitors from all over Texas who come to celebrate the state flower, the bluebonnet. Named the "Bluebonnet Capital of Texas," Burnet is famous on the Hill Country Wildflower Trail for having some of the best natural crops of bluebonnets anywhere in the state. (The Brenham area comes in a close second.) The second week in April is the Annual Blue-bonnet Festival.

WHERE TO STAY

$$–$$$ 📷 **Canyon of the Eagles Lodge.** While driving the winding road to this
☼ hilltop lodge, it's easy to believe you've taken a wrong turn. But after a few glimpses of sparkling Lake Buchanan, you dead-end right into this state-managed nature preserve and its low-frills guest lodge. This is a great spot for bird-watchers, as you'll have a good shot of seeing the endangered black-capped vereo and golden-cheeked warbler, as well as the glorious bald eagles that nest here from fall to early spring. Most cabins offer spectacular views of the lake and come equipped with comfortable queen beds and full bathrooms. (Plans to update some of the guest accommodations were underway at this writing.) Nature-focused children's programs are offered in summer and during spring break. **Pros:** Dining lodge has panoramic views, pets are welcome. **Cons:** Accommodations are somewhat primitive, outdoor dangers on trails (bugs, snakes, and poison ivy). ✉ *16942 RR 2341,* 📷 *800/977–0081* ⊕ *www.canyonoftheeagles.com* 🛏 *62 rooms* ⚘ *In-room: refrigerator (some), no TV, Wi-Fi. In-hotel: pool, public Wi-Fi, children's programs (ages 3–12), some pets allowed* 🚭 *AE, D, MC, V.*

LLANO

36 mi northwest of Marble Falls via Hwy. 71.

The greatest attraction to Llano is the drive out there. Whether you're heading north from Fredericksburg on Highway 16 or east from Mason on Highway 29, you'll see some of the most beautiful panoramas of rugged hill country in the region. Perhaps the most inspiring features of the scenery are the dramatic granite outcrops that burst from the landscape in pink, speckled domes.

Llano's history is a rather slow and quiet one, which has translated into a refreshing personality trait of the town. Established in 1856 in compliance with a state legislative act to establish Llano County, the city was a frontier trading center that didn't experience much economic growth until the late 1880s when discovery of iron deposits in the northwest part of the county drew financial interest from Dallas and northern states. The discovery spurred a number of charters for a dam, an electric power plant, an iron furnace and foundry in anticipation of what many saw as the next "Pittsburgh of the West." But the mineral resources, with the exception of the perpetual granite quarries, soon proved too shallow to sustain economic growth, and Llano's small blip on the industrial map soon faded.

Much of the town's identity today rests in the ranching, farming, and granite industries. Visitors are often attracted by the relaxed atmosphere and activities along the picturesque Llano River. The town square has a historic feel; it's sprinkled with galleries, antiques and gift shops, and a museum of Hill Country wildlife.

Talking Texan

Texans use the word "y'all" a lot. You'll hear it in pretty much any type of conversation, and you'll likely incorporate it into your vocabulary before heading home. (It really is a useful word, and it sounds so nice—at least when Texans say it.) There are a few other sayings and pronunciations that are unique to the Lone Star State:

SAYINGS

"He's all hat and no cattle": Used to describe someone who is all talk and no action.

"This ain't my first rodeo": I wasn't born yesterday.

"You can put your boots in the oven, but that don't make them biscuits": Say what you want, but that doesn't make it true.

"We've howdied, but we ain't shook yet": We've made a brief acquaintance, but have not been formally introduced.

PRONUNCIATION

Burnet: "Burn-it"

Pedernales: "Pur-dah-nallis"

Guadalupe: "Gwaa-dah-loop"

Manchaca: "Man-shack"

San Felipe: "San Fill-a-pee"

SPORTS & THE OUTDOORS

HUNTING

Though considered a controversial pastime in certain parts of the country, hunting is a favorite hobby among many Texans, and the Llano Basin has the highest density of whitetail deer in the Unites States. As a result, Llano Country is considered by many hunters to be the Deer Hunting Capital of Texas. In fall, when hunters head to West Texas through Llano, you'll see big pickup trucks towing trailers with deer blinds, feeders, ATVs, and camping gear. In fact, banners are strung across the main streets welcoming hunters to town. There are a number of leases available for hunting deer, quail, dove, and turkey in the Llano area as well as exotic game ranches that attract hunters from across the nation.

Those interested in a lease can check the lease list at the Llano Chamber of Commerce. Hunting licenses and a Hunter's Education certification are required for all in-state and out-of-state hunters. Hunting and fishing licenses are available at most sporting-goods stores, gun shops, and some department stores across the state. See the Texas Parks and Wildlife Department Web site (⊕ *www.tpwd.state.tx.us/huntwild)* for more details.

SHOPPING

Llano isn't quite the shopping hub that Fredericksburg or Boerne are, but near and along the town square you can find a number of gift shops such as the **Sagebrush** (*112 E. Main St.*) and Create (*110 E. Main St.*), and antiques-lovers will enjoy **Llano Railyard Antiques** (*502 Bessemer*), **Antique Station** (*107 Grayson St.*), and **Across the Street Antiques** (*400 Bessemer*). If you have time, be sure to stop in at the famed **Fain's Honey**

(*3744 S. Hwy. 16*), where you can choose from a selection of natural raw honey, creamed honey, sorghum molasses, and cane syrup.

WHERE TO EAT

CAFE
¢–$
✕**Acme Café.** If you want to go where the locals go, head over to the town square for lunch at the Acme. The average fare here is just about anything you'd find at a typical diner. The cheeseburger with a side of steaming, crispy fries is pretty hard to beat, especially when followed by peach pie. ⊠*109 W. Main* ☎*325/247–4457* ▭*AE, D, MC, V* ⊘*Closed Sat.*

AMERICAN
$$–$$$
✕**The Badu House.** Originally the National Bank of Llano, built in 1891, this stately manor later served as the family home to N.J. Badu, a French immigrant who studied the mineralogy of the Llano Basin. In recent years, the Badu House has been tastefully transformed into a restaurant focusing on local cuisine. If you like wild game, don't miss the grilled Bandera quail. Beneath the skin the meat is tender. and the accompanying chipotle and honey glaze gives the dish a nice kick. The back patio has live music on weekends. ⊠*601 Bessemer Ave.* ☎*325/247–1207* ▭*AE, D, MC, V* ⊘*Closed Sun. and Mon.*

AMERICAN
¢
✕**Chrissy's Homestyle Bakery.** At this tiny little bakery housed in an old historic building, the enchanting aroma of fresh-baked pies and pastries envelops you the second you walk in the door. The question of what to order immediately overwhelms you as you scour the glass cases showcasing pies, sweet and savory kolaches, and cookies. May we suggest the German-style sweet pretzel and the cream cheese–poppy seed kolache? Of course, the jalapeño, cheese, and sausage kolaches and cinnamon rolls are amazing as well, but you'll have to get there before the hunters, fishers, and early travelers do; they go fast. ⊠*501 Bessemer Ave.* ☎*325/247–4564* ▭*AE, D, MC, V* ⊘*Closed Mon.*

BARBECUE
¢–$
✕**Cooper's BBQ.** This Texas legend is serious about barbecue, and it expects no less from its clientele. Just look for the smokestacks rising from the tin-roof portacache and the swarm of Texas-size pickup trucks lining the parking lot. The menu is literally what's on display in the open pits that greet you at the entrance. Pick your meat from brisket, sausage, smoked turkey, ribs, or whatever else they have on hand for the day and step in line for the typical barbecue sides including coleslaw, potato salad, and plenty of doughy white bread. Park your tray where you can find a seat at one of the long picnic tables in or outside, but not before grabbing a few pickles, onions, and a bowl of beans from the serve-yourself condiment bar. ⊠*505 W. Dallas* ☎*325/247–5713* ▭*AE, D, MC, V.*

WHERE TO STAY

$–$$$
🏨**Railyard Bed and Breakfast.** Don't let the name fool you; you won't be sleeping on the tracks. The Railyard will eventually have a train that will take visitors from Llano to Kingsland for views of the granite outcrops and the rolling hills. This bed-and-breakfast has four separate houses happily situated in close proximity to the rail line, within easy walking distance of restaurants and the town square. Each cottage is uniquely decorated with tasteful antiques and vintage furniture. **Pros:** Within walking distance of shops, charming private cottages. **Cons:**

View of the railroad isn't very picturesque; if you aren't an antiques fan, the decor may be a little much. ⊠ *502 Bessemer Ave.,* ☎ *325/247–3827* ➟ *4 cottages (8 bedrooms total)* ☁ *In-room: kitchen, DVD, Wi-Fi.* ☰ *AE, D, MC, V* ⦿ *CP.*

MASON

35 mi west of Llano via Hwy. 29.

You don't just find yourself in Mason; you have to want to get there. Nestled in the rolling hills at the very northwest corner of this region, this pristine town was once a bastion of civilization for hunters on their way to or from various excursions, but today it's one of the Hill Country's best-kept secrets.

Originally established as a fort in 1851 by the United States government as one of many posts from the Rio Grande to the Red River to encourage growth in the region and protect settlers from Kiowa, Lipan Apache, and Comanche tribes, the town of Mason endured a tumultuous history for the better part of the Civil War under Confederate control. Following the federal government's reoccupation in 1866, the town began to see a resurgence through cattle ranching that remains a major part of the town's industry today.

Among the many things to see and do around the town, visitors shouldn't miss a trip to Ft. Mason. Just up Post Hill, this historic site played a pivotal role in the success of the town by protecting settlers from Indian raids through the late 1870s, and by providing employment opportunities for residents. The fort is also known for producing some of the Civil War's most notable generals, including Albert Sidney Johnston, William J. Hardee, and Robert E. Lee.

SPORTS & THE OUTDOORS

BAT WATCHING

One of the largest Mexican free-tailed bat colonies in the world is found in the hills of Mason County. Managed by the Texas Nature Conservancy, **Eckert James River Bat Cave** (☎ *325/347–5970* ⊠ *$5* ⦿ *Late May–mid-Oct., Thurs.–Sun. 6–9*), a maternity bat cave, is home to more than 4 million Mexican free-tailed bats. Only females inhabit the cave, inside which they bear and rear their young each spring; they depart from the cave in mid-October. You can watch in the evening and morning as the entrance to the cave swarms with female bats leaving and returning from an evening hunt to feed their pups. Stand clear of the entrance, unless you don't mind bat guano (droppings) or having thousands of female bats buzz by. The best way to glimpse this phenomenon is from a safe distance a few hundred yards away.

BLUE-TOPAZ HUNTING

Mason County has the great fortune of being the only place in Texas where you can find blue topaz, the state gem. It is naturally found in many of the granite outcroppings in the area. You can try your hand at panning for the rare blue gem from streambeds and exploring ravines.

Bluebonnets: the Pride of Texas

CLOSE UP

Ever since men first explored the prairies of Texas, the bluebonnet has been revered. American Indians wove folktales around this bright bluish-violet flower; early-day Spanish priests planted it thickly around their newly established missions; and the cotton boll and cactus competed fiercely with it for the state flower—the bluebonnet won the title in 1901.

The prized flower pops up across the fields of the Hill Country in March, usually peaking in April. Nearly half a dozen varieties of the bluebonnet, distinctive for flowers resembling pioneers' sunbonnets, bloom through-out the state, even as far west as Big Bend National Park. In fact, from mid-January until late March, at least one of the famous flowers carpets the park: the Big Bend (also called Chisos) Bluebonnet has been described as "the most majestic" species, as its deep-blue flower spikes can shoot up to 3 feet in height. The Big Bend bluebonnets can be found beginning in late winter on the flats of the park as well as along the Camino del Rio (Highway 70), which follows the legendary Rio Grande between Lajitas and Presidio, Texas.

Back in the Hill Country, those out for a springtime Sunday-afternoon drive

Scenic drives bring you close to the Texas bluebonnet (lupinus Texensis).

can see the violet-blue flowers along the road or at several attractions, including Fredericksburg's Wildseed Farms, right off Highway 290 as you enter town from the east, and Austin's Lady Bird Johnson Wildflower Center (4801 La Crosse Avenue). Farther north, in Burnet, the self-proclaimed Bluebonnet Capital of Texas, there's a bluebonnet festival each April.

For information on viewing the blue-bonnets, call the Wildflower Center (☎512/292–4100) or the Texas Department of Transportation Hotline (☎800/452–9292) from March to May.

—Marge Peterson

Two Mason County ranches open their property to the public for topaz hunting, but you have to call in advance to make an appointment. Mike Seaquist of **Garner Seaquist Ranch** (✉*108 Fort McKavitt* ☎*325/347–5413* 🖱*$15* ✆*Feb. –Oct.*) will meet you in town and take you to his working ranch for a day of topaz hunting. Be sure to wear comfort-able shoes, and bring a shovel. The **Lindsay Ranch** (✉*460 Lindsay Rd.* ☎*325/347–5733* 🖱*$10* ✆*Feb.–Oct.*) also offers topaz hunting.

FLY-FISHING
Though the Guadalupe River has received much acclaim for its vast angling opportunities, the Mason County side of the Llano River is little slice of heaven for fly-fishers. It's one of the longest remaining

wild rivers without flood control or electric generation in the country. Anglers will delight in the copious amounts of largemouth bass, bluegills, and Guadalupe River smallmouth bass (the state fish of Texas). And if you're lucky, you'll get a hit from the beautiful Rio Grande perch, a dark gray perch dotted with brilliant sapphire spots. Large outcrops of granite protrude from the river depths, easily creating navigable rapids and great deep pools. Some of the river is wadable, but a kayak or canoe is advised.

> **NOTABLE NATIVES**
>
> Mason was home to novelist Fred Gipson, who wrote the classic *Old Yeller*. Also with ties to the area is historical fiction and nonfiction writer Scott Zesch, who wrote the critically acclaimed *The Captured*, about children abducted by Apache Indians in the Mason area. Zesch's father, Gene Zesch, is known in the Southwest for his whimsical wood carvings. Original Zesch carvings are on display in the Director's Room of the Commercial Bank in Mason.

ROCK CRAWLING

Though going vertical on massive boulders in a four-wheel drive vehicle is a site normally seen in Moab, Utah, rock crawling is actually possible at the Katemcy granite outcropping on the Kruse Off-Road Park 10 mi north of Mason. Off-roading adventurers will find a number of trails and obstacles to master on this 800-acre property.

Katemcy Rocks at Kruse Off-Road Park (⊠ *Kruse Off-Road Park* ☎ *325/347–6333* ⊕ *www.katemcyrocks.com* ☞ *$30* ۞ *Feb. –Oct.; call for days and times*).

ARTS & ENTERTAINMENT

The **Odeon Theater** (⊠ *122 S Moody St.* ☎ *325/347–9010*), in the town square, is a Texas landmark. In continuous operation since 1928, the theater is both a movie theater and a venue for live shows.

WHERE TO EAT

AMERICAN
¢–$

✕ **The Cat's Meow.** Sandwiched between the Underwood Antique Mall and the Mason Gallery is one of Mason's oldest buildings. Originally a 19th-century saloon, the Cat's Meow is now a superb little café catering to what owner Cathy Terrell calls the "three S's"—soups, sandwiches, and sweets. Her signature chicken salad bursts with almond slivers and red grapes, while the turkey sandwich with cranberry-apple chutney evokes holiday comfort food. ⊠ *106 S. Live Oak* ☎ *325/347–5225* ▤ *AE, D, MC, V* ۞ *Closed Sun. No dinner Mon.–Sat.*

TEX-MEX
¢–$
★

✕ **Santos Taqueria y Cantina.** There's a certain positive energy when you enter this family-run place where you can watch fresh gorditas hand-pressed in the open kitchen and owner Santo Silerio's grandmother stirring up a fresh batch of creamy chili con queso. Be sure to try a squash gordita. A magical thing happens when squash, onions, tomatoes, cilantro, poblano peppers, and a few special ingredients are simmered together and served in a hot pocket with queso blanco and some sautéed chicken. Order the corn gorditas rather than the flour. Though it takes a few extra minutes, the old adage is true: good things come to those who wait. ⊠ *205 San Antonio St.* ☎ *325/347–6140* ▤ *AE, D,*

MC, V ⊘ *Closed Mon.–Wed. No dinner Sun.*

AMERICAN
¢–$

✕**Willow Creek Café.** Seated in the heart of the town square, this cheery café seems to keep a steady flow of business as it serves everything from club sandwiches to hand-battered, chicken-fried steaks. Friday night is fried catfish night—you'll have to fight locals for a table, but the fried crunchy fish is worth it. The café opens at 5 AM. ⊠*106 Fort McKavitt St.* ☎*325/347–5365* ☐*AE, D, MC, V.*

WHERE TO STAY

$$

⛭**Gamel House.** On the town square, the Gamel Guest House is one of the first houses ever built in Mason. Erected in 1869 by cattle baron John W. Gamel, this guesthouse has a tranquil sitting area off the back porch beneath a shady oak tree The small, two-bed, two-bathroom cabin is well appointed with antiques, including the Gamel family's original dining-room table and claw-foot bathtub. Those who love feeling like they've stepped back in time will feel right at home here. Those who like a little more modernity may feel a bit cramped. It costs $150 per night for the entire house with a two-night minimum. **Pros:** History buffs will love the stories surrounding this property, rooms are comfortable. **Cons:** A little too close to the main roads of town, not ideal for children due to the antique furniture. ⊠*224 San Antonio St.* ☎*325/347–5531* ⊕*www.masontxcoc.com/member/zesch/gamel.htm* ⇱*1 cabin (seeps 4 (⛶In-room: kitchen, refrigerator, dial-up* ☐*AE, MC, V* |◉|*CP.*

$$–$$$$

⛭**Raye Carrington on the Llano River.** If you enjoy fly-fishing or birding, this may be just the ticket. Each suite or cabin on the property feels secluded, while the common areas allow for family-style breakfasts and grilling your dinners by the river. You can also use this as a base for kayaking, mountain biking, and hiking. Guided fishing and casting instruction is available. **Pros:** Rooms are simple and comfortable, perfect place to commune with nature, fly-fishing fans won't want to get off the water. **Cons:** Poor cell-phone reception, dinner options are going into Mason or grilling for yourself. ⊠*8603 Lower Willow Creek Rd., 2 mi west on Willow Creek Rd. of U.S. 87 N* ☎*325/347–3474 or*

> ### GAMEL GOLD
>
> Legend has it from family members that still reside in Mason today, that there is gold buried somewhere on the Gamel property. In the mid-1800s, cattle baron John Gamel was leaving town for a cattle drive. Having sold a number of cattle in a recent business transaction, Gamel did not have time to deposit his funds—at that time, gold was the primary form of tender. He left the gold with his wife and told her to hide it until he returned.
>
> One afternoon, she was tending her garden and a man jumped from behind a bush and startled her to the point that she had a stroke. Unable to speak, and severely brain damaged from the trauma, Mrs. Gamel passed away before her husband could return; and without being able to tell anyone where the gold was.
>
> For many years, family members had to fend off gold diggers from looting the property. Though the gold has never been found, the current owners of the Gamel property, Patsy and Gene Zesch strongly advise against trying your hand at "tilling the soil."

3

866/605–3100 ⊕www.llanoriver.com ⇋4 cabins (sleep 2–5), 5 rooms (sleep 2–3) ⌂In-room: no phone, refrigerator, no TV. In-hotel: public Wi-Fi, no-smoking rooms ☰AE, D, MC, V ⦾BP.

THE HILL COUNTRY ESSENTIALS

Research prices, get travel advice, and book your trip at fodors.com.

TRANSPORTATION

BY AIR

You can access the Hill Country from either the Austin Bergstrom International Airport or San Antonio International Airport (⇨San Antonio, Austin & the Hill Country Essentials at the back of this book for airport maps). Hill Country towns begin within 25 to 30 mi of either airport. From Austin's Bergstrom International Airport, follow U.S. 290 west until the terrain changes from flat to steep and rolling. To get to northern towns such as Marble Falls, Llano, and Burnet, exit U.S. 281 and head north. Fredericksburg, Boerne, Comfort, and Bandera are all farther west from 281, but are easily reached with a little map navigation. New Braunfels, Gruene, and San Marcos are easily accessed from 1–35 between Austin and San Antonio. From San Antonio's International Airport, U.S. 281 North and I–10 West will both take you into the heart of the Hill Country.

Information Austin-Bergstrom International Airport (⊠ 3600 Presidential Blvd., Austin ☎512/530–2242 ⊕ www.ci.austin.tx.us). **San Antonio International Airport** (⊠ 9800 Airport Blvd., San Antonio ☎210/207–3450 ⊕www.ci.sat.tx.us).

BY CAR

This is the land of the open road. The best—and really—the only way to access the Hill Country is by car (or by motorcycle, which is an increasingly popular method). The towns are small enough that parking is not a problem. And though it's not encouraged, you're probably pretty safe leaving your car unlocked. Locals joke that they can spot an out-of-towner when they hear the "beep" of a car alarm.

CONTACTS & RESOURCES

EMERGENCIES

In an emergency dial 911. Each of the following medical facilities has an emergency room open 24/7. A new 120-room hospital, Lake of the Hills, is being built just outside Marble Falls. It is part of the Scott & White health-care system based in Temple, Texas, which is known for its top-notch medical facilities. It is expected to open in 2010.

Hospitals Hill Country Memorial Hospital (⊠1020 S. Hwy. 16, Fredericksburg ☎830/997–4353). **Seton Highland Lakes Hospital** (⊠3201 S. Water St., Burnet ☎512/715–3000). **Seton Marble Falls Healthcare Center** (⊠700 U.S. 281, Marble Falls ☎830/693–2600). **Sid Peterson Memorial Hospital** (⊠710 Water St., Kerrville ☎830/896–4200).

VISITOR INFORMATION

Bandera Convention & Visitors Bureau (✉ *126 Hwy. 16 S, Bandera* ☎ *800/364–3833* ⊕ *www.banderacowboycapital.com*). **Boerne Convention & Visitors Bureau** (✉ *126 Rosewood Ave., Boerne* ☎ *830/249–8000* ⊕ *www.boerne.org*). **Castroville Chamber of Commerce** (✉ *802 London, Castroville* ☎ *830/538–3142 or 800/778–6775* ⊕ *www.castroville.com*). **Comfort Convention & Visitors Bureau** (✉ *630 Hwy. 27, Comfort* ☎ *830/995–3131* ⊕ *www.comfort-texas.com*). **Fredericksburg Convention & Visitors Bureau** (✉ *302 E. Austin, Fredericksburg* ☎ *830/997–6523* ⊕ *www.fredericksburg-texas.com*). **Johnson City Chamber of Commerce** (✉ *803 Hwy. 281 S, Johnson City* ☎ *830/868–7684* ⊕ *www.lbjcountry.com*). **Kerrville Convention & Visitors Bureau** (✉ *2108 Sidney Baker, Kerrville* ☎ *830/792–3535 or 800/221–7958* ⊕ *www.kerrvilletexascvb.com*). **Lake Travis Convention & Visitors Bureau** (✉ *1415 RR 620 S, Suite 202, Austin* ☎ *877/263–0073* ⊕ *www.laketravischamber.com*). **Llano Chamber of Commerce** (✉ *700 Bessemer, Llano* ☎ *325/247–5354* ⊕ *www.llanochamber.org*). **Luckenbach Convention & Visitors Bureau** (✉ *412 Luckenbach Town Loop, Fredericksburg* ☎ *830/997–3224* ⊕ *www.luckenbachtexas.com*). **Marble Falls** (✉ *916 2nd St., Marble Falls* ☎ *830/693–2815* ⊕ *www.marblefalls.org*). **Mason County Chamber of Commerce** (✉ *108 Fort McKavitt, Mason* ☎ *325/347–5758* ⊕ *www.masontxcoc.com*). **New Braunfels Chamber of Commerce** (✉ *424 S. Castell Ave., New Braunfels* ☎ *800/572–2626* ⊕ *www.nbjumpin.com*). **San Marcos Convention & Visitors Bureau** (✉ *202 N. C.M. Allen Pkwy., San Marcos* ☎ *512/393–5900* ⊕ *www.sanmarcoscharms.com*). **Wimberley Convention & Visitors Bureau** (✉ *14100 RR 12, Wimberley* ☎ *512/847–2201* ⊕ *www.wimberley.org*).

3

San Antonio, Austin & the Hill Country Essentials

PLANNING TOOLS, EXPERT INSIGHT, GREAT CONTACTS

There are planners and there are those who, excuse the pun, fly by the seat of their pants. We happily place ourselves among the planners. Our writers and editors try to anticipate all the issues you may face before and during any journey, and then they do their research. This section is the product of their efforts. Use it to get excited about your trip to San Antonio, Austin & the Hill Country, to inform your travel planning, or to guide you on the road should the seat of your pants start to feel threadbare.

GETTING STARTED

We're really proud of our Web site: fodors.com is a great place to begin any journey. Scan Travel Wire for suggested itineraries, travel deals, new openings, and other up-to-the-minute info. Check out Booking to research prices and book flights, hotel rooms, rental cars, and vacation packages. Head to Talk for on-the-ground pointers from other travelers.

∎ RESOURCES

ONLINE TRAVEL TOOLS

Texas Tourism The Web site ⊕www.traveltex. com has wonderful driving tours and trip-planning tools as well as an extensive events calendar.

The Handbook of Texas Online (⊕www. tshaonline.org), by the Texas State Historical Association, is an incredible resource for information about any Texas hamlet, town, or city (from Abbott to Zybach)—and pretty much any other topic about Texas you can think of.

The Texas Commission on the Arts (⊕www. artonart.com) maintains an events calendar.

The Texas Governor's office (⊕www. governor.state.tx.us) covers far more than politics—it's devoted to promoting music and the arts throughout Texas.

Texas Highways (⊕www.texashighways.com) focuses on exploring the Lone Star State.

The Texas Historical Commission (⊕www. thc.state.tx.us) has a wealth of information on the rich history of the Lone Star State.

Billing itself as the "National Magazine of Texas," **Texas Monthly** (⊕www.texasmonthly. com) has its finger on the state's pulse, with coverage on politics, shopping, arts and culture, and Texas travel.

The Texas Parks and Wildlife Department (⊕www.tpwd.state.tx.us) is a source for nature-lovers.

∎ THINGS TO CONSIDER

SHIPPING LUGGAGE AHEAD

If you're planning to fly to Texas and rent a car once there you're there, then shipping your luggage in advance via an air-freight service is something you may want to consider. It can be a great way to cut down on backaches, hassles, and stress at the airport. There are some things to be aware of, though.

First, research carry-on restrictions; if you absolutely need something that isn't practical to ship and isn't allowed in carry-ons, this strategy isn't for you. Second, plan to send your bags several days in advance. Third, plan to spend some money: it will cost at least $100 to send a small piece of luggage, or a golf bag.

Some people use Federal Express to ship their bags, but this can cost even more than air-freight services. All these services insure your bag (for most, the limit is $1,000, but you should verify that amount); you can, however, purchase additional insurance for about $1 per $100 of value.

Contacts Luggage Concierge (☎800/288–9818 ⊕www.luggageconcierge.com). **Luggage Express** (☎866/744–7224 ⊕www. usxpluggageexpress.com). **Luggage Free** (☎800/361–6871 ⊕www.luggagefree.com). **Sports Express** (☎800/357–4174 ⊕www. sportsexpress.com) specializes in shipping golf clubs and other sports equipment. **Virtual Bellhop** (☎877/235–5467 ⊕www.virtual bellhop.com).

TRIP INSURANCE

We believe that comprehensive trip insurance is valuable if you're booking a very expensive or complicated trip or if you're booking far in advance. Who knows what could happen six months down the road? But whether or not you get insurance has more to do with how comfortable you are assuming all that risk yourself.

Trip Insurance Resources

INSURANCE COMPARISON SITES		
Insure My Trip.com	800/487–4722	www.insuremytrip.com
Square Mouth.com	800/240–0369 or 727/490–5803	www.quotetravelinsurance.com
COMPREHENSIVE TRAVEL INSURERS		
Access America	800/284-8300	www.accessamerica.com
CSA Travel Protection	800/873–9855	www.csatravelprotection.com
HTH Worldwide	888/243–2358 or 610/254–8700	www.hthworldwide.com
Travelex Insurance	800/228–9792	www.travelex-insurance.com
Travel Guard International	800/826–4919 or 715/345-0505	www.travelguard.com
Travel Insured International	800/243–3174	www.travelinsured.com
MEDICAL-ONLY INSURERS		
International Medical Group	800/628–4664 or 315/655–4500	www.imgglobal.com
International SOS	215/942–8000 or 713/521–7611	www.internationalsos.com
Wallach & Company	800/237–6615 or 540/687–3166	www.wallach.com

Comprehensive travel policies typically cover trip-cancellation and interruption, letting you cancel or cut your trip short because of a personal emergency, illness, or, in some cases, acts of terrorism in your destination. Such policies also cover evacuation and medical care. Some also cover you for trip delays because of bad weather or mechanical problems as well as for lost or delayed baggage. Another type of coverage to look for is financial default—that is, when your trip is disrupted because a tour operator, airline, or cruise line goes out of business. Generally you must buy this when you book your trip or shortly thereafter, and it's only available to you if your operator isn't on a list of excluded companies.

If you're going abroad, consider buying medical-only coverage at the very least. Neither Medicare nor some private insurers cover medical expenses anywhere outside the United States (including time aboard a cruise ship, even if it leaves from a U.S. port). Medical-only policies typically reimburse you for medical care (excluding that related to preexisting conditions) and hospitalization abroad, and provide for evacuation. You still have to pay the bills and await reimbursement from the insurer, though.

Expect comprehensive travel insurance policies to cost about 4% to 7% or 8% of the total price of your trip (it's more like 8%–12% if you're over age 70). A medical-only policy may or may not be cheaper than a comprehensive policy. Always read the fine print of your policy to make sure that you are covered for the risks that are of most concern to you.

▌ TRAVEL INTO MEXICO

Other than long lines, crossing into Mexico isn't much of a hassle—just bring your passport. Don't carry a single bullet or even a pocketknife into the country; Mexican law is harsh on weapons possession. U.S. driver's licenses are valid in Mexico, but cars must be driven only by their owners or by those with signed documents from a rental agency. (Do *not* bring a rental car into Mexico without your rental agency's blessing—this can void your contract, making you personally responsible for any damages that occur on the other side of the border.) Taking public transportation or walking across the border are your best options.

Keep in mind that when you travel in Mexico, you're under Mexican law and fully liable. Things that seem minor here—like insulting someone, littering, being tipsy in public, or making a rude gesture—can be criminal south of the border. Just be respectful, and you'll probably be okay.

Reentering the United States is more vigorous than crossing the border into Mexico. If you're traveling with children, keep in mind that both parents must consent to the travel. If one is not present, the child must have a notarized permission letter, preferably with times and itinerary of travel, and proof of their relationship to the child. (This precaution is meant to safeguard children from abduction.)

GOVERNMENT ADVISORIES

▌TIP➔ **If you decide to take an extended trip into Mexico from Texas, consider registering with the State Department (⊕ *https:// travelregistration.state.gov*), so the government will know to look for you should a crisis occur in Mexico while you're visiting.**

CUSTOMS & DUTIES

You're always allowed to bring goods of a certain value back home without having to pay any duty or import tax. But there's a limit on the amount of tobacco and liquor you can bring back duty-free, and some countries have separate limits for perfumes; for exact figures, check with your customs department. The values of so-called "duty-free" goods are included in these amounts. When you shop abroad, save all your receipts, as customs inspectors may ask to see them as well as the items you purchased. If the total value of your goods is more than the duty-free limit, you'll have to pay a tax (most often a flat percentage) on the value of everything beyond that limit.

Because of tighter restrictions on traveling between the United States and Mexico, customs lines have lengthened. The average wait varies depending on time of day and time of week, and can range 5–45 minutes. Customs is usually relatively painless, but you will have to pay a tax on items totaling more than $200 to $1,600, depending on circumstance. Educate yourself beforehand, because should you exceed the total amount by even $20, you'll have to pay tax on the whole lot.

Alcohol and cigarette imports are limited, and those bringing them over the border must be of age. For some purchases, such as Mexican medicine and eyeglasses, you are required to have a prescription, and drugs not approved by the FDA are usually banned. It's OK to bring some fresh foods across the border—like fish you've caught—but other foods (like most fruit) will have to be tossed before your step back on to U.S. soil. A safety note: stay away from Mexican candies; many have a high level of lead.

U.S. Information U.S. Customs and Border Protection (⊕ www.cbp.gov).

DRIVING IN MEXICO

If you go south of the border, be aware that your American insurance probably won't cut it in Mexico—no matter how great your coverage is—since Mexican law requires insurance that covers personal injury. Credit cards often provide some coverage, as does AAA, but your best bet is to get a tourist card for identification purposes, and to buy Mexican insurance either online or at the stores on the border. That way, you can drive with a clear conscience and no worries.

If you have an accident in Mexico, be aware that you might go to jail while authorities try to figure out who is at fault. Also, keep in mind that Mexican insurance won't spring you from jail if you're found to be criminally at fault (for example, if you were deemed to be drinking and driving or criminally negligent).

INSURANCE

Driving in Mexico requires Mexican insurance—period. Getting in a minor fender bender without it can result in your car getting impounded, and you might even get arrested. Also, be aware that driving while intoxicated or under the influence of any drug automatically invalidates your insurance in Mexico!

ROADSIDE EMERGENCIES

Green federal repair trucks are paid to cruise the Mexican highways. Services from the "Green Angels" is free (and you can call them from anywhere in Mexico), but you'll have to pay if your car needs supplies or parts.

Emergency Services (Mexico) **Green Angels** (☎English-speaking, 01–55–5250–8221).

SHOTS & MEDICATIONS

Everyone entering Mexico should be up-to-date on their booster shots, regardless of age. This isn't a requirement, but it's a good precaution. The Centers for Disease Control maintains pertinent updates and requirements for Mexico on their Web site—consult it and speak with your physician before a long trip south of the bor-

der. All visitors should pay attention to how their food is cooked and drink only bottled water.

Health Warnings National Centers for Disease Control & Prevention (CDC; ☎877/394–8747 international travelers' health line ⊕www.cdc.gov/travel). **World Health Organization** (WHO ⊕www.who.int).

TRAVEL TO MEXICO	
Passport	Must be valid at the time of reentry.
Visa	Tourists and business travelers staying more than three days and six months, respectively, require an application.
Vaccinations	Hepatitis A, typhoid, and even rabies shots have been recommended (but are rarely needed) in border towns. If venturing farther south, antimalarial drugs may be needed.
Driving	U.S. driver's license is fine. Temporary Mexican insurance should be purchased.
Departure Tax	None if walking or on a bus. If you're driving, you'll need to pay $15 for a permit, which should be displayed in the windshield. (Some areas also require a tourist card.)

PASSPORTS & VISAS

PASSPORTS

A passport verifies both your identity and nationality. U.S. passports are valid for 10 years. You must apply in person if you're getting a passport for the first time; if your previous passport was lost, stolen, or damaged; or if your previous passport has expired and was issued more than 15 years ago or when you were under 16. All children under 18 must appear in person to apply for or renew a passport. (Note that even though Texas feels like a whole 'nother country, you don't need a passport to enter Texas!)

■TIP➜ Before your trip, make two copies of your passport's data page (one for someone at home and another for you to carry separately). Or scan the page and e-mail it to someone at home and/or yourself.

U.S. Passport Information **U.S. Department of State** (☎877/487-2778 ⊕http://travel.state.gov/passport).

U.S. Passport & Visa Expediters **A. Briggs Passport & Visa Expeditors** (☎800/806-0581 or 202/338-0111 ⊕www.abriggs.com). **American Passport Express** (☎800/455-5166 or 800/841-6778 ⊕www.americanpassport.com). **Passport Express** (☎800/362-8196 ⊕www.passportexpress.com). **Travel Document Systems** (☎800/874-5100 or 202/638-3800 ⊕www.traveldocs.com). **Travel the World Visas** (☎866/886-8472 or 301/495-7700 ⊕www.world-visa.com).

BOOKING YOUR TRIP

Have you ever wondered just what the differences are between an online travel agent (a Web site through which you make reservations instead of going directly to the airline, hotel, or car-rental company), a discounter (a firm that does a high volume of business with a hotel chain or airline and accordingly gets good prices), a wholesaler (one that makes cheap reservations in bulk and then resells them to people like you), and an aggregator (one that compares all the offerings so you don't have to)? Is it truly better to book directly on an airline or hotel Web site? And when does a real live travel agent come in handy? Read on.

■ ONLINE

You really have to shop around. A travel wholesaler such as Hotels.com or Hotel-Club.net can be a source of good rates, as can discounters such as Hotwire or Priceline, particularly if you can bid for your hotel room or airfare. Indeed, such sites sometimes have deals that are unavailable elsewhere. They do, however, tend to work only with hotel chains (which makes them just plain useless for getting hotel reservations outside major cities) or big airlines (so that often leaves out upstarts like jetBlue and some foreign carriers like Air India).

Also, with discounters and wholesalers you must generally prepay, and everything is nonrefundable. And before you fork over the dough, be sure to check the terms and conditions, so you know what a given company will do for you if there's a problem and what you'll have to deal with on your own.

Booking engines like Expedia, Travelocity, and Orbitz are actually travel agents, albeit high-volume, online ones. And airline travel packagers like American Airlines Vacations and Virgin Vacations—well, they're travel agents, too.

But they may still not work with all the world's hotels.

■TIP➜ To be absolutely sure everything was processed correctly, confirm reservations made through online travel agents, discounters, and wholesalers directly with your hotel before leaving home.

An aggregator site will search many sites and pull the best prices for airfares, hotels, and rental cars from them. Most aggregators compare the major travel-booking sites such as Expedia, Travelocity, and Orbitz; some also look at airline Web sites, though rarely the sites of smaller budget airlines. Some aggregators also compare other travel products, including complex packages—a good thing, as you can sometimes get the best overall deal by booking an air-and-hotel package.

■ WITH A TRAVEL AGENT

If you use an agent—brick-and-mortar or virtual—you'll pay a fee for the service. And know that the service you get from some online agents isn't comprehensive. For example Expedia and Travelocity don't search for prices on budget airlines like jetBlue and Southwest. That said, some agents (online or not) *do* have access to fares that are difficult to find otherwise, and the savings can more than make up for any surcharge. What's more, travel agents who specialize in a destination may have exclusive access to certain deals and insider information on things such as charter flights. Agents who specialize in types of travelers or types of trips can also be invaluable.

■TIP➜ Expedia, Travelocity, and Orbitz are travel agents, not just booking engines. To resolve any problems with a reservation made through these companies, contact them first.

Online Booking Resources

AGGREGATORS

Cheapflights	www.cheapflights.com	compares airfares.
Kayak	www.kayak.com	looks at cruises, airfares, and vacation packages.
Mobissimo	www.mobissimo.com	examines airfare, hotels, cars, and tons of activities.
Qixo	www.qixo.com	compares cruises, airfares, vacation packages, and even travel insurance.
Sidestep	www.sidestep.com	compares vacation packages and lists travel deals.
Travelgrove	www.travelgrove.com	compares cruises and packages and lets you search by themes.

BOOKING ENGINES

Cheap Tickets	www.cheaptickets.com	discounter.
Expedia	www.expedia.com	large online agency that charges a booking fee for airline tickets.
Hotwire	www.hotwire.com	discounter.
lastminute.com	www.uslastminute.com	specializes in last-minute travel.
Luxury Link	www.luxurylink.com	has auctions (surprisingly good deals) as well as offers on the high-end side of travel.
Onetravel.com	www.onetravel.com	discounter for hotels, car rentals, airfares, and packages.
Orbitz	www.orbitz.com	charges a booking fee for airline tickets, but gives a clear breakdown of fees and taxes before you book.
Priceline.com	www.priceline.com	discounter that also allows bidding.
Travel.com	www.travel.com	allows you to compare its rates with those of other booking engines.
Travelocity	www.travelocity.com	charges a booking fee for airline tickets, but promises good problem resolution.

ONLINE ACCOMMODATIONS

Hotelbook.com	www.hotelbook.com	focuses on independent hotels worldwide.
Hotel Club	www.hotelclub.net	good for major cities worldwide and some resort areas.
Hotels.com	www.hotels.com	big Expedia-owned wholesaler that offers rooms in hotels all over the world.
Quikbook	www.quikbook.com	offers "pay when you stay" reservations that let you settle your bill at checkout, not when you book.

Agent Resources **American Society of Travel Agents** (☎703/739–2782 ⊕www. travelsense.org).

ACCOMMODATIONS

Most hotels and other lodgings require you to give your credit-card details before they will confirm your reservation. If you don't feel comfortable e-mailing it, ask if you can fax it. However you book, get confirmation in writing and have a copy of it handy when you check in.

Be sure you understand the hotel's cancellation policy. Some places allow you to cancel without any kind of penalty—even if you prepaid to secure a discounted rate—if you cancel at least 24 hours in advance. Others require you to cancel a week in advance or penalize you the cost of one night. Small inns and B&Bs are most likely to require you to cancel far in advance. Most hotels allow children under a certain age to stay in their parents' room at no extra charge, but others charge for them as extra adults; find out the cutoff age for discounts.

■TIP➔ Assume that hotels operate on the European Plan (EP, no meals) unless we specify that they use the Breakfast Plan (BP, with full breakfast), Continental Plan (CP, continental breakfast), Modified American Plan (MAP, breakfast and dinner) or are all-inclusive (AI, all meals and most activities).

Texas Lodging **Texas Hotel Association** (☎800/856–4328 ⊕www.texaslodging.com ✉1701 W. Ave., Austin).

BED & BREAKFASTS
Reservation Services **Bed & Breakfast.com** (☎800/462–2632 or 512/322–2710 ⊕www. bedandbreakfast.com) also sends out an online newsletter. **Bed & Breakfast Inns Online** (☎800/215–7365 or 615/868–1946 ⊕www. bbonline.com). **BnB Finder.com** (☎888/547–8226 or 212/432–7693 ⊕www.bnbfinder.com).

HOME EXCHANGES
With a direct home exchange you stay in someone else's home while they stay in yours. Some outfits also deal with vacation homes, so you're not actually staying in someone's full-time residence, just their vacant weekend place.

Exchange Clubs **First Home Exchange** (⊕www.1sthomeexchange.com); links people from all over the world; free registration. **Home Exchange.com** (☎800/877–8723 ⊕www.homeexchange.com); $59.95 for a 1-year online listing. **HomeLink International** (☎800/638–3841 ⊕www.homelink.org); $90 yearly for Web-only membership; $140 includes Web access and two catalogs. **Intervac U.S.** (☎800/756–4663 ⊕www.intervacus. com); $78.88 for Web-only membership; $126 includes Web access and a catalog. **Seniors Home Exchange** (⊕www.seniorshomeexchange.com); links travelers from across the globe, available only to seniors; membership fees range from $59 to $79 for three years.

AIRLINE TICKETS

Most domestic airline tickets are electronic; international tickets may be either electronic or paper. With an e-ticket the only thing you receive is an e-mailed receipt citing your itinerary and reservation and ticket numbers. The greatest advantage of an e-ticket is that if you lose your receipt, you can simply print out another copy or ask the airline to do it for you at check-in. You usually pay a surcharge (up to $50) to get a paper ticket, if you can get one at all. The sole advantage of a paper ticket is that it may be easier to endorse over to another airline if your flight is canceled and the airline with which you booked can't accommodate you on another flight.

▌ RENTAL CARS

When you reserve a car, ask about cancellation penalties, taxes, drop-off charges (if you're planning to pick up the car in one city and leave it in another), and surcharges (for being under or over a certain age, for additional drivers, or for driving across state or country borders or beyond a specific distance from your point of rental). All these things can add substantially to your costs. Request car seats and extras such as a GPS when you book.

Rates are sometimes—but not always—better if you book in advance or reserve through a rental agency's Web site. There are other reasons to book ahead, though: for popular destinations, during busy times of the year, or to ensure that you get certain types of cars (vans, SUVs, exotic sports cars). Also, make sure a confirmed reservation guarantees you a car, as agencies sometimes overbook.

▌**TIP**➔ Make sure that a confirmed reservation guarantees you a car. Agencies sometimes overbook, particularly for busy weekends and holiday periods.

All major Texas airports offer reliable rental-car service through the major chains, with several classes of vehicle available. If you stick with the reputable national chains, you'll find cars in excellent condition and in many categories, from fuel-efficient economy vehicles to spacious SUVs. If you're planning on off-roading, you'll have to look for local outfitters in the areas that allow all-wheel-drive vehicles

If possible, stick with reputable national chains that you trust. The vast distances between the attractions and cities in Texas mean that you'll want support if you have car problems.

Most national rental agencies have car seats available—but check beforehand because they aren't available in each franchise (and fees vary). No matter what, Texas state laws requiring children younger than five, or under 36 inches, to be restrained in a car or booster seat firmly secured in the back of the vehicle. The state further recommends that children shorter than 4 feet, 9 inches still be secured in booster seats in the back.

A valid U.S. driver's license is acceptable in Mexico, but you may need a visa when driving several miles outside a border city. You also need temporary Mexican insurance when driving.

CAR-RENTAL INSURANCE

Everyone who rents a car wonders whether the insurance that the rental companies offer is worth the expense. No one has a simple answer. It all depends on how much regular insurance you have, how comfortable you are with risk, and whether or not money is an issue.

If you own a car and carry comprehensive car insurance for both collision and liability, your personal auto insurance will probably cover a rental—but read your policy's fine print to be sure. If you don't have auto insurance, or if you have just the bare minimum, then you should probably buy the collision- or loss-damage waiver (CDW or LDW) from the rental company. This eliminates your liability for damage to the car.

Some credit cards offer CDW coverage, but it's usually supplemental to your own insurance and rarely covers SUVs, minivans, luxury models, and the like. If your coverage is secondary, you may still be liable for loss-of-use costs from the car-rental company (again, read the fine print). But no credit-card insurance is valid unless you use that card for *all* transactions, from reserving to paying the final bill.

▌**TIP**➔ Diners Club offers primary CDW coverage on all rentals reserved and paid for with the card. This means that Diners Club's company—not your own car insurance—pays in case of an accident. It *doesn't* mean that your car-insurance company

Car-Rental Resources

AUTOMOBILE ASSOCIATIONS

U.S.: American Automobile Association	315/797–5000	www.aaa.com;
		most contact with the organization is through state and regional members.
National Automobile Club	650/294–7000	www.thenac.com
		membership is open to California residents only.

MAJOR AGENCIES

Alamo	800/462–5266	www.alamo.com
Avis	800/331-1212	www.avis.com
Budget	800/527–0700	www.budget.com
Dollar	800/800–4000	www.dollar.com
Enterprise	800/261–7331	www.enterprise.com
Hertz	800/654–3131	www.hertz.com
National Car Rental	800/227–7368	www.nationalcar.com
Thrifty	800/847–4389	www.dollar.com

won't raise your rates once it discovers you had an accident.

You may also be offered supplemental liability coverage; the car-rental company is required to carry a minimal level of liability coverage insuring all renters, but it's rarely enough to cover claims in a really serious accident if you're at fault. Your own auto-insurance policy will protect you if you own a car; if you don't, you have to decide whether you are willing to take the risk.

U.S. rental companies sell CDWs and LDWs for about $15 to $25 a day; supplemental liability is usually more than $10 a day. The car-rental company may offer you all sorts of other policies, but they're rarely worth the cost. Personal accident insurance, which is basic hospitalization coverage, is an especially egregious rip-off if you already have health insurance.

■TIP➔ You can decline the insurance from the rental company and purchase it through a third-party provider such as Travel Guard (⊕ *www.travelguard.com*)—$9 per day for $35,000 of coverage. That's sometimes just

under half the price of the CDW offered by some car-rental companies.

■ VACATION PACKAGES

Packages *are not* guided excursions. Packages combine airfare, accommodations, and perhaps a rental car or other extras (symphony tickets, guided excursions, boat trips, reserved entry to popular museums), but they let you do your own thing. During busy periods packages may be your only option, as flights and rooms may be sold out otherwise.

Packages will definitely save you time. They can also save you money, particularly in peak seasons, but—and this is a really big "but"—you should price each part of the package separately to be sure. And be aware that prices advertised on Web sites and in newspapers rarely include service charges or taxes, which can up your costs by hundreds of dollars.

■TIP➔ Some packages are sold only through travel agents and online agents.

Each year consumers are stranded or lose their money when packagers—even large ones with excellent reputations—go out of business. How can you protect yourself?

First, always pay with a credit card; if you have a problem, your credit-card company may help you resolve it. Second, buy trip insurance that covers default. Third, choose a company that belongs to the United States Tour Operators Association, whose members must set aside funds to cover defaults. Finally, choose a company that also participates in the Tour Operator Program of the American Society of Travel Agents (ASTA), which will act as mediator in any disputes. And fourth, do not book through a single person who seems well intentioned. Well intentioned they may be, but incompetence may rob you of both your money and your high hopes.

You can also check on the tour operator's reputation among travelers by posting an inquiry on one of the Fodors.com forums.

Organizations American Society of Travel Agents (ASTA ☎800/965–2782 or 703/739–2782 ⊕www.astanet.com). **United States Tour Operators Association** (USTOA ☎212/599–6599 ⊕www.ustoa.com).

▌GUIDED TOURS

Guided tours are a good option when you don't want to do it all yourself. You travel along with a group (sometimes large, sometimes small), stay in prebooked hotels, eat with your fellow travelers (the cost of meals sometimes included in the price of your tour, sometimes not), and follow a schedule. Plus a knowledgeable guide can take you places that you might never discover on your own.

Whenever you book a guided tour, find out what's included and what isn't. A "land-only" tour includes all your travel (by bus, in most cases) in the destination, but not necessarily your flights to and from or even within it. Also, in most cases prices in tour brochures don't include fees and taxes. And remember that you'll be expected to tip your guide (in cash) at the end of the tour.

Recommended Companies Hotels.com (⊕www.hotels.com), a big Expedia-owned wholesaler, offers rooms in hotels all over the world. **Quantrill** (⊕www.quantrill.com) offers motorcycle tours (bikes provided) of the entire Route 66 pathway from Chicago to Los Angeles. **Quikbook** (⊕www.quikbook.com) offers "pay when you stay" reservations that allow you to settle your bill when you check out, not when you book.

TRANSPORTATION

▊ BY AIR

The two airports in Central Texas are in San Antonio and Austin. You can easily access the Hill Country from either. See the Essentials section at the end of each chapter for local airport information.

▊TIP➔ If you travel frequently, look into the TSA's Registered Traveler program. The program, which is still being tested in several U.S. airports, is designed to cut down on gridlock at security checkpoints by allowing prescreened travelers to pass quickly through kiosks that scan an iris and/or a fingerprint. How sci-fi is that?

Airline Contacts Alaska Airlines (☎800/252–7522 ⊕www.alaskaair.com). **American Airlines** (☎800/433–7300 ⊕www.aa.com). **Continental Airlines** (☎800/523–3273 ⊕www.continental.com). **Delta Air Lines** (☎800/221–1212 for U.S. reservations ⊕www.delta.com). **Frontier Airlines** (☎800/432–1359 ⊕www.frontierairlines.com). **jetBlue** (☎800/538–2583 ⊕www.jetblue. com). **Northwest Airlines** (☎800/225–2525 ⊕www.nwa.com). **Southwest Airlines** (☎800/435–9792 ⊕www.southwest.com). **Spirit Airlines** (☎800/772–7117 ⊕www. spiritair.com). **United Airlines** (☎800/864–8331 ⊕www.united.com). **USAirways** (☎800/428–4322 ⊕www.usairways.com).

Airline Security Issues Transportation Security Administration (TSA; ⊕www.tsa. gov) has answers for most airline security questions.

▊ BY BUS

Only one major bus line goes to every Texas city: Greyhound. Purchasing your ticket in advance and traveling on a weekday can dramatically slash the price of a ticket. Most Texas cities have municipal bus systems. While this is a cheap method of getting around, it can take a bit of time.

See the Essentials section at the end of each chapter for local bus information.

Bus Information Greyhound (☎800/231–2222 ⊕www.greyhound.com).

▊ BY CAR

The state has a fantastic network of interlacing highways and smaller, meandering roads. Just be aware that distances are great here—Texas is the largest state in the Lower 48. The drive from Houston, in the east, to El Paso, in the west, is 745 mi—about the distance from New York City to Charleston, South Carolina!

ROAD CONDITIONS
Most roads in Texas are smooth and well maintained. Frontage roads run parallel to many highways, which makes it easy to merge into and out of traffic. Be aware that U-turns are a way of life in Texas—lanes on some Texas highways will lead you to a U-turns, and U-turns are permitted from most left-turn lanes. As you motor along, you'll see abbreviations like FM (which means Farm-to-Market; most of these routes were originally in rural areas); RM means Ranch-to-Market (and springs from the same roots); IH means Interstate Highway; and Loop (LP) means a bypass around a city.

In rural areas, traffic tends to move quite a bit more slowly. This is a law-and-order culture, and that attitude even bleeds into the way people drive—it's not uncommon for commuters to drive a steady 5 mph under the speed limit. Take a deep breath and wave when you pass. (Whatever you do, don't make rude gestures—that'll get you a ticket in Texas.)

When you're on the highway in urban areas, be aware of the overhead signs—some of the major highways can be five- or six-lanes across, and it's pretty easy to unintentionally end up in an exit lane.

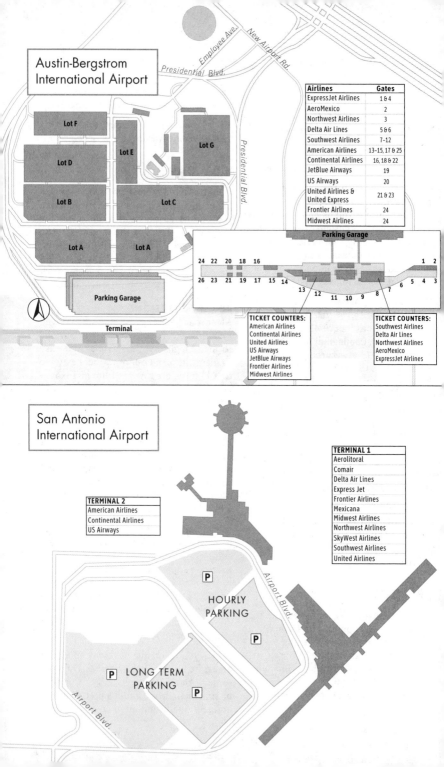

Austin-Bergstrom International Airport

Airlines	Gates
ExpressJet Airlines	1 & 4
AeroMexico	2
Northwest Airlines	3
Delta Air Lines	5 & 6
Southwest Airlines	7–12
American Airlines	13–15, 17 & 25
Continental Airlines	16, 18 & 22
JetBlue Airways	19
US Airways	20
United Airlines & United Express	21 & 23
Frontier Airlines	24
Midwest Airlines	24

Lot F
Lot E
Lot G
Lot D
Lot B
Lot C
Lot A
Lot A
Parking Garage
Terminal

Presidential Blvd.
Employee Ave.
New Airport Rd
Presidential Blvd.

Parking Garage

24 22 20 18 16   1 2
26 23 21 19 17 15 14   13 12 11 10 9 8 7 6 5 4 3

TICKET COUNTERS:
American Airlines
Continental Airlines
United Airlines
US Airways
JetBlue Airways
Frontier Airlines
Midwest Airlines

TICKET COUNTERS:
Southwest Airlines
Delta Air Lines
Northwest Airlines
AeroMexico
ExpressJet Airlines

San Antonio International Airport

TERMINAL 1
Aerolitoral
Comair
Delta Air Lines
Express Jet
Frontier Airlines
Mexicana
Midwest Airlines
Northwest Airlines
SkyWest Airlines
Southwest Airlines
United Airlines

TERMINAL 2
American Airlines
Continental Airlines
US Airways

HOURLY PARKING
LONG TERM PARKING
Airport Blvd.
Airport Blvd.

Some highways have two posted speed limits—one for day driving (the white sign with black lettering), and one for night driving (the black sign with white lettering). The night speed limit is usually 5 mph below the daytime speed limit.

Even though this is Texas, the roads can get frosty during the winter months. Beware of driving on overpasses when the temperature hits 34° or below, as the road can quickly get slick. And if there's an ice storm, be especially careful; slow down, and leave lots of distance to stop.

TRAVEL TIMES BY CAR		
From	To	Distance, Est. Travel Time
Austin	Gruene	47 mi, ¾ hr
Austin	Fredericksburg	77 mi, 2¼ hrs
Austin	San Antonio	79 mi, 1¼ hr
Austin	Houston	165 mi, 3 hrs
Austin	Dallas	195 mi, 3½ hrs
San Antonio	Laredo	159 mi, 2 hrs
San Antonio	Houston	197 mi, 3 hrs
San Antonio	Dallas	275 mi, 4¼ hrs
San Antonio	South Padre Island	291 mi, 5 hrs
San Antonio	El Paso	580 mi, 8 hrs

ROADSIDE EMERGENCIES

In Texas, help is just a 911 call away. The highway patrol is always cruising the highways and byways and will likely spot you.

Emergency Services AAA (☎800/222–4357 ⊕www.aaa.com). **Texas Highway Patrol** (☎512/424–2000 ⊕www.txdps.state.tx.us).

RULES OF THE ROAD

In Texas, littering is verboten (thanks to decades of the "Don't Mess with Texas" ad campaign), so don't throw anything out your car window. (Even a flicked cig-arette butt can spell big trouble, particularly if there's a drought.)

All front-seat passengers must wear seat belts, and children younger than age five or under 36 inches tall must be restrained in a car- or booster seat firmly secured in the backseat of the vehicle. The state further recommends that children shorter than 4 feet 9 inches be secured in booster seats in the backseat. Also, be aware that some parts of Texas have passed laws against using cell phones while driving.

Standard driving laws apply. A right on red is okay (after a full stop), as long as there's no sign telling you not to.

Police are scrupulous about enforcing the drinking and driving laws; a blood alcohol level of .08 or higher (sometimes less, if you're driving erratically) will result in your arrest. If you're caught driving under the influence (even if it's a first offense), you can lose your license for a year, spend six months in jail, and/or pay a $2,000 fine. A third offense can get you 2 to 10 in the pen. And if you're under 21 and have any alcohol in your system, you'll automatically lose your license.

▌ BY TRAIN

Amtrak's Texas Eagle Line runs between Chicago and Dallas, Fort Worth, Austin, and San Antonio, with links to other parts of the state.

Prices tend to be extremely reasonable, with some coach tickets costing about $50, and sleeper tickets costing less than $200. Customers can make a custom guide on the Texas Eagle Web site that explains the high points of each station and town. Check online for money-saving specials, including buy-one-get-the-second-half-off fares. Customers can choose whether to ride coach, or book a sleeping room for two or for four.

Information Amtrak's Texas Eagle (☎800/222–4357 ⊕www.texaseagle.com).

ON THE GROUND

▮ BUSINESS HOURS

Business hours in urban areas of Texas and in Mexico can stretch after sunset, particularly at chain stores and shopping malls. Even in the smallest towns, the malls close at a decent hour (usually 9 PM, unless it's Sunday), but the smaller shops often close as early as 5 PM. Some shops in Texas close for lunch (usually from noon to 1 or 2 PM). Religious holidays above and below the border are stringently observed; these include Easter and Christmas, and sometimes Ash Wednesday and Good Friday.

▮ EATING OUT

RESERVATIONS & DRESS

Regardless of where you are, it's a good idea to make a reservation if you can. We only mention them specifically when reservations are essential (there's no other way you'll ever get a table) or when they are not accepted. For popular restaurants, book as far ahead as you can (often 30 days), and reconfirm as soon as you arrive. (Large parties should always call ahead to check the reservations policy.) We mention dress in our listings only when men are required to wear a jacket or a jacket and tie.

▮ FISHING PERMITS

Texas stores, sporting-goods shops, and hunting outlets all sell fishing permits, and they are also available online. The only time you won't need one when fishing is on the first Saturday in June, or if you're a nonresident under 17 or mentally disabled. Otherwise, fees start at $15. The **Texas Parks and Wildlife Department** (☎713/948–3350 ⊕*www.tpwd. state.tx.us*) has a list of businesses that vend the licenses.

▮ HEALTH

Ailments that might strike, depending on the time of year, include sunstroke, heat exhaustion, and dehydration. These are easy to prevent by simply donning hats in the sun, slathering on SPF 30 regardless of season, and packing bottled water.

In Mexico, malarial insects tend to infest deeper down in the country, so generally the most visitors have to fear is a case of incontinence due to lower sanitation standards for water and food. Wash your hands frequently, and use hand sanitizers. Make sure your food is thoroughly cooked, don't buy food from street vendors whose cooking methods you haven't watched, and avoid any meat product (particularly pork) that may have sat in the sun for 30 minutes or longer. Do not buy any Mexican folk remedies, as they might contain high levels of lead. Stick with what's proven—bring your own aspirin or Tylenol, cold remedies, and headache medicines. Also bring Imodium A-D or Pepto-Bismol in case an upset tummy attacks. Also, make sure immunizations are up to date for both kids and adults.

▮ MONEY

Prices in this guide are given for adults. Reduced fees are often available for children, students, and seniors.

ATMS & BANKS

ATMs are available throughout Texas. If you travel across the border, you can easily get pesos by using an ATM at a Mexican bank (note, however, that your own bank will probably charge a fee for using ATMs abroad, and the foreign bank may also charge a fee). You'll usually get a better rate of exchange at an ATM than at a currency-exchange office—or even when changing money in a bank. And extracting funds as you need them is a safer option than carrying around a large amount of cash.

CREDIT CARDS

Throughout this guide, the following abbreviations are used: **AE**, American Express; **D**, Discover; **DC**, Diners Club; **MC**, MasterCard; and **V**, Visa.

It's a good idea to inform your credit-card company before you travel, especially if you're going into Mexico and don't travel internationally very often. If you don't, the credit-card company might put a hold on your card owing to unusual activity—not a good thing to find out halfway through your trip.

Reporting Lost Cards **American Express** (☎800/528–4800 in the U.S., 336/393–1111 collect from abroad ⊕www.americanexpress.com). **Diners Club** (☎800/234–6377 in the U.S., 303/799–1504 collect from abroad ⊕www.dinersclub.com). **Discover** (☎800/347–2683 in the U.S., 801/902–3100 collect from abroad ⊕www.discovercard.com). **MasterCard** (☎800/627–8372 in the U.S., 636/722–7111 collect from abroad ⊕www.mastercard.com). **Visa** (☎800/847–2911 in the U.S., 410/581–9994 collect from abroad ⊕www.visa.com).

TRAVELER'S CHECKS

Some consider this the currency of the caveman, and it's true that fewer establishments accept traveler's checks these days. Nevertheless, they're a cheap and secure way to carry extra money, particularly on trips to urban areas. Both Citibank (under the Visa brand) and

American Express issue traveler's checks in the United States, but Amex is better known and more widely accepted; you can also avoid hefty surcharges by cashing Amex checks at Amex offices. Whatever you do, keep track of all the serial numbers in case the checks are lost or stolen.

Contact **American Express** (☎888/412–6945 in the U.S., 801/945–9450 collect outside the U.S. to speak to customer service ⊕www.americanexpress.com).

▌TIPPING

In Texas, normal tipping rules apply—but don't tip 20% unless the service was truly wonderful. Tipping protocols in Mexico don't vary wildly from tipping in the United States—except that the percentage expected is lower. In Mexico, 10% (or a little more) for waitstaff is perfectly adequate for good service. When staying in hotels, tip the maids by leaving a dollar or two (or, even better—the peso equivalent) on the pillow to thank them for good service. Gas attendants who squeegee down the windows or perform other services while filling the tank should be tipped a dollar or two. Don't tip cab drivers; the tip is usually already figured in the fare. (Though do include something extra if your driver performs a special service, like an impromptu tour.)

FOR INTERNATIONAL TRAVELERS

CURRENCY

The dollar is the basic unit of U.S. currency. It has 100 cents. Coins are the penny (1¢), nickel (5¢), dime (10¢), quarter (25¢), half-dollar (50¢), and golden or silver $1 coins. Bills are denominated $1, $5, $10, $20, $50, and $100, all mostly green and identical in size; designs and background tints vary. You may come across a $2 bill, but the chances are slim.

CUSTOMS

Information **U.S. Customs and Border Protection** (⊕www.cbp.gov).

DRIVING

Driving in the United States is on the right. Speed limits are posted in miles per hour (usually between 55 mph and 70 mph). Watch for lower limits in small towns and on back roads (usually 30 mph to 40 mph). Most states require front-seat passengers to wear seat belts; many states require children to sit in the backseat and to wear seat belts. In major cities rush hour is between 7 and 10 AM; afternoon rush hour is between 4 and 7 PM. To encourage carpooling, some freeways have special lanes, ordinarily marked with a diamond, for high-occupancy vehicles (HOV)—cars carrying two people or more.

Highways are well paved. Interstates—limited-access, multilane highways designated with an "I–" before the number—are fastest. Interstates with three-digit numbers circle urban areas, which may also have other limited-access expressways, freeways, and parkways. Tolls may be levied on limited-access highways. U.S. and state highways aren't necessarily limited-access, but may have several lanes.

Gas stations are plentiful. Most stay open late (24 hours along major highways and in big cities) except in rural areas, where Sunday hours are limited and where you may drive for long stretches without a refueling opportunity. Along larger highways, roadside stops with restrooms, fast-food restaurants, and sundries stores are well spaced. State police and tow trucks patrol major highways. If your car breaks down on an interstate, pull onto the shoulder and wait for help, or have your passengers wait while you walk to an emergency phone (available in most states). If you carry a cell phone, dial *55, noting your location on the small green roadside mileage marker.

ELECTRICITY

The U.S. standard is AC, 110 volts/60 cycles. Plugs have two flat pins set parallel to each other.

EMBASSIES

Contacts **Australia** (☎202/797–3000 ⊕www.austemb.org). **Canada** (☎202/682–1740 ⊕www.canadianembassy.org). **Mexico** (☎202/728–1600 ⊕www.embassyofmexico.org). **United Kingdom** (☎202/588–7800 ⊕www.britainusa.com).

EMERGENCIES

For police, fire, or ambulance, dial 911 (0 in rural areas).

HOLIDAYS

New Year's Day (Jan. 1); Martin Luther King Day (3rd Mon. in Jan.); Presidents' Day (3rd Mon. in Feb.); Memorial Day (last Mon. in May); Independence Day (July 4); Labor Day (1st Mon. in Sept.); Columbus Day (2nd Mon. in Oct.); Thanksgiving Day (4th Thurs. in Nov.); Christmas Eve and Christmas Day (Dec. 24 and 25); and New Year's Eve (Dec. 31).

MAIL

You can buy stamps and aerograms and send letters and parcels in post offices. Stamp-dispensing machines can occasionally be found in airports, bus and train stations, office buildings, drugstores, and convenience stores. U.S. mailboxes are stout, dark-blue steel bins; pickup schedules are posted inside the bin (pull down the handle to see them). Parcels weighing more than a pound must be mailed at a post office or at a private mailing center.

To receive mail on the road, have it sent c/o General Delivery at your destination's main post office (use the correct five-digit ZIP code). You must pick up mail in person within 30 days, with a driver's license or passport for identification.

Contacts **DHL** (☎800/225–5345 ⊕www. dhl.com). **Federal Express** (☎800/463–3339 ⊕www.fedex.com). **Mail Boxes, Etc./ The UPS Store** (☎800/789–4623 ⊕www. mbe.com). **United States Postal Service** (☎800/275–8777 ⊕www.usps.com).

PASSPORTS & VISAS

Visitor visas aren't necessary for citizens of Australia, Canada, the United Kingdom, or most citizens of European Union countries coming for tourism and staying for fewer than 90 days. All Mexican residents will need a tourist visa for entry into the United States, and special permits are required for those who wish to travel beyond the border area. If you need a visa, the cost is $100, and waiting time can be substantial, depending on where you live. Apply for a visa at the U.S. consulate in your place of residence; check the U.S. State Department's special Visa Web site for further information.

Visa Information **Destination USA** (⊕www.unitedstatesvisas.gov).

CELL PHONES

The United States has several GSM (Global System for Mobile Communications) networks, so multiband mobiles from most countries (except for Japan) work here. Unfortunately, it's almost impossible to buy a pay-as-you-go mobile SIM card in the United States—which allows you to avoid roaming charges—without also buying a phone. That said, cell phones with pay-as-you-go plans are available for well under $100. The cheapest ones with decent national coverage are the GoPhone from Cingular and Virgin Mobile, which only offers pay-as-you-go service.

Contacts **Cingular** (☎888/333–6651 ⊕www.cingular.com). **Virgin Mobile** (☎No phone ⊕www.virginmobileusa.com).

INDEX

PHOTO CREDITS 6, *Al Rendon/SACVB. (left),Texas Tourism.* 7 *(right), Kenny Braun/Texas Tourism.* 8, *Texas Tourism.* 9, *Tomas del Amo/Alamy.* 11 *(left), SeaWorld San Antonio.* 11 *(right), Al Rendon/SACVB.* **Chapter 1: San Antonio:** 21, *Terrance Klassen/age fotostock.* 28, *Six Flags Fiesta Texas.* 32, *maxlucado.com.* 33, *Lakewood Church.* 39, *SeaWorld San Antonio.* 52, *Kheng Guan Toh/Shutterstock.* 53, *Wendy T. Davis/Shutterstock.* 72, *Hyatt Regency.* 73, *Hotel Valencia.* **Chapter 2: Austin:** 105, *LBJ Library.* 111, *Kenny Braun/Texas Tourism.* 130, *Peter Horree/Alamy.* 132, *Chris Kraus.* 144, *Eric Gevaert/Shutterstock.* 145, *Elke Dennis/iStockphoto.* 166, *Hilton.* 167, *The Driskill Hotel.* **Chapter 3: The Hill Country:** 209, *Carol Barrington/Aurora Photos.* 231, *Michael Page/Becker Vineyards.* 245, *Bill Heinsohn/Alamy.*

NOTES

NOTES

NOTES

NOTES

NOTES

NOTES

NOTES

NOTES

NOTES

NOTES

NOTES

NOTES

ACKNOWLEDGMENTS

During the research and reporting of this guide, there are many we wish to thank for their assistance. The writers and editors gratefully acknowledge the many convention and visitors bureau representatives, like Dee Dee Poteete and Tonya Hope from the San Antonio CVB, Daryl Whitworth of the Fredericksburg CVB, and Beth Krauss of the Austin CVB; Meredith Spurgeon Michelson, who handles public relations for the state; the many restaurant and hotel employees who took the time to show us their properties; those who gave us tours of some of Texas's noteworthy attractions, such as Fran Stephenson at SeaWorld Texas; and last but definitely not least, we thank the many residents of Central Texas who shared with us their insights on the land they love.

ABOUT OUR WRITERS

Although he now calls the Big Apple home, **Tony Carnes** (*Texas Megachurches*), a senior writer at *Christianity Today* magazine, was born in the Hill Country. He and his wife, Darilyn, go back often to, as President LBJ called it, this "special corner of God's real estate."

Jessica Norman Dupuy (*The Hill Country, Austin's Arts & Entertainment*) is an Austin-based freelance writer specializing in food and travel. Raised in the Texas Hill Country, she enjoys the outdoors, savoring different cuisines, and any chance to travel abroad—or to the Rocky Mountains in a pinch. She is a contributor to *Texas Monthly*.

Specializing in the arts and travel, **Wes Eichenwald** (*Austin*) is a freelance writer and editor who has lived in Austin since 2002 (following previous lives in New York, Boston, and Ljubljana, Slovenia). His writing has appeared in numerous outlets, including the *Chicago Tribune* and the *Los Angeles Times*. Along with their two young children, Wes and his wife enjoy discovering hidden corners and new places to eat, shop, and explore in the Texas capital.

Writers **Lisa Miller & Larry Neal** (*Famous Texans CloseUps*) usually save their pithy writing for press releases and op-eds. But these two Texans, who work together in the nation's capital, had fun writing up the bios of some of the state's most famous characters, from music greats like Willie Nelson to genteel souls like Lady Bird Johnson.

A graduate of Northwestern University's Medill School of Journalism's master program, **Roger Slavens** (*San Antonio Dining & Lodging*) is a new resident to San Antonio. When he's not working as a writer and editor, he spends his time with his family, checking out the fun places to eat and explore in their new city.

Texas native **Kevin Tankersley** (*San Antonio Sports & the Outdoors*) roots for the Bears of Baylor University, his alma mater and where he teaches writing in the journalism department. He has worked as a photographer, writer, reporter, and sports information director. He and his wife, Abby, have a daughter, Sophie, and a son, Brazos. They live in Waco.